CW01064268

30127 05754518 3

FAMILIAR EVIL

Rannah Gray

IN COLLABORATION WITH
MARY JANE MARCANTEL
AND THE BRITISH SURVIVOR
KNOWN AS ETHAN

The
LISBURN
PRESS

The Lisburn Press
www.TheLisburnPress.com

THE LISBURN PRESS
3115 OLD FORGE DRIVE
BATON ROUGE, LOUISIANA 70808

FAMILIAR EVIL
Copyright © 2015 by Rannah Gray

All rights reserved. No part of this book may be reproduced or transmitted in any form, or by any means, electronic or mechanical, including photocopying, recording, or by any information storage and retrieval system, without written permission from the publisher, except in the case of brief quotations embodied in critical articles or reviews.
For information, contact The Lisburn Press.

PUBLISHED IN THE UNITED STATES OF AMERICA

Visit our website at TheLisburnPress.com.

First edition published November 2015

Cover design by Sarah Powell
Text design by Kim Springfield
Edited by Patricia Stallman

Library of Congress Cataloging-in-Publication Data is available.

ISBN: 978-0-578-17072-5

For information regarding special discounts for bulk purchases, please contact The Lisburn Press Special Sales at info@LisburnPress.com.

Printed in Canada

This book is printed on acid-free paper.

IN MEMORY OF

NATHAN S. FISHER

FOR ETHAN

CONTENTS

AUTHOR'S NOTE

This is a true story.

I never imagined I would be involved in a story like this—one that would change my view of the world forever. The story you are about to read covers 365 days. During that year of my life, it was on my mind every single day. I felt, at times, fear, apprehension, and ultimately determination to speak up about a child predator who was living among us—not simply accepted, but, in some circles, celebrated. Scott Rogers sold himself as a friend of every good cause, herald of all good news. He was, in fact, a dangerous criminal.

I never expected that the simple act of writing a letter to the editor would land me in the middle of an international criminal investigation, but thanks to the Internet, all of our lives are now interconnected. What happens to one of us can in turn affect any person on this planet. If you think that sounds far-fetched, just wait until you see how easy it truly is to have your life completely changed by a happenstance.

This book was written—first and foremost—for the British survivor known as Ethan and for the boys of Bury. For those young boys in Bury St. Edmunds, England—and we will never know how many there were—who suffered unspeakable sexual, physical, and psychological abuse at the hands of Scott Rogers. Although he changed his name several times, he could never escape his true character. He was a master manipulator. A child predator. A monster.

But this is not his story.

This is a story about Ethan, who reached out to me for help across the Atlantic Ocean and six time zones, and found someone who is today proud to call this remarkable man a friend. He is the best proof that a powerful intellect, inherent goodness, and a keen sense of humor are perhaps the best tools for surviving terror. *I am so very proud of you—it was the journey of a lifetime and you never lost sight of its true purpose—protecting children.*

This is also a story about Jake, one of the strongest, most determined men I have ever met. *I hope the past becomes a faded memory, washed away by the love and support of your beautiful family.*

It is a story about unbelievable coincidences and how strange new friendships became treasured gifts—bonds that help temper the sadness that comes with the discovery of horrific abuse, and ease the anxiety that goes with challenging the forces of evil.

It's a story about making tough life decisions…standing up for yourself…standing up for someone else…putting your faith in a complete stranger…making friendships for life.

This story is also told for Tim and Paul and all the others whose lives were interrupted by abuse. I have been fortunate to meet six men who were victims of Scott Rogers, including Mathew Hodgkinson, who died from a self-inflicted gunshot wound. Each has given me tremendous insight into the man who deceived law enforcement, Child Services, families, and community and religious leaders on two continents.

Five living survivors have cooperated freely with me to tell the story, providing invaluable information and a look behind the disguise of their abuser. Because those who live in England prefer to remain anonymous, I have changed their names for the purpose of this book. I have met each of them in person, however, and they have given an extraordinary behind the scenes look at the man and his crimes. We also know of other survivors who continue to suffer as a result of Scott's abuse and whose experiences we chose not to reveal out of respect for their privacy and continued healing.

My thanks to Mary Jane Marcantel, a paralegal whose skills and persistence to find the truth are unmatched. From the minute she began helping me find the best place to report information about possible crimes, she has been professional and caring, with a laser focus on justice within the law. She moved seamlessly from being a researcher brought on board to help develop legal strategies, to assisting with every aspect of this book, to a trusted friend.

My sincere appreciation to Jim Brown and The Lisburn Press for wanting this story told, and to Jim for the best advice I was given: "Go to England and get the rest of your story."

And that's where I found it—drenched by the tears of survivors, buried in the pained expressions on their faces. But that is also where I witnessed the courage of good men, the power of loving families, and the strength of the human spirit.

Heartfelt thanks to:

Nathan Fisher and his wife Francine. Nathan provided expert legal and strategic advice in addition to his loyal friendship. Francine, a safe haven for the most confidential discussions.

Val Marmillion, innocent co-target of Scott Rogers' attempt to discredit those of us who did not fall for his manipulative ways. *Your integrity is always an inspiration.*

Sarah Powell, Compose Digital Design, for making the journey to Bury St. Edmunds with me to help document its beauty and walk in the footsteps of this story, and for your kind heart and loyal friendship.

Assistant U.S. Attorney for the Western District of Louisiana, Luke Walker—a true hero. Your dedicated public service makes the world a safer place for children.

Allyson Hoffine, Inspector for the U.S. Postal Inspection Service, for your tireless work and commitment to the survivors of Scott Rogers' abuse. Your sensitivity made a difference in their ability to finally speak up about what he took from them.

East Baton Rouge Parish Mayor-President Melvin L. "Kip" Holden, for your friendship, your instincts to do what is right, and your unwavering commitment to children.

Leslie Todd, LCSW-BACS, for your professional insight into the actions of a child predator and for sharing with our readers the clinical side of the issue.

Jim Engster, for your friendship, and for providing the perfect venue for the Boys of Bury to reveal their truth. No one else could have conducted that interview.

JoAnne Moreau and Tuesday Mills, for your help with fact checking and your amazing ability to find the truth.

Don Moreau, for sharing your knowledge and expertise to help us navigate through the language of law enforcement and the mind of a predator.

Stuart Poulton, for your cooperation and for providing background information to complete the story. *Best wishes on your journey going forward.*

Tim, for trusting me to meet and talk about your painful experiences. *As always, I wish you continued healing and a good life.*

Gemma and Paul, for sharing your perspectives and giving us a glance behind the curtain at the Academy of Dance and Performing Arts.

Paul Derrick, head of news content for the *Bury Free Press*, for assistance researching background on Bury St. Edmunds and Scott Rogers.

Lieutenant Don Kelly, Baton Rouge Police Department, whose sharp police instincts kept the Baton Rouge Police safe from manipulation by Scott Rogers, for your help with background information important to telling this story.

Sue Kaplan for your support and encouragement; Patricia Thomas for your support and for the best thing you offered—prayers for the children.

Shannon Fay Borghardt for legal advice; Adrian Randall for assistance and a lifetime commitment to stopping those who abuse children; Darla O'Connor for sharing your story.

Patricia Stallman, talented editor, for your encouragement, your help in assuring our story is clearly told, and for making me appreciate the Oxford Comma.

Everyone has a family by either birth or choice. I happen to think mine is extraordinary. Thanks to my late father, Huey P. Gray, for his love and kindness and for teaching by example that we should help others when we can. To my Mom, Dorothy Simmons Gray, for her amazing courage and for giving me the love and support to do whatever was needed to help the children and make sure the truth was told. Thanks to the rest of my family—my sister Abby and her husband Kurt; my brother, Mike and his family: Angel, Melissa, Sammy, Madelyn, Katherine, and Samuel—and to Daniel.

I have learned that strong families sustain us even when they don't know it, and I could not have done this without your listening, reading, advising, entertaining, helping, humoring, supporting, distracting, and all the other great things that families do.

Rannah Gray

INTRODUCTION

"SCOTT ROGERS IS A PREDATOR"

Day 57
Lafayette, Louisiana
October 23, 2013

Assistant U.S. Attorney Luke Walker leaned back in his chair, narrowed his eyes, and listened closely. Like two women seated before a judge, Mary Jane and I didn't waste any time getting to the matter at hand.

When she opened her notebook, removing copies of the emails and news articles Ethan had sent me from England, I suddenly thought, *What am I doing?* Just two months ago, I had never heard of Ethan. Then, one day, as I was leaving my office in Baton Rouge for a press conference with the Mayor, that first email on Scott Rogers popped up in my inbox. Now I was sitting in a federal courthouse in Lafayette, 60 miles from home, sharing a story that seemed unimaginable. *That's why I'm here. I believe Ethan is telling the truth.* So I began the story I had by now repeated several times.

I have worked around Louisiana politics long enough to hear all the rumors, tales, and outright lies that I needed to develop pretty good instincts about people. On top of that, I'm a skeptic by nature. Mary Jane Marcantel is a paralegal, which means she will research, investigate, and ask questions until she finds the truth.

As I studied Luke Walker carefully listening to what we had learned about Rogers' past, I began to think we had finally found someone who understood. *You are exactly what I've been looking for*, I thought. Everything Mary Jane had told me about Walker rang true, and I began to relax for the first time in two months. *He's going to help!*

Walker wears the mantle of an Assistant United States Attorney so well that you easily imagine him convicting drug dealers, bank robbers, and corrupt politicians. And he does all of that. But his serious demeanor also reflects extensive work convicting those who engage in child pornography, human trafficking, and child molestation. He is patient and focused, and as we talked, he glanced at the photos in the old newspaper clippings we had brought, politely allowing us to tell our story. He interrupted only to clarify a point, then settled back in his chair as we continued.

Just a few months before we drove across the Atchafalaya River Basin from Baton Rouge to ask for his help, the U.S. Department of Justice had honored Luke Walker with its Child Protection Award at a Washington, D.C., ceremony. Now we were sitting across from him—Luke Skywalker, the comparison he hears all too often but still smiles courteously to acknowledge. And like the fictional character he calls to mind, Luke Walker is a hero…in this case a champion for the survivors of child sex abuse.

When Luke finally spoke, he had processed the information we had presented to him, and he laid out the plan to save the two little boys who now lived with Scott Rogers in Baton Rouge.

For two long months, I had been looking for the right person, the person who had the authority and the will to act on what Ethan had sent me. *At last, someone with the power to do something is going to help us!*

"There are two types of child sex offenders," Luke Walker said. "One we call *situational*," and he explained how those offenders, finding themselves alone with a child, may experience urges and molest the child, an act outside their normal behavior. "The other type we call *predators*," he explained, "always hunting for the next victim, always looking to get control of a child.

"This is the most dangerous kind," he said, as I hung on every word.

Then he sat up in his chair, leaned forward, and looked squarely at Mary Jane and me before speaking with the confidence that comes from 25 years of confronting society's most reviled criminals.

He tapped his index finger on the copies of old news articles he had spread out on his desk, bringing our focus back to the reason we were there.

"Scott Rogers is a predator."

The Boys of Bury

ETHAN *in his own words*

A LONG WALK HOME

Bury St. Edmunds, England
1990

It was a winter evening when I left the Academy that night. It was very cold. My lips were dry. It must have been 7 p.m. I stopped outside the door and wondered what I should do. I can't go home. I was in complete shock. I felt a silent panic that grew inside me. I started to walk. I couldn't think straight. I knew I had just been abused, I knew how wrong it was. Was it my fault? I let it happen. What do I do? I had my personal stereo with me. I put some music on and started to walk. Not in the direction of home—I walked towards the Abbey Gardens. I didn't know how to deal with this. I was so scared. I was in so much trouble. One way or another, I got to the Abbey; it was closed, and so I jumped a wall and found myself inside. Alone. I walked over to a tree, I sat down.

I kept going over what happened. I couldn't stop it. If I tell anyone I'll never have a normal life, my family will never have a normal life. If I tell anyone, everyone will soon know. My brother will get bullied. I can't tell a soul. Ever. If I keep it secret, it will be as if it never happened.

I felt like a massive betrayal. I couldn't think of anything worse. Was it my fault? What do I do? I didn't know. I needed more time to think but Mum would be getting worried if I didn't make it home soon.

I have to put this right. I felt butterflies intensify in my stomach. I wanted to cry but I couldn't. Somehow I have to make this right. Maybe it won't happen again. I can get through this. I have to get through this. I have to survive it.

I closed my eyes. I mustered up all the strength I had. I swore to myself—If I can survive this, I will put this right. I pulled myself together and stood up. I jumped back over the wall and slowly walked home.... I felt a massive change. I didn't have time to do anything else. But start to act. Start to lie. Start to live a separate life.

As soon as I walked through my front door, I became someone else.

CHAPTER ONE

BURY ST. EDMUNDS

March 27, 2015
Bury St. Edmunds, England

As you leave London in the afternoon and drive north into the countryside, through the small towns and ancient villages, you pass children pushing their scooters and riding skateboards on the sidewalks after school. Just west of Bury St. Edmunds, around Newmarket, the landscape is green with grassland and home to more than 3,000 racehorses. My Louisiana friends who are racing enthusiasts have taught me that Newmarket is the international birthplace of thoroughbred racing. It is also the home of the legendary Tattersalls auction, where over 10,000 of the world's finest horses are sold annually.

East of Bury, Suffolk County stretches all the way to the North Sea, where the coastline has suffered erosion as dramatic as coastal Louisiana, leaving behind ghost towns, their residents evicted by the sea.

Around Bury, farmers grow sugar beets, wheat, barley, and vegetables in the sandy soil and sell their produce in surrounding market towns.

Most Bury St. Edmunds families know each other, and most weekends revolve around activities at historic churches or the local community theatre. The Theatre Royal promotes a talent show called "Bury's Got Talent" that asks the question, "Are you Bury's next star?" *This is almost the same appeal Scott Rogers made! Performing arts in Bury are as popular as sports in Louisiana,* I thought. *The promise of fame must be a powerful allure.*

Local pubs and restaurants serve food from the area farms, and a thriving tourist trade helps support a genteel way of life. Narrow cobblestone streets dotted with blooming flowers and park benches beckon you outdoors, where children play and couples stroll until twilight falls.

When I made the journey to Bury in March 2015, as I settled into the back seat of the taxi out of London, I tried to imagine Ethan's childhood. He should have been safe here from the evils of the world.

With a population of just over 40,000, Bury still holds farmers markets in the town center twice a week and offers, in addition, Britain's largest brewery and smallest pub. Greene King Brewery, which produces some of the country's favorite beers, dates back to 1799 and stands just across the street from the Theatre Royal. And if you want to grab a beer with a few of your closest friends, you can squeeze into The Nutshell, serving customers in the town center since 1867. With the *Guinness Book of World Records* proclaiming it Great Britain's smallest pub, The Nutshell is a popular tourist stop as well as a local favorite.

On the outskirts of town, a tall British processing plant that turns sugar beets into refined sugar occasionally sends its sweet, earthy aroma wafting through the streets of Bury, a scent so common that the locals tend to forget about it until a visitor inquires. With a scent more reminiscent of vegetables boiling on a stovetop than cookies baking in an oven, to Bury residents, sugar beets are simply the smell of money.

Bury grew up as a market town around the Abbey of Bury St. Edmunds, which dates to the 11th century. The Abbey's ruins still remain near the St. Edmundsbury Cathedral, and just down the street, in St. Mary's Church, Mary Queen of France, the favorite sister of King Henry VIII, is buried. Queen Mary, who loved market day in Bury St. Edmunds as much as today's visitors, kept her own pavilion on Angel Hill, just across from the Abbey Gardens, where a tony boutique hotel called *The Angel* stands today.

Local establishments like The Abbey Hotel give you a glimpse of the rich history and charm of the area, as visitors climb narrow staircases to sleep in 600-year-old rooms and wake to proper English breakfasts.

In 1214, in the heart of Bury St. Edmunds, the Barons of the time met at the Great Abbey, where they forced King John to sign the Magna Carta, thus giving the small town over 800 years of English history to celebrate. When I walked through the Abbey Gardens that March day, the ruins looked like the perfect playground for energetic young boys like Ethan and his friends to re-enact the adventures of their favorite action heroes from movies like *James Bond* or *Commando. What a perfect imaginary battlefield—open spaces to run and lots of places to hide!*

With its impeccable landscaping, rich arts and culture, and polite residents, Bury St. Edmunds is Middle England, and its values are much the same as Middle America's. The town, which centers on conservative beliefs and moral principles, is a place where residents live by conventional English standards, far different from the more progressive views of nearby Londoners. And while Americans might think of England as relatively small in size compared to the United States, residents there typically refer to living in the United Kingdom, or the U.K., which consists of England, Scotland, Wales, and Northern Ireland.

Located less than a two-hour drive from London, one of the world's leading financial and cultural centers, Bury is what Americans think of as a quintessential English town. Or as Paul Derrick, head of news content for the *Bury Free Press* told me when I visited his office, "It's the sort of town you would see on a chocolate box." *But life in Bury was far from picture perfect,* I thought. *Just 20 years earlier a quiet evil was at work here, tearing families apart and stealing the innocence of children.*

In this idyllic setting, in 1983, Scott Rogers and his wife Mandie opened the Academy of Dance and Performing Arts, where they taught young boys and girls to act and dance and encouraged them to dream of starring on stage, television, and in movies. While Scott had no credentials to teach dance, he used Mandie's to establish the Academy, with himself serving as a choreographer and the school's principal.

When the two initially started teaching, they held dance classes at the Mildenhall and Lakenheath Air Force Bases, which primarily support U.S. Air Force personnel. This tie to the Americans living in Suffolk County gave Scott the appearance of some unspoken connection with the United States. Later, the Academy got its official start in the village of Hopton, near Bury St. Edmunds, with just half a dozen students.

Soon, Scott acquired studio space in the back half of the old train station in Bury and moved all instruction there. The station provided space for dance and music studios, changing rooms, offices, a small theatre, and a shop where students could pay their fees and purchase uniforms. Mandie taught the classes, such as ballet, that required formal training, and Scott began choreographing performances for festival competitions. The two of them developed the Academy into a thriving business with eight full-time and seven part-time staff.

On December 19, 1984, Mandie gave birth to a daughter, Kimberly Anne Mary Rogers, who grew up around the Academy in the company of her parents.

During my visit in 2015, I met former dance student Gemma at a diner in Central London. I knew I would like her when I saw her waving cheerfully to my taxi driver from the sidewalk, eager to direct him to the closest parking garage. She had spotted him circling the block several times and called my cell phone to ask, "Is that you in the silver people carrier? Just tell your driver to look for me and I'll show him where he can park." Before we even spoke, we were laughing together at his obvious frustration with London's Friday afternoon traffic as we hurried down the windy street into the diner.

Gemma had attended the Academy from the time it opened in 1983 until after Scott's 1993 trial for sexual assault and gross indecency with a young male student. I knew she could help fill in the blanks for the story that had overshadowed normal life for me during the past year.

"Scott was very creative, very good at choreography," she told me. And while she had enjoyed many sleepovers at Scott and Mandie's house, she said, the girls always slept away from the boys, so she had never witnessed the abuse. As for Scott's dance instruction, Gemma told me, "He knew what he was doing. He didn't have any formal qualifications, but he taught the festival groups, and we won every competition. Because he was successful at winning the festivals, the talented kids wanted to come study with him. So he had some exceptional dancers."

Gemma, I learned, is now a young professional living in London with a career that has taken her throughout the world. She smiles with the enthusiasm of a young girl when she shares the good memories of the Academy kids, but her eyes reflect a tender sorrow when she considers the abuse she now knows some of her classmates suffered. "He was very narcissistic," Gemma explained of Scott. "But also very charismatic and very manipulative. He learned how to keep you on edge so you would behave the way he wanted. It was a beautiful example of how a narcissist behaves: Make people feel very, very special so they live in your world. Then absolutely knock them down so they will do anything they can to get back into that circle. And just constantly keep them on edge."

Once students from the surrounding area began attending the Academy, some of those parents allowed their children to transfer to the same Bury schools the other Academy kids attended, so that working out before and after school, as well as on weekends, was easier to schedule. Because of the long hours the students were happy to put in, the next step had been for Scott to invite his favorite students to stay overnight at the house he shared with Mandie and their young daughter, Kimberly. As Scott flattered the parents about their children's promising futures, many agreed to the sleep-overs. Scott, after all, was an elder in the local Mormon Church, and his young wife and daughter were always conspicuous around the Academy; the parents, therefore, felt fortunate that such a man took a keen interest in their children.

At its peak, enrollment stood at 800 or more students, and Academy dance teams were good enough to win local competitions routinely, helping Rogers recruit more students from the nearby towns.

As the Academy continued to grow, Scott decided to take in, as a foster child from Child Services, a 10-year-old boy named Jake. To convince authorities to place the boy with him, Scott took advantage of problems Jake's parents were having in a custody battle. As time passed, he taught Jake the skills of a great dancer, paired him with a beautiful dance partner, and promoted him as the pride of the Academy. And Jake evolved as one of the Academy's success stories: handsome, talented, and eventually starring in London's West End productions and national touring shows.

But before Jake realized his dreams of performing in some of the world's most renowned theatres, Scott forced him to live a nightmare, one that almost cost him his life.

The Boys of Bury

ETHAN *in his own words*

Bury St. Edmunds, England
1985

My early years were great. My brother and I had the run of the village and often went out looking for adventure at an early age. We got into all kinds of mischief, always ending up at home at the end of the day for a bath and a good telling off. We became well known around the village. There was a lot to do, ditches to play in, trees to climb, and a park and a field. And other village kids...we were friends with some and not so friendly with others.

There were a few who often wanted to fight. This was my first experience having a fight. My brother and I looked out for each other; sometimes we ran, sometimes we fought, but we never got too beaten up and sometimes we even won. I remember my first fight, a circle of kids, tops off, fighting in the middle of a circle on the field. I'm not too sure any of us really knew what we were doing, throwing random punches, pushing, and wrestling.

I liked it. I liked Bury. I liked the primary school. I liked my bike. I liked my brother and I liked being a kid.

C H A P T E R   T W O

THE EMAIL

Day 1
Baton Rouge, Louisiana
August 28, 2013

Late summer in Baton Rouge brings forth a heat that rises in waves from the pavement. The August sun radiates through the air, making everyone appear to move in slow motion. That heat is the first thing I remember about Wednesday, August 28, 2013.

The cheerful morning TV news anchors had warned us that the humidity would be *oppressive*, not exactly a word I wanted to hear for the outdoor press conference I had scheduled later that day. When you work in public relations, you find yourself involved in a wide variety of subjects, and today's promised pure fun. Not surprising, when I decided to leave my office and walk the six blocks down North Boulevard to Town Square for a final check of the set-up, it was the hottest time of the day. In a couple of hours, we would announce the first Baton Rouge New Year's Eve celebration, when a 10-foot lighted Red Stick would drop at midnight from the very place where we would meet the press that August day. The Red Stick—or *Baton Rouge*—is a reminder both of our city's French heritage and of the wooden stake Native American hunters drove into the Mississippi River bank to mark the boundaries of their hunting grounds. Draped with the pelts from their hunts, the Red Stick was dark red, stained by the blood of their kill. That spot high on the riverbank marked what is now Louisiana's Capital City.

Our firm, Marmillion/Gray Media, had produced the advertising campaigns for Baton Rouge Mayor-President Kip Holden's three successful elections. Recently, I had volunteered to take on this project, working with him to create *Red Stick Revelry,* a signature event for the city. We had raised private funds from local companies and planned the day's announcement to include, in addition to Mayor Holden, a number of the city's top business leaders, whose generosity had funded the inaugural event.

Then, just before leaving my office, I heard the computer's familiar *ping* that signaled a new email, and for a minute considered reading it on my phone as I walked. But something made me stop and go back to my desk. Not recognizing the sender, I clicked the message and saw that the subject line read "Scott Rogers," admittedly not my favorite topic.

I had met Rogers only one time, with a mutual client about concerns she had over his work. Scott had become very emotional, even weeping in what I felt was some sort of strange, dramatic performance meant to distract from his inability to perform in a professional business setting. To those of us at the meeting, he lost all control.

I started reading the email, and while it was only about 10 lines long, every sentence packed a punch. One shocking statement could barely sink in before I read the next. I kept thinking, *Who sent this? Why is he contacting me?* The words started running together as I began reading it a second time: "I knew Scott Rogers in the 90s…sexually abusing boys as young as 12…. I'm extremely confident he will still be abusing…children may be in danger."

While the sender's name was at the top of the email, the message was signed simply "E." *Who is this? How did he find me?*

With its U.K. email domain, I was somewhat surprised it escaped getting caught by a spam filter, or lost in the black hole of junk mail. But this email had reached its intended target. And although the words struck me as bizarre—and I had no clue who was reaching out to me—I had an instant feeling they were all true. Something about the puzzling message made sense…and I suspected I was about to learn the answer to questions that had lingered about Scott Rogers since my first recollection of him. While he had portrayed himself as a friendly TV host who supported local charities, law enforcement, and the faith community, I had always felt that something about his mysterious arrival in Baton Rouge didn't add up. While I found his charade fake and pretentious, I knew he had attracted a small but loyal following. *This is someone who knows Scott Rogers! But why contact me?*

I quickly hit the print key, got up from my desk, and walked to the window overlooking North Boulevard to wait for the copy. When the whir of the printer stopped, I reached for the page, folded it in half, tucked it into my purse, and headed out the door. The mystery that was Scott Rogers was about to unravel. What I didn't know at the time was: A monster was living among us.

CHAPTER THREE

THE ATTORNEY

Day 1
Baton Rouge, Louisiana
August 28, 2013

During the press conference in Town Square, I noticed Nathan Fisher and his young associate, Shannon Fay, standing in the shade, listening. One of Louisiana's top criminal defense attorneys, Nathan is best known for wearing colorful bow ties and walking his defendants out of jail. But what I had really come to respect over the years was his deep interest in all of his clients, not just fighting for them in the courtroom, but also putting them on a better path in life. He is the most loyal friend a person can have, as generous with his time as he is with his money, willing to do whatever he can to help. I was glad to see Nathan, his face shaded by the straw hat he was wearing to elude the sun's piercing rays. I knew he was the only person I could trust with the email that waited in my purse.

Just before the line-up of speakers announced the New Year's celebration, I walked over to the covered area where Nathan stood. "I need to talk to you. Can I see you after this?" I asked, hoping he could sense the urgency in my voice.

"Yeah," he said, studying me for some hint of what was going on. "I'll be at the office."

I hurried away, trying to put the contents of the email out of my mind. Town Square was the perfect place for our big announcement, but the sooner we got everyone out of the heat, the better. The Mayor, who had shown up with a cast on his hand from recent surgery, recruited me to stand with him at the podium to help with his notes. We were only two blocks from the Mississippi River, which occasionally hurled warm breezes our way like the burst of hot air that escapes from the open door of an oven. As I helped the Mayor turn the pages of his remarks so they did not go fluttering away on a gust of heat, news outlets were sending out our announcement as "Breaking News." After months of planning, I was feeling good that we had reached this day, but in the back of my mind, I couldn't stop thinking about that email. *What did this stranger want? His message was chilling. Of all times to be standing here in front of everyone!*

After the press conference, I spoke briefly to some of the people who had gathered. Since Mayor Holden had taken office, most residents considered Baton Rouge a boomtown; the crowd that summer day welcomed news of the city's first official New Year's celebration. A majority-white voting population had elected Holden as Baton Rouge's first African-American mayor, which was unusual for a Southern city.

My business partner Val Marmillion and I had called Holden prior to the 2004 election and told him we believed he could win—and we wanted Marmillion/Gray Media to help elect him. In addition to Val's national work, he and I had formed an advertising and public relations firm to handle Louisiana projects that had both local and national interests. Together we had produced national award-winning advertising campaigns and videos on local market budgets, often beating our competition and their substantial national production money. Our success made the clients happy and gave us the opportunity to work together.

Although Val was born in Houma, Louisiana, he had spent most of his professional career outside the State. He had served as Chief of Staff to former U.S. Senator John Breaux when he was a Congressman, and managed Breaux's successful campaign for the Senate in 1986. Then, after spending time on

Capitol Hill in Washington, Val moved to Los Angeles, where he built a successful public relations firm later acquired by global giant Ogilvy & Mather. Unhappy working in the corporate environment, he started another boutique public relations firm and produced groundbreaking public education campaigns for national clients.

Through it all, he remained drawn to Louisiana, his home. When the State of Louisiana hired him to create the America's WETLAND Foundation to draw attention to Louisiana's coastal land loss, he began spending more and more time in the State. At that same point, he and I decided to look for opportunities to work together.

Since Kip Holden had run for Mayor twice unsuccessfully, even some of his staunchest supporters had lost hope and discouraged him from trying again. As a man who can find the sunny side of any situation, however, he felt our call offering assistance had come at the perfect time. The result was our joining his campaign and helping him develop a winning strategy and a lasting trust.

Once elected, the Mayor became something of a rock star, tremendously popular with the public, as he set Baton Rouge on course to achieve national rankings for its strong economy and resurgence. The city's success meant few would admit they hadn't supported Mayor Holden in his first successful election, and by the time he ran for a second term in 2008, his victory included winning every single precinct in East Baton Rouge Parish. *That certainly silenced those who called his first election a fluke!*

Sticky from the heat but excited about the success of the day, I slipped away from the lingering crowd at the press conference, quickly walking the two blocks from Town Square down St. Ferdinand Street past the courthouse to the Law Offices of Nathan Fisher. *He will know how to handle the email,* I thought, *how to respond to the sender, what to do.* So after a quick *hello* to the receptionist, I almost ran up the stairs to the office where Nathan sat behind his desk, on the telephone, motioning for me to come in and take a seat. I waved to Shannon down the hall to join us. She had started working for Nathan as a young college student, but was now a savvy lawyer in her own right, and even though he didn't yet know it, I knew Nathan would want her in the discussion.

Nathan has handled some interesting cases. As I sat waiting, I remembered that, as a young lawyer, he had helped New Orleans District Attorney Jim Garrison investigate the assassination of President John Kennedy. I recalled his years representing LSU athletes, free of charge, when they were involved in local incidents. Nathan was so committed to the law that at times he represented the occasional sex offender, determined that even the worst criminals deserved the best defense available.

Perhaps the Danziger Bridge case in New Orleans, however, truly defined his career in terms of his relentless pursuit of justice. Ronald Madison, a young developmentally disabled man, who, his family said, had the mental capacity of a 6-year-old child, and his brother Lance, a former NFL receiver in the 1980s, had sought refuge at the bridge after the rising storm waters of Hurricane Katrina flooded their home in 2005.

When the New Orleans Police received a call reporting gunshots on the bridge, they responded and fired on a family walking across it, killing one and injuring four others. Hearing the shots, the Madison brothers fled the area, but police tracked them down and fired on both of them. With Ronald shot in the shoulder, Lance made the decision to run for help. When the officers caught up to the injured Ronald, one shot him in the back and another stomped on him before he died. Nathan initially stood alone against the strength of the New Orleans Police Department in the aftermath of the devastating storm, defending Lance Madison, whom police had charged with attempted murder of the eight police officers, even though he was unarmed. In the chaos following Katrina, Lance, a respected FedEx employee for 25 years, had been shackled and jailed for almost a month before Nathan could get him released.

In his pursuit of justice for the Madison family, Nathan would not be deterred. Months turned into years as he investigated the case, collecting evidence, conducting interviews, and ultimately, in 2010, taking what he had learned to the Justice Department to help it indict the officers. In what the U.S. Department of Justice called one of the most significant police misconduct prosecutions in U.S. history, five New Orleans Police officers were convicted in 2011 on a total of 25 civil rights violations that earned them sentences of six to 65 years behind bars. Three other officers involved in the cover-up pleaded guilty to various lesser charges. Because of wrongdoing by some members of the prosecution's team, the complicated case remains in appeals today.

Nathan's client, Lance Madison, was cleared of all charges against him. Six years passed, however, before he delivered a stirring statement to the officers at their sentencing—a statement describing the devastation that their actions had caused his family. Throughout those six years, Nathan had kept a quiet resolve, as he and his associate Shannon worked diligently in pursuit of the truth for the Madison family. The Danziger Bridge case epitomizes how Nathan worked throughout his life— quietly, tirelessly, and always with an eye on finding the truth. And even though the journey towards justice was slow and frustrating, he always believed that the power of the United States Government would ultimately set things right.

If we have a sex offender in our midst, Nathan will know what to do, I thought. *I know I can count on him.*

My mind drifted back to the conversation he was having on the phone with a client, sternly asking questions to make sure he had done everything that Nathan had instructed. I glanced around the office, which is a shrine to the 1970s: contemporary chrome and black leather furniture, an original Woodstock poster framed and leaning against the wall, along with artwork, certificates, and basketball memorabilia from his son Ari's coaching career at nearby University High School and LSU.

As he ended his telephone conversation, he turned his focus to me and said, "What's up, kiddo?" I pulled the folded paper out of my purse, opened it, and handed it to him. As Nathan read, I was lost in thought about the shadowy figure of Scott Rogers, who had already caused so much trouble. *I had finally managed to put my own problems with Scott Rogers out of my mind. Now this!*

CHAPTER FOUR

THE CONTRACT

Spring 2009
Baton Rouge, Louisiana

Nathan Fisher knew the story of Scott Rogers well. That was another reason I needed his guidance. To understand how completely crazy it was for me to receive the email, you would have to know the twists and turns that led to this moment in 2013. You would have to know the roster of people who play local politics, some in opposition to Mayor Holden. As I had learned, his challengers don't mind taking shots at him or anyone around him.

Just two years earlier, Val and I had completed a project for the East Baton Rouge Parish Mayor's Office of Homeland Security and Emergency Preparedness (MOHSEP, pronounced *Mo-Sep* in the world of bureaucratic acronyms) and its director, JoAnne Moreau. The MOHSEP project brought us into our only contact with Scott Rogers and 1stCo, a Delaware corporation with a generic Internet presence identifying it as a TV and video production company.

Rogers hosted *The Around Town TV Show*, a 1stCo production that aired Saturdays and Sundays on local station WAFB-TV at 5 a.m. Almost a parody of the British sitcoms that still sometimes appear on PBS stations in the U.S., *The Around Town TV Show* featured Rogers as the effusive host gushing over a line-up of elected officials, government agency employees, and non-profit directors—with an occasional program sponsor thrown in. In recent years, Scott's daughter, Kimberly Scott Rogers, known as *Kimmy,* served as co-host, with Celeste Gill, who promoted herself as "Chef Celeste," serving as resident chef for the show and eventually replacing Kimmy as co-host. *Two Brits and an African-American chef trained in Hawaii—there was nothing "Around Town" about the show's hosts! But they all worked very hard to create the appearance that they were just like everyone else.*

We had learned that while Scott called all the shots, he had at times put the company in the name of his daughter and often led people to believe that two younger men, Mathew Hodgkins and Stuart Poulton, ran it. Both of these young men had moved to Baton Rouge with Scott, and both, we learned later from Ethan, were from Bury St. Edmunds, the same small English town where Scott had lived and taught dance. The corporate records listed, as president of the company, A. Martin; as treasurer, Mathew Hodgkins; and as agent for process, Lexlee Overton, who was Rogers' attorney and a recurring guest on the show. *Martin* was Scott Rogers' given name at birth, before he changed it several times, so at first Nathan and I thought "*A. Martin*" might be an alias for Scott, as so little was known about his mysterious arrival in Baton Rouge. We were not sure at this point of Scott's reasons for changing his name, but knew he had created a new identity for himself when he moved to the States.

Actually, we learned later, the *A. Martin* listed on the corporate papers for 1stCo was Angela Hills Martin, a student at the Academy in Bury St. Edmunds, who had also come to the U.S. with Scott and some of the others. She started *The Around Town TV Show* with him and remained a close friend, serving on the 1stCo Board of Directors. Later, Angela married and moved to nearby St. Tammany Parish.

Lexlee Overton is a personal injury attorney who runs a non-profit organization called *Lexlee's Kids,* for which Rogers frequently emceed events and which he promoted on his show. Lexlee's website claims that she dedicates a large part of her practice to helping children whom others have injured or wrongfully harmed. I would understand the irony of this statement as I learned more about her client, Scott Rogers.

The one project that brought Val and me in contact with 1stCo resulted in our filing suit against the company when Hodgkins billed the city-parish for work our firm had performed and then, at Scott's instruction, kept our fees. Nathan had referred me to a civil attorney to handle the suit, and Overton had represented 1stCo. Now faced with the new information in the email I had received from Ethan, Nathan and I wondered if Scott had chosen Overton because, as he built his network of contacts related to child welfare and law enforcement, her foundation focused on children and therefore served his unspoken purpose well.

I met MOHSEP Director JoAnne Moreau when I volunteered to help Mayor Holden with the overwhelming media response to Hurricane Katrina in 2005 and subsequently spent long hours in the Emergency Operations Center. Moreau is absolutely one of the best in the country at her job, with the national ratings to prove it. Married to Don Moreau, a retired Louisiana State Trooper who had served East Baton Rouge Parish as the Coroner's Office Chief of Operations, she reminds you often that she is the daughter of a German mother, as if to explain her inner strength, or perhaps to warn you of it. She is honest, loyal, focused, and determined to do what is right. Her job puts her in charge of coordinating the city's emergency response efforts from hurricanes to chemical spills to epidemics, and she will stand toe to toe with any law enforcement agent who may disregard the proper protocols. If a discrepancy in procedure occurs, the smart money is on JoAnne to get it right. Despite the intensity of her job, she also has the charm and sense of humor she needs to hold a large team together during the most difficult of times.

When the levees broke in New Orleans after Hurricane Katrina, leaving thousands stranded in attics and on rooftops, it was Baton Rouge that began receiving the 911 calls when the

New Orleans system collapsed. It was Baton Rouge that deployed a trained urban search and rescue team and propped up six local government bodies so that they could resume somewhat normal business operations. And it was Baton Rouge's response to Katrina, led by Mayor Holden and JoAnne, that a White House official said deserved a gold medal for compassion.

Sometime after Katrina had revealed the public's lack of knowledge on disaster response, JoAnne approached Val and me about helping her develop a public education program on emergency preparedness. She explained that one of the federal government's primary goals is to get information out from local governments to the public, so that residents are ready to deal with disaster. Katrina had uncovered so many weaknesses and vulnerabilities in Louisiana that JoAnne wanted to prepare Baton Rouge for any scenario.

She told me that 1stCo principal Scott Rogers had proposed producing a series of educational videos for broadcast on television and in hospital waiting rooms throughout the city. Though she was open to considering that idea, JoAnne wanted Val and me to develop a comprehensive public education campaign to manage the overall messages, so that accurate and consistent information reached the public. She understood the level of Val's work nationally, she knew he represented a number of local government organizations, and she wanted to be sure her department's programs met or exceeded national standards.

When Val and I discussed possibly combining the two projects, JoAnne quickly said that our firm, Marmillion/Gray Media, and 1stCo needed to decide whether to work together on a proposal. For her part, she wanted tight control over the messages. We offered to give 1stCo a call to discuss JoAnne's project and see whether working together was an efficient plan, and I scheduled a meeting with Scott Rogers at the 1stCo studio. Though I had never met him or seen his TV show, from the promos that aired for his program, I had not taken him very seriously. But if he had a TV studio that could produce quality work, I assumed we could at least talk to him to see if we might work together.

Val and I were excited about helping JoAnne build a program to help prepare communities and local officials for natural disasters like Katrina, and if 1stCo could contribute, we were willing to work with its crew.

For our meeting with Scott Rogers, Val and I arrived at Entrance 3 on the back of Cortana Mall, walked past a Chinese food buffet, and rang the buzzer on the locked door of *The Around Town TV Show* studio where 1stCo operated. We were entering for the first time the strange and uncomfortable world of Scott Rogers.

Cortana Mall had enjoyed its heyday in the 1970s and '80s, when it served as the region's primary shopping mall and one of the country's largest. But since 1997, when a second shopping center, the Mall of Louisiana, opened in Baton Rouge, Cortana had struggled to keep up. As a number of storefronts were empty within the expansive mall, we imagined that the space for *The Around Town TV Show* studio was available for rent at quite a reasonable price.

Arriving at the studio door, I rang a doorbell and a British voice came through the speaker box by the door. After we identified ourselves, we heard a buzzer, the door clicked, and some unknown person invited us to enter. In the entryway, framed photographs and certificates from local politicians and non-profit agencies, all recognizing Scott Rogers for hosting various charity fundraising events, lined the walls. As we walked past Scott's glory wall, we entered a small studio with sets for *The Around Town Show.*

A young barrel-chested man with a round face and slight beard appeared through a door from the back of the studio, calling out in his British accent, "Hello, I'm Mathew Hodgkins." He invited us into the studio to take a seat at a round, high-top table set up in the middle of the studio floor. Val and I glanced at each other briefly, then perched uneasily on round, wobbly bar stools with no backs under the bright studio lights. *What's going on?* I thought. *It's as if he is carefully positioning us on the set as part of a show.* With more comfortable options available, I found it odd that Rogers had set a table for us in the middle of an empty studio.

Surrounding us were the sets where he staged *The Around Town TV Show*, which only added to the eerie feeling that we had wandered upon a replica of classic America. A model kitchen for the cooking segment lined one wall, and a sofa and chair, with plastic plants alongside, provided another set. Finally, completing the display was a talk-show-style desk where Rogers sat to introduce the show, to close with interviews of his most prestigious guests of the hour, or to tape silly promos for upcoming shows.

Neither Val nor I had ever seen the program; however, because the promos occasionally aired late at night, we both had a vague idea of who Scott Rogers was. I was also somewhat familiar with him from his appearances in the community and had always thought him an oddity. His humor came across as forced, as he tried much too hard to promote his so-called "positive news show," or as his slogan proclaimed, "Unity in the Community." Looking around, I couldn't help wonder how he could convince enough businesses to sponsor his program to pay for the studio space, much less cover the salaries of his staff and crew.

As the three of us balanced awkwardly on our stools, I began to wonder if Mathew had to seat us before Scott would make his entrance. I felt very strongly that Scott was stage-managing us. Now that we had taken our places, I asked, "Is Scott joining us?"

"No, you will be meeting only with me," Mathew replied, offering no further explanation. In fact, Mathew was the only person we saw in the studio on that visit. Although he made reference to others who, we assumed, were there, everyone else remained out of sight.

As we sat under the intense TV lights, Val and I began by explaining that JoAnne had asked us to work with her to develop a new brand and public education program for emergency preparedness, and that she had also expressed some interest in a 1stCo proposal to produce videos for emergency events. We emphasized JoAnne's concern that the messages the two firms produced be consistent, and we wondered if our working together with 1stCo would help accomplish that efficiently. We described the scope of what JoAnne had asked us to do and told Mathew we would not mind working with 1stCo on the video production to help coordinate the information both firms communicated to the public. "What do you think?" I asked Mathew. "It doesn't matter to us—we are just looking for the most efficient way to achieve our goals." At the time, we knew what JoAnne wanted us to do for her department. If the 1stCo piece worked out for them, that would be fine with us. We could help them more than they could us, so the decision of whether to work together didn't really matter to us.

"That's fantastic!" Mathew said under the heat of the bright lights, a little too enthusiastic for my taste. "You clearly provide services that we do not, and this would be a great opportunity for us." *I guess the whole group tries hard to project that excessively positive tone*, I thought. Though Mathew said very little, speaking in a programmed but professional manner, he seemed eager to work with us.

"We can submit separate proposals or we can submit one together," I said. "We're fine either way. I just know the two have to be closely coordinated to work as smoothly and efficiently as JoAnne would like."

"Yes, let's submit together," Mathew said. "I think this is a *terrific* idea." *There it is again. Why does he sound so rehearsed?*

"How would you like to handle the proposal?" Val asked.

"Would you like 1stCo to be the lead consultant," I added, "or would you like us to lead?"

"It doesn't matter to us," Mathew replied. "Whatever works best."

Since we were unsure of the quality of 1stCo's work, I preferred for us to have as much control as possible, but when we learned that the cost of the 1stCo proposal was about three times more than ours, I told Mathew that it probably made more sense for 1stCo to serve as lead consultant, with our firm as a sub-consultant.

"Yes, we would like that," Mathew quickly agreed. "I can easily combine the two proposals for JoAnne and send you a copy."

"We typically sign a contract for our services," Val said. "Would you like us to provide a sub-consultant agreement between our two firms?"

"I don't think that is necessary," Mathew said. "Since we will both invoice the client for our work on a monthly basis and JoAnne will oversee our work, I don't think we need a separate agreement."

After a polite, albeit peculiar meeting, Val and I told Mathew we would look forward to receiving the combined proposal and working with him. During our discussion, we noted that the 1stCo staff was using relatively new HD cameras and appeared to have the necessary lighting and equipment for videotaping the segments we planned.

As if the invisible people inside *The Around Town TV Show* studio could still hear us, Val and I left the mall and walked the short distance to my car in complete silence, not speaking until we were about to open our car doors. "Did you have the feeling we were being recorded?" Val finally asked.

"Yes!" I said, looking at him over the top of the car. As we opened our doors to get in, I finally realized why I'd had such an uneasy feeling in the studio and why we had both walked in silence well into the parking lot before either of us had said a word. "And where do you think Scott Rogers was?" I asked.

"In the back, watching us," Val said matter-of-factly.

Beginning in May 2009, we worked with 1stCo to produce a television series for East Baton Rouge Parish Homeland Security, programs that provided information on how to prepare for any disaster, including hurricanes, floods, fires, and chemical spills. The program aired on the local government channel, Metro 21, and was available online, and the Parish provided it free of charge to anyone teaching others how to prepare for disasters. Val and I developed the "Red Stick Ready" brand and a public education campaign that both the National League of Cities and FEMA recognized as a National Best Practice. In fact, FEMA produced a training video showcasing our campaign as a model for training local elected officials around the country to deal with the public and the media during emergencies.

Even though the coordination with 1stCo was sometimes awkward, working with JoAnne and her staff was a pleasure. She had a small, close-knit team that logged incredibly long hours and genuinely seemed to enjoy its work.

Part of our task for the monthly television program included rewriting 1stCo scripts that Scott had reportedly written, scripts that used British lingo and an awkward cadence that sounded unnatural for our local audience. While we never had any direct contact with Scott, never saw him or spoke to him, when the project began, Mathew set up a single blind email address. He asked that we use it instead of communicating with any of the 1stCo staff individually, so that Scott could monitor all of our communications, a step we found very strange.

Both Mathew and Stuart Poulton, who also worked on the project with us, often mentioned him, reporting *Scott would want this* or *Scott would want that*. But he never attended any project meetings. We simply coordinated our work with Mathew and Stuart, under the direction of our client. When we rewrote scripts and sent them back to the generic email address, we never knew who received our work or how they reacted.

We occasionally taped a segment for the Red Stick Ready program on a set in the 1stCo studio, but while Mathew and Stuart often implied, in conversation, that Scott was in another part of the studio, he never made his presence known. And though he had initially asked to host the program, JoAnne preferred to tape in her own building to underscore for the public where and how her department operated. Because she wanted the information to come directly from trusted local government officials, she preferred that she and the Mayor serve as spokespersons. We agreed that interjecting a British TV host would only confuse people.

Later we learned that when Scott landed a similar contract with the local public library system to produce a monthly cable

TV program, he had asked to serve as the on-air host. The library staff members, however, knew they did not wish to present library information through the filter of an ostentatious British personality. When denied the opportunity to wrap himself around the impeccable reputation the library enjoyed, Scott assigned the project to Stuart and rarely participated.

A few years earlier, Scott had also approached the popular then-Baton Rouge Police Chief Jeff LeDuff, praising him for his interview skills and pushing him for a regular segment on *The Around Town TV Show* that would include crime prevention tips. But keen observation and good police instincts intercepted Scott's attempt to cozy up to the Chief. Baton Rouge Police Lieutenant Don Kelly, then a sergeant in the department, accompanied LeDuff to his first interview on the set.

Kelly had joined the Baton Rouge Police Department in 1986 after working as a reporter. For most of his career, he served as a public information officer for the department, giving news interviews and assisting police chiefs with media training and responses. He has an independent streak and is known for speaking his mind.

"We drove over to Cortana Mall together," Kelly explained, "and I had the luxury of sitting back and watching the production while the Chief did his interview. I had worked in television before becoming a cop, and I wanted to see what this show was all about. I was curious about the equipment they were using, how many people worked on the show. It was a small Sunday morning public affairs show, and when I was in the business, you didn't spend any money on those shows."

Kelly was impressed, however, with the quality of the broadcast equipment; the production was much more sophisticated than he had anticipated.

The most unusual aspect was that Scott had the crew produce the interview live to tape, meaning they shot everything in real time, taking no breaks between segments.

"Every show I've seen done like this was shot in segments, and then you piece it all together in post-production. They did the entire show as if it was airing live. They would run from one set to another, like what you see on *Saturday Night Live.* Number one, it's silly—it's a waste of energy—and I didn't know why they did it that way. It was more like watching a live play than a pre-recorded television production and it struck me as very theatrical, with Scott clearly in the roles of director and star."

But Sergeant Kelly's observation of Scott Rogers in action concerned him much more than the way Rogers produced the show.

"I watched Scott Rogers—he was like a circus ringmaster, in control, telling everyone what to do, controlling everyone in that studio, and they were deferential to him—I'd never seen anything like that," Kelly said. "One thing that really struck me was that everyone on the set was wearing identical black t-shirts with a screen-printed "Around Town TV Show" logo and "Crew" on the back...every person on the floor was dressed alike. Usually it's the opposite...TV people are independent sorts. The last thing they would do is put on uniforms like a NASCAR pit crew.

"Watching Scott as a performer, so over the top, gushy, and phony, it was hard to take him seriously," Kelly said. "It was like a parody. I thought at the time, *'I don't buy this act for a minute.'*"

Kelly was even more uncomfortable with the interaction on the set between Scott and his daughter. "There was an overall sense of the way they looked at each other, the way they talked to each other, touched each other...more like lovers, or a boyfriend-girlfriend relationship. When we left and got into the car, Jeff said, 'What did you think?' asking about his interview. I said, 'Chief, I have to tell you, I feel like I just left a cult. The matching t-shirts, the way he controls everyone, you just don't see talent doing that at this level—maybe in Hollywood, but not at a little nickel and dime TV show. There is more going on here than meets the eye. The really weird thing was his daughter—it was creepy. I even wondered if she was really his daughter. I'm telling you, this guy is either a serial killer or a pedophile. We need to stay away from him.'

"I felt like I had just left Jonestown," Kelly said, recalling the American cult leader Jim Jones, who, in 1978, orchestrated a mass suicide of more than 900 followers, including 200 children, just as authorities began to investigate his compound in Jonestown, Guyana. His name is still synonymous with the inconceivable hold some charismatic leaders have over their followers, getting them to "drink the Kool-Aid" they knew would kill them.

A few weeks after Kelly's first close-up encounter, retired Baton Rouge Police Lieutenant Richard Sobers contacted him. Kelly had been surprised to see Sobers working on the set of *The Around Town TV Show,* wearing the same matching crew shirt as the others. The retired officer was calling to say that the show wanted to begin a regular segment on crime prevention and that Rogers had assigned Sobers to coordinate it. He suggested they set up situations that would allow police officers to demonstrate how easily a criminal can break into a house or automobile. Kelly agreed to organize a demonstration for the show and shortly afterward arranged for a few more. But soon Sobers began asking for the police demonstrations more frequently, even suggesting weekly segments for Scott's television program.

Kelly called Sobers to tell him that work demands would not allow the Baton Rouge Police Department to help produce a weekly segment for *The Around TV Town Show,* since participation would involve his own time in scheduling officers and would also pull officers from their work details.

"Look, Buddy," Kelly told Sobers. "This is getting to be too much. We're very busy, we're dealing with deadlines and hard news, and I just don't have the time to devote this many resources to one little cable TV show."

Kelly recalls, "I just did not have time to pull detectives off of cases and set up sites for taping. We had to pull back. Maybe we could have done it once a month, but not once a week. I didn't think the payoff was much. I didn't know anyone who actually watched the show."

Sobers obviously reported Kelly's response to Scott Rogers, because soon after explaining why the department could not provide weekly content for the show, Kelly received a call from an irate Rogers.

"Scott had an extremely over-the-top reaction," Kelly remembers. "He was pissed—that's the only way to put it. My conversation with Richard Sobers was not controversial. It was basically to tell him that I have only this many people, so many hours in the day.

"But now the curtain was pulled back and I was not dealing with the syrupy Mr. Rogers anymore. I was dealing with someone who was abusive, demeaning, condescending—not just yelling, but intent on taking me to task. This guy on the phone with me was psychotic—totally the polar opposite of what he had portrayed, which I had never believed in the first place."

At one point in his conversation with Rogers, Kelly, mentioning that Mathew had contacted him, referred to the young man as one of Scott's employees, which only angered Rogers more. Scott exploded at him, saying, "This is how stupid you are! Mathew doesn't work for me...I work for Mathew, but you didn't know that, did you, Sergeant Kelly?"

After Rogers screamed at him, Kelly recalls trying to calm him down and finally simply saying goodbye and hanging up. A few minutes later, the phone rang, and as caller ID showed Rogers was calling again, Kelly asked a fellow officer in the public information department to answer. The officer placed Rogers on hold and turned to Kelly with the news that Scott was calling to ask for Chief LeDuff's telephone number.

"I'll take it," Kelly responded. Picking up the phone, Kelly confronted Rogers, "What do you want, Scott? You want the Chief's cell phone number? His home phone number? Am I supposed to be scared of this because you're reporting me?"

Rogers shot back, "You obviously have a problem with me, and Chief LeDuff and I have always been quite good friends, and I want to see if the problem extends to him."

"I knew the Mayor had done the show a couple of times, and I thought at the time he might be close to Rogers. I didn't know. So I gave Rogers the number and called Jeff to tell him I had just had the weirdest conversation with Scott. 'I knew that guy wasn't right,' I told LeDuff, 'and now I've seen this side of him. This guy is bad news, Chief—we just need to stay away from him.'

"I wish I could say I had a crystal ball and I knew everything," Kelly says now. "I thought there was a potential he was molesting his daughter. Every time I saw him with the Better Business Bureau or as Grand Marshal of a parade, it made me mad because I thought, *This guy is a pervert—he is a pedophile.* I had no evidence, but that was my impression. I knew he was a phony and a hypocrite and something was just not right about him. I didn't want my kids around him. I didn't want my department around him...and I was fortunate I had a good relationship with my boss and he listened. I never envisioned what a monster Rogers turned out to be."

Kelly had to watch while other law enforcement agencies allowed Scott to portray a close friendship and association with them on his TV show and at public events. When he tried to caution them about allowing Rogers to serve as emcee at the community's most respected public safety events, some colleagues even teased him about his strong feelings against the man.

Meantime, Scott Rogers was doing what he had always done—fooling the exact people a community depends on to protect children from men like him. Experts will tell you that this is one of the most effective tools a child predator uses: He will first spend time with parents, law enforcement, Child Services employees, and anyone else whose approval he needs to gain physical control of children. *He was seducing the gatekeepers!*

CHAPTER FIVE

THE MELTDOWN

November 2009
Baton Rouge, Louisiana

When Val and I began working on the Homeland Security project with 1stCo, none of us was aware that Lieutenant Don Kelly had forewarned the Baton Rouge Police Chief about Scott Rogers. In fact, even more time passed before I actually met Scott and witnessed his bizarre Jekyll and Hyde behavior first hand.

For almost a year, when we taped segments for the *Red Stick Ready* project in the *Around Town* studio, JoAnne also had an eerie feeling that someone was watching us. During our visits, Kimmy, her manner always overly attentive, would suddenly appear from the back of the studio and join us before JoAnne's TV appearance. Her focus honed in on JoAnne—talking to her, flattering her, and even brushing her dark brown hair.

"You look lovely," Kimmy gushed as she straightened JoAnne's jacket and checked her makeup. Kimmy is an attractive, full-figured blonde with a penchant for performing. JoAnne recalls her singing, on her father's show, a sultry version of "God Bless America" in the style of Marilyn Monroe's "Happy Birthday, Mr. President." For the taping of that segment at Louisiana's Old State Capitol Building, Kimmy stood, wearing an evening gown, on the dramatic winding staircase under a brightly-colored stained glass dome. Scott showcased that performance several times on the *Around Town Show.*

Though Scott, we assumed, must dispatch his daughter from the back of the studio to focus on the client, at that point he had never actually shared his own presence. Then suddenly, one day, when we were all talking in the studio, a man's voice with a British accent reverberated over the speakers in response to something one of us had said, and we froze.... Scott was in fact watching us and listening to every word we said. *So creepy!*

Later, a MOHSEP staff member said she felt Scott had created a special caste system around his ego by assigning each of his crew one of us to ingratiate. She had observed, for example, that Scott spoke only to JoAnne, as if reserving his charm for the person highest in the hierarchy. Mathew made frequent phone calls to check in with JoAnne's deputy director, Tuesday Mills, and, as I seemed to have the best rapport with Stuart, he and I coordinated guests and schedules. Kimmy was clearly the emissary Scott sent to schmooze JoAnne, who was much too perceptive for such obvious manipulation.

When JoAnne, in her friendly and open way, asked the 1stCo production crew, "Where's Scott?" one of the group would say, "He's out back blowing a fag," laughing at her reaction as they explained the British slang for smoking a cigarette.

During the time we spent at the studio, Scott never made a single appearance, even though his people usually acknowledged he was "in the back." I later learned from a reporter for the U.K.'s *Daily Mail* that many people in Bury St. Edmunds said they had never met Scott when he was living there, even though they were aware of his presence in the town. Scott seemed to have a way of pushing others out front to speak for him, while he conducted most of his business behind the scenes. He was the host of a community television program, yet he never even welcomed his client, JoAnne, when she visited his studio.

One day in September 2009, as we walked out of the studio after taping a segment for the *Red Stick Ready* program, JoAnne received an email announcing a new partnership between *The*

Around Town TV Show and the Governor's Office of Homeland Security and Emergency Preparedness, or GOHSEP— pronounced *Go-Sep*—to produce a monthly television segment. Staring at her phone, JoAnne, along with Tuesday Mills and me, sat in the food court area across from the studio and read the message again. We were only about 20 feet from where we had worked for the last hour, and no one there had said a word about Scott's State-level partnership, which, we assumed, would duplicate the information we were producing with 1stCo for the local program. The three of us sat quietly as occasional shoppers walked by and the fast food restaurants in the adjacent food court prepared for their lunch crowds, the smell of chicken stir-fry in the air.

As we re-read the email, JoAnne recalled that she and I had attended a luncheon meeting on disaster management at LSU, where the GOHSEP director had complimented her on the program we were producing but had made no mention of his interest in something similar. In fact, the role of the State agency had never been to communicate directly with the public on a local basis. Rather, that office had produced statewide communications and then worked closely with local parishes to get information to the communities.

"Can you believe they didn't mention a word about this?" JoAnne asked incredulously. She read aloud from the press release, "'When the producers of the show offered this opportunity for GOHSEP to take part in a monthly segment to help educate the public on ways to keep their families safe from all-hazards, we jumped at the opportunity, said GOHSEP Director Mark Cooper.'

"What are they doing?" she asked. The press release stated the first segment would focus on preparation for the H1N1 virus and a possible pandemic, a topic we were currently researching in pre-production for the *Red Stick Ready* program.

JoAnne was quite concerned that Rogers was charging both the city and the State for the content 1stCo produced for her program. His secrecy aroused her suspicions: *Why else had he decided not even to discuss with her his involvement with the State office...on a project so similar in scope to her own?* Her department's close working relationship with the State is critical to her operations. She did not want Scott to cause any conflicts between the two agencies.

That evening, JoAnne sent a brief email to Mathew requesting a meeting with the 1stCo staff about the announcement of its new partnership with GOHSEP. He replied with a rambling email six paragraphs long that feigned only a mild awareness of the press release and described the GOHSEP arrangement as routine guest appearances on future programs. In a tone that sounded more like Scott than Mathew, he ended with a smug question, "Are you sure you want to meet tomorrow over a guest interview segment on our *Around Town* production? I am not sure how this interview segment has a bearing on production of *Red Stick Ready* or the Mayor's Office. Please let me know if this helps clear this up for you."

JoAnne replied, "Yes, I believe it's necessary."

JoAnne met the following morning at her office with Mathew and Stuart to address her questions. *Scott had sent the scouting party out!* In typical fashion, they returned to the studio and Mathew sent a lengthy written response, after they discussed the meeting with Scott.

"Dear JoAnne," he began. "First, thank you for spending time with Stuart and me to explain your feelings and position this morning. There was a lot of information that you shared with us that we were oblivious to and that came as a total surprise to us both.

"Second, I have had a chance to share your conversation in the meeting today with Scott," Mathew wrote. Although Mathew and Stuart had met with JoAnne, it was clear they could not make any decisions until they first met with Scott. Mathew continued by saying, "Scott saw this new segment as an association between this parish and state." Of course, that would make a strong case for discussing a program that involved her department with JoAnne before announcing it.

"I know Scott has been trying for some time now to arrange a meeting with you and to spend some time with you, JoAnne, on another project," Mathew continued. "Had this requested meeting been arranged, this may have provided you both an opportunity to discuss this new segment idea (and for Scott to have received your input—since none of us at 1stCo were aware of any potential problems you described to us.)"

Was he trying to blame JoAnne for Scott's screw-up? Good luck with that!

"We are going to spend some more time together with Scott after our shoots today, and perhaps over the weekend (as a group) to review everything and to possibly make some suggestions that might help remedy your concerns. Of course, it was never our intention to cause you concern or worry."

But soon, JoAnne's instincts proved correct.

After she identified the topic she wanted to cover each month, our firm worked with her to determine the best spokespersons, research the information they would present, and invite them to appear on the show. Then we handed off the segment so that 1stCo could schedule the interviews.

Now that 1stCo was also producing a segment on emergency preparedness for GOHSEP, the program content we had developed and the guests JoAnne selected began to appear on the State's *Around Town* segment even before our local program aired.

Scott's use of our work for another project surprised all of us. While the local and State emergency management departments coordinate closely, 1stCo's commandeering of our content struck us as unethical, if not illegal. When you produce work for a client, sharing it with another client without permission—whether or not the second client is also paying you for the content—is unheard of. Though we assumed that the arrangement Scott had announced could involve a new contract, his press announcement touted a partnership. *Was GOHSEP paying him to do the same work? Or was he simply giving the State a segment on his show remarkably similar to the one JoAnne was paying him to produce? Either way, why hadn't he discussed his new arrangement with JoAnne?*

Scott's connection to GOHSEP was Veronica Mosgrove, GOHSEP's public information officer who was now co-hosting the emergency preparedness segment on *The Around Town TV Show* with Scott. Veronica is an icy blonde former television reporter in her mid-40s who has had a close relationship with former Baton Rouge Police Chief Greg Phares, now an investigator with the Louisiana Inspector General's Office.

Veronica grew up in New Orleans and worked in television in several markets before landing in Baton Rouge. In 2007, she was the weekend anchor and "nightside reporter," often covering crimes, for local television station WBRZ, and Phares was losing an election to current Sheriff Sid Gautreaux. In her coverage of the race for sheriff, her loyalty to Phares got her in hot water. Mosgrove reported, on air, stories that sent Gautreaux calling on the management at WBRZ to question her objectivity. After a couple of complaints, the station assigned another reporter to cover the campaign for sheriff.

I didn't know Phares before the sheriff's race, but I had worked closely with the Baton Rouge Union of Police, which had a strong relationship with Mayor Holden. During Gautreaux's earlier tenure as the Police Chief of Baker, a small municipality within East Baton Rouge Parish and therefore within Mayor-President Holden's jurisdiction, he had been a friend and political ally of the Mayor. Holden, after his first-term election, asked me to help Gautreaux organize his own team and prepare for a tough campaign against an incumbent sheriff. Soon Gautreaux asked me to take on campaign management responsibilities in addition to producing TV spots and other advertising.

Since the previous sheriff, who had served for 23 years, had resigned a year before his term expired, Phares was serving as interim sheriff until the election. Campaigns against incumbents are never easy, and this one was more than a little nasty. Many of those who supported Phares were angry that the very popular Mayor-President was lending his support to the challenger.

But Mayor Holden felt strongly that one way to help his friend was to duplicate the winning team that had successfully managed his own campaign against an incumbent mayor just a few years before. Gautreaux welcomed the support, recognizing the Mayor's popularity throughout the Parish, especially in the suburban neighborhoods of the southern part, where Gautreaux had never run.

I knew that Greg Phares had been controversial since his days as Baton Rouge police chief from 1992 until 2001, when his steely demeanor and quick temper defined him. During the time two serial killers were preying on women in Baton Rouge, residents, including some victims' parents, criticized Phares for not alerting the public soon enough.

In an interview with WVUE television station in New Orleans, Phares told reporter Kerry Cavanaugh he did not launch a public awareness campaign when police suspected the first serial killer because the victims were primarily prostitutes who already lived a high-risk lifestyle. When he suspected a second serial killer, Phares said he "addressed a local running club on jogging safety" but decided not to sound a public alarm. Murder victim Christine Moore's father told the reporter he did not believe his daughter would have gone running alone the day she was killed if she had known the risks.

"If you ask the families of these victims, many will tell you the serial killer isn't the only one with blood on his hands," Cavanaugh said, showing a poster with the photos of three victims.

"The right judgment call to make back then was that there was a serial killer out there," Moore's father said. "And that judgment call wasn't made, so that's something he has to live with. All I know is what I have to live with."[1]

Lynne Marino, the outspoken mother of victim Pam Kinamore, who was killed in 2002, never held back in her criticism of the police investigation. In 2007, she called Sid Gautreaux and asked to record a radio spot for him in his campaign against Phares. Gautreaux asked me to talk with her because she wanted to make sure her spot was well written and

---

[1] Fruggidy, dir. "Phares Knew About the Serial Killer." You Tube. 14 November 2007. Web. 9 September 2015.

effective. My conversation with Mrs. Marino echoed what we often saw in her interviews with the media—a devastated mother inconsolable over the death of her beautiful daughter. While we were hesitant to use a grieving mother in a political commercial, Mrs. Marino was adamant to be heard. She also wanted to deliver a clear and concise statement and welcomed help writing and editing her comments. I gently explained that, because of my involvement with the Gautreaux campaign, I could not do anything that would influence her choice of words. I felt sure the Phares campaign would hit back and accuse Gautreaux of exploiting a victim's grief-stricken mother, but Mrs. Marino was not easily dissuaded. I encouraged her to trust her instincts, to say what she wanted to say, and her statement would be fine.

From my conversation with Mrs. Marino, I knew she would speak from the heart. A few days later, in the final weeks of the campaign, she recorded a 30-second commercial and asked the Gautreaux campaign to air it. Her words were more compelling than those any professional media consultant could have written.

"This is Lynne Marino," she began. "I lost my daughter, Pam Kinamore, who was murdered by the Baton Rouge serial killer. There is no excuse for the fact that Greg Phares kept his knowledge of a serial killer hidden from the public. How many of our children would be alive today if we had only known what monsters were out there? This Saturday I'm asking you to vote for a change in the Sheriff's Office. Greg Phares didn't do the job then. How can we trust him to do it now?"

Powerful words from a source the Gautreaux campaign never anticipated.

Phares' most effective opponents, however, were local law enforcement associations whose members worked tirelessly behind the scenes in support of the more affable Gautreaux. One of those more active volunteers was the former officer who had first encouraged Phares to say publicly that a serial killer was operating in Baton Rouge.

The sheriff's race was bitterly fought, with Phares leading Gautreaux in the primary by 46 to 37 percent, and Gautreaux coming from behind in the runoff to win by a margin of 52 to 48. A small group of us worked late nights with Gautreaux to pull together a winning coalition. Known as a night owl, Gautreaux, with his wife Suzi, routinely dropped by my house for late night strategy sessions during the stressful campaign before driving to their home in the more rural part of East Baton Rouge. After his election, however, Gautreaux distanced himself from Mayor Holden; those close to the new sheriff bristled at the credit many gave the Mayor for Gautreaux's victory.

Because he was filling the unexpired term of the former sheriff, Gautreaux took office immediately after the election. The transition was therefore faster than the usual change in leadership, and even more personal and difficult for the previous sheriff's longtime employees. To make room for the new administration, they had to leave quickly. Regime change is never easy and can leave deep wounds.

Then, less than a year later, in her reporting on Mayor Holden's 2008 re-election campaign, Mosgrove followed the same pattern she had used against Gautreaux. Once again, station management received complaints about her bias, this time against Holden. The Mayor's supporters assumed her reporting retaliated for his hand in Gautreaux's election; as manager of both campaigns, however, I felt that Veronica simply did not like either of them.

After her sudden departure from television, Mosgrove had landed at GOHSEP, where she openly declared herself a sworn enemy of the Mayor. "She told me she considers it a badge of honor that she is his enemy," a friend of the Mayor reported.

Now Veronica and Scott Rogers were in a position to poke at the Mayor a little. They did not simply duplicate the information that the Mayor's Office was distributing through the program we had launched for East Baton Rouge Parish; they began to undermine the smooth relationship between two public safety agencies. 1stCo was producing the same content for both the city and the State. The difference was that Scott was getting from Veronica what the City of Baton Rouge had flatly refused: He was co-hosting the State's segment with her. He had successfully created the appearance of close ties with the Governor's Office, a tactic that helped him sell himself as a credible source of information to the public and other State agencies.

At the same time, from her position at GOHSEP, Veronica could impact the critical relationship between the State and local emergency management departments, and, more important, between the Governor's Office and the Mayor's Office.

Meanwhile, to get to the bottom of Scott's freewheeling use of her program content, JoAnne invited the 1stCo team and me to her office on November 13, 2009, to discuss her ongoing concerns. This was the only time I was ever in a meeting with Scott Rogers, and it is a meeting none of us will ever forget. Watching his reactions, I could not imagine how he had managed to interact successfully with enough businesses to recruit the program sponsors he needed to pay for the production of his own show.

At the Emergency Operations Center, large video screens line the walls, providing continuous news and weather updates for first responders, who sit side by side at computers and phones to receive information from the field. From there, we could see through the glass walls into the Executive Overwatch room. From this hub, with its video and computer monitors and a clock showing multiple time zones, city-parish administrators track local emergencies as they unfold.

Both the Operations Center and the Overwatch are located on the second floor of the building where the glass walls allow a view of the activities that take place in the emergency call center on the main floor below. From this building, the city dispatches firefighters, city police, sheriff's deputies, paramedics, and other first responders. Here, at the EOC, one of the most somber environments for a meeting, JoAnne led the way into the Executive Overwatch and sat at the head of the long conference table. Tuesday Mills and I followed, taking our seats on the side closest to the door. Scott Rogers, wearing a suit, walked around the table to sit opposite from Tuesday and me, and a more casually dressed Mathew Hodgkins followed him. Scott sat completely upright in his chair, mentioning that he had back problems. He was restless and tense, and did not make eye contact with any of us at the table. Scott Rogers was about to put on an emotionally charged performance more suitable for the stage.

Mathew sat quietly by, stoic, showing no emotion at all, deferring to Scott to respond to JoAnne's questions.

When JoAnne asked why—in the State's segment of *The Around Town TV Show*—1stCo was using program content prepared for her project, Scott delivered a meandering monologue we struggled to follow. "I don't work for 1stCo," he began. "I'm simply a consultant to the company. I am not responsible for decisions made by 1stCo."

At that point, he attempted to describe 1stCo as an entity completely separate from *The Around Town TV Show*, which he hosted. Scott denied any contractual agreement with the Governor's Office and insisted that Veronica was simply appearing on his *Around Town Show* "as a guest," as were the other guests Mathew and Stuart had interviewed for JoAnne's project. Pure coincidence, he claimed, that the same people with whom 1stCo taped interviews, at JoAnne's direction, appeared on *The Around Town Show*—before their segments aired on the *Red Stick Ready Show* for East Baton Rouge Parish.

"Well, if you were interested in providing information on emergency preparedness on your TV show," JoAnne asked Scott, "why didn't you offer that opportunity to our department as a simple courtesy? After all, I am your client and we are already working together. If you want this content shared with your audience, is that invitation open to me, too?"

Scott's face went blank. He didn't have an answer, but he began to realize he had painted himself into a corner. Time for a distraction: His face turned red, sweat beading on his upper lip.

"Scott, who should I contact about the decision made by 1stCo if you are not the person in charge?" JoAnne asked. Scott began to fidget in his chair. Since the company's official corporation filing with the State then listed his daughter Kimmy as president, JoAnne asked if she should address her concerns with Kimmy.

"1stCo is run by a board of directors," Scott said. "I am only responsible for *The Around Town TV Show*, which is an independent broadcast." Without providing any names, he began blathering about 1stCo's corporate structure, but he could not tell his client who was responsible for decisions at 1stCo. *He would not name a single administrator or board member. Why is everything shrouded in secrecy?*

That is because, in reality, Scott Rogers was 1stCo's sole decision maker.

Mathew, Stuart, and Kimmy did exactly what he told them, while other board of directors members changed periodically and only rubber-stamped Scott's actions. None of what he said in the meeting made any sense, and as JoAnne continued asking simple questions, he eventually began hyperventilating, breathing heavily, as if he needed air. At one point, he pushed his chair back from the table and stood up as if he were leaving. Then he sat back down and continued, his voice strained as he started to cry, which seemed to us a gross overreaction.

I later learned that when Scott felt he was trapped, he used what some of his former students called his "fake crying voice" in an attempt to elicit sympathy or to make them feel guilty for upsetting him. Paul, a former Academy student I met later—in London in 2015—believed Scott often used this tactic any time he felt pressure.

When I attempted a couple of times during the meeting to comment, hoping somehow to calm the commotion he had roused, Scott would wail, "You don't UNDERSTAND!" and he would wipe his face with his hands as if to dry his tears.

I had to admit, he was right about that: I did not understand why he couldn't see the clear conflict of using—in a second project—work we had produced for East Baton Rouge Parish. *Was he charging both government agencies for the same work?* But while his behavior seemed unethical to us, to him the problem was our failure to understand. The whole ordeal made me think that the principles involved in working for government agencies escaped him. In addition, I believed he was unaware of the unprofessional impact of his theatrics. But mostly, that meeting left me with the realization that Scott Rogers was a ticking time bomb.

His anger over JoAnne's questions was palpable; his dislike for me unmistakable. I felt he somehow blamed me for JoAnne's concerns, as if I had pulled back the curtain and exposed his questionable behavior. In fact, the day GOHSEP sent out the press release about its partnership with *The Around Town Show*, Scott most likely had been in the back of the studio, fully aware the announcement had been made, while JoAnne sat in the front. We would later learn this was exactly the kind of chaos he savored. He enjoyed creating conflict as long as he controlled the outcome.

Even though I had tried to ignore the drama and focus only on what Scott was saying, nothing made sense. As his agitation increased, JoAnne and I exchanged glances, trying to get a read on where the meeting was going.

Finally, when Scott said, "I believe I need to speak with my attorneys…" I knew it was time to end the discussion. Closing my book where I had been taking notes, I said, "I've always believed that when one party in a business meeting says he has to speak to his attorney, it's probably best to end the discussion and let the attorneys for both sides continue it later."

If Scott mentioned calling his lawyer as a scare tactic or some sort of threat, I thought, *JoAnne wasn't about to be bullied. If he thinks he needs an attorney to get out of this conversation, he must have something to hide.*

JoAnne announced that she didn't feel the meeting was going anywhere but would give Scott an opportunity to get back to her with a plan to resolve her concerns. After he left the building, Scott phoned JoAnne while we were still processing his emotional meltdown. He claimed he had lost a large diamond ring during the meeting, a gift from Kimmy that had sentimental value, and asked that we look for it.

Just when I thought our dealings with Scott Rogers couldn't get any weirder, there we were on the floor of the Executive Overwatch room, looking for a diamond ring none of us believed he had actually lost. We crawled around under the long conference table as if we might find Scott's diamond! *Who's crazy now?* I thought. If Scott had in fact lost a large diamond, surely he would have returned to retrace his steps. An expensive diamond ring also seemed like an odd gift from a daughter; more likely Scott had called JoAnne away from the rest of us to speak alone with her and play the victim, free of the distraction of Tuesday and me. The story of the lost ring seemed to her a ploy to garner some sympathy. *If he just wanted to control us in some way, he definitely succeeded!*

Most of us will experience someone losing his temper in a business meeting, or becoming overly emotional under stress. But the meeting with Scott Rogers in the Emergency Operations Center exposed a personality that worked hard to deceive and exploded when questioned. *What was he hiding? Why would Scott jeopardize his lucrative contract with JoAnne by acting so combative? He must have a bigger plan.*

CHAPTER SIX

THE POLITICS

September 2010
Baton Rouge, Louisiana

After the dramatic meeting with Scott Rogers at the Emergency Operations Center, JoAnne had considered canceling the entire contract with 1stCo rather than ever again deal with him. But with only a few months remaining for the project, she instead scaled it back to the parts she could most easily complete. Our firm finished its portion of the work, submitted our final invoices to 1stCo as the contract provided, and I exchanged pleasantries with Mathew about working together. Meanwhile, Scott was building a network of contacts and aggressively pursuing work for 1stCo. To understand how he could be so effective after moving to Baton Rouge from England, you must examine the connections and how he leveraged one project to secure the next.

Though Scott never admitted it, we later learned he signed a contract with GOHSEP to work with Veronica Mosgrove on a pilot series of public education videos—almost the exact services for which the Mayor's Office was paying him. In truth, 1stCo had signed a $9,950 contract with GOHSEP in April 2010, followed by an almost identical $11,500 contract with GOHSEP in October 2010, with the scope of services for both very similar to what the company was producing for JoAnne's department.

Veronica Mosgrove would eventually sit at the center of a long, drawn-out dispute between her office and the Mayor's Office over the management of federal grants. That dispute ended only when the Governor appointed a new homeland security director, a former parish president with keen political instincts on how governmental bodies operate. The new director moved quickly to restore the strong working relationship the State had previously enjoyed with the Mayor's Office. He made quick changes in his department, and, within a short time, everyone who had orchestrated the feud against East Baton Rouge Parish was gone. Veronica was one of the first to depart. The new director saw to it that the petty and potentially dangerous political games, in an area of public safety where State and local officials must work closely together, came to an end.

Veronica's next stop was Press Secretary to the Louisiana Commissioner of Agriculture and Forestry, and within 60 days 1stCo signed its first contract with that department: $36,586 to develop a 30-minute quarterly television show on Louisiana's crops, "Cooking Up Louisiana's Treasures." The contract was announced by the Agriculture Department in a press release on September 28, 2012, as a "collaboration" with 1stCo Productions of Baton Rouge. The programs featured Chef Celeste from *The Around Town TV Show* and Agriculture Commissioner Mike Strain. The Specialty Crop Block Grant Program at the U.S. Department of Agriculture provided funding for the programs. Later, 1stCo received a $6,500 contract through the agriculture department to produce a cooking show that promoted Louisiana crawfish. *In a state so rich in chefs and filmmakers, Louisiana had tapped a British trio and a Hawaiian-trained chef to teach local residents about the importance of "home grown."*

On the exact date that 1stCo began its contract with the Governor's Office of Homeland Security and Emergency Preparedness, it signed a $49,500 contract with the Secretary of the Louisiana Department of Health and Hospitals. Top officials from that department had also worked closely with JoAnne and appeared on her program. Now Scott had signed them up for four

30-minute videos for the Bureau of Primary Care and Rural Health, dedicated to improving the health of residents in rural and underserved areas. This contract was also 100 percent funded with federal monies, while another contract for $7,500 was funded with State public health dollars. Secretary of State Tom Schedler, a frequent guest on the *The Around Town Show*, sent a special proclamation for the show's 10th Anniversary program. He appeared on the show several times, once even accompanied by his family. He too signed a contract with 1stCo.

Scott was even able to secure a contract with the Governor's Program on Abstinence, a State office that promotes an abstinence lifestyle to reduce teen pregnancies and sexually transmitted diseases. At the time of Scott Rogers' contract with the abstinence program, its director was busy running a scheme to execute fraudulent contracts totaling more than $50,000, which she directed to accounts that she, along with members of her family, controlled. Gail Dignam was convicted of mail fraud and sentenced to serve 70 months in a federal prison and pay restitution. The Office of Inspector General for the United States Department of Health and Human Services, the Louisiana Legislative Auditor, and the FBI investigated the case.

"Ms. Dignam has left a path of corruption and deceit across our country," said William W. Root, Assistant Special Agent in Charge for the Inspector General for the U.S. Department of Health and Human Services. She "took advantage of charities and DHHS grants to serve her own self-interests, and America is tired of the fraud, waste, and abuse of [its] tax dollars."[2]

FBI Special Agent in Charge David Welker added, "As always, when [public servants seek] to enrich themselves at the expense of the public they serve, the true victims are the citizens who cannot take advantage of the program which was defrauded."

---

[2] "Former Director of the Louisiana Governor's Program on Abstinence Sentenced to Serve 70 Months in Prison." FBI: New Orleans Division Press Releases. 1 March 2012. Viewed 9 September 2015. https://www.fbi.gov/neworleans/press-releases/2012/former-director-of-the-louisiana-governors-program-on-abstinence-sentenced-to-serve-70-months-in-prison

Unknown to the federal agents, working along with Ms. Dignam, using federal funds to promote sexual abstinence, was Scott Rogers, a child sex predator.

While the FBI carefully reviewed files and contracts Ms. Dignam had awarded, Scott was working his relationships with her and other public officials to build up 1stCo, using federal and State dollars to support his secret lifestyle. To his delight, he fooled them all.

Scott Rogers had gained traction with the contracts he secured to produce videos distributed through cable outlets and the Internet, but his most loyal patron was Veronica Mosgrove, who worked with 1stCo at two State departments. *It's amazing how far Scott's reach extended into law enforcement and state officials! He had convinced powerful people to believe his stories.*

We completed the Homeland Security contract in September 2010, the same month Baton Rouge Mayor Pro-Tem Mike Walker, serving his final term on the Metro Council, made a dramatic break with Mayor Holden and began opposing him publicly. Walker is a tall beefy man, plain spoken, with a soft Southern drawl that belies his quick temper. But his advisers took advantage of his short fuse and persuaded him to go down a path where we never expected him to go.

A man who had served 12 years on the Metro Council, he appeared one of the Mayor's closest allies. But after the tragic murder of Alexandra Engler—a young mother living in Beauregard Town, a small historic neighborhood near downtown Baton Rouge—he made an unusual move.

While Mayor Holden comforted the victim's family, Walker held a press conference just outside the Mayor's Office to blame Holden for the city's crime rate. He suggested the city-parish withdraw almost a million dollars from its reserve fund, held primarily for recovery from hurricanes and other natural disasters.

"I think everyone realizes we have an emergency situation in East Baton Rouge Parish," Walker railed. "Whether you wanna call it that or not, that's what it is."[3]

The murder was one of the worst Baton Rouge had seen in years: An African American man with a long criminal record had broken into the Engler home, killing Alexandra and injuring her 9-year-old daughter, shooting her in the back as she attempted to run away. The murder rocked Baton Rouge and presented ugly overtones in a city that still struggles with a racial divide.

Holden had worked hard to bring the races together for the first time, but nothing arouses racial tension like a black man killing a young white mother, shooting her young daughter, then carrying their TV out of the house with no regard for their lives. Add to that the man's avoiding jail for his last violation because a judge sentenced him to read the Bible and mow lawns for neighbors to learn how to be a better person. Clearly that attempt at rehabilitation hadn't worked.

Now that Walker had gone on the offensive, everyone knew he had made the decision to challenge Holden for Mayor in 2012. Since Walker was term limited and could not run for his Council seat again, Holden had often said maybe he could work in the Mayor's administration when the time came. He knew Walker wanted to continue community involvement in some way, and he wanted to find a spot for him. But working for the Mayor is not what Walker wanted—he wanted the Mayor's job. And we soon learned he was willing to shut down city government if that might level the playing field for his run at the office.

By January 2011, Val and I thought our final invoices from our work on the emergency preparedness project should have been paid, since the city-parish was always prompt, and we were anxious to close out our work with 1stCo. On Friday, January

---

[3] "Mayor, Councilman disagree over curbing crime." WAFB. 5 October 2010. Viewed 9 September 2015. http://www.wafb.com/story/13274680/mayor-councilman-disagree-over-curbing-downtown-crime?clienttype=printable&redirected=true

14, I emailed Mathew to ask when he expected final payment, and he replied quickly. "Payment arrived Wednesday, I believe. I will be processing your payments Monday. Thank you, Rannah, and all the best to you, too."

By February 11, after noticing the payment still outstanding in our books, I checked in by email again. After a series of strange exchanges, in which Mathew seemed very evasive, he finally told me that Scott Rogers had decided to withhold our final payment until he confirmed that we had completed the work. Of course, I knew that wasn't true, because the MOHSEP staff had already verified the work as complete and had signed off to JoAnne that the invoice was ready for payment.

In a few more back and forth emails with Mathew, I pointed out that Scott had not been involved in our work enough to know what any of us had done, but, more important, the client had paid the invoice because the client was in possession of our completed work product. And since Scott now had our fees sitting in his account, his withholding them amounted to theft.

Scott was doing what I later learned he always did—provoking us for his own entertainment, like a cat toying with a mouse. I could feel his sway in how Mathew talked around the subject, clearly uncomfortable. I assumed Scott might be embarrassed because of our meeting and his meltdown—I knew I would be. But I let Mathew know I would turn the bill over for collection by the end of February. These people were weird, and now I sensed they were trying to make up some crazy excuse for keeping our fees; I wasn't going to play that game. I wanted nothing more than to end our connection with Scott Rogers, but that didn't mean I would just let him steal our money. *I don't want to be snared by Scott's crazy trap! Should we just write it off as a bad debt? Is that what he is counting on?*

I learned later that Stuart had been driving Scott a few days after his meeting with JoAnne at the Emergency Operations Center and witnessed Scott get angry with the Mayor for not supporting him. Scott knew from our meeting that JoAnne might cancel the contract, so he wanted to make sure the Mayor wouldn't allow that. Of course, JoAnne had discussed the matter thoroughly with the Mayor after our meeting, and he had agreed with her completely, quickly telling Scott as much on the phone. Again, Scott grew agitated at not getting his way and began to raise his voice. The Mayor continued to tell him he supported JoAnne's decision. Then, after two warnings for Scott to calm down, Mayor Holden informed him it would be "three strikes and you're out" if he continued yelling into the phone, so when Scott went on another rant, the Mayor hung up.

Now the petulant child was unleashed. Furious that he was not able to entangle the Mayor in his web, Scott decided to get even. First, he would cause the city problems by keeping our fees, which in his mind would create a bookkeeping nightmare for the city-parish and somehow reflect poorly on JoAnne. And second, he would rip us off. He was a master at creating turmoil, so he went to work doing what he had done best his entire life— turning people against each other.

He invited Metro Council members, starting with the Mayor's challenger Mike Walker, to serve as guests on his TV show, flattering them profusely on the air, which is always intoxicating for politicians. Richard Sobers, the retired Baton Rouge police officer who had tried to schedule police segments for Scott's show, was still working as a volunteer on the set of *The Around Town TV Show* and now openly campaigning for Mike Walker for Mayor. Later, Sobers was very active in a non-denominational church Scott formed after he became an ordained minister through an Internet course.

The 1stCo studio was Scott's spider web, where he could spin his mischief and malice. Sitting on the set prior to the interviews, he disparaged Mayor Holden and gathered information about the Council members, especially those he might use to cause problems for the administration. As those close to Scott knew, he derived great enjoyment from weaving this plot against the Mayor.

As Scott drew the Council members into his web, however, the young man operating the soundboard for the television program sat listening through his headphones. He had lived under Scott's control since the age of 12, when, back in England, Scott had begun sexually abusing him. Still, he had remained loyal to his mentor. He told me later, however, that he began to see what Scott truly was—a master manipulator.

Soon, rather than pay our firm for its fees and expenses on JoAnne's project, Scott began trying to return the fees to the city-parish, though administrators told him they had no reason to accept the money. He somehow continued to imagine that he could wreak havoc on the city's financial reports, and since he could not trick either JoAnne or Mayor Holden into joining him as his disciples, he rolled the dice with Mike Walker. *Scott was trying his hand at Louisiana politics!*

The Boys of Bury

PAUL *in his own words*

London, England
2015

He got close to all the people who have the power, all the stand-ups in the community. He was there hosting everything, being the center of attention. In plain sight! It's that classic behavior, saying, "If I'm here and you can all see me being this wonderful person, there's no way you're going to question me. But if I hide away in my tower, then you'll think I'm a weirdo." Like a Michael Jackson character...he related to Michael a lot, by the way.

CHAPTER SEVEN

THE NEWSPAPER

June 2011
Baton Rouge, Louisiana

Scott had now built his own enemies list: He no longer liked Holden because the Mayor wouldn't go along with Scott's manipulation. JoAnne had caught him in an unethical move and questioned him, so he would have to cause her some trouble. He somehow blamed me—either for agreeing with JoAnne or for my association with the Mayor, so he was more than happy to cause problems for me. *It's what he does. It's second nature to him to create chaos. He can't wait until we are ensnared in his web.*

Soon Mike Walker's statements against the Mayor began showing up in stories by local reporter Greg Garland, who, early in his career, had worked at *The Advocate*, Baton Rouge's daily newspaper, before moving around the country and writing for newspapers in Florida and Maryland. When Garland returned to Baton Rouge and *The Advocate* after a 20-year absence, Executive Editor Carl Redman assigned him to cover City Hall. Thus began a long period of coverage in which Garland criticized the Mayor and his administration.

Scott Rogers prided himself on feeding information to reporters while keeping his own name out of their stories, and he could find no better place to begin than with Garland. The two shared the added benefit of Veronica Mosgrove on the inside of her department's feud with the Mayor's Office. It was not uncommon for Garland to call the Mayor's Office for a response before anyone there had learned of an action by Mosgrove's department.

In October 2011, Mike Walker appeared on *The Around Town TV Show* to cook banana pudding with Scott, and in December 2011, Rogers invited the entire Metro Council to attend a holiday luncheon and the taping of a special Christmas edition of the show.

By the beginning of 2012, when Walker officially announced his candidacy, he attended the Mayor's annual State of the City address at noon before driving to *The Around Town TV Show* studios for his own press conference announcing he would run against Holden. To kick off Candidate Walker's campaign, Scott and his team had produced a melodramatic video that Walker said moved him to tears. Though Scott was stepping into the world of local politics in Baton Rouge, time and time again he proved himself tone deaf when it came to the Louisiana political climate.

Through 2011 and 2012, Walker wasn't the only local elected official with whom Scott Rogers was building a close relationship. He had long been a friend of Sheriff Sid Gautreaux, going back to Gautreaux's days as Baker police chief. Rogers had met him shortly after arriving in Baton Rouge, while covering Baker's Buffalo Festival, an annual event named for the local high school mascot. On his TV program, Rogers claimed he had served Baker as a reserve police officer and that Gautreaux had helped him get his first concealed gun permit. He even joked on the air about flashing his Baker police badge, should a police officer stop him. "I was assigned a desk job when I was working as a reserve officer with the Baker Police Department," Scott said with a cheeky smile, "because if I rode with an officer, when he made a stop, there were just so many problems with people asking for my autograph. So they had to give me a desk job." *Unbelievable! He will say anything to enhance his celebrity status.*

When Gautreaux won the race for sheriff, Scott's interest shifted from the small-town Baker Police Department to the Sheriff's Office and its parish-wide influence. Gautreaux became a frequent *Around Town TV Show* guest, hosting cooking segments and naming Rogers a chaplain for the Sheriff's Office. According to the Sheriff, Rogers requested work with the Crime Victims Services Division, led by Sgt. Carolyn Stapleton. At every opportunity, Scott Rogers positioned himself to serve as master of ceremonies for programs to benefit or recognize victims of crime.

He read a poem at Gautreaux's annual *Evening of Remembrance* for crime victims and served as emcee for the *Walk a Mile in Her Shoes* fundraiser to end rape, domestic violence, and sexual abuse. His work with the Sexual Trauma Awareness and Response (STAR) organization, formerly the Rape Crisis Center, is likely the most ironic. While hiding a secret past as a sex offender, Rogers brazenly strapped on bright yellow high heels to emcee a program in support of rape victims.

In 2012, Rogers also managed the unsuccessful re-election campaign of Dr. Shannon Cooper, East Baton Rouge Parish Coroner, charging him over $22,000 for campaign services and consulting. Rogers had befriended Dr. Cooper's wife Pam and had convinced the couple to hire him as a political consultant. JoAnne Moreau's husband Don, Chief of Operations for the Coroner's Office, had to watch his boss lose re-election because of Rogers' strategic decisions, which were so poor that some thought he had deliberately sabotaged Dr. Cooper's campaign. *Why did he decide to inflict his special brand of chaos on his friend Pam Cooper? Again those close to Scott told us he didn't need a reason to create conflict—he did it simply because he could.*

Meanwhile, Rogers continued courting the Metro Council, trying to enlist Mike Walker's help in getting the Council to hand over management of the city-parish government access television channel, Metro 21, to 1stCo. Scott had floated the idea to others, touting the radio studio he had built in *The Around Town TV Show* studio, but he had failed to interest anyone. Then an announcement came from the Metro Council office that

Rogers had offered all of the Metro Council members free airtime on his *Around Town TV Show* to talk about what they were doing for their districts. To land a contract to produce the Metro 21 channel programming, he needed seven Council votes in favor, and he was starting to work to get them.

Soon *Advocate* reporter Greg Garland called me about our contract with MOHSEP. Getting Garland on board Scott's grudge wagon was like throwing fresh red meat to a hungry wolf.

Around the same time, Greg Phares, now a criminal investigator for the Louisiana Inspector General, and Veronica Mosgrove, public information officer for the Governor's Office of Homeland Security and Emergency Preparedness, visited Scott Rogers at his *Around Town* studio in Cortana Mall to talk about Mayor Holden and our contract with MOHSEP. Phares questioned Scott about Mayor Holden for more than an hour and followed up with several shorter visits, according to a 1stCo employee. Later, Phares took FBI Agent Jeff Methvin to JoAnne Moreau's office for an interview on the matter of the 1stCo contract. *What on earth is this about?* we thought. We could not believe Phares could convince an FBI agent to take up Scott Rogers' personal vendetta. *Did Phares actually take Scott seriously?*

But JoAnne is not easily intimidated. She answered the FBI agent's questions completely. She had nothing to hide and welcomed the opportunity to tell him the whole truth. Ironically, Phares' association with Scott Rogers and Veronica Mosgrove would ultimately have a chilling effect on where I would turn with the frightening information I had received from England. *How could I approach the FBI for help?*

When Greg Garland visited my office in early June 2011 to discuss the story he had gotten from 1stCo about our Homeland Security contract, I noticed immediately that he had a hard time making eye contact. This was not just because he is short in stature, but also because he seemed to have made up his mind about his story before arriving. He took very few notes during my interview. At one point, when I was answering a question and he was staring at his notepad, I noticed that his head bobbed as if he were falling asleep. When I said, "Are you okay?" he quickly ended the interview and said he didn't have any more questions for me. Despite my annoyance, I was actually worried about his walking back to City Hall in the summer heat.

"Are you sure you're okay?" I asked. "Do you want me to give you a ride? I'm not sure you should be walking in this heat."

But Garland seemed embarrassed by his lapse and, quickly gathering up his note pad, said, "No, it's actually better if I walk. I'll call you if I have any further questions." His story ran on the front page of *The Sunday Advocate* on June 19, 2011, with the paper giving it as much play as possible. It was full of inaccuracies, overblown, and damning of JoAnne and me, not to mention the false accusations against Mayor Holden. The article featured a seven-year-old color photo of the Mayor and me standing together talking during his first successful mayoral campaign. *When is the last time a newspaper published a seven-year-old photo on page one?*

The focus of the story was the unfounded accusations attributed to Mathew Hodgkins that somehow the Mayor had forced him to work with us. Of course, I didn't think the Mayor would even know who Mathew Hodgkins was, but that didn't matter. After all, let's not let the truth get in the way of a good story. Although Mathew had told me he would like to work together because our two firms did not perform the same type of work, he claimed in *The Advocate* story that 1stCo would have preferred to do our work in addition to the video production it had provided. *News to me! He certainly was excited to work together when we met on the set of The Around Town Show.*

Scott Rogers' name did not appear in the article, even though he had concocted the entire story and pushed Mathew out on the ledge to take the fall by making Scott's claims on the record. I knew that was how the story had come about, and later, a person who was present confirmed how Scott had manipulated the news story by using both Garland and Mathew, and how very pleased he was with himself that Garland had left his name out. Little did Garland know, Scott had every reason to keep his name out of print, now that anyone in the world could read *The*

Advocate online. And once again, Scott had choreographed events to turn out just as he wanted. *The master manipulator— he used a seasoned investigative reporter to get his story in the paper!*

Ironically, after our firm had managed the Mayor's election in 2004, I had always avoided any conversations with him about any work Val and I pursued in Baton Rouge. Since I never spoke to him about anything our firm did for other clients, I didn't even have to stop and think before answering questions about business links to the Mayor. I knew without hesitation that he had not had anything to do with any work we were performing in Baton Rouge.

Now I was getting caught in the political war that Greg Garland and some Council members were waging on a daily basis against the Mayor. While he had very few questions for me, Garland called every local client we worked for and several that we didn't, asking them if the Mayor had ever recommended us. All of them replied *no*, but an aggressive investigative reporter crawling all over your business definitely sends a chill. Garland had earned the reputation that if he was calling, you could expect a negative story, so you should hope to avoid him altogether.

Having to fight for our reputation against such an unfair and unethical opponent was enough to discourage my business partner, Val, from working in Baton Rouge, and who could blame him? He had a great reputation and had enjoyed success throughout the country. Why should he put up with petty games? But since I lived in Baton Rouge, I felt I had no choice but to speak up in our defense.

I was so angry—disgusted, really—that the daily newspaper in Louisiana's Capital City could get its facts so wrong, content to harm reputations in the process. We worked hard, tried always to produce our best work, and charged very reasonable professional fees. Val and I were protective of our professional reputations, because in our work, honesty and ethics are important.

I wrote a letter to the editor in an attempt at least to set the record straight and correct Greg Garland's mistakes. My avenue of protest was small consolation, since letters are limited in length and run on the editorial page, whereas the story against us ran on the front page of the Sunday paper, and it doesn't get any bigger than that.

Still, a few days later, I submitted my letter through *The Advocate's* website and waited a couple of days for someone to call and confirm its receipt. When that didn't happen, I called the paper and inquired when it might run, only to be told that my letter to the editor was actually sitting on Executive Editor Carl Redman's desk.

That seemed odd to me. I knew the editor wasn't the person at the newspaper who actually decides which letters get published. This wasn't a good sign. But I was determined to get a correction published, so I placed a call to Redman, who had always defended Greg Garland to the Mayor's Office against any criticism of his work, and I waited for his return call. It came that evening. He said that he had my letter but would not publish it unless I made some changes, a requirement I considered strange. "I'm not going to run it as it is, Rannah," Carl said flatly.

For starters, he told me I could not introduce in my letter any information that was not in the original news article. "What?" I asked. That seemed odd, and incredibly unfair. If Garland had got his news story right, I wouldn't need to provide any new information. One of my main complaints was that while Scott Rogers had made the decision to withhold our final payment, and I had shared this information with Greg Garland during my interview, Scott Rogers' name was nowhere to be found in the article. Garland had protected him. *What am I missing? Why is everyone covering for this guy?*

Over the next few days, I submitted four versions of my letter, each time having to remove language I felt was important to the truth, before Redman agreed to publish it. In the end, he actually drafted part of the letter himself, sending it back to me and saying that if I could agree to the version of my letter to which he had contributed edits, he would publish it. I agreed, because I felt if I pushed any further, he would simply refuse to run any response at all. *The power of the press.* If he refused to publish my letter, I had no other recourse to set the record straight. The newspaper was my only outlet. I couldn't afford to push him to the point where he just refused to publish anything at all. I wanted any small inch of the paper I could get; I wanted to set the record straight.

Probably the worst error in the story had to do with Garland's reporting that I would not say how much another public agency, completely unrelated to the Scott Rogers story, was paying us on another contract. Besides providing him a copy of the contract, I had also explained it to him and he had reviewed it with the client. I knew he had every single bit of information, but chose instead to insinuate that we must be charging more than the contract allowed, which was completely false. That contract was the result of a competitive selection process for which we submitted a bid; in no way could the compensation differ from what the contract allowed. Not only that, Garland never gave any indication that he did not understand the payment terms before publishing an outright lie about them—perhaps he was napping during that part of our meeting. After I had explained this egregious mistake in detail to Redman, so clearly that he couldn't help seeing the error, he told me he would talk to Garland.

"It's too late," I said. "The damage is done." *How could they be so cavalier and allow a reporter to draw conclusions that simply weren't true?*

I knew I had to stay focused on clearing up the 1stCo contract issue in my letter, because, while Garland had made other errors, I believed they were the result of sloppy reporting and his own bias. But with the 1stCo accusations, I felt Scott Rogers was deliberately making false claims against us in an effort to harm our firm and our reputations in the community. *My mistake was in looking for a rational explanation for Scott's behavior. This is what he does; logic doesn't apply.*

That night, I opened my kitchen pantry and began rifling through newspapers in the recycling bin to read the past week's published letters to the editor. *Since when are letters to the editor prohibited from introducing new information? That's almost all they do!* After working to earn two degrees in journalism at LSU and an internship at *The Advocate,* I had worked for the

Louisiana Secretary of State and Louisiana State University. I left public service to start my own public relations firm and, as a small business owner, took great care every day to make sure our work met and exceeded the highest standards. *Who was this man making up stories about me to tell the press? Why was the paper printing the lies he told them when the truth was so easily available? It was as if a cloud of cynicism had permeated The Advocate, leaving its editorial staff to stand by whatever Greg Garland wrote, regardless of whether I could prove his inaccuracy.*

I never dreamed I would find myself fighting an uphill battle to get the truth into a newspaper I grew up reading and respecting.

Before *The Advocate* would publish my letter, I had to provide a copy of 1stCo's corporate charter from the Secretary of State's Office showing Kimberly Scott Rogers listed as president, since my letter stated that she served in that capacity. Incredibly, Redman took issue with my saying the story contained any accusation against the Mayor until I pointed out to him that the 1stCo contract was with the *Mayor's Office* of Homeland Security and Emergency Preparedness; that it was signed by *Mayor Holden*; and that the story included two photographs of the *Mayor* and me with numerous references to ties between us. *No accusations against the Mayor by Greg Garland? Come on!* Redman partially conceded and allowed the line about accusing Mayor Holden to stand if I would say the accusations against him were an extension of those against JoAnne. *Seriously?* I knew the Mayor was likely more a target of Garland's than I was, but I felt I had to stand up for myself.

"Your letter says that Scott Rogers decided the non-payment. The story clearly says the decision was based on his recommendation," Redman wrote in an email to me, even though Rogers was not named, identified only as "operations manager." Of course, this information was news to us, since Scott had emphatically told us he did not work for 1stCo. I could tell that Scott had successfully entwined Greg Garland in his confusing explanations to the point that Garland wrote exactly what Scott wanted him to write. *I wonder if he saw it coming. He was played by Scott Rogers.*

"I suggest your letter say something like: 'The non-payment was based on the recommendation of someone who had collected the funds from the city-parish, never spent a single day working on the project with us, and yet somehow recommended withholding our final payment,'" Redman proposed to me.

Fortunately, in our phone conversation, Redman agreed Garland's article should have named Scott Rogers, so I was able to add, "That person is Scott Rogers, host of *The Around Town TV Show*, who identified himself to us as merely a consultant to 1stCo, a Delaware corporation whose president is Scott Rogers' daughter, according to the Louisiana Secretary of State's Office. Rogers is referenced in *The Advocate* as its 'operations manager' but the paper omitted his name in the June 19 front-page story." *That person is Scott Rogers...at least I was able to get his name in the newspaper to shed a little light on what he had done.*

When we finally had a version of my letter that *The Advocate* agreed to publish, Carl said, "You know, Rannah, I know you're angry with Greg, but this story didn't come from him. It came from two Council members who brought the story to him."

"I know," I said. "I've heard that Mike Walker and Chandler Loupe have made it clear they are going after Mayor Holden, and I suppose I'm just the latest to get caught in the middle. But that doesn't mean they're right or that what they are doing is fair or that *The Advocate* should help them."

To me, the newspaper staff had a responsibility to work until it got the story right. If Greg Garland was an investigative reporter, why did he arrive at my office with his mind made up?

When I later learned just how pleased Scott Rogers was at getting the story published without the inclusion of his name, I began to understand just how devious he was. I also learned that some of his crew members, who were growing tired of the verbal abuse they all endured, were secretly delighted when my letter to the editor was finally published, exposing Scott as the one who manipulated the news coverage. "She doesn't buy his bullshit," one laughed, enjoying my success in getting his name in the newspaper.

My final letter didn't say everything I wanted it to, but it was the best I could get past Carl Redman. Under the confusing headline, "Pact Story Misleading, Gray Says," my letter appeared on June 28, 2011, nine days after the original story ran. I drew little satisfaction from its publication, mainly disappointed that I had to work so hard to get it in print…just to have a voice in my own story. *At least I was able to get Scott's name in the paper!*

"That person is Scott Rogers…" was finally published, and those five words were the most critical in the entire letter. As it turned out, that one letter to the editor would change lives forever.

Dear Editor:

I feel it necessary to respond to *The Advocate's* troubling and misleading article regarding public contracts and our firm. The simple truth is, I have never had a conversation with Mayor-President Kip Holden before or since his election about prospective business of any kind for our firm.

Last December, a number of our clients informed us an *Advocate* reporter called them to ask if Mayor Holden had recommended our company to them, and our clients informed the reporter he had not. At that very same time, a curious thing happened. After telling us, "We will be processing your payments Monday," 1stCo, Inc., a company we were working with on a project for the city-parish, abruptly reversed its position and decided it would not pay for work we had completed.

Since we started our company, this is the only time we have had to refer an invoice to attorneys for collection. This nonpayment was based on the recommendation of someone who had collected the funds from the city-parish, never spent a single day working on the project with us, and yet somehow recommended withholding our final payment.

That person is Scott Rogers, host of the "Around Town TV Show," who identified himself to us as merely a consultant to 1stCo, a Delaware corporation whose president is Scott Rogers' daughter, according to the Louisiana Secretary of State's Office. Rogers is referenced in *The Advocate* as its "operations manager," but the paper omitted his name in the June 19 front-page story.

Since a 1stCo representative stated in your story that they "preferred to provide those services," referring to the marketing and public relations services provided by our firm, it seems they had a clear financial motive in accusing Homeland Security Director JoAnne Moreau, and by extension Mayor Holden, of forcing them to work with our firm.

As often happens, people who feed stories to reporters end up boasting of their efforts, and for six months, we have heard about this looming story.

Our firm worked with the city-parish to develop a nationally recognized public education campaign for emergency preparedness, implementing a unique brand through a television show and public outreach. We are proud of the work we have done, and take great exception to the implications in the story.

We were involved in the production of every television program, considerable script writing and editing, selection of guests and postproduction quality reviews as well as all public outreach surrounding each month's program and topic.

Your article leaves us with this question: A two-page story in the Sunday edition of *The Advocate*, a seven-year-old front-page photo, a false allegation by 1stCo, the failure to name Mr. Rogers—when did reporters go from covering news to actively participating in its creation?

Rannah Gray
President, Marmillion/Gray Media
Baton Rouge[4]

Now, two years after that letter was published, I was sitting in Nathan's office as he leaned over his desk, holding a copy of the email I had received a few hours earlier.

"Rannah, I recently read your article on pact story misleading…" the email began.

Would Scott Rogers ever realize that by trying to damage my reputation, he had put himself on a collision course with a past he had worked two decades to hide? What would he do when he found out his actions were about to open the door to reveal dreadful secrets he had kept hidden for 20 years? Would he even remember this man, Ethan, who was emailing me now? The truth would prove more shocking than I could imagine.

---

4 "Pact Story Misleading, Gray Says." The Advocate. 29 June 2011. Viewed 9 September 2015. http://theadvocate.com/news/opinion/259534-63/letter-pact-story-misleading-gray.html

CHAPTER EIGHT

THE CONNECTION

Day 1
Baton Rouge, Lousiana
August 28, 2013

Nathan carefully read the email I had handed him.

Rannah,

I recently read your article on pact story misleading. I knew Scott Rogers in the '90s...he was a dance Principal of a school called The Academy of Dance and Performing Arts. The company and the individual were bad news...very bad news. He was accused of sexually abusing boys as young as 12. The 1st Co. company you mentioned is owned by his daughter but more interestingly Stuart Poulton and Matt Hodgkins, who are also co-owners, were kinda "kidnapped" by him and fled to the US in the late '90s... their families never saw them again!...he was cleared by a court for the one case that was brought against him for sexual abuse. There were more boys who were abused and I am extremely confident that he will still be abusing. He is a very clever nasty little man.

I can send you newspaper stories on the above case if you're interested or can raise the awareness for any parents of children that may be in danger.

Yours truly,
E

When I handed Nathan a copy of the email, I didn't give him any background, so as he started to read, he said, "What's he talking about, 'Pact Story Misleading'?"

"My letter to the editor!" I said as I sat on the edge of my chair in front of his desk. "That's the headline *The Advocate* put on it. Can you believe? I didn't remember at first either—Pact Story Misleading! I thought at the time the headline was terrible."

He turned back to reading and I watched him staring at the paper.

In the two years since I had written that letter, Mayor Holden had easily won re-election over his challenger, Mike Walker, who ran an embarrassing campaign that ended with a desperate racist ad against the Mayor. The final fistful of mud Walker slung was a completely made up story about the Mayor riding around in a limousine with Louis Farrakhan, who had recently addressed students at local historically black Southern University. The truth was that Mayor Holden did not even know Farrakhan was in the city, but that didn't stop the Walker campaign from hiring a limousine and showing up in front of City Hall late one night to film it speeding away.

As luck would have it, one of the Mayor's staff was leaving City Hall after working late and saw Walker's political consultant directing the limousine driver for the shot.

Soon, a ridiculous commercial aired, implying that the Mayor had provided limousine service for Farrakhan on his stop in Baton Rouge. Local business and community leaders were so appalled at what Walker was attempting that they held a press conference to denounce him. Mike Walker had transformed from one of Mayor Holden's closest friends to one of his ugliest foes, ruining, along the way, the good feelings many people had about him. Most people chalked it up to bad political advice, but Mike had to own his decision to play that race card.

Meanwhile, our firm waited until the campaign was over to file suit against 1stCo for keeping the fees and expenses it owed us. I had imagined that a lawsuit during the 2012 election cycle would likely result in another front-page story, whereas after the election most people would ignore it.

On May 8, 2012, our attorney sent a certified letter to 1stCo giving it 30 days to pay our fees without further legal action. On May 14, Mathew Hodgkins, who identified himself as general manager of 1stCo, Inc., and "Around Town Media," wrote a letter to the Governor's Office of Homeland Security and Emergency Preparedness. He acknowledged that the Mayor's Office of Homeland Security and Emergency Preparedness had requested the services we had provided in the final months of the contract. He now claimed, however, that he could not verify our performance of the work and had therefore withheld payment. In his letter, Mathew further acknowledged that he had attempted to return our fees to MOHSEP unsuccessfully and was now attempting to give them to the State. Three days later, Scott Rogers' attorney, Lexlee Overton, wrote to our attorney and claimed that we did not have a contract with 1stCo and stated that 1stCo planned to give our fees to GOHSEP.

Of course, that didn't make any sense at all, since Mathew had long ago invoiced the Homeland Security department for the work both 1stCo and our firm had performed; further, JoAnne's staff had signed off, confirming all of the work had been done, and Scott had deposited the check he'd received for the fees. It dawned on me that scamming money from business contracts might be more routine for Scott than I imagined.

Soon after we filed suit in City Court, Lexlee Overton filed on behalf of 1stCo to move the suit to State Court and then immediately relinquished our fees that her client had held for almost three years and deposited the money with the court.

Meantime, Councilman Chandler Loupe had begun a law practice with Overton and moved into her office on North Boulevard, next door to our office. To me, Baton Rouge, at times, has the feel of a town much smaller than it is, and this was definitely one of those times. I call this strange occurrence *the Mayberry effect*, after the 1960s-era Andy Griffith TV Show set in the fictional small town of Mayberry. This experience is similar to the Six Degrees of Separation game, in which people can be connected to someone else in a maximum of six steps, using their relationships to others. In Baton Rouge, with a population of more than a quarter of a million people, you don't expect everyone you meet to be connected to someone you know. But if you lived in tiny Mayberry, those links would be commonplace.

All Val and I wanted, however, was to clear our names of the unfortunate twist of fate that had brought us into contact with Scott Rogers and never deal with him again.

When 1stCo finally deposited our fees with the court, our attorney told us the case was basically over and all that remained was for our suit to make its way through the District Court docket, which he estimated could take another year or two because of the backlog. He suggested that we forget about our legal problems with 1stCo and said he would let us know when our fees were paid and, honestly, I hadn't thought about the whole mess in months when I received Ethan's email. But that craziness was the first thing on Nathan's mind.

"Rannah, before you answer this guy, you need to consider that Scott Rogers could be writing this to get you to say something you shouldn't," Nathan said as he leaned back in his chair. "You don't really know who is contacting you."

"I know," I said, "but I have to tell you I have a strong feeling this person is legitimate. It just makes sense."

"Well, we need to think about what you're going to say when you reply," Nathan said. "First of all, ask him to send you the newspaper articles he mentioned." Nathan turned back to the email and began reviewing it again.

"He mentions that Rogers was cleared by the court in one case. We need to see if we can get those court records. He mentions that other boys were abused…see if he can get any records of those cases, too. We need more information."

"Okay, I will ask him to send us anything he can get," I said. Shannon, who had seen me at the press conference and knew I was anxious to talk to Nathan, was taking notes, reading the email and agreeing with him that I had to be careful.

"Don't say anything that isn't factual," Nathan cautioned me. "In other words, you should not say anything about Scott Rogers that would leave you open to a charge of slander. Only say what you know to be public and factual."

That night, I went home and carefully composed the first of many emails to Ethan.

"Thank you for reaching out to me," I began. "I would be very interested in seeing the newspaper articles you mentioned."

I told him I was familiar with Mathew and Stuart and knew that Scott had adopted a young boy since moving to Baton Rouge.

"Do you know if the court records in the U.K. are public records?" I asked. "You mention that other boys were abused…. Were these other cases made public? Copies of the documents would be extremely helpful."

I was so nervous about replying to the first email that I drafted my response and waited until morning to read it to Nathan. He had rightfully made me feel guarded about the unknown person with whom I was communicating. After receiving that first email, I had Googled the writer's name and found a person who appeared to be from the area where the news stories about Rogers originated. His company's website included the photograph of a young man with movie-star good looks by the same name. His picture had a haunting quality; he appeared to look at a far distant target instead of the camera. A brief description said he had worked his way through the ranks and helped the company achieve impressive growth.

"*Is this you, Ethan?*" I wondered. He appeared about the right age, and I couldn't help thinking I could see a slight look of melancholy in his steel blue eyes. He seemed lost in his own thoughts when the photo was taken.

Nathan quickly reminded me that the person emailing me could be using a fake name, or even someone else's, and that I should proceed with extreme caution.

Little did I know, Ethan's hopes fell when I did not respond immediately to his first email. He began to regret sending it, especially using his real name. He felt he had acted too impulsively, and had made a mistake revealing himself to a stranger.

Meanwhile, Nathan and I talked again about my response the next day and I sent my first reply late that night. I awoke the next morning to another email from Ethan. We soon fell into a routine of emailing back and forth on a daily basis: I asked questions, and he provided more and more information. Because of the six-hour time difference, I would wait to send an email just before going to bed and awaken to find a reply from Ethan when he started his day the next morning.

His first response concerned Scott Rogers' adoption of a little boy in England. "It's very alarming that he has adopted another child. It's also very worrying that he has so much involvement with children, although not surprising," he wrote.

In the year that I corresponded with Ethan, this focus remained constant, never wavering from his primary concern. Any time new developments occurred in the investigation of Rogers, Ethan's first question always addressed the safety of children. His unease about matters I was only beginning to understand was heartbreaking. In just his second email, he wrote, "It would be a little weird telling someone I don't know huge details about my life, but then I don't feel...I have much choice!" *He's going to tell me something I don't want to hear. I could feel it.*

He went on to disclose how, in the late 1980s, Rogers had adopted a young boy, Jake, who was about 10 or 11 years old. Ethan wrote that until the boy ran away to London in the mid-1990s, Scott sexually abused him for many years.

He told me about another boy, Tim, who in 1992 or '93 complained to his parents of Scott's sexual abuse during a sleep-over, a charge that resulted in Rogers' arrest and trial. "Scott was cleared, but there were several counts that were undecided and a re-trial was in the cards, but Tim could not bear to go through it all again," Ethan wrote.

"Mathew Hodgkins' real name is Mathew Hodgkinson; he was Scott's 'boyfriend' at the age of 13...he slept with Scott on numerous occasions. His parents had to force him to move to

France with them…they even had to lock him in a room to keep Scott from getting at him. It did not work," he wrote.

I could hardly believe what I was reading, but with every sentence, I grew more and more convinced that Ethan was telling the truth. Why would anyone make this up? I found it daunting to imagine the difficulty of telling a total stranger secrets you have kept for 20 years, but Ethan's descriptions were clear and consistent. Remembering Nathan's warnings, I knew I could not be naïve. I had to read everything carefully, pay attention to any discrepancies, and handle my communication with Ethan as I would anything else. I had to keep asking myself: *Do his facts add up? What can he prove in black and white?* But no matter how many times I read every single word he wrote, my instincts told me Ethan was who he said he was, and he was telling me the truth.

CHAPTER NINE

THE GRENADE THROWER

Day 2
August 29, 2013

After the initial email describing Mathew and Stuart as "kinda kidnapped," Ethan told me he felt Scott Rogers had brainwashed Stuart, then announced to the boys at the Academy, when Stuart was only 15 or 16 years old, that Stuart was gay. Ethan said that Stuart's parents, who had not seen him since he was 18, missed him very much. He described Stuart as a buddy at the Academy. He said they had hung out together, sneaked cigarettes between classes, and talked about girls. He was, Ethan said, surprised when Rogers announced that his friend was gay.

"Scott was accused of running a cult at one point," Ethan wrote. "He had a special circle of pupils between the ages of 12 and 16."

He mentioned Rogers' wife Mandie and their daughter, saying that Scott mistreated Mandie, who didn't seem to know what was going on. "She lost her daughter Kimberly to him when he left Bury St. Edmunds.

"Scott is extremely charming, manipulative, calculating, and very clever," Ethan continued. "He befriends the parents and then the kids. He will still be abusing children. Whilst I knew Scott I know for a fact that he abused at least five people aged between 11 and 16. I have no doubt that there were many more.

"All this information may be hard to prove...I hope you may be able at least to alert people to the dangers in some way," Ethan wrote. "What do you have in mind?"

What did I have in mind? I had so many thoughts swirling around in my head, and at the same time, I had nothing. I had no plan. At this point I wasn't sure what to do with the information. This was the first hint I'd had of what I believed Ethan wanted me to do: Warn people so that they would not let Scott hurt any more children.

Yes! Of course we need to do that. But how? I had filed a lawsuit against 1stCo based on Scott's decision to make off with our fees. Now I was supposed to start telling people he was a child sex abuser they could not trust around children. Oh, and by the way...those two men who work for him? Kidnapped! I couldn't imagine telling anyone Ethan's story. This new information was too incredible. *But somehow, I believed it. But I could not believe it just because I wanted to,* I thought. *Because I felt Scott had tried to hurt me, I must be completely certain Ethan was telling me the truth. Someone could easily assume I was out for revenge against Scott. I could not react too quickly, or make any assumptions that were not supported by facts. I had to be careful for both Ethan and myself....*

Ethan began to realize that his habit of throwing grenades without thinking through the consequences had placed him in the eye of a storm now brewing. After providing me some information, he was thinking maybe he could just hand off this problem to me and ease out of the picture, hoping I would alert someone and word would get out about Scott. Anything to keep Scott away from children.

What do I have in mind? I kept thinking. I had no idea what to do! But one thing I knew: With each piece of new information Ethan shared with me, I grew more certain this was a very serious, and possibly dangerous predicament. I knew that since Scott was now here in Baton Rouge, Ethan was looking to me for an idea—some remedy for his concerns. But at this point I had a lot more questions than answers for Ethan.

Still, I knew this: I wouldn't take any action unless I was certain I had the facts to support it.

The Boys of Bury

ETHAN *in his own words*

Bury St. Edmunds, England
1985

The summer was amazing. We hung out in the Abbey Gardens, skateboarded, biked around, played football, rounders, cricket...Charlie and I used to go down to the Abbey Gardens with a big box of matches and genie them, normally with some grasshoppers in.

Over the summer Charlie and I started going to a drama class, it was on a Saturday. We would reenact Dirty Harry scenes. I loved acting, it was the one thing I was really good at, drama. I excelled in it. Mum and Dad decided to take it to another level. Mum found a Saturday drama club at somewhere called The Academy of Dance and Performing Arts.

I was pretty nervous on the first one. I didn't know anyone, it was a little odd going somewhere on a Saturday. I stood outside, the class started at 2:15 p.m. All of a sudden the door opened and I walked into a busy class, probably about 15 of us.

Sitting on a chair in the middle of the room was a man. My first impression was that he looked like a bender, a bit odd, he was wearing ballet shoes, with socks and long hair, a waistcoat and trousers pulled up too high. He introduced himself as Scott, and the class began....

CHAPTER TEN

THE CHURCH

A few months before Ethan contacted me, I learned Scott Rogers had started a non-denominational church, the 13:34 Church of Christianity, in his television studio at the mall. When a friend of mine—who worked for a non-profit, of course—appeared for her *Around Town* interview, she found a church sanctuary. Another generic website revealed no names, only times for services and vague statements about the church's tenets.

The name *13:34 Church* points to the Book of John, Chapter 13, Verse 34: "A new command I give you: Love one another. As I have loved you, so you must love one another."[5]

This verse appears in the chapter leading to the Last Supper, when Jesus predicts the betrayal by Judas and Peter's denial. "My children, I will be with you only a little longer. You will look for me, and just as I told the Jews, so I tell you now, where I am going, you cannot come."

Verse 35 continues, "By this everyone will know that you are my disciples, if you love one another." Was Scott Rogers using even the Bible to gather around him a flock that would carry out his twisted ideas of devotion? This behavior was

---

[5] "John 13: New International Version." Bible Gateway. The Zondervan Corporation. Viewed 9 September 2015. https://www.biblegateway.com/passage/?search=John+13

starting to sound more and more like a cult—exactly what Ethan said parents and teachers in London accused Scott of running in the U.K. Now that Scott Rogers had a church of his own, was he using it to attract families and children while hiding his true objectives? Of course, I had no idea at the time that Scott Rogers had been active in the Mormon Church in the U.K., even traveling to the U.S. when he was younger to perform his year of missionary service before returning as an elder.

Scott's first sermon in a Baton Rouge pulpit came with an invitation to speak at the Unity Church of Christianity, a diverse congregation that describes itself as active supporters of the lesbian, gay, bisexual, and transgender (LGBT) community. Strangely, Scott reacted violently when people assumed he was gay. Then, as he gained confidence in his ability to preach, he pulled his so-called family together and announced that he planned to get ordained online and start his own church. The first service at the 13:34 Church in Cortana Mall drew about 50 people from the Unity Church. He had found a new outlet for his powers of persuasion. As he had in the past, Scott put Mathew and Stuart to work doing renovation and construction, this time building a sanctuary at the 1stCo studios in the mall. After years of working for Scott, they were now talented carpenters, and with free labor, Scott could hold down his costs.

Louisiana is no stranger to cases of child sex abuse by unlikely offenders, especially religious leaders. The first modern-day case of sex abuse by a Catholic priest, in fact, came to light in the 1970s, when a bishop learned that Father Gilbert Gauthe had molested altar boys in South Louisiana. The priest finally pleaded guilty in 1984 to 34 counts of child molestation and possession of child pornography. Gauthe had molested at least 37 boys in four parishes.

After the Catholic Church settled over $20 million in claims by victims, cases involving priests' abuse and bishops' cover-ups began to fall like dominoes around the world.

Gauthe's story unfolded to horrified Catholics, revealing the quiet, unassuming priest as an evil and aggressive predator who threatened to send his victims straight to hell and kill their parents, should they tell. In the course of his trial, we also learned that when Gauthe was around 9, an older boy had molested him, and Gauthe later preyed upon young boys around that same age.

Ironically, Gauthe had confided to his brother, also a pedophile eventually arrested and jailed in the U.K., that he had gravitated to the priesthood because it offered unlimited access to young boys.

Now England had sent us one of its own worst predators in the form of a Peter Pan character who touted "Unity in the Community." We had a television host who stole into our homes in the early hours on weekend mornings, wrapping himself up in positive news and all that is good. The truth now revealed a very different story. Assuming I believed Ethan, which I did, how would we alert Baton Rouge to Scott Rogers?

Everything I do, I try to base on logic and facts. Now I was supposed to warn people that a man who had befriended them was a child molester. What proof did I have?

Well, I could say, I got this email from someone I've never met, who lives in England, but who I believe is real and honest and just trying to stop Scott Rogers' abuse of children. *Yeah, right!* I wouldn't blame anyone who thought that answer more than a little odd, who thought this stranger had pranked me.

I could find nothing rational in this recent turn of events…and yet, with Ethan's second email, I grew even more convinced he was telling me the truth. I asked questions, he provided answers. No drama. Nothing evasive. He just answered my questions.

"Please feel free to contact me should I be of any further help," Ethan closed his second email. And a few emails later, "Good luck with all." *As my Cajun friends would say, Lâche pas la patate! Don't drop the hot potato! I could tell he wanted to hand off this problem to me as quickly as possible. You've got to hang in there, Ethan.*

It was as if he had wrapped up a package, tied a bow on it, and delivered it to me. Now he was thoughtfully offering his assistance, should I need help unwrapping my present, which he was definitely hoping I didn't. *You better believe I need help,* I thought. I hoped this mysterious stranger wasn't about to disappear just as he was giving me enough information to do something, although I had no idea what.

Believing Ethan was one thing. Taking action was another entirely. I knew I had to be careful. If he could just provide some evidence that supported his account of Scott's crimes, I was willing to trust my instincts and try to connect Ethan with someone who could help. As he revealed more about Scott Rogers, I began to realize that Scott was even more dangerous than what I knew. But I needed to know more. I needed *proof.*

After all, Rogers had surrounded himself in Baton Rouge with friends in law enforcement, some who believed in him enough to allow him easy access to their departments. His friendships with high-ranking law enforcement officials gave Scott a certain legitimacy, despite his peculiarity. If I was going to warn anyone about Scott, I needed as much information as possible.

I knew one thing: I would find Scott Rogers hiding behind powerful people and he would use that power to retaliate.

CHAPTER ELEVEN

THE PAST

Day 3
August 30, 2013

Within two minutes of my emailing Ethan to ask for the newspaper articles he had mentioned in his first email, he began sending a series of emails containing attachments that, unfortunately, I could not open. I quickly emailed back, since at that point it was 11:30 p.m. in the U.K., and I was anxious to read what he was sending.

"Try these," said Ethan, and soon I began receiving photographs of yellowed news articles pasted into a scrapbook. Ethan, it appeared, was taking photos with his iPhone and emailing them straight to me.

I felt bad for him, as the hour was getting close to midnight there, and we kept having problems getting copies to me that I could read. I suggested he send them through a file-sharing program like Dropbox or wait until the next day, but he emailed back, "Don't worry. I can handle it. If this one doesn't work, I'll Dropbox it."

The easy back and forth rhythm of our emails gave me the comfortable feeling of speaking with a trusted colleague. Except that he wasn't. He was someone I had never met, someone in a foreign country, someone telling me that a child molester living in my community had fooled almost everyone, including our highest-ranking law enforcement officials.

Initially, I oversimplified everything I said, the common misstep Americans make when talking to someone from another country. But from the beginning, Ethan understood everything and replied quickly. Talking to Ethan was like talking to someone I saw every day. But the feeling was more than familiarity; I had the inexplicable sense that we saw things the same way, had the same values, processed information alike, reacted to news similarly. Intuition is hard to describe, but I had this strong feeling about the kind of person he was from day one.

I have always been a skeptic, listening carefully to what people say to get a read on them through what they reveal about themselves. So it came as a surprise to me that I found myself trusting Ethan so quickly.

Because some of the articles Ethan emailed me blurred when I enlarged them, I had trouble reading them. I kept emailing back and forth with him late into the U.K. night, as he sent first one page of an article, then the second, then another and another. I knew it was getting later there, but I was so anxious to see the material that I hoped he would stick with emailing until all of the articles came through. Ethan very patiently sent one page at a time, checking to make sure I could read each one before sending another.

While he was sending the photographs, I offered the few details I knew about the circumstances of the child living with Scott Rogers. I told him Scott hosted a weekly television show and that Kimberly appeared on the show with him, while Mathew and Stuart worked in production. I told him Scott had started some sort of non-denominational church in the mall, in the same space as his studio.

I knew the young boy had either emotional problems or a learning disability, because Scott had described him publicly as "feral" when he adopted him. I didn't know what he meant by that, because I doubted the child had truly been raised without human contact. Using that term to describe a child with any type of disability was certainly inappropriate. I also remembered hearing Scott describe, in a television interview a few years back, how his adopted son was frightened by Halloween, so he planned hayrides and other activities for him that were less unsettling than scary costumes and noises.

Within the past year, I told Ethan, I had also attended a community event during which Scott, serving as the emcee, spoke of his wife's leaving him when Kimberly was born and of how he had raised her as a single father. Scott often told people Mandie had no maternal instincts—the same attribute he accused his own mother of lacking—and claimed she had rejected both Kimberly and him.

Ethan assured me the story was completely false, as Kimberly had been around 8 at the time of Scott's trial, living in the same home with her parents, who were still married.

I promised Ethan I would take the newspaper articles to an attorney for advice. As I printed them out and began reading, I couldn't help wondering, *Who are you, Ethan? You have saved these newspaper articles in a scrapbook for 20 years.* I was starting to get a sinking feeling that Ethan knew a lot more about Scott Rogers, details I wasn't anxious to hear. At the same time, with every email, I grew more and more comfortable communicating with him.

I kept thinking, *He is telling the truth. I can feel it. And if this information is true, what am I going to do with it? He has reached out to me from across 5,000 miles and six time zones and he hasn't wavered one bit when I've asked him for more information.*

I began printing the photos as they came in, until I was holding in my hands copies of old newspaper clippings from 1993, articles from the *East Anglian Times* and *Bury Free Press,* that gave me a chill. The clippings were attached to lined notebook paper in a scrapbook or journal full of pages, some of the larger articles unfolded to reveal a neat handwriting on the pages behind the photographs. The edges of the pages were worn and turned back.

The book lay open on a bright red quilt covered with small white stars. A man's hand held the book open in each photograph. *Was this some sort of a diary or journal that Ethan had kept? Why have you kept this all these years?* I thought. *Why are these articles so important to you?*

The collection detailed the charges brought against Scott Rogers in Bury St. Edmunds when Tim, one of his Academy students, accused him of sexual assault. Scott was arrested and charged with one count of committing a serious sexual offense, three counts of indecent assault, and two counts of indecency. Scott's assaults on the 13-year-old boy had included sodomy, masturbation, and oral sex.

The news articles Ethan had kept for 20 years described Scott's arrest and trial. Over the course of the next year, I would learn more about the court case and why many people believed the jury reached the wrong verdict. As more information came to light, the bizarre world of Scott Rogers began to unfold.

In the articles Ethan provided, the young boy who filed the charges described how Scott, who was 31 at the time, sexually assaulted him when he was a student at the Academy of Dance and Performing Arts. The boy's name was not published because of his age. First, the boy said, Rogers, before sexually assaulting him, pressured him—or as the article reads, "pressurised him"— to say in front of the other students that he was gay. *He was brainwashing them.*

The trial convened at Inner London Crown Court, with Sandra Stanfield prosecuting and Ann Curnow, Queen's Counsel, defense attorney for Rogers. Curnow, who passed away in 2011, was a trailblazer among women attorneys in the U.K. and, as the London Times noted, "renowned for her powerful cross examinations."[6]

Stanfield described how Rogers spent most nights sleeping with students or with a young boy, Jake, "a sort of adopted son," instead of with his wife Mandie. When he wasn't sleeping downstairs with the boys from the Academy, Scott forced Jake to sleep on the floor of the bedroom he shared with Mandie, which Jake felt made her angry with him. Scott used the excuse

---

[6] "Ann Curnow." The Times: Obituaries. Times Newspapers Limited. 9 June 2011. Viewed 9 September 2015. http://www.thetimes.co.uk/tto/opinion/obituaries/article3055408.ece

that Jake was afraid of the dark, but Jake despised Scott and longed to sleep as far away from him as possible.

At the time of Scott's arrest and trial, living with him and Mandie in their house on Fornham Road were Kimberly, 7, adopted son Jake, 19, and Academy students Claire, 16, and Mathew Hodgkins, 14.

At the trial, prosecutor Stanfield walked the jury through a description of how Rogers trained his Academy students to behave.

"He insisted that pupils bowed on his entering or leaving a room," she said. "And Russian wedding rings were given to favored pupils so they could become married to the Academy and never do anything to harm it."

She explained that Rogers had accepted Tim, the plaintiff, on a trial basis and agreed to put him up at the Academy while he was studying there. On and off the witness stand over five days, the young boy, now 15, described how the abuse began on the living room floor after Rogers ordered Mandie, Kimberly, and the other students to go to bed.

Rogers had spotted Tim dancing at a festival and approached his father to say the son had potential but needed to dance with boys to build strength. He suggested the father enroll his son in the Academy.

"He started to say things to make me think I was gay," Tim testified at the trial, "and said I wasn't really interested in my girlfriend. I was feeling pressurized by the things he was saying. At first I said I wasn't, but then—I don't know why I said anything—I said I was gay."[7]

Rogers then began to assault him, he testified, on three separate nights during June and July of 1991. Rogers had convinced parents that he had set up important auditions in London for the boys at the Academy and that they would have to spend the night at his home so he could rehearse late with them and make sure they arrived for the audition on time. The

---

[7] "PRINCIPAL ASSAULTS DANCE PUPIL." Bury Free Press. Johnston Publishing Limited. (n.d.)

boy reported that the sexual assaults took place in Rogers' living room and during an audition trip to London.

Detective Adrian Randall and Detective Sergeant Stephen Gooda had taken the young victim's statement on April 28, 1992. On the morning of Thursday, April 30, the two went to Scott's home on Fornham Road to arrest him.

When Randall began to explain to Scott why they were there, he was able to say only, "I'm arresting you," before Scott interrupted in an excited tone, "I knew this would happen! I have been expecting this. That's the problem with being successful— people are jealous." Detective Sergeant Stephen Gooda told the jury that after Rogers learned the reason for his arrest, he said, "I can't believe this is happening. We've had this before; they called the social services."[8]

Later in an interview at the Bury Police Station, Rogers told the detectives he was not gay, the detective told the court; however, he told them he was "very demonstrative" and often hugged and kissed people. He told the detectives that when Tim and he spent the night together in the living room of the Fornham Road house that he shared with his wife, Mandie, the 13-year-old boy had molested *him*.[9]

Prosecutor Stanfield said the young boy acknowledged that what was done to him was done with his consent; however, "the law has particular care for children and regards children under 16 to be incapable of consenting to acts of sexual assault."[10] *The boy was only 13 years old! How could he possibly understand what was happening?*

I was amazed to read that U.K. law would allow a young boy accusing a person of sexual assault to endure such intense questioning on the witness stand. Rogers' defense attorney went after his young accuser, charging him with seducing Rogers. Curnow admitted that Rogers had slept with the young boy, but claimed that Rogers actually awoke one morning to find the boy

---

[8] "Sex charge dance teacher expected arrest." Bury Free Press. Johnston Publishing Limited. (n.d.)

[9] Ibid.

[10] "Dance academy head denies sex abuse of boy, 13." Bury Free Press. Johnston Publishing Limited. (n.d.)

trying to seduce him by touching him on the outside of his boxer shorts.

"No, that did not happen," Tim replied as he gave evidence on the fifth day of the trial.[11]

Of the sexual assaults, Rogers' attorney said the boy came on to him twice. She offered no explanation as to why Scott Rogers hadn't resisted sexual advances by a minor or why, if the advances had in fact occurred, he would put himself in that position a second time. While this defense was preposterous, its success confirms the effectiveness of Ann Curnow in defending Scott. Another strategy kept the young victim in and out of the witness box over five consecutive days.

The victim did admit to writing in his diary that he wished Scott Rogers was his father. "But Scott does that," he explained. "He makes all his pupils look at him as a father figure. His way of thinking is to pull you out of your family.

"He did that to me and my sister," Tim continued. "He tried to pull us out of our families. He tried to work me away from my father. He told us we should stand up to our parents and that if they ever hit us, we should hit them back."[12]

When Curnow then asked Tim if he had a "crush" on Scott Rogers, he answered, "No," and denied her claim that he had made up the accusations against Scott. According to news reports of the trial, the young victim said he did not tell anyone about the sexual assault until six months later, when the experience caused problems with a new girlfriend.

Charlotte Elliott, principal of the Central School of Dancing in Norwich, which the young victim had attended before leaving to study with Rogers, testified that the boy was a "very promising dancer; good looking with a good physique." She said further that when he later came back to her school for extra lessons, he complained of groin and back injuries and told her Rogers had "forced him through" an exam too early. Former Academy students, including Ethan, told me it was common for Scott to force a class at the Academy to do splits, and if one

---

[11] "Dance school head is called victim of lies." Daily Times. 12 June 1993, 35.
[12] Ibid.

student could not get all the way down to the floor, he would announce that no one could get up until the last student achieved a perfect split. This group punishment caused great pain for the students and also helped Scott turn them against each other.[13]

Mrs. Elliott, a fellow with the Imperial Society of Teachers of Dancing, one of the world's leading dance examination boards, testified she did not recognize, on leaflets promoting the Academy, two of the three sets of initials Rogers had put after his name as dance instructor credentials.

Curnow then called to the stand a parade of 17 character witnesses, including members of the clergy, to discredit the young victim. Dr. Stuart Tovey, whom Curnow identified as a "genito-urinary expert," told the jury that medical evidence made it "unlikely to be physically possible" for the sexual offense to have taken place. At the time of the trial, Dr. Tovey was listed as a consultant physician in charge of the Lloyd Clinic, the department of genito-urinary medicine at Guy's Hospital in London.[14]

Later, the young men who attended the Academy told me Scott often boasted to them about the size of his penis, and was apparently willing to bring in a doctor to testify about its size…to quash the suggestion that he could have sexually assaulted a child without leaving damaging evidence. *He was fighting for his life…he would do anything…and say anything.*

A mother of two students—a 13-year-old boy and 9-year-old girl, both of whom attended Rogers' dance Academy—also testified in support of Rogers. When defense attorney Roderick Newton asked, "Do you have any qualms about leaving either of your children with him?" she replied, "Not in the least, no." The woman went on to describe Rogers as "an extremely giving person" who was "kind and considerate."[15]

Under cross examination, she told prosecutor Stanfield that her son had stayed with Rogers overnight at his home but

---

[13] Sex charge dance teacher 'expected arrest.'" Bury Free Press. Johnston Publishing Limited. (n.d.)

[14] "Pupils' mother praises accused dance teacher." East Anglian Daily Times. Archant Community Media. (n.d.)

[15] Ibid.

denied he had slept with him. When Stanfield then asked whether Rogers had ever given her son any gifts, such as a Russian wedding ring, she again denied any inappropriate behavior toward he son.

After 13 days of testimony, a jury of eight men and four women deliberated for seven hours before finding Rogers *not guilty* of the most serious charge, "committing a sexual offense on a 13-year-old boy," but hung on five other counts of indecent assault and indecency. Judge Bryan Pryor "regretfully" discharged the jury. Prosecutor Stanfield said her decision on retrying Scott on the five undecided charges would come after at least seven days. The trial in London had been highly publicized and covered daily by the tabloid press.

On Tuesday, July 20, 1993, Stanfield reported to the court that no re-trial would take place. After the ordeal of the first trial, the young victim's parents refused to allow him to give evidence in a second. Judge Colin Smith then entered "not guilty" on the books for the remaining charges.

The verdict seemed to shock people, especially Scott Rogers himself, who dramatically fell weeping into Mandie's arms as he left the court and told reporters, "The verdict left us quite surprised. I said goodbye to my daughter this morning and told her I would not be coming back if the people did not believe me."

He added, "Yes, I hug the children, but it is because I like to be a polite and considerate person. If that is seen as a crime in today's society, then it is a sad day indeed."[16]

When I met her in 2015 in London, former Academy student Gemma thought about how Tim must have felt 20 years ago to see Scott escape conviction for molesting him. "He would have counted many of us as friends and yet those people weren't on his side," she explained, "and actually, probably disliked him because he was taking away their Scott from them. So not only did he have the horror of having to come out and talk about it, but he didn't get believed either. You lose on all counts—for

---

[16] "Teacher cleared of sex charges." East Anglian Daily Times. Archant Community Media. (n.d.)

being the person who was actually trying to do the very best for thousands of people."

After reading over the news articles from Ethan, I stopped by Nathan's office to give him and Shannon a copy. He didn't want me to email the material to him, so at this point we were still printing everything we shared.

My next question to Ethan was whether he knew if the prosecutor, Sandra Stanfield, was still active, as Nathan thought she might recall more information about the trial. I also asked if Ethan knew any of Scott's victims who might be willing to talk to someone in the United States, should the need arise. I kept thinking that should the appropriate officials look into the safety of the children now under Scott's control, they would benefit from speaking to a person with direct knowledge of his actions, rather than merely reading 20-year-old newspaper clippings on a messy trial that recorded a predator "not guilty."

In reading the news articles about the trial, I was struck by parallels to the Scott Rogers we knew in Baton Rouge: In the U.K., he had adopted a young son, even though he had a biological daughter; 17 character witnesses had testified for him, people he had collected, people in positions to help him cover up his activities, people who included clergy, local officials, and respected physicians. Thinking about those with whom he surrounded himself in Baton Rouge, the similarities were uncanny and no doubt the result of a deliberate pattern.

Research tells us pedophiles have an almost uncontrollable desire to have sex with children. Their behavior is highly repetitive to the point of compulsion. According to a number of studies, the average male pedophile who molests boys will abuse as many as 260 victims during his lifetime, with over 90 percent of convicted pedophiles arrested again for the same offense after their release from prison.

Yello Dyno, a company providing educational tools for teaching children to be aware of potential sex offenders, reports on characteristics of child sex offenders. Dr. Mace Knapp, Nevada State Prison psychologist, is quoted saying, "The serial killer has the same personality characteristics as the sex offender against children." When you begin to understand how prolific child predators are, the real danger sets in.[17]

If the charges against Scott in the U.K. were true, then, as Ethan said, Tim wasn't the only young boy Scott abused. *How many more victims were out there?*

In Bury, Scott offered his popular dance students to perform free of charge for local events, which he felt put local community leaders in his debt. He gave the appearance of generosity, when what he was providing the town was no more than an opportunity for him to spend more time with the young boys. This professed good will benefitted him as much as it did the events.

In Baton Rouge, in addition to several law enforcement officials, Scott had befriended Rabbi Barry Weinstein, who remained close to him. Dr. Chuck Williamson's Eye Center and Cosmetic Surgery Center sponsored *The Around Town TV Show,* and Williamson's daughter, Shelly Williamson Esnard, was a regular guest on the program. She sometimes demonstrated cosmetic procedures on Scott, who often talked on the air about the work he'd had done on his face, teeth, and body. *As he worked to keep his name off the Internet, he was changing his physical appearance as well.*

The sponsors who seemed the most entrenched with Scott were Better Business Bureau President Jim Stalls and Events Coordinator B.J. Militello, who taped regular segments for *The Around Town Show.* Scott also served as emcee for BBB programs, hosted membership luncheons at his home in St. Gabriel, and frequently reminded viewers that he was the Bureau's marketing consultant. Other recurring sponsors of *The Around Town TV Show* included Neighbors Federal Credit Union, Louisiana Lottery, and Dana Vutera and Associates Insurance Agency.

The close-knit group of volunteers Scott had gathered around him included Frances and Charles Bennett, who served as greeters for *The Around Town TV Show* for years, even acting

---

[17] "Statistics." Yello Dyno. Viewed 9 September 2015. http://yellodyno.com/Statistics/statistics_child_molester.html

as surrogate grandparents to Scott's adopted son. I knew Frances from my days working at the LSU Athletic Department, when she and Charles regularly attended our sporting events and we discovered that she and my uncle had been high school classmates. After making that connection, when we ran into each other, we often caught up on people we knew in common.

Frances, in her mid-70s, and Charles some ten years older, have been full-time community volunteers for over 20 years. Even after Charles recovered from a stroke, he served on the 1stCo Board of Directors, and he and Frances were involved with Scott's television show, church, and family.

On one occasion, she started to tell me how she and Charles volunteered for Scott on *The Around Town TV Show*. At the time, Scott had just orchestrated *The Advocate's* front-page news article about me, so I quickly changed the subject, saying, "Frances, you and I will have to agree to disagree about him." I found it hard to accept her devotion to Scott, especially considering she was a regular on the set when he was shooting his weekend program. Scott frequently spoke harshly to the production crew when taping those programs, saving his cruelest reprimands for Stuart, reprimands Frances had witnessed. Though this behavior left some people thinking Scott was not the positive person he tried to portray, they fell victim to his charm and took his outbursts as signs of a perfectionist. *His power of persuasion was obviously very effective!*

I never had a reason to take a close look at Scott Rogers, but of all the people in law enforcement and social services with whom he had aligned himself, had any one of them looked into his background? Did no one think his living arrangements—three unrelated men and a young woman adopting a little boy—unusual? Did anyone ever wonder why, in this age of social media, a media company would intentionally keep such a low online profile?

How was it possible that Scott could get so close to high-ranking law enforcement officials without anyone running a background check? *What does the FBI say? "Trust, but verify."* Scott may have been the subject of a culture of whispers, but he should have been, at some point, vetted by a culture of questions.

The sad truth, when it comes to child sex abuse, is that the uncomfortable nature of the subject too often silences those in a position to help children. Pedophilia is an unspeakable crime. We must learn to see it when it is in front of us, to name it, and to speak out about it.

CHAPTER TWELVE

THE UNMASKING

Day 4
August 31, 2013

It was the beginning of the Labor Day weekend, and the 90-minute drive from Baton Rouge to our family home in rural Mississippi provided a short break from the revelations of the last few days. Because cell phone and data service is so spotty in the country that I often can't receive emails or calls, the drive is a peaceful respite from Baton Rouge. Evergreen Oaks, which has been in my family since my mother's ancestors built it in 1850, is where I grew up with my older brother Mike and younger sister Abby. For the long holiday weekend, I escaped to the country, still thinking about Ethan and all he had told me.

Just before I left town, he emailed me, "Do you think you could get Stuart's email address? If anything good can come out of this, it would be to get Stuart home. I knew Stuart and was very good friends with him…I may be able to get him to open up…."

Soon after reaching out to me, Ethan had run into Stuart's mother in Bury St. Edmunds, and she had asked him if he knew where her son was. "I miss him so much," she told him. Ethan didn't tell her he had discovered that Stuart was now living with Scott in Baton Rouge. Nor did he disclose he had reached out to a stranger there to warn people about Scott's past and how he had left Bury with Stuart and Mathew. But seeing her pain amplified his interest in helping Stuart escape Scott's control.

Of course, good-hearted people may have trouble believing that a man actually removed children from their families. It's only natural to think that when the children grew older, they would surely want to return to their parents. To accept the truth, you must consider that no child could stand up to the brainwashing techniques Scott used. He subjected the boys to hours and hours of questioning, punishing them physically or sexually until they gave him the right answers. And so they became dependent—emotionally, financially, totally—on their abuser. He cut them off from their families early on, and controlled every aspect of their lives. *They lost all control to him.*

When I returned to Baton Rouge and Internet service on Sunday night, I replied to Ethan, providing all of the contact information Stuart includes in the signature of his emails: his email address at 1stco.com, along with his office telephone, fax, and cell phone numbers. I warned Ethan, however, that because others, including Scott, read the emails we had sent to Stuart, he should carefully consider how to contact him. Ethan agreed he would move cautiously. "I will tread very carefully and keep you posted on a response," he said.

A few days earlier, just as I was leaving town for the long weekend, Nathan had run into former investigative reporter John Camp and thought he might be a good resource for what I should do with the information Ethan had sent me. When he asked if I were willing to meet with Camp after the holiday, I quickly agreed.

Camp had worked as a highly respected investigative reporter for local television station WBRZ before moving on, in 1989, to a ten-year stint as senior correspondent for CNN's newly-created investigative reporting team. He was a respected, award-winning journalist, with four Peabody awards—the Pulitzer Prize of broadcasting—to his credit. He was a hard-nosed investigative journalist, a rare breed today.

Nathan scheduled the meeting at his office on Tuesday, September 3, and Camp joined him, Shannon, and me on the black leather sofas to review the emails and news articles. As I explained how Ethan had contacted me, Camp's take was to use the material in a news story, "Who is Scott Rogers?" He felt that would open the door to exploring the U.K. trial that had brought Rogers to the United States, and provide the reason for making that information public. He pointed out that Rogers had simply appeared in Baton Rouge and immediately befriended a large number of elected officials and community leaders, all the while living in guarded secrecy. In addition, Camp agreed that questions begged asking, such as: What was the relationship of Rogers with the other two men in his household? How did Rogers choose Baton Rouge as his domicile? Camp considered those questions a worthy entrée for an exploration of Rogers' life. He mentioned that he was mentoring an investigative reporter to whom he could give the story, and that he still had contacts at WBRZ he thought would find the articles interesting. He also offered that a friend and colleague with a broadcast network in London might also help.

During the promotion of a book he had written, Camp said, Frances Bennett, the volunteer greeter at Scott's show, had invited him to appear as a guest. When Rogers interviewed him, Camp thought, like JoAnne and me, that the atmosphere on the set was odd. He joked that Rogers' praise of him was so over the top that it made him uncomfortable.

When Camp expressed interest in communicating directly with Ethan, I said I would have to see if Ethan was comfortable with that. At this point, we were only five days into my daily emails with Ethan, so I didn't know how he would feel about sharing his story further. When I sent Ethan Stuart's contact information, I took that opportunity to provide background on Camp's career and to ask Ethan if he would feel comfortable communicating with him by email.

And lastly, I asked Ethan to send any other newspaper articles he could find, since the earlier ones had not covered the trial's verdict as much as Scott's arrest and the trial itself.

Noting that the time in the U.K. was around 12:30 p.m., Ethan promised to dig out and send over all of the newspaper articles he had not previously emailed. He then asked me to send Camp's email address and said he would be glad to contact him.

I asked Ethan if he had heard that before moving to Baton Rouge, Scott had been involved in a dance company, perhaps "The Seventh Sign," in Dallas. This was something Nathan had run across when I first had my legal problems with Scott; he had asked a private investigator he used on his criminal cases to look into Scott's past. The investigator came back to Nathan and told him that something didn't add up in Texas. "Nathan, something is just not right," the man said. "The trail goes completely cold on Scott Rogers in Texas. I'm telling you, if I could go over there and spend some time on the ground, I could find out, but something is just not right."

Ethan replied that while he was not aware of a Dallas company, he thought that Rogers, after leaving Bury St. Edmunds, had started a "Seventh Sign" dance company in Kent.

Another religious reference! When you hear people casually mention cults, common sense dictates that you not take most references literally, but more and more, the web surrounding Scott Rogers was starting to look like an actual *cult*. The name *Seventh Sign* evokes the story of the Apocalypse in Revelation, the last book of the Bible.

The United States Conference of Catholic Bishops interprets the Book of Revelation as difficult to understand because "it abounds in unfamiliar and extravagant symbolism," using imagery, colors, and numbers rather than literal descriptions to convey its meaning. In describing the end of the world, the number *seven* is used extensively to depict perfection.[18]

The word *apocalypse*, which derives from the Greek word for "unveiling" or "uncovering," refers to God opening seven sealed scrolls that describe the end of time. A 1988 movie, "The Seventh Sign," depicted the apocalypse in modern times with the warning, "An ancient evil has been awakened and there is nothing you can do to stop it…except pray."

---

[18] "The Book of Revelation." United States Conference of Catholic Bishops. Viewed 9 September 2015. http://www.usccb.org/bible/revelation/0.

The seven seals follow the wrath of God, through war, famine, plagues, earthquakes, and other disasters that result from mankind's disobedience of God's laws. The seventh sign is considered the calm before the storm: a half-hour of silence after the final battle between good and evil.

Did Scott find untold meaning in The Seventh Sign? Did he believe the children could calm the chaos in his mind—the turmoil caused by his own evil acts?

Ethan promised to continue looking for contact information for any attorneys involved in Rogers' U.K. trial. Soon, however, he was emailing back, asking if he could trust Camp, saying he did not want Camp to include him in any news stories.

"Yes, you can trust him," I replied, "but I understand your hesitation, because his success is the result of his tenacity in seeking the truth. Just be very clear with him that you do not want your name used in any way, and he will respect that. He was one of the top investigative reporters in the U.S. and will protect a source of information. If he asks you anything you're not comfortable answering, just don't answer."

That night, Ethan began emailing more news articles by continuing to photograph the pages in his scrapbook. As we again went back and forth on the size, he was patient and accommodating to make sure we got what we needed. On September 4, Ethan sent 15 or more emails containing news articles, along with an update on his communication with Camp.

By the next day, he and Camp had exchanged introductory emails, and Ethan had forwarded me the chain to read. Identifying his role as that of a "consultant," Camp told Ethan he found Rogers an intriguing character whom he had met only once as a guest on his television show, which he noted had a very small viewing audience. When you are promoting a book, however, Camp wrote, you don't count the number of people you're reaching.

In his emails to Ethan, Camp wondered about the U.S. allowing Rogers to adopt a child, about his forming a church—perhaps as a tax dodge—and about his "mysterious influence on public officials." About the adoption of a young boy, Camp wrote, "He does not seem like the kind of guy who would be allowed to adopt a child. That is the most intriguing public policy angle I've seen so far." He asked Ethan directly, "What is your interest in Scott? You seem to have a lot of information and insight into his character and history." Camp finished by assuring Ethan that if we must tell a story, he would find the proper medium.

After considering Camp's angle and having listened to Nathan's opinion on the information I had received, I explained to Ethan the two schools of thought on the direction we should take. One was the legal path, which meant that to get law enforcement authorities in Louisiana to look into Rogers' practices, we would need some solid information to prove he had committed a crime in the United States. From the first day, legal prosecution had been Nathan's preferred approach because he believed, as others did, that Rogers was still committing crimes against children.

To take legal action against an abuser, I wrote to Ethan, will eventually require "a person who is brave enough to speak up. I realize that would be difficult for a victim of sexual abuse."

The second school of thought was to give all of the information to the news media and hope for stories that would at the very least prompt the appropriate officials to look into the safety of Rogers' adopted son. This second option was what Ethan had hoped might happen: News reports of Rogers' history would make people question his current behavior and encourage the involvement of the authorities.

I worried, however, that because the U.K. had ultimately acquitted Scott of the charges there, and because 20 years had passed, the news media here might not move eagerly to cover the account of his past. And depending on who broke the story, Scott had made enough friends in the Baton Rouge media that he might cry foul, claiming that the young victim in the U.K. had not told the truth and that he himself had suffered as a result. This much I knew: The predator would put on quite a performance to convince people he was the victim. It's what they do.

The National Association of Adult Survivors of Child Abuse provides information to help prevent abuse and help victims recover. In talking about child predators, it points out, "An adult molester's ability to lie, exaggerate, minimize, rationalize and manipulate people greatly exceeds the ability of a child to sort through fears and emotions and think reasonably about the molester." Experts point out that once children become emotionally attached to their molester, they begin to feel responsible for him, even believing that they are more to blame for the abuse than the molester is. "At this point, the molester's psychological manipulations may begin to shift from positive to negative. Criticism or 'silent treatment' may replace praise and flattery. Threats may become more frequent than pronouncements of love."[19]

In the blink of an eye, the predator can paint himself as the victim, outraged and threatening or pained and weeping. The process is deliberate and carefully planned, but always manipulative.

Ethan felt the legal route to ending Scott's abuse of children would prove very difficult. He said if "someone" came forward, it would be "word against word," and asked whether authorities in the U.S. could take action if that someone were in the U.K., or would that person's disclosure just remain the problem of the U.K. authorities?

He mentioned that he could try to contact men who had lived with Scott when they were boys, as well as Jake, Scott's older adopted son in the U.K., to ask if they might help.

In connecting Ethan with Camp, I realized I had not clearly communicated that Camp was now living in Louisiana, and Ethan had the impression he was in the U.K. Once he understood that Camp was in "Barton Rouge," as he called it, he was more comfortable speaking with him. But he was not as interested in talking to the celebrated investigative reporter if that might lead to a news story in the U.K.

Two clear paths had emerged for uncovering the truth about Scott Rogers, but both involved significant obstacles. Nathan wanted to continue looking for a legal option because that was

---

[19] "Recovery." National Association of Adult Survivors of Child Abuse. Viewed 9 September 2015. http://www.naasca.org/010111-Recovery.htm

right in his wheelhouse. That path seemed safer to me, but also more difficult. Going to the press afforded Ethan more anonymity but might prove ineffective.

Scott disguised himself in public, wearing the mask of a model citizen—a friend to law enforcement. Our task required that someone with tremendous courage and firsthand knowledge strip away that mask and reveal the truth. But could anyone who had lived through a child predator's psychological abuse find the strength to step forward? Or would the pain of recalling the abuse outweigh the desire to stop the abuser?

CHAPTER THIRTEEN

THE CULT

Day 8
September 4, 2013

At our request, Ethan began thinking of others who might have knowledge of Scott Rogers' abuse. "There are two I can think of, one lives in the States," he wrote. "She lived with Scott during the time when the abuse was going on…I believe she was also abused and is aware of everything that went on with the boys. The other is Scott's adopted son, but I think it may be difficult to get him to help. What kind of confidentiality could you/we offer?"

I had to laugh. There he was again, giving me ownership of this dilemma, or trying to. At least this time he was including himself. I had no idea at this point the confidentiality anyone could expect, because I had not yet figured out who should receive this information. More and more, I thought the appropriate authorities needed to take a look at whether any children should be living with Scott, Kimmy, and two other men. But I felt Ethan believed we should simply put the information about the U.K. trial into the hands of the media as a way of warning the public. I just wasn't sure the media would find the story we knew was there.

In response to my daily questions, Ethan continued to send information. He explained more about the people surrounding

Scott Rogers. Mathew, or Matt, as he always called him, and Stuart, or Stu, were dancers at Rogers' Academy, he said, with Matt already living full time at Scott's house when Ethan first met him. Though Stuart joined the school later, Scott quickly brought him in as a permanent member of the "family," as Ethan described the group. He said Scott always told the children at the Academy that he loved them, always said how special they were to him, and spent a lot of time earning the trust of their parents. Extra kids were always staying at Scott's house, the boys sleeping in one room with Scott and the girls in another with Mandie and Kimberly.

Ethan said that at one time Mathew's parents took him away, because they knew what was going on between Rogers and their son. Though they moved to France and even kept Mathew locked in his room for a while, he escaped and returned to Scott. Ethan later reported that, to help Mathew escape, Scott mailed him a stuffed animal with a fake passport and cash sewn inside. When Mathew went back to Scott's house and his parents then sent the police looking for him, Ethan said, Scott hid Mathew in a special hiding space he had built between the walls, so that the police would not find him. Ethan recalled that by the time Mathew turned 18, his parents could do nothing more, and Mathew continued living with Scott and his family.

Ethan felt that Scott had brainwashed Mathew and Stuart at an early age and somehow forced them into staying with him. He reported that the trial severely damaged Scott's reputation and finances; clearly, the school could not survive the scandalous stories that emerged, despite the lack of a conviction. Scott took Mathew, Stuart, and a girl named Angela Hills and moved to Kent, until he managed to get everyone visas and they relocated to the United States, first Dallas and then Baton Rouge. Ethan said that while he knew of other people Scott had abused, he did not feel comfortable telling me their names, because he did not know if they would want to reveal their involvement with Rogers, even to expose him as a rapist and pedophile.

"It's very difficult with abuse," Ethan wrote. "It's hard to open up, especially about sexual abuse, as there was brainwashing going on and that lasts a long time. People are not necessarily willing to tell the world that they were abused; a lot of time has passed."

Oh, no, I thought. *He knows this all too well.*

Ethan also found a BBC news article about Prosecutor Sandra Stanfield that led us to believe she might still be active, and another article outlining the school's attempt to fight off the cult label after the trial. As we began to learn about the efforts by parents and county officials in Bury St. Edmunds to keep Scott from getting control over children, we began to understand just how dangerous he was.

After Scott's trial rocked the small town of Bury, Academy parents formed a support group to shut down the dance school. They learned from each other that as Scott would get the children to tell him secrets about their parents, he would then use that information to tell parents stories on each other. His strategy was to keep the parents from developing friendships, which would no doubt lead to their talking more often. He had succeeded in creating hard feelings among some parents who, based on Scott's stories, refused to speak to each other. This manipulation kept the parents from sharing sooner their concerns about him and his influence over their children.

On November 9, 1995, the Suffolk County Council issued a highly unusual statement warning parents of the "perceived risk" of sending their children to the Academy of Dance and Performing Arts. Though Rogers had gone to court to keep information about the school private, the Suffolk County Council won a long legal battle to speak out and warn the parents of the 500 remaining students. The Court of Appeal in London prevented the Council only from including Scott's name. A few hours after the decision by the Court, Suffolk authorities released the following statement:

> Suffolk County Council believes that parents of children attending the Academy of Dancing and Performing Arts, or considering sending their children to the academy, should be aware of the following information.

In 1993, at the conclusion of a case heard in the High Court, a number of findings and observations were made regarding the academy and the conduct of a senior member to which the local authority are not at liberty to refer.

Suffolk County Council had concerns about the unhealthy atmosphere at the academy and an environment in which some pupils moved their allegiance from their parents to that senior member and the academy. This occurred unbeknown to their parents.

The local authority felt that the situation was reminiscent of those cases in which parents sought to extricate a child from the influence of a religious or supposedly religious cult.

There was also considerable anxiety felt as to levels of intimacy that existed between the senior member and pupils.

The academy had produced written material stating that it had close links with social services. It is no longer the case that such links exist.

In view of the above information, Suffolk County Council's social services department cannot recommend that children attend the academy and would wish to alert parents and carers to the perceived risk.

Suffolk County Council's education department would also wish to alert parents and school governors to the use made by the academy and its staff of premises in the area for the teaching of dance and other activities.

These classes are held sometimes in schools and sometimes elsewhere. Suffolk County Council wishes to make it clear that it does not recommend that children attend these classes.

Tim's mother, who had watched her son go through the trial, spoke to the press when the Suffolk County Council statement was released. Her son and daughter had attended the Academy for only six weeks when he complained to his parents of Scott's abuse. In other words, a new student said that Scott had molested him three times in a six-week period. In the short time he was there, she told reporter Chris Evans with the *Daily Mail*, her son was "spellbound by the atmosphere."[20]

Scott had spotted her son, recruited him to the Academy, and molested him, all within a few weeks.

His mother claimed Scott told the students heartbreaking stories that reduced them to tears. Scott often included stories of how his father had physically abused him. "My son and daughter used to bring home these stories on sheets of paper which I found lying about the house," she said. "It was then that I realized something should be done." When she confronted her son about the stories, he told her Scott had sexually assaulted him.

Two years after the trial, Tim's mother told the *Daily Mail* her son was still haunted by his experience at the Academy. "He finds it very difficult to trust people and he feels very insecure in himself," she said. "Something should be done about that place," she said on the day the Council's statement appeared. "It's no exaggeration to say it was like a cult which divided families. I think it should be closed."[21]

On November 10, 1995, the *Bury Free Press* published the statement on its front page. At the time, Rogers charged fees of up to 1,500 British pounds a year for part-time courses, claiming the school's students had moved on to appear in West End Theatre productions in London and on television.

---

[20] "Six weeks changed my son's life." Daily Mail. Associated Newspapers Limited. 11 November 1995, 5.
[21] Ibid.

But the damage was done. Soon, local schools where Scott had been teaching classes, in addition to those at the Academy studio, banned him from their premises.

By now, Scott and Mandie had divorced although she remained living with him in the house on Fornham Road. A few months before their September 25, 1995, divorce, Scott told some of his inner circle that he had met a Texas woman named Diane Palladino through an Internet chat room. After the Suffolk County Council issued its statement, Scott flew to Dallas to meet her in person. *Could he be plotting an exit strategy?*

Once they had met, Diane visited Scott in the U.K. for several months, even taking a job temporarily at Lakenheath Air Force Base. Some of the Academy students, including Ethan, remember meeting her.

When Greg Hadfield, senior investigative reporter for the *Daily Mail,* saw the Suffolk County Council's press release, his Fleet Street reporter instincts kicked in. Finding the statement unusual, he suspected more to the story and planned to get up to Bury St. Edmunds quickly.

The *Bury Free Press* published a series of articles that included interviews with parents and students about the bizarre, cult-like behavior at the Academy. To accompany several pages of stories on the Academy, Editor David Williams included a special front-page editorial in the November 17 issue entitled, "At last…we can tell you what we believe you ought to know," with a photograph of the Academy labeled "The Academy—A Public Warning."[22]

A page-one editorial spotlighting a newspaper series of this type was unprecedented; Williams, however, had been hearing complaints from parents for two years and felt the public had a right to know what led to the Suffolk County Council's statement. "In more than 40 years of journalism, I have never seen a statement quite like it," wrote Williams, noting that public authorities are normally over-cautious. He explained that his newspaper's exposé was based on interviews with families who

---

[22] "At last we can tell you what we believe you ought to know." Bury Free Press. Johnston Publishing Limited. 17 November 1995.

were all one-time supporters of the Academy, some fervently so. Though they had not spoken out because they feared legal action by Scott, who was quite litigious, they all signed statements to the newspaper giving the *Press* permission to tell their stories.

By this time, Scott had purportedly handed over the reins of principal of the Academy to a trusted employee, a young woman who was only 18 years old. In an effort to keep the school open in its waning days, the young principal sat for an interview with the *Bury Free Press* and denied the cult label. On November 17, 1995, the *Bury Free Press* published her claim that Scott had little to do with the Academy any more, teaching only about three classes a week. The newspaper had requested that Scott participate in the interview, but the new principal appeared with a school parent and said that Scott was in London choreographing a show. The reporter pointed out that two hours after the interview, Scott was with the principal in Bury preparing for a show with Academy dancers.

It was this same young principal who drove to France to bring Mathew back to Scott against his parents' wishes. In 1995, a school mom, working at the Academy, told the *Bury Free Press* that when Mathew's parents took him to France, Scott got the students to write letters to him every day. Scott would send the letters by overnight delivery, pressuring Mathew to return. Finally, in a carefully orchestrated effort, the young Academy principal left to pick up Mathew. The school mom described Scott nervously pacing around the Academy, worried that something might go wrong and cursing the principal for taking so long. Finally, Scott got the phone call he had been waiting for: His young protégé had Mathew with her. She arranged to meet Scott at a service station so he and Mathew could reunite, and Scott persuaded the woman at the Academy to go with him. As the woman got out of Scott's car to enter the principal's for the ride back to the Academy, she saw Mathew walk straight over to Scott and kiss him warmly on the mouth. The woman said Scott had kissed Mathew at the Academy and she had not thought it unusual, since Scott was very affectionate with all the students. Then she noticed another driver at the service station, filling up his tank when he observed the young boy kiss Scott on the lips. He looked shocked. And suddenly, the woman realized that Scott's behavior was strange.

When she got into the car to drive back to the Academy, the first thing the young principal said to her was, "When are they coming to arrest me?"

A former student, Paul, later described to me how some parents of Academy students were so devoted to Scott that they brought him gifts of flowers and fruit baskets to win favor with him. Like the students, some of the parents were also spellbound by Scott, and he enjoyed manipulating them as much as he did the children. "I remember being in his office and one of the mothers came in with this big fruit basket," Paul told me, and Scott said, 'Oh, thank you so much.' And then he looked at me as she left and said, 'Your mum will be doing this for me soon.'" The predator was seducing the parents.

Paul described the time of the trial as strange. "Scott was very frantic. He spoke in a crying voice, you know, when people aren't really crying but they talk in that kind of whimpery 'I'm so wounded' voice? He did that a lot of the time. 'Why are they doing this to me? They're persecuting me. They're so cruel. They're just jealous of my success. They want to bring me down. I'm so close to all of you and they don't understand it. And we all have a really good relationship.'"

When I heard Paul explain this, it had a familiar ring. Scott had used the same tactic when JoAnne confronted him. "You don't understand! Why are you doing this to me?" he whined to her. This was apparently how Scott Rogers handled problems— make people uncomfortable or even embarrassed for questioning him and maybe they will go away.

Paul recalled feeling very uneasy with the behavior surrounding Scott, but not brave enough to stand up at the time and say, *This is wrong. This isn't a normal set-up.*

"And knowing that people like Mathew and Stuart were getting more and more estranged from their real families, and spending less and less time with them, it felt wrong," Paul said. "I remember Mathew and Stuart went from calling Scott 'Scott,' to calling him 'Dad.' Then even as a child, you think, *That's not okay.*"

Paul said Scott began spending a lot of one-on-one time with him, talking endlessly and even massaging his legs, which Scott told him would improve his dance technique, even though Paul had no interest in dancing. He had entered the Academy to study voice and acting. Though he joked with me, just as Ethan had, about not being a dancer, he indicated that Scott had pushed him into taking the dance classes. Only later did he fully realize that the massaging was inappropriate. Then, when Paul was 17, Scott made his first sexual advance on him after having a couple of drinks, a ploy he often used as an excuse for initiating his inappropriate behavior. If the boy resisted, Scott would blame it on the alcohol and dismiss it.

After Paul left the Academy, Scott called him to work on a show he was producing in Malaysia, where he had taken Kimmy and the students from his inner circle at the Academy to live for several months. "The show that we had in Penang, in Malaysia, was an international dance show with Scott's dancers and Thai Ladyboys," he explained. The Ladyboys are cross-dressing or transgender males who appear as female performers in cabaret shows and are often active in the Thai sex trade.

In Penang, all of the boys stayed in one room with Scott, while the girls, including Kimmy, stayed in another. Scott had connected with a wealthy Chinese businessman who wanted the British dance company to perform at the opening of a huge nightclub, so the students expected an extended stay.

Mathew acted as Scott's spokesperson, reminding the students what they should and shouldn't do. "Think about your behavior when you're out in public," he told them. "Remember that you're representing us. You have to be very professional." Most of them were working illegally on visitors' visas, so Scott no doubt wanted to avoid too much attention.

One student who traveled to Malaysia with Scott said the dance performances were the public reason he took the Academy students to countries like Malaysia to perform. But the secret behind the trips was that he was arranging to sell some of the boys to men for sex after the shows.

Like many of Scott's schemes, the deal soon soured. He told the students the Malaysia group didn't want to pay what it cost him to provide a professional show, so he packed them all up and returned to Bury. "The whole thing fell apart," Scott told them. "They were refusing to pay what we wanted. We needed to go home right away." Scott had talked to the group about going to Australia for a while until the talk about the Academy died down, then going back to Malaysia at some point.

"I didn't really understand any of that," Paul said. "But I'm sure it was something shady."

Academy students describe how Scott created competition among them for his attention, always setting goals for them to achieve. He once said he wished he could take all of his favorite students and move to a deserted island where they could all live together. Then he would point out which students he would choose, devastating those he did not pick. *Silent treatment replaces praise! The psychological abuse was well orchestrated.*

Some of Scott's former favorites tell stories of his affectionate behavior with the students, cuddling with them at sleepovers at his house, hugging and kissing them and getting them to massage him. "Some evenings, if Scott said he'd had a stressful day—many a time this would be because of a row with one of the parents—he would sit in a chair and students would be stroking his arms and legs, round his ears, neck, and shoulders, tickling him and caressing him," one former student told the *Bury Free Press* at the time of the Council's statement. "He loved his hair being combed. He'd take his vest off and roll up his shell suit trousers so we could stroke him." Shell suits were a British fad in the late 1980s and early 1990s. Similar to a track suit or warm-up, they were made of brightly-colored polyester fabrics and famously worn by Jimmy Savile, the BBC television personality whose pedophile exploits exploded in the headlines after his death in 2011. "About half-a-dozen boys and girls, ages around 12 to 16, would do this," the former student recalled.

Dr. Anna Salter, Ph.D., is a widely respected authority on child sex offenders and victims. She has conducted training sessions in all 50 states and serves as a consultant to the Wisconsin Department of Corrections. Her description of how child predators develop emotional bonds with children by grooming them matches Scott's tactics. Dr. Salter has said the first physical contact between a predator and a victim is often nonsexual touching designed to identify limits. This could include putting an arm around the child's shoulder, brushing his hair, and touching him in a way that appears accidental. This nonsexual touching desensitizes the child and breaks down inhibitions, allowing the predator to move to the next step of more overt sexual touching. Scott's Academy students have described his cuddling and hugging them and massaging their legs, and having them brush his hair and massage his shoulders and legs in return. When the students spent nights at his house, Scott encouraged wrestling and tickling on the floor as they watched movies together. In fact, he engaged in anything involving touching that could appear nonsexual. The predator gradually broke down the children's barriers.

As always, Scott had his supporters, even among parents. Angela Hills' mother Catherine, who was 40 at the time of the Suffolk County Council's statement, denounced it and said the warning made no difference to her. "The council is just harping on about old news which I am fully aware of," she told the *Daily Mail*. Catherine said she had been involved in 16-year-old Angela's classes from the beginning and was "extremely pleased" with them. "I have no qualms at all about her being there. Parents are readily encouraged to come along and watch classes," she told Greg Hadfield, when he delved into the story behind the Academy for the *Daily Mail*.[23]

Hadfield, who knew that other parents had every reason for grave concern over Scott's influence on their children, flew to France to sit down with Mathew's parents. "Their son's story was the most painful of many painful ones I heard," he later told me. "It's a story that has stayed with me. We should have done more at the time."

---

[23] "This is not a cult says dance school starmaker." Greg Hadfield. Daily Mail. Associated Newspapers Limited. 11 November 1995.

The Boys of Bury

ETHAN *in his own words*

Bury St. Edmunds, England
2015

Dance training was very tough. Ballet was the hardest discipline. We were expected to be at the Academy any free time we had to train, we even had a 2-hour class before school at 7 a.m. There was me, Jake, Stuart and Mathew, we would work out under Scott's supervision. I was flat in splits after just one week, put through a strict programme over 7 days, eventually I was doing splits on a chair. You were pushed beyond your limits. You could never stop mid-way through anything, if that happened you would have to either do more or have the whole class focused on you.

Punishments were dished. A lot of classes were used to humiliate, bully or hurt. In some respects, that was dance, it was competitive, it was hard work, and you learn to take that kind of physical abuse.

But nothing was as bad as hearing your name called out as you were summoned to his office.

CHAPTER FOURTEEN

THE ABUSE

Day 10
September 6, 2013

As I read the news articles Ethan sent me, my list of questions grew. I knew we needed more information before we could prove whether Rogers had committed any crimes. "Do you know the name of the newspaper that published the articles?" I asked Ethan, "Or anything about Chris Mills, the reporter who covered the trial?" I thought we had to look for every possible source of additional reliable information to substantiate Ethan's concerns. He worried that "word against word" may not convince anyone that Scott was a danger, and I agreed.

"What about family members of the victim in the trial? Do you know them?"

I told Ethan that for Camp to build a news story required solid information, or Scott could simply claim that the report was old news, that people in the U.K., jealous of his success, had tried to smear his good name but that the courts had cleared him.

Ethan replied with the names of the newspapers that had covered Scott's trial, including the *Daily Mail, East Anglian Daily Times,* and *Bury Free Press.* He knew both the victim in the trial and his sister, he said, and that the parents had not spent much time at the Academy, as they lived in the next county over.

At any rate, Ethan felt that the main victim was Scott's adopted son, Jake. "I believe he was the most affected by Scott's abuse," he said, revealing that Jake, who now uses his real name, instead of the adopted name Scott gave him, is settled with a wife and children.

Ethan also mentioned that a young woman, Natalie, who had also lived with Scott and was very close to him, "got engaged to Jake when the court case was going on. This was a distraction technique Scott came up with," Ethan said. "The engagement was over when the trial finished." Ethan felt Natalie might open up, should the right person approach her.

He mentioned two other boys whom he knew Scott had also abused at the time, but he was not sure where they now lived.

Although Nathan had known John Camp for many years, I knew and respected another journalist—Jim Engster—from his work covering LSU sports and Louisiana politics. Coincidentally, Jim and I had worked in both of those arenas, and crossed paths often. I know him as an honest man and one of the most objective people in journalism. Jim hosts a popular radio program, *The Jim Engster Show,* which showcases his entertaining interviews with newsmakers, authors, and political figures from around the country.

I invited Jim to have lunch with Nathan and me at Serop's, Baton Rouge's best Lebanese restaurant and a favorite gathering spot for attorneys, judges, and politicians, in addition to regular customers just looking for good food. I had previously agreed to talk to John Camp in confidence, because he is such an experienced investigative reporter. I knew he would know how to verify information. Now I was about to confer with another journalist to ask his advice on what to do with Ethan's information, but I also trusted Jim Engster to keep what we were about to tell him confidential.

When I arrived, the restaurant was already packed with the Friday lunch crowd. Nathan, a close friend of the owners, had arranged for a private table tucked behind the half-wall near the entrance so that we could talk without being overheard. Nathan never gets a menu at Serop's and only occasionally actually places an order. Usually the servers just bring him his favorites automatically. Since we were all regulars, we ordered quickly, and I began telling Jim, under Nathan's watchful eye, the story of a young man from the U.K. and his report on Scott Rogers.

Jim knew Scott well. During his many appearances on Scott's television show, Jim had experienced a definite discomfort with the host. Because Jim ran a respected program on the local public radio station, Scott pursued a reciprocal invitation to appear on the Engster show each time Jim appeared on his, and that exceeded Jim's comfort level.

Jim is also close to many of the people in Scott's orbit— Veronica Mosgrove, local rabbi Barry Weinstein, conservative political activist Elizabeth Dent Sumrall, and others, all Scott's regular guests and close friends. The Rabbi even co-hosted Scott's program occasionally, and Mrs. Sumrall presented, in a regular segment on *Around Town,* topics of interest to senior citizens. She had also attended an elaborate birthday party Scott threw at his home for his young son and referred to the guest list as a "who's who of Baton Rouge."

One of Jim's most fascinating talents is his instant recall of dates and noteworthy facts. Even though we don't see each other often, he always remembers my birthday and the birthdays of friends we have in common, as well as many dates and facts pertaining to local, national, and world events, and people from many arenas, including politics, the arts, and sports. His amazing memory makes his interviews some of the most interesting anywhere.

As I explained to Jim how I had received the information from Ethan and why I wanted his reaction to it, he pointed out that Scott had pressured him to appear on Jim's radio program as an expert.

"Well, what subjects are you an expert on?" Jim said he asked Rogers.

"What do you need an expert on?" Scott replied.

Jim said he knew Scott had a permit to carry a concealed weapon, so when the topic of gun control came up on his radio program, while he had no problem finding any number of people who were staunch gun rights advocates, he knew no one who might agree to debate in favor of gun control and decided to try Scott.

When he called him, Jim explained that the topic for the day was gun control and that he would like to have a discussion that covered both sides. Scott quickly accepted.

"Which side do you want me to cover?" Scott asked him.

Jim and I laughed at the notion that Scott presented himself as an expert but apparently considered the subject matter irrelevant. Clearly, Scott Rogers could take on whatever role he needed to assume. He could wear any mask, portray any character.

After looking at the emails and clippings and talking, over lunch, with Nathan and me, Jim said one idea was to invite Scott to appear as a guest on his radio program and confront him with the news articles about his trial.

"Oh, wow!" I said. "After you tell me he carries a concealed weapon, you want to confront him with his secret past as a pedophile on live radio sitting just a few feet away from him?"

While I admitted that the plan would make for a dramatic show, I told Jim I didn't feel we had all of the facts we needed to proceed. Jim's insight was good, however, and Nathan and I promised to stay in touch as we continued to look for the appropriate person to receive our information and act on it.

While we were talking, Jim took out his phone and did a quick search for both Scott Rogers and Richard Scott Rogers, the name he had used for Jim's radio program. In just a few minutes, he found several listings for Scott, associated either with Baton Rouge or *The Around Town TV Show,* that included different dates of birth, some showing him two years younger than other records indicated he was. Jim was surprisingly quick searching several online databases; he pointed out that Scott's changing both his name and birth date made finding him online more difficult. As we finished lunch, the discussion at the table again turned to the question of why Ethan had been looking for Scott Rogers for so many years.

"Is he a victim?" Jim asked.

"I haven't asked that," I replied. "You know, it's not an easy thing to ask. I'm afraid I know the answer, but I don't want to hear it."

Though only about ten days had passed since I had received Ethan's first email, he and I were at times emailing several times a day. I would ask a question and he would answer. I would ask for more information, and he would find it. He was so reliable in responding that I could feel myself growing more and more committed to his cause.

He seemed to me a nice young man, and communicating with him came easily. He was nothing like the members of Scott Rogers' so-called *family,* all of whom gave the impression they had something to hide, secrets to keep. Ethan was open, answering whatever I asked. The only problem was, I was afraid to ask the tough questions.

That night, after the lunch with Nathan and Jim, I thought about where all these inquiries were leading. I knew that to help Ethan, I would have to start asking more difficult questions. Any information we could help him gather would be worthless to him unless it helped move his search forward.

I emailed Ethan to bring him up to date on what I had learned, and before signing off I asked, "Have you pursued this effort before over the years, or was contacting me your first step?"

I fell asleep thinking about the conversation at lunch with Jim. *Is Ethan a victim?* I hoped not, but my instincts told me he was. Ethan's primary concern was to stop Scott's abuse of other children. I knew for us to help him, we would eventually have to know as many facts as we could find. When I woke the next morning, Ethan had responded to my question.

"The last time I saw Scott, Jake had just run away. Scott was a mess, he told me what he had done to Jake, it was extremely disturbing. Matt had to silence him as he 'said too much.' I never saw him again after that…. Ever since, I have been looking for Scott and actually found that he had set up in Barton Rouge a few years ago, but never knew what to do next. Then I found the article and made contact with you."

What had Scott Rogers told him that was so "disturbing" he never saw him again? So upsetting that it consumed his thoughts for 20 years and caused him to spend the last 13 years looking for him?

Ethan's explanation of Mathew's attempt to silence Scott for saying too much about what he had done to Jake was frightening. I was still getting to know this person I emailed daily, and he was sharing something so personal and damaging, I felt I needed simply to listen. I wanted Ethan to tell his secrets when he was ready, without my peppering him with a lot of questions that went to the very core of a person's being. But I also knew if he wanted me to help him, I would have to push ahead to find out more. This information was critical, considering that the English court had allowed Scott to escape punishment for his crimes. For Ethan's claims to have any credibility, we needed to know what had happened.

I read the end of Ethan's email again. *If I am understanding him correctly, after hearing what Scott Rogers said he had done to Jake, Ethan never saw Scott again and has been looking for him ever since.* More and more, each day, I believed I would eventually learn what had sent Scott Rogers to the United States.

The feeling you get when a young man begins to tell you about sexual abuse is hard to describe. What kind of depraved person would steal the innocence of a little boy by forcing sex on him at the age of 12 or 13? What confusion must rise in the mind of a young boy who spends his days talking with his friends about girls and flirting with girls, then finds himself alone with a male teacher who forces sex on him?

Every story you hear about abuse is the same: Victims never talk about the abuse while it is going on—they typically don't report it and they don't tell each other. They experience tremendous guilt because their abusers tell them what is happening to them is their fault. They often turn to alcohol or drugs to escape the feelings of shame. A survivor of child sexual abuse finds that it affects later adult personal relationships. Victims are extremely cooperative with anyone who helps them hold their abusers accountable. And they never forget their loss of innocence. They never forget what the abuser took from them.

Nathan and I talked about Ethan's description of the last time he saw Scott. "You have to ask him for more details," Nathan said. "You need to ask him what happened. That's the only way we can know what to do. That's the only way we can do anything to help him. You just *have* to ask."

"I will," I said. "I just know where this is going and I hate to hear it."

The day after our lunch with Jim, I wrote Ethan an even more detailed email, asking him to explain what he meant about the last time he saw Scott. As had become my daily routine, I sat down at the computer and wrote Ethan late at night, asking the questions Nathan and I had discussed during the day. I use my office at home for writing anything that requires channeling my right brain creativity and intuition, since left brain logic and reasoning comes more naturally to me. I was meeting with Nathan and calling him every day, so I had to confine my research to evenings.

My home office is an upstairs back porch I enclosed with floor-to-ceiling windows on one wall and, on another, a large stained glass window that sprinkles soft blue light over the Mexican tile floors. One friend calls my office *the birdcage* because it hangs high on the house among the oak trees that shade Baton Rouge's Garden District. I do my best writing surrounded by nature, perched at my desk with a large computer monitor providing the only light. To gather my thoughts, I move away from the computer to an overstuffed reading chair, as if shifting out of reach of the keyboard frees my mind to think. The birdcage is the place where I allowed myself to think about what Ethan had heard Scott confess, and what I would have to ask him. I knew I had to probe further than I would ordinarily, but Nathan was right: The only way we could help Ethan was if we knew the truth.

"When you mentioned that Scott told you what he had done to Jake, I assume you mean of a sexual nature," I finally wrote.

"I wonder about the context of a conversation like that. Was he drinking? Distraught over Jake's running away? Bragging? I have a hard time imagining why he would tell you that he had harmed Jake...or did he not think his action was harmful? I understand the information was extremely disturbing, but please help me understand as specifically as you can."

I reminded Ethan that if we were to give the story to a news media outlet in Baton Rouge, we would need to say what we believe Scott had done beyond the U.K. accusations, which had not resulted in conviction.

"Please tell me as much specifics as you are comfortable telling," I asked.

When I woke each morning, I walked straight to my office upstairs, sat down at the computer, and opened an email from Ethan that had arrived around 4 a.m. The morning after I pressed him for details on Jake, Ethan's response hit me like cold water thrown in my face, snapping me awake in the early morning hour. "Oh, no..." I actually said out loud as I read his words, putting my hand over my mouth as I spoke.

I know that deep inside I already knew enough to expect what was coming, but seeing the words on the screen, my hands went up to my face, and I leaned forward on my elbows as I read Ethan's email.

"Rannah, I popped over to Scott's house as I had heard that Jake had run away. Scott was in his living room with Matt, Stuart, and a girl called Angela Hills who also moved to the States with Scott.... Scott was very low, he had scratches or attempted cuts on his arms, he was red faced and very emotional. He then went on to tell me, with everyone present, how he had spent the night with Jake, locked him in a hotel room, and had sex with him...he was kind of remorseful, although he continued to say how amazing he thought the sex was. Matt then tried to get Scott to be quiet as Mandie (his wife) was in the other room! Scott was almost ranting, he was on medication and very emotional. As I said, Jake was gone and never came back, thankfully. I never saw Scott again after that...Scott left town soon after and moved to Kent, U.K., before moving to the States."

As Ethan began to reveal those details, the story began to take on a whole new depth of reality. *He raped that young boy! Then he told the other students about it! What kind of monster was he? He was abusing the other boys in the room, too, but what about Angela? She had remained close to Scott all these years....*

Throughout everything I had learned about Scott Rogers, from his manipulation of a news story in an attempt to smear Mayor Holden and me, to his courting law enforcement officials and children's advocates, all in a vain attempt to make himself look better to others, I had considered him merely a fraud...someone pretending to be this benevolent person helping children. I never bought that. Nothing about the man ever seemed real or honest to me, which was enough to make me uncomfortable. Now, however, I found myself getting angry, which is admittedly rare for me. Scott Rogers disgusted me, and the violent nature of his abuse shocked me, especially considering the way he was still fooling so many people. The idea of his locking a young boy in a hotel room and raping him made me sick.

There could be no question now: We were dealing with a monster. Scott Rogers, the silly little man who masqueraded as an advocate for children, was in reality a sexual predator. Who knew how many young boys he had molested or raped? Or what was going on in the house where he lived now with two grown men and a little 9-year-old boy? Now that we knew what we faced, the only question was: How would we stop him?

CHAPTER FIFTEEN

THE FRIENDSHIP

Day 11
September 7, 2013

In one of the first emails I received from Ethan, he had asked me for Stuart's email address; from my description of the Stuart I knew, Ethan felt he might walk away. Maybe his reason for contacting me was to free Stuart from what he knew was an abusive life. Ethan had described Stuart as a friend at the Academy. The two sounded like a couple of typical high school boys...that is, until Scott Rogers dragged Stuart in front of the other students and forced him to tell them he was gay. That took Ethan by surprise.

Although I had cautioned Ethan about emailing Stuart, since we had always believed Scott read his emails, he knew Stuart's parents and wanted to re-connect them with their son.

On September 7, Ethan shared with me an answer he had received from Stuart in reply to his email. Briefly mentioning their teenage years, Stuart said he was surprised not only to hear from Ethan after 18 years, but surprised "that you seem to think I've been trapped in a basement for all this time," he wrote.

"Just so you know, I have a passport, my job has me traveling frequently, I have been back to the U.K. several times, my family does have my email address, and they have contacted me—also, they wrote me out of their will. I have no interest investing time and effort finding out why.

"I am happy to stay in touch and share what we are both up to these days. (I always smile when I think about the stuff we got up to), but I have to be honest...after your message I am really concerned that your first contact with me had such a weird tone. Were you serious about the whole 'saving' me crap, or can we stay in touch?" Stuart wrote.

"Do you think Stuart wrote that email back to you?" I asked as soon as I read it. I had an instant feeling he had not. I had worked with Stuart for a year, emailing with him on a regular basis, and to me, the language and the tone didn't even sound like him. Admittedly, I knew him only in the context of work and had no idea how he would respond to questions about his life at home with Scott, but Stuart always managed to keep things on a lighter note, even when deflecting the conversation away from anything personal. To me, that response had an angry and sinister tone I had never heard in him. And the phrasing was completely different from the way Stuart spoke.

A few years back when we had worked with Stuart on the monthly television show for the East Baton Rouge Homeland Security department, if anything ever came up on the weekend that we thought we should video for the show, it was Stuart I called. I would apologize for bothering him on the weekend, and he would cheerfully say, "No problem, I was just entertaining the nephew."

At the time, I knew nothing about the family circumstances of Scott Rogers or the others around him, so I assumed they were in some way truly related. Initially, I had no idea that Stuart meant Scott's adopted son when he referred to his *nephew*. Even though we began to understand that Scott, Mathew, Kimmy, and Stuart were all living together, I still thought they might be related in some way. *Was Kimmy Scott's biological daughter? Could the little boy actually be her son, even though Scott claimed the child was his son? Was Stuart possibly Scott's brother or brother-in-law?* It was impossible to figure out how the members of this so-called "family" were related. Stuart had allowed us only a brief peek behind the curtain of secrecy into the Scott Rogers home, revealing that the male members were perhaps related only in their devotion to Scott.

In April 2010, when the Hurricane Hunter, a special weather plane that tracks tropical storms, scheduled a visit to Baton Rouge, JoAnne Moreau wanted to feature it on the *Red Stick Ready* television program. The Hurricane Hunter, with its fascinating array of weather equipment, flies directly into the eye of a hurricane to get readings that help the National Weather Service determine the storm's strength and predict its path. JoAnne and her staff were working with local schools to arrange tours for children so that they might learn more about hurricanes, and we planned a press briefing and interviews for the monthly program.

I remember that Stuart was on hand videotaping the children, as well as Mayor Holden speaking with the pilots, and local National Weather Service officials explaining how the airplane helps communities prepare for storms. On the tarmac, Mayor Holden was having a great time entertaining the schoolchildren, who circled around him with questions and requests for photographs and autographs. "Look at him," JoAnne laughed as she watched the Mayor with the children, "He's like a rock star to them."

At lunch inside the Baton Rouge Airport terminal, speakers from the National Weather Service made brief presentations to the press, as Stuart captured the activity for our television program. He ended up sitting next to me at lunch, in the back of the room, eating late, after the presentations. At one point, as we were finishing up, Stuart turned to me and said, "Rannah, would you consider going to lunch with me? You seem to be involved in a lot of projects in the community, and I would like to talk to you about other job opportunities that may be out there."

This took me by surprise, but Stuart seemed very sincere. "Of course," I said. "I would be happy to go any time. But I'm surprised that you would consider leaving 1stCo."

Stuart explained that he didn't exactly mean that he would leave 1stCo, but that he might take on other jobs in addition to his work there. I wasn't sure if that is what he actually meant, or if he retreated when I questioned him about leaving Scott's employment.

Since Stuart had opened that door, however, I decided to ask a question we had all discussed in 1stCo's absence. "Stuart, I've always wondered how you manage living here and traveling back to visit your family," I said. "Is there a time of year when business here is slow, at Christmas or in the summer, when you all shut everything down and go home? Or do you stagger your visits and go at different times?"

"We don't," Stuart replied.

"You don't go home?" I asked.

"No," he said.

"Does your family visit you here in the States?" I pressed.

"No," he said.

"Do you have family back in England?" I asked.

"Oh, yes," he said.

"When is the last time you saw them?" I asked.

"About 16 years ago," he said.

"Oh, no…" I said, realizing that something was terribly wrong, as 16 years ago he must have been a very young man. "Why haven't you visited your family?"

"Because I'm afraid if I go home, then I won't be able to get back into the States," he said haltingly.

"You mean because of your visa?" I asked.

"Yes," he replied. "I was very close to a girl when we lived in Texas, and she wanted to get married so that I could get citizenship, but I decided not to do that."

Having helped a young student at LSU deal with immigration issues in the aftermath of 9-11, when anyone who wasn't a U.S. citizen was under a cloud of suspicion and deportation was a very real option, I felt the need to caution him.

"I'm not trying to pry into your personal life," I told him, "but marrying to get citizenship is against the law, and they take that very seriously," I said.

"Oh, I know," he said. "In the end, I couldn't do it…mainly because I cared too much for her to let her risk it."

That seemed as far as he wanted to go with the conversation, and we went back to talking about hurricanes and airplanes.

"Well, let me know any time you want to go to lunch," I said.

"Okay, thanks," Stuart replied as he picked up his empty paper plate to drop it into the waste receptacle. "I'm going to go shoot some more video before I leave."

Stuart never again mentioned getting together outside of work. The next time I saw him, it was as if we'd never had that conversation.

Now he was telling Ethan that he had visited the U.K. often and traveled freely.

"What are your thoughts on Stuart's reply?" I asked Ethan. "It is not consistent with what he told several of us here."

"Stuart's response…it's a tricky one," Ethan said. "Stuart knows what Scott is, Stuart abandoned his family years ago for no real reason. They are good people, they love him. I guess Stuart is too far gone. He is 34 now, so he has the intelligence and the resources to get out of town and leave Scott if he wanted to. I thought perhaps Scott had access to his phone but then, I sent a text to his mobile so he would have a chance to delete or respond differently. I'm considering calling him and seeing how he reacts to a call. He has been with Scott a long time. What is Scott to him? I don't know anymore, it's very odd. As is the whole situation."

Then, within 24 hours, Ethan received another message from Stuart.

"I have had a more positive response from Stuart regarding his family and he says he is going to make contact and let them know how he is doing…I've passed him all contact details." *Maybe Stuart isn't lost,* I thought. *Maybe hearing from a friend he hadn't talked to in 20 years was the lifeline he needed to get out of a bad situation.*

But Ethan and I had no way of knowing that at the *Around Town Show* studio, a copy of every email that hit the company server was automatically routed to Scott Rogers. He read every email they received and every one they sent. He insisted that he know where they were at all times, so they either checked in every 15 minutes or Scott dispatched an employee to find them.

Stuart later told me that when he received Ethan's email, Scott stood over him and dictated what he should say in his reply. Ethan was offering his childhood friend help in getting home, even financial assistance to buy an airline ticket, but Scott knew Stuart wasn't going anywhere. Even though Stuart regularly inquired of Scott about the status of his green card application, he was always told not to worry about it, that he would be fine. That was easy for Scott to say. Stuart's green card was finally issued in 2012 and when it came in, Scott locked it in the 1stCo safe at the studio and never told Stuart. For two years, Stuart would worry about his immigration status, not knowing that he had received his green card and Scott had it hidden away. *Keep them on edge. It's the only way to control them.*

And despite telling Ethan he would do so, Stuart did not follow up with his parents to let them know he was okay.

Scott paid Mathew and Stuart for working at 1stCo by direct deposit to checking accounts he could access. Once he deposited the funds into their accounts, he transferred the majority of the money into a separate account that he alone controlled, leaving them only a small allowance, as little as $500 a month. This ploy would document, for immigration purposes, that each of them had a job and income, and still allow Scott to control them by limiting their access to money. Control the money and control their ability to escape—experts later told us that human traffickers often use this tactic, and that law enforcement representatives look for it when considering felony charges.

When Paul, the former student who knew Mathew and Stuart from the Academy and their work in Malaysia, heard about their employment arrangements, he commented, "He gave them money for candy." That is what it amounted to: the small allowance you would give a child. Their lack of money kept them dependent on him.

Because Ethan had kept our conversations confidential, should I run into Stuart at a public event he would have no idea I was beginning to learn the truth about his past.

Even after our very unpleasant experience working with Scott, I had attended a few events for which he had served as emcee. One was "Meanwhile, Back at Café du Monde…" a dinner theatre presentation of monologues about food, which Baton Rouge native Peggy Sweeney McDonald produced. The concept involved gathering chefs, local celebrities, restaurant owners, and other people of interest and asking them to deliver a brief but entertaining monologue about their experiences with food.

I had met Peggy through mutual friends when she came by my office before launching the live event, and I had recommended several chefs and local celebrities who ended up contributing monologues for her shows. When I attended a Baton Rouge performance to see my close friend Daniel Brockhoeft, a classically trained New Orleans chef, deliver his monologue, I discovered the emcee for the night was none other than Scott Rogers. Of course, Scott would emcee an arm wrestling match if it meant photo opportunities with local officials. Stuart had accompanied him, shooting video, I assumed for *The Around Town TV Show*. To my surprise, Stuart saw me and immediately rushed over to hug me warmly.

"How are you doing?" he said with what seemed genuine sincerity. "I miss seeing you."

"Me, too, Stuart," I replied and gave him a hug.

As we watched Scott open the show that night with his own monologue, our table was surprised to see Scott Rogers, who usually behaved in a silly, juvenile manner, deliver a raunchy monologue that really missed the mark for that dinner audience.

He spun a tale of how his wife had abandoned him and his infant daughter Kimmy when she was only a week old, and since he knew nothing about taking care of a baby, he had fed her solid food, which led to his regaling the audience with bathroom humor about the results of his mistake. The story didn't sound even remotely true, and Rogers' awkward attempt to win over an audience fell flat. Nothing about his performance was funny, and, more and more, I was uncomfortable just being in the room with him.

We left that night without speaking again to Stuart. I imagined that since our contract dispute with 1stCo was ongoing, embracing me in plain sight of Scott might cause Stuart some difficulty, and I admired his courage before a very controlling employer. Little did I know Stuart was just beginning to exercise some small acts of defiance in the face of Scott's control. And he was feeling Scott's wrath.

Now I was wondering about the real Stuart. Was he the one who seemed to long for independence from Scott? Who had a clear sadness in his eyes when talking about the girl who had wanted to marry him to help him remain in the U.S.? The one whose face lit up when he saw a familiar face across the room and rushed over to hug me?

Or was he the Stuart who pushed back on any suggestion that his life was anything less than fantastic, filled with the excitement of international travel and professional success?

Or considering the bizarre story of how he came to the United States…was he both?

Though Stuart had been Ethan's friend, something about the hold Scott had on him made him mysterious, elusive. And yet, while Ethan had his own problems with Stuart and the role he had played in supporting Scott, especially knowing about his violent abuse of Jake, the memory of their friendship at one time in their lives seemed to make him hope that Stuart was not lost.

"Stuart could be the key for the future," Ethan said. "If he leaves, he may open up later. It is possible to find others who may talk, too. I would not rule this out."

The question for which none of us knew the answer, however, lingered: Could anyone get through to Stuart now?

The Boys of Bury

PAUL *in his own words*

London, England
2015

I remember Scott used to have a lot of one-to-one time with the pupils in his office where he would chain smoke menthol cigarettes and talk to you. He had this way of saying, "What are you thinking?" which he used to do a lot. All the time. So when you're an awkward teenager and you are unsure of yourself, he saw that as a weakness or an opportunity to sort of befriend me and maybe manipulate me in some way or another. There would be lots of long conversations.

But part of my early dance classes with him was that he used to have one-to-one time with me where he would massage my legs and things like that, as a way to help my dance technique. Now, of course, looking back, I realize how incredibly wrong that was. But at the time, it felt like, "Oh, this is just what happens."

As a 38-year-old man, to look back at that behavior at the Academy, you realize that's not okay. And being a victim of abuse from Scott—maybe not to the extreme that the others were—but certainly I felt the humiliation, the sexual advances, and the manipulation was very much there.

CHAPTER SIXTEEN

THE PROSECUTOR AND THE JUDGE

Day 14
September 10, 2013

Ethan was able to recall certain details about his years at the Academy before and after Scott's trial, and the newspaper articles he sent helped fill in some of the blanks. But we were just beginning to understand fully this very disturbing story and the dangerous man at its center.

Nathan and I were having extensive discussions about what we should do. In matters of this nature, the first place I would instinctively turn would be to law enforcement. But we had a dilemma. I wasn't in a position of choosing which area law enforcement agencies to rouse. Instead, we were faced with eliminating the agencies where we felt Scott had unusually close ties. I didn't feel comfortable going to the Louisiana State Police because Scott presented himself publicly as a close friend of Colonel Mike Edmonson, who is the superintendent. East Baton Rouge Parish Sheriff Sid Gautreaux had appointed Scott a reserve deputy and chaplain for his department, so I didn't feel his office was the best choice. I couldn't go to the FBI because Scott had managed to convince them to investigate me. I couldn't go to the U.S. Attorney in Baton Rouge because he would engage the FBI. I couldn't go to the Baton Rouge Police because they most likely did not have any jurisdiction. *There has to be a law enforcement agency to hand this off to!*

One of the first steps Nathan asked me to take was to share Ethan's emails and the news articles about the trial with Sue Bernie, the sex crimes prosecutor for the East Baton Rouge Parish District Attorney. He hoped she would be able to offer us some help and direction. Nathan had great respect for Bernie and had often faced her in the courtroom. Nathan felt someone should determine whether Rogers was committing crimes here in Louisiana similar to those Ethan described in the U.K.

Nathan knew sex offender behavior, and he didn't think Scott Rogers would have simply stopped abusing children.

The meeting with Sue was sobering. We found her in her cramped City Hall office filled with LSU women's basketball memorabilia. I had worked at the LSU Athletic Department for 13 years as Associate Athletic Director in charge of marketing, radio and television programming, and ticket sales for 20 college sports teams, and I knew Sue as one of the staunchest supporters of the Lady Tigers basketball program. When you consider all the serious criminals she deals with through her work, you realize she pours an equal amount of energy into supporting her favorite team. Now seeing her office, I realized just how much she enjoyed the balance that sports must provide for her.

Sue's opinion was the same as Nathan's: People who sexually abuse children do not stop. She was very concerned that Scott had adopted a little boy in Baton Rouge, especially since the newspaper articles from the U.K. mentioned that he had previously adopted a son there. Sue also expressed concern about his starting a church, which she feared he could use to recruit young boys. She reiterated that since Mathew and Stuart were now adults, the State's only legal concern involved the child.

When Sue retired from her job in 2015, she had 30 years' experience as a sex crimes prosecutor, working with thousands of children and adult victims of sexual and physical abuse. Though she still says the real heroes are the victims of sexual abuse who work with prosecutors like her to bring their abusers to justice, the Louisiana Foundation Against Sexual Assault recognizes her work annually by presenting the Sue Bernie Justice Award to deserving recipients.

I listened closely as she described for Nathan and me the behavior patterns of sex offenders. As she reviewed the articles, we walked over to her computer and I pulled up some photographs I had found online of Scott and his little boy at various charity events. Taking a look at the child, Sue feared Scott was very possibly already sexually abusing him or grooming him for abuse. She worried about the child's developmental disorder's preventing him from understanding the abuse and reporting it. We were not presenting her with any evidence of child abuse, but only with the articles of a previous trial that had ended in a hung jury and ultimate acquittal, so we weren't giving her anything to prosecute. Her experience with abusers and their victims, however, added legitimacy to her concern for a victim. She encouraged us to gather more information and said she would help if law enforcement were to investigate and bring her charges that she could prosecute.

"Why don't you try to find someone who can go to his church and report anything unusual?" she asked. She worried that without the dance academy Scott had used in England to gain access to young boys, he might attempt to use church activities here.

She felt strongly that the news articles and photographs clearly exposed a child sex predator.

Leaving Bernie's office, I had no doubt she had seen in the articles the face of a very dark and evil man. If her instincts and experience told her that Rogers was still abusing children, no doubt could remain in my own mind, and she seemed very confident. But I was just beginning to understand the difficulty of finding the right hands in which to place this information. We were dealing with a master manipulator, a man who had built a network of influential supporters both here and in Bury, so we knew to take great care as we moved toward finding someone who could rescue the child and warn the public.

Each night, I reported whatever I had learned during the day to Ethan; at the end of this day, I told him we needed more information before we could say definitively that the little boy

Scott had adopted was in danger. I asked Ethan again for contact information for the prosecutor or for anyone associated with the prosecution of Scott Rogers in the U.K., as Nathan was eager to consult a person with legal knowledge of the trial.

Even though Ethan had provided me his cell phone number in his last email, I didn't feel I was ready just yet to speak with him directly. I first had to accept my own evolving sadness that he was more than likely a victim himself. From the beginning, Nathan and I had discussed that possibility, but I hadn't wanted to accept it. I knew now that I not only had to face Ethan's abuse, but prepare myself to talk about it.

After meeting with Sue Bernie, I emailed Ethan that night that the Scott Rogers story seemed to be one of a sexual predator getting away with his crimes and continuing to commit them. "I will never pry," I wrote, "but I hope you or someone close to you was not a victim. Regardless of what happened, you were very brave to reach out to a stranger who lives so far away. I assure you that I will do my best to prevent him from harming another child."

And I meant every word. As it began to sink in that Ethan was, in all likelihood, a victim of Scott's abuse, I imagined the uncertainty he must feel in talking about something so personal with someone he had never met. But I was also struck by the bravery it must take for him to want so badly to stop his abuser from hurting other children. Whatever he had to say, I knew I had to be ready to hear it.

If Nathan and I found any credible evidence that Scott Rogers was sexually abusing children, I would have to do something. I didn't know what; I would just deal with that when the time came. Meanwhile, we needed Ethan to find contact information for any of the U.K. prosecutors, as they could no doubt estimate how serious a threat Scott presented here and whether we should not only take Ethan's concerns seriously but plan a strategy for action.

The oddity that was Scott Rogers—weeping during a business meeting, spying on community leaders at his television studio, fabricating a tale of a lost ring to distract attention from his behavior, living with two unrelated young men and the young male child he had adopted, suddenly starting a church—somehow deflected the depth of his evil. *Distract and deflect! A pattern that had worked for him in the past.*

His slight, elfin appearance and British accent conveyed a strange daintiness, an eccentric immaturity, and thus a person who presented no danger to others, especially children. Many people who noticed his peculiar nature, perhaps influenced by stereotypes, simply assumed he was gay and uncomfortable admitting it. They did not presume he was dangerous.

While many overlooked his peculiarity, it also called up a somewhat typical Southern response. On our hands and knees in the Emergency Operations Center, searching for a ring we knew did not exist, all of us were paying homage to that old Southern solution to awkwardness: "Let's just not talk about *that*." Rogers' extreme emotional state threw us off, so we did what he asked! For much too long, we did not question Scott Rogers' strangeness; we ignored his unusual living arrangements. Nathan always said the British accent made people somehow feel he was intelligent, perhaps more cultured than they. One acquaintance of Scott even attributed the three unrelated men living together to "a cultural thing," as if this exotic creature with his foreign accent was more comfortable living with others from a similar background. To overcome their suspicion that something wasn't right, some people just chalked up Scott's oddity to his being British. Our nature leads us to respect people's privacy, but Ethan had pulled back the curtain for us and now we faced something very sinister. *So what would we do? Was Scott Rogers operating, in Louisiana's capital city—and in plain sight—a child sex abuse ring?* While I realized the question was shocking, I knew that such evil could be exactly what faced us.

Nathan had also asked if I would be willing to meet with Federal Judge James Brady, whom we've both admired since long before he was appointed to the bench. Nathan has to appear before him with clients, which limits the subjects of their conversations outside the courtroom, but they are longtime friends. I've known and admired the Judge since his early days as State Chairman of the Louisiana Democratic Party.

Judge Brady had been influential in the 1986 election of former U.S. Senator John Breaux. After sharing the Breaux campaign trail with him and orchestrating a close win over Breaux's fellow Congressman Henson Moore, Val also knew Judge Brady.

Appointed by President Bill Clinton, Judge Brady had just taken senior status on the bench when Nathan suggested I meet with him and share my story about Scott Rogers and the mysterious man from England who had contacted me. Judge Brady could not give me any legal advice, Nathan cautioned, but he knew I respected Brady and was having a difficult time deciding what to do with the information I had received. I told him I had no problem conferring with Judge Brady, and Nathan called to schedule the meeting.

Arriving at the federal courthouse in downtown Baton Rouge, carrying a folder that contained copies of the news articles and emails from Ethan, I found Judge Brady in his office sitting behind his desk. I took a seat in a chair across from him and noticed that the void between us felt unusually wide, with him settled comfortably behind the massive wooden desk and my chair positioned a good distance from its opposite edge. Before we began, he reminded me that although he could not give me any legal advice, he was happy to visit with me.

As I began explaining about someone in the U.K. contacting me with evidence that Scott Rogers, living here in Baton Rouge, was a child molester, Judge Brady's expression grew very serious. I held up news articles from the trial to show him, but he made no effort to lean forward across the great divide to look more closely. Uncomfortable with the whole story as I told it to him, I hurried through it to the end and he quickly advised me, in a very paternal federal judge-like way, to turn everything I had over to the U.S. Attorney's Office.

"Rannah, you are not law enforcement and you don't want to give something like this to the press," he said. "Give it to the appropriate authorities and let them handle it." That is exactly what I wanted to do; but I was having trouble finding that appropriate authority.

I sensed the conversation was over before he changed the subject and said, "Now, did you ever see a photo of '*Me Too Moore*?'" He was referring, of course, to a large puppet Val had ordered made in the likeness of Congressman Moore and had sent around to press conferences in the final stretch of the 1986 campaign. With the puppet, he had demonstrated that whatever Congressman Breaux said he had accomplished, Congressman Moore also claimed as part of his record. *Me Too Moore*, the puppet, provided great comic relief and press attention in the final days of the campaign and helped push the smooth talking Cajun Congressman Breaux to victory over the more staid Moore.

I was so glad Judge Brady had given us a reason to talk about something else that I gratefully followed him into his conference room where we shared a laugh at the photo of what may be the only official campaign puppet in America. And since I had heard many stories about *Me Too Moore*, but had never seen him, the photograph was an unexpected treat.

Since you cannot bring a cell phone into the federal courthouse, I had to wait until I got to my car to phone Nathan. The walk back felt twice as long as earlier. I thought I had made Judge Brady ill at ease, but I conceded to Nathan that his advice was good. "Nathan, I felt like I brought a skunk to the garden party!" I teased him. "You sent me to see Judge Brady and I feel I made him uncomfortable, which is the last thing I wanted to do."

At that moment, I realized Nathan might have had an agenda I wasn't aware of. Something told me he was hoping Judge Brady would advise me to disengage from this growing saga and because of the respect I had for him, I might finally listen. Nathan had already told me that other people, whose opinions I valued, thought I should avoid having anything to do with pursuing the truth about Scott Rogers. Now he had played the Brady card, and I had to admit it was an ace. If I wouldn't listen to Judge Brady, Nathan knew I wasn't going to walk away, no matter what.

I knew I should do exactly what Judge Brady said, and in a perfect world, the U.S. Attorney is precisely where you would take the information Ethan had given me about Scott Rogers. I could not, however, let go of one worry: Should I hand over this information to the U.S. Attorney in Baton Rouge, Nathan had explained to me, that office would bring in the FBI to investigate Scott Rogers. But wait—Scott Rogers had somehow managed to get Greg Phares to investigate JoAnne Moreau and me, and Greg had already brought in a local FBI agent. *Did they believe Scott Rogers' stories?* We were afraid that if anyone mentioned Scott's past problems to the wrong person, he would pack up his family and disappear into the night. We knew he had done just that in the U.K. and in Texas. We didn't know it yet, but he had done the same thing in Baton Rouge in 2008, when he had disappeared with the family for a year.

Accepting that the FBI posed a risk was especially hard for me, since my sister worked at FBI Headquarters in Washington and you would ordinarily feel that bringing in the FBI is as good as it gets. Nathan had cautioned me that if I told my sister about my communication with Ethan, she could not discuss it with anyone at the Bureau. He wanted to avoid any chance of information leaks.

If a child molester, with a history of violent sexual abuse against young boys, was now operating in our community, committing the very same crimes he had before, I knew I could not walk away. Knowing he had persuaded a British Child Services agency to place a little boy in his custody, a child who had endured the worst abuse by Scott, was even more frightening. Scott was following the same pattern in Baton Rouge, working hard to develop close ties with Child Services, adopting a little boy.

I just didn't feel I could turn Ethan's information over to law enforcement agencies where Scott had already successfully made inroads. *Would they take these accusations seriously? People don't like to be fooled, and they don't like to look foolish. Scott was manipulating so many people...playing so many games. I imagined that finding out the truth would make some people very angry.*

CHAPTER SEVENTEEN

THE SILENCE

Day 14
September 10, 2013

As the amount of information on Scott Rogers' past grew, Nathan talked to a few colleagues in the legal community he trusted, then reported their advice sparingly to me. One attorney, a woman, suggested he tell me to leave it alone and not get involved. I was amazed a woman would not be concerned enough about the safety of the little boy in Scott's custody to find a way to help. Nathan considered her a friend, and I could tell he was disappointed that she didn't have the same feeling about stopping Scott from hurting other children that he did.

Another he asked for help said she wanted nothing to do with exposing Scott Rogers and I shouldn't either. The subject matter was simply not something she was going to touch. Still another attorney, this time a man, said he just didn't want to get involved. I couldn't believe that these attorneys would suggest I ignore the strong possibility of a crime, especially one against children. For those with experience in criminal law, it was clear that a pedophile was highly likely to continue committing crimes against children. But they didn't want to be the ones who intervened. It was almost as if they were so uncomfortable with the subject of child sex abuse that they immediately shut down any discussion. We were learning that the subject is, in fact, so very difficult that those who are powerless to act, by their own fears or repulsion, prefer the rest of us to follow suit.

This particular crime evokes a reaction much different from the response to most crime—which is to reject, expose, and punish. This crime is the unspoken sin, so contemptable that some people feel sullied by simply discussing it.

Despite the discomfort I was causing, however, I continued to seek someone who would put the safety of the little boy living with Rogers first—ahead of Scott's perceived celebrity or law enforcement connections. I wanted someone who was responsible for the safety of children to advise me on how to handle the information Ethan had provided about Scott.

In April 2015, Jerry Sandusky's adopted son, Matt, spoke in Summit, Mississippi, in my home county of Pike, about his being sexually abused throughout his childhood by his pedophile father, the Penn State football coach and convicted serial child molester. Child Services had placed Matt Sandusky in Jerry's family, an environment that included the respected Penn State football program, and where Matt and other boys fell victim to another high-risk sport, the continuous, nearly open sexual abuse of children.

Matt told how his father created the appearance of decency by raising money for charities and starting a camp for underprivileged youth. As he sat through his father's trial and listened to other boys testify about the abuse they suffered, Matt realized for the first time, at the age of 33, that he was not the only survivor.

"If *you* are ashamed to talk about it, how can we expect victims to not be ashamed?" Matt Sandusky asked the audience.

The main lesson I was beginning to learn about child sex abuse was that very few of us are able to discuss it…or even to mention it. "These people fool everybody," Matt Sandusky explained, "And because the subject is awkward, hard, uncomfortable…we can't have a conversation about child sex abuse. And this allows them to abuse."

Thinking about what he had said, I find a strange dichotomy in the way people react to the abuse of animals versus the abuse of children, both innocent victims of a senseless crime. To the mistreatment of animals, we see people respond with outrage and action. But to the sexual abuse of children, the response all too often is silence and distance.

The younger Sandusky described how his father, at his Second Mile Camp for boys, pushed other adults away so the kids relied only on him. "I did not have one person looking out for me," Matt said. "No one ever had my best interests in mind. Have the courage to protect a child," he pleaded.

I didn't know any of this when I received Ethan's first emails. And although Nathan considered all three attorneys he had approached good friends as well as good resources, he knew I would not like their advice. But he wanted me to hear all opinions, not just those with which I would agree, so I could make the best decision. He spent time assuring me that all three considered me a friend, too, that they were among the best attorneys around, and that they had based their advice on what they felt was best for me.

That conversation was tough for both of us. Nathan wasn't arguing for their viewpoint; he was just presenting their opinions. I knew I had to take him seriously.

"I hear you, and I appreciate their concern for me," I said, "but if we honestly believe Scott Rogers is sexually abusing children, doing *nothing* is not an option. It's just *not*, Nathan. You know that. After all, as an attorney, if you honestly believe Rogers is committing a crime, aren't you obligated to report it to the authorities? How can anyone suggest I do nothing at all?"

"I hear you," he echoed. "I just wanted to let you know what they said…. I want to be sure we think about everything and protect you, too."

"I know, but look at what Ethan has sent us. And remember how Sue Bernie reacted when she saw it. So now Scott has adopted a little boy here, just as he did there. Only this one is autistic. If Scott is abusing him, he may not be able to tell someone. I just can't do *nothing*...I can't."

This was so hard. I respected everyone Nathan had consulted on my behalf, especially Judge Brady, but I just couldn't imagine ignoring Ethan's disclosures. As awful as I found the stories about Mathew and Stuart, they were now grown men in their mid-30s. Even if Scott had indeed brainwashed them in their childhood, I didn't think I had any right to interfere in their personal lives now. But the little boy was another matter. What if Scott chose him because of his communication disorder? What if the abuse had already begun? How could I ignore that? *How could anyone?* I knew we had to have proof and not just suspicion, but Sue's reaction carried a lot of weight with me, and she seemed confident that our fears were justified.

I knew Nathan was just trying to protect me, and I had to weigh everything the attorneys had advised. But I also knew that our meeting with Sue Bernie had convinced him, too, that something was very wrong in the Scott Rogers household. He knew the little boy in Scott's custody was in danger. And I knew he wouldn't be satisfied ignoring that danger any more than I was.

But our problem was even harder than simply choosing to do something. The big question was, what could we do?

By now, I told Nathan, I needed to share the U.K. articles with JoAnne Moreau. Although he was hesitant for me to talk to anyone about Ethan's contacting me, he understood that I felt *The Advocate's* article had wronged JoAnne as much as it had me. After what Scott had put her through, I thought we had to tell her that she was dealing with a man who was dishonest and quite possibly dangerous. A man who would manipulate the truth to cause problems for anyone he couldn't control.

JoAnne shouldered the burden of running a city-parish department, which meant that she had to go before the Metro Council for approval on her department's spending. I wanted to share the truth with her.

I visited JoAnne's office, bringing along an envelope with copies of the news articles Ethan had sent me. One of her first comments was that in her conversations with Stuart, he had indicated that he missed his family and had talked about his hometown, once even looking it up on a map and showing her where he had grown up. When she asked whether he traveled home often to see his family, he said he did not, as Scott held his and Mathew's passports and would not allow them to return. Just as he had told me, he told JoAnne that, to achieve legal residence here, he had considered marrying a girl when the group lived in Texas in order to become a U.S. citizen, but had decided that was not a good option.

Like me, JoAnne thought we were finally finding the answers to a lot of our questions about Scott Rogers. All of a sudden, the secrecy made sense.

We were in agreement that while Mathew was very stoic and revealed nothing, Stuart was friendlier, more open and pleasant, and might possibly speak more freely if given the opportunity.

I asked JoAnne to share the news stories with her husband, Don, who knew more about Scott Rogers than I did. He had watched Scott cost his boss, the parish coroner, his elected office and send the FBI to interview his wife. Don Moreau had occupied a front row seat to witness the very worst of Scott's petulant and vindictive behavior.

And as a retired Louisiana State Trooper, he definitely knew more than I did about pedophiles.

JoAnne and Don agreed we were finally learning the truth about Scott Rogers' mysterious arrival in Baton Rouge and his efforts to ingratiate himself to the people he thought could shield him from scrutiny. But they also believed we should be extremely cautious in deciding where to take the information we had received. Don believed Scott Rogers could be dangerous.

I had already received a lot of advice to stay out of Ethan's search for answers. But people I trusted had also reassured me that Scott was a classic child predator. I went back to Nathan and told him I had given very serious thought to his counsel.

"Do you believe Scott Rogers is a pedophile?" I asked him.

"Yes," he replied without hesitation.

"So do I," I said. "And I have to say again…doing *nothing* is just not an option. I don't know what to do, but I have to do something."

At least I had put that decision behind us. I knew Nathan would support it because, deep down, he felt the same way. And Nathan had the strongest sense of justice of anyone I knew. Now that we had put to rest the question of whether or not we were going to go any further with Ethan, it was time to decide what we would do with his explosive information.

"We are not going to look the other way," I told Nathan, echoing William Wilberforce, in 1784 a Member of Parliament, a man who worked for 26 years to abolish the British slave trade. He died just three days after the assurance that a law outlawing slavery in most of the British Empire would pass. Today, people often use one of his more famous quotations as a reminder that modern-day human trafficking and even animal welfare initiatives are rooted in the same call to action that we must find in ourselves: "You may choose to look the other way, but you can never say again that you did not know."

CHAPTER EIGHTEEN

THE PROBLEM SOLVER

Day 15
September 11, 2013

Early the next morning, Nathan called me. "Would you consider talking with Mary Jane Marcantel?" he asked.

I had met Mary Jane several times over the past 20 years and knew her to be a valuable member of criminal defense teams for some of Louisiana's most notable trials. Mary Jane is a paralegal with a bright investigative mind, brimming with energy and speaking with the precision of a seasoned news commentator. In conversation, she leaves you with the distinct feeling that she is rapidly processing everything she sees and hears and revealing only exactly what she plans to share and not a word more. She is short in stature, but tough as nails.

"Yes," I quickly said. "I would be very comfortable talking with her."

Nathan knew we were all in now and needed more information before we could move forward, and he reminded me that Mary Jane had been instrumental in the arrest and conviction of Joey Smith, a local businessman who had murdered his second wife, possibly a girlfriend, and most likely his third wife, who remains missing after disappearing years ago. Though the women in his life, no question, didn't live long, charging him with anything had been very difficult. I had heard about the case for years as he eluded arrest.

A few minutes after we ended our conversation, and before Mary Jane started her work day, her phone rang and caller ID showed it was Nathan Fisher. She and Nathan had known each other for years and had worked together on cases, and Mary Jane's daughter had been friends with Nathan's son Ari in high school. But his early morning call was unusual.

Her interest was piqued as she answered the phone and, after saying *hello,* Nathan told her he had a situation that required her assistance.

"Do you have a few minutes to talk?" he asked.

"Sure," Mary Jane said, as he began to tell her our story. Nathan explained to Mary Jane that he had a personal friend named *Rannah Gray*; he asked if Mary Jane knew me.

"I do," she replied.

He went on to tell her he was calling about an English fellow named *Scott Rogers* whom he described as a con artist. He explained that I had received an email from someone in the U.K. I had never met, telling me that Scott had sexually abused children there 20 years ago. He told Mary Jane I had gone to a federal judge and others for advice. Then he said he woke up in the middle of the night with the idea to call her and had already asked me if I would be willing to talk to her. Nathan explained that we needed assistance with a plan to help a child in Scott's custody, a little boy he had adopted.

Mary Jane's notes:

Rannah does not need a last name, even though when people introduce her or speak her name, it's always "Rannah Gray." For those who have any knowledge of politics in Baton Rouge, Louisiana, "Rannah" will suffice. You know who she is. I had seen her at political gatherings; I had seen how she talks to people, how she addresses them. She dresses and walks like a Southern lady. She is gracious and cordial. She does not argue or fight with anyone even though she is, by her own right, a power broker in Louisiana and the City of Baton Rouge. She is a consummate public relations person, which is how she makes her living.

I, on the other hand, am aggressive, brash, outspoken. I am very short, very Italian, with the temperament that goes with my heritage. Growing up, I missed the lessons from my beauty queen mom on how to behave like a proper Southern lady. As a child, I was a tomboy who enjoyed playing and competing with the boys.

*My dad, who was old enough to be my grandfather, was a successful businessman with a car dealership. Later in his life, he owned two race cars, which, 40 years ago, I drove at dirt track racing, taking home the trophies. Because my dad was 21 years older than mom, he did not understand a woman's wanting to **do** anything but be married or **be** anything but a teacher or a nurse. He allowed me go to college only to study one of those professions.*

After I got to campus, I changed my major to business without his knowing.

And while I married and had two children, for 35 years I have been a single working mom who still has more fun playing with the boys.

For the last 30 years I have worked in a man's world, assisting lawyers with criminal defense work on most of the major political cases in the State of Louisiana. I also work street crime cases, like murder, rape, and drugs. While I am not an attorney, I am fortunate to have worked with some of the best.

My mentor was Camille Gravel. He was a legend in my hometown of Alexandria, where he practiced law. He served as executive counsel to three Louisiana governors and as head of the National Democratic Party. I went to work for him on a federal case with international ties when he was sixty-two years old, and I worked for him as the first paralegal in the State. He included me in all of his cases, and he represented people from all walks of life, from governors to street-crime defendants, sometimes pro bono. I traveled the State with him, from courthouse to courthouse. My education and connections in the legal world came from that journey with him.

Nathan explained to me that he and Rannah had been trying to figure out how to proceed with the Rogers case. They needed someone who knew both behavior and the law. I found the situation interesting, and I agreed to the meeting. I was not sure what kind of plan they were considering or how I could help.

This was not the first time an attorney had approached me to work with the prosecutors and law enforcement I normally oppose. About 20 years ago I worked a murder-for-hire case in which a husband paid his drug runner to kill his second wife, and was the suspect in the disappearance and presumed death of his third wife, who remains missing. This same man was running drugs out of Columbia into Louisiana with the help of his girlfriend, who also wound up dead under mysterious circumstances. He had large insurance policies on both wives. I had to figure out what door to open to get the feds involved in the investigation, since they don't have jurisdiction over a murder unless it involves a federal law. The drug operation was that door.

The feds credit me with discovering the crucial piece of evidence that resulted in the husband's plea to federal drug charges, and his indictment and successful prosecution for a 10-year-old cold case involving the second wife's murder. To this day, we are still trying to locate the third wife, who disappeared from the residence and has never been found...but that is another story.

My ability to think outside the box and my success with that murder-for-hire case caused Nathan to call me for help.

Because of the nature of the Rogers case, and because of who Scott Rogers was and all the people he knew, we had to keep quiet as to what we were doing. So we decided I would meet with Rannah at her home on September 11, 2013, the evening after I returned from a scheduled meeting in Lafayette, Louisiana, with Luke Walker, an assistant United States attorney.

Little did I know on that day the role he would play in my new case.

I called Mary Jane, and she suggested we meet later that afternoon at my house. I printed a copy of the news articles and Ethan's emails to help walk her through what we knew at this point. As she parked in front of my house, I saw her through the glass panes on my front door and I was on the porch to meet her before she reached the front gate.

I had spread out, on my dining room table, copies of the news articles and emails and was ready to share the information Ethan had provided as well as some that Nathan and I had gathered. My brain works best running along a linear path, so I started from the beginning. A friend once told me that I open with, "First, the earth cooled…" which is a nice way of saying that my stories are long and detailed. And so I began.

Mary Jane's notes:

I drove to Rannah's Garden District home with its gracious porches and balconies. Her home fit her—a Southern lady!

She gave me copies of a few rag-tag newspaper articles from 20 years ago, most of which contained no dates. Reading them, however, I had a sense of when events had occurred. Someone had not only collected the articles, but had, years ago, pasted them into some sort of scrapbook or journal. A guy from the U.K., with long-ago ties to Scott Rogers, had sent them to Rannah. There had to be a reason he had kept these articles. Had Rogers tormented and sexually abused him?

We knew he was not the boy in the articles, the survivor of Rogers' crimes in the U.K. Though the clippings were aged and yellowed, the words were clear. They told a horrific story of an adult, Scott Rogers, who had abused a young male child. The articles implied, further, that this child was not Rogers' only victim. I wondered if the guy who had contacted Rannah was one of them.

Rannah told me the story of how she had received an email from this person in England, a man who had tracked Rogers for

20 years and found him here in Baton Rouge. She told me the action she had taken since that first email and what she had learned from each person she consulted. I began to piece together all of Rogers' contacts.

Nathan, Shannon, and Rannah had not yet come up with a plan to move forward and wanted my thoughts.

Mary Jane and I talked for hours, stopping only briefly to get a glass of water for each of us. I found her reaction very similar to Sue Bernie's—she believed we were dealing with a pedophile who was most likely continuing to abuse children. She wanted to read over the material again and take some time to think about it, but promised to get back in touch with me.

By the time she got up to leave, the night sky had seeped through the oak trees and painted Wisteria Street in darkness. The street light across from my house cast its golden shadow on her car as I turned on the front porch light and walked her to the front gate. As I walked back inside, I remembered that Nathan was waiting for a call, so I hurried to let him know Mary Jane and I had met.

At this early point, unaware of where this journey might lead, he was always careful to protect my identity. He had decided that Mary Jane would work for him, as she had on other cases, and that he would represent me, which meant my communications with her would be protected by attorney-client privilege. He was thinking ahead, laying the groundwork for what he hoped would be a criminal charge against Scott Rogers.

Nathan and I had been very careful in limiting any discussion of Scott Rogers, seeking assistance only in strict confidence. We had met with two seasoned journalists, several attorneys, a sex crimes prosecutor, and a judge. The consensus among them was that something should be done. I wanted to hand this information off to whoever was responsible for protecting the little boy in Scott's custody. But so far, I had not found that person or agency I felt we could trust. Now Mary Jane was about to get involved, and I would soon learn she was jumping in with both feet.

CHAPTER NINETEEN

THE AWARD

Mary Jane's notes:

*After I'd read and digested the articles Rannah had given me, a statement by Rogers jumped out: his claim that the 12-year-old victim who testified against him at trial had come on to him, not once but twice. He was blaming his juvenile victim for the sexual assault. A 12 year old cannot legally sexually assault an adult, and pedophiles **always** blame the victim.*

Neither Nathan nor Rannah nor I had a clue what we could do, if anything. We did not know whether Rogers' criminal conduct was continuing, even though logic says that if he was a pedophile 20 years ago, he was still a pedophile.... The question was: Who were his current victims, if any? And was his adopted son one of them? We knew we needed to investigate Scott Rogers, but we knew our search would be tricky.

Louisiana is known for its good food, and I've been told that I'm a very good cook. In Louisiana, we have a saying, 'First you make a roux,' meaning that you have the ingredients for the first step, the base for what you will cook. Not only did I not have the ingredients for the roux, I had no pot in which to make it.

We knew that whatever we discovered when looking into Scott Rogers, we were limited in where we could take any criminal allegations. We would have to take care that we did not make any missteps; we did not know whom Scott knew, in what capacity, and the degree of those connections and the power that went with them. And if you make that misstep, payback in Louisiana is a bitch.

The first place I decided to check Scott Rogers was with the courts in the 19th Judicial District—East Baton Rouge Parish. I found a civil suit in which a person identified as a 1stCo employee had been employed by The Silver Sun, a small jewelry store in a strip mall in the eastern part of the city, to keep its books.

I knew I had to get the depositions of Scott Rogers and Mathew Hodgkinson from that litigation.

I then decided I would look into Rogers on the Internet to see what I would find. For a man as well established and connected in the Baton Rouge community as he was, for a man involved in television and public relations work, for a man involved in the community's politics, he had left very little trace. In this day and age, anonymity on the Internet is hard to achieve, but Rogers had done just that.

"Why?" I wondered.

The only information I found was that the Louisiana Department of Children and Family Services had given Rogers an award for serving as a foster parent, and that through his fostering work, he had adopted a male child with a disability. When I saw that, based on the trial in the U.K., I was flabbergasted.

Because of the nature of my criminal work, over the years I have learned that people who are pedophiles remain pedophiles for life. Is it possible that pedophiles can change? Not really. Learning how to control their urges is highly unlikely.

A pedophile is like an alcoholic. If you are an alcoholic, you are an alcoholic for life. Counselors encourage alcoholics to stay away from people who drink and places serving alcohol. And while alcoholics may learn to control their drinking, they are known to relapse.

Because pedophiles cannot stop their sexual urges, the courts list them on a sex registry and order them to stay away from children.

In one hand, I had 20-year-old news reports of Rogers' trial for molesting a male child, along with some indication of other *victims. And his defense was that the child was at fault for sexually assaulting* **him***. Yet in the other hand, I had accolades that the Department of Children and Family Services, which is responsible for the protection and wellbeing of children, had thrown at Rogers for all his good work with foster children. And the department was encouraging others to emulate Rogers in fostering and adopting. It was as if Scott Rogers were two different people.*

When I found that the Department of Children and Family Services had honored Scott Rogers as a model foster parent, I literally got up from my desk and walked out my front door to talk to myself, to walk off my anger, and to figure out how in the world this had happened. As I walked, I could see the buildings that house the people who placed Scott Rogers' young adopted son in the home of a pedophile.

I live and work in Spanish Town, the oldest neighborhood in Baton Rouge. Founded in 1805, it sits at the base of the Louisiana State Capitol and adjacent to Capitol Park, the site of most State office buildings. Spanish Town is as close to the New Orleans French Quarter as it gets.

Over 30 years ago, this unique neighborhood held the first Baton Rouge Mardi Gras Parade that now brings over 150,000 people into downtown Baton Rouge with its irreverent commentaries on politicians, sports figures, and major news events. Spanish Town residents are diverse in race and economics, as well as sexual orientation.

When I moved here over 20 years ago, the neighborhood was a predominantly-gay community. I know that if you are gay, you are not a pedophile any more than you are if you're straight. A pedophile is sexually attracted to children.

Just as it had started its own Mardi Gras parade, the neighborhood began, in 1997, the Spanish Town New Year's Eve celebration with about ten people cooking in a small kitchen. By 2012 the party had grown to almost 300 in attendance for an upscale progressive dinner party for our downtown neighbors. In 2013, the City of Baton Rouge held its first New Year's Eve party downtown, the culmination of the event that Rannah announced on the day the man from the U.K. made his first contact with her.

As I walked around Spanish Town, all I could think was why, in this day and age, this State of Louisiana agency, whose mission is the protection of children, would not have found out about Rogers' past. It was inconceivable.

I also knew that Rogers had ties to the law enforcement offices that would have conducted his background check, and I wondered if those ties had anything to do with their failure to discover his past. As I walked and talked to myself and pondered the situation, I knew right then and there that something was screwy with his application to the State of Louisiana Department of Child Services. I just did not know what.

After finding Rogers' award on the State of Louisiana's website, I called Rannah. "You are not going to believe this shit!" I said, and read her the press release from Child Services. Rannah and I talked about Scott's adopted son and how he had a disability and how Rogers had called him a "feral child." We talked about how Rogers could have adopted a child and whether someone could have helped him circumvent the background check. Then I learned that Rogers had asked various people with political connections to write character references on his behalf. The Louisiana State Police conducts criminal history checks for the State agencies; that would include a check on Rogers' criminal history to determine whether he qualified for foster or adoptive parenting. The discovery of his arrest and trial in the U.K. for child sex abuse should have kept him from fostering or adopting children here. The State Police runs the checks on teachers, childcare employees, and nursing home employees.... I hope it does a better job on them. ·

A few days after taking home everything I gave her to study, Mary Jane had her own epiphany. Whether you are Catholic or Protestant, if you live in Louisiana you don't have an "aha moment" like people in the rest of the country…you have an epiphany. In searching for information about Scott Rogers online, she found the November 2, 2012, press release on the Louisiana Department of Child Services website, honoring him with its Media Advocate Award at a ceremony during which U.S. Senator David Vitter made the presentation. Rogers was identified as an adoptive parent whose "passion for fostering and adoption led him to complete the required training to become a certified licensed foster parent himself."[24]

Child Services Department Secretary Suzy Sonnier said Rogers "has led by example and is an advocate like no other in the Department of Children and Family Services working to place foster children in permanent adoptive homes. From raising funds and securing sponsorships for Christmas events, successfully encouraging other families to become involved in fostering and adoption, to making a lifelong commitment to his adoptive son, his dedication to making a difference in the lives of Louisiana's children is clear."

Mary Jane's notes:

*Just how detailed a background check could Child Services have conducted? Did it in fact conduct **any** check? In an investigation, the agency would have talked to Mathew Hodgkinson, Stuart Poulton, and Scott Rogers' daughter Kimmy. All of them knew about the allegations of sexual misconduct with children in the United Kingdom, and none of them ever disclosed it. In fact, two of these individuals, as minors, were themselves victims of Scott Rogers. Did Child Services or the Louisiana State Police ever ask them if Scott's information was true?*

The next question is: If Child Services had found anything negative on Rogers, would the agency have given him children anyway?

---

[24] "DCFS celebrates adoption awareness month with families and children at Governor's Mansion." Louisiana Department of Children and Family Services. 2 November 2012. Viewed 9 September 2015. http://www.dcfs.louisiana.gov/index.cfm?md=newsroom&tmp=detail&articleID=497

After talking with Rannah, I went back to do some more research. I looked up the Louisiana laws on the requirements for becoming a foster parent and an adoptive parent. You have to declare your residency and give your social security number. One question addressed arrest records on all adult members in the household. Any answer of "yes" required a detailed explanation.

If Rogers had completed the Child Services application truthfully, he would have included his arrest and the outcome of the trial from 20 years ago. In that event, I could only hope that someone's brain in Child Services would have engaged to get the details of his criminal history and deny him as a foster or adoptive parent. But even if Rogers had lied about his past, his place of origin would be listed, as well as the date of his citizenship. You would think that someone at State Police Headquarters would have picked up the phone and called the police in Rogers' U.K. hometown. If the investigation started, however, with the date Rogers entered the United States in 1990, or the date he became a citizen in 2006, then nobody even considered his earlier life and his misconduct in the United Kingdom. Not the best background check by Louisiana State Police.

*What about the application for citizenship? I knew that Rogers was not a citizen when he came into the United States, so I did a quick Google search. One of the questions on the application is: "Have you ever been arrested or convicted of a crime and if so to give the details." I assumed that Rogers would have answered that question falsely. Still, how could any background check by the federal government **not** have resulted in information on his arrest and trial in the U.K.? The federal investigators who review applications for U.S. residency and work permits are employees of the same federal agency that checks the records of a non-citizen entering the United States. That federal agency would have known, based on those records, that he had come from the U.K. and could have picked up a phone and called the U.K. to check him out.*

I could not imagine that any person who had been tried for sexually abusing a child could get through any citizenship approval process. So I assume that he falsified information in that application. But he also could have been just plain lucky and the federal investigators could have missed truthful statements of his arrest and trial for sexually abusing a child in the U.K. Either the citizenship investigation did not catch the lies or the federal investigators ignored his answers and approved him for citizenship. I chose to believe what was behind door number one, though I was not sure why.

I also guessed that once Rogers became a citizen of the United States, he bootstrapped his way to foster parenthood by saying the federal government had cleared him. That way, Child Services needed to check him only from the time of his citizenship until the time of his application for foster parenting. Scott, I came to know, was a master manipulator, always using one stepping stone to gain advantage to the next.

With this piece of information, I could tell Mary Jane felt she had found something significant. While we had assumed Rogers would have hidden his arrest when applying for U.S. citizenship, Mary Jane discovered he had applied for a license to be a foster parent and was an adoptive parent. She knew that the forms and process for those applications would be exhaustive and that Scott could not have avoided the question, "Have you ever been arrested for a crime?" We would just have to find a way to get access to those records!

While the process to obtain federal records through the Freedom of Information Act is long and complicated, Mary Jane is a master of seeking Louisiana public records in her line of work. We were finally hopeful that she would uncover something we could give to the authorities that would allow them to look into Scott's unusual living and parenting arrangement.

Mary Jane's notes:

After gathering these blank forms, I talked to Nathan about going forward with a public records request to Child Services. We needed information on Rogers and his application to the State to become a foster parent and then an adoptive parent. Though I wrote the initial letter, Nathan decided that one of his employees would sign it in an attempt to keep the request low key. We sent that letter, and Child Services, claiming that the information was an exception to the public record law, immediately rejected that request. Because I had not made that request over my signature, I could not call and talk to the person who rejected it. So I phoned Nathan about sending a second letter, this time over my signature.

We did all we could to keep Rannah out of the forefront of our investigation.

CHAPTER TWENTY

THE CALL

Day 27
September 23, 2013

After a few weeks of daily communication between Ethan and me, I had learned a lot about Scott Rogers, supported by the professional opinions of attorneys, a private investigator, and an expert in the prosecution of child sex abuse cases, all of whom felt that, from what they could observe, Ethan's story was true. Now with what Mary Jane had found, I realized Scott Rogers was likely a serious threat to children in Baton Rouge.

After my first contact from Ethan, I had made the decision to record and watch Scott's *Around Town TV Show* each week, hoping to learn more about him. Since the show aired only at 5 a.m. on Saturdays and Sundays, I imagined the audience was very small, even though the program aired a second time on the city-parish governmental access television channel, Metro 21, which is set aside by the local cable franchise company for programming by local governments. When the Mayor's chief administrative officer questioned whether *The Around Town TV Show,* a for-profit business, met the requirements to air on the government access channel, Councilman Loupe—who after the 2012 election had replaced Mike Walker as Mayor Pro-Tem—decided Scott Rogers' *Around Town TV Show* would continue to air on Metro 21 as a public service.

Despite my having to watch two hours a week of Scott Rogers, who we now believed was a both a pedophile and a complete hypocrite, watching *The Around Town Show* on a weekly basis proved worthwhile. Every week, Rogers actively sought out law enforcement officials and non-profit organizations, especially those that advocated for children, to appear on the program. He prodded them on air to invite him to emcee their events and to come on the show to promote their work, as if his program could deliver a large and influential audience, rather than the narrowcast viewers it reached. His mastery as a con artist was beginning to come into clearer focus for me, now that I was paying attention to him. Just as he targeted young boys, he targeted the law enforcement officials. They were his prey…and they were falling into his trap.

Nathan now felt I should talk to Ethan by phone to figure out how his inquiries were going, and I agreed we needed a conversation to discuss our next steps. I emailed Ethan a lengthier update of all of my meetings, describing the feelings among the group of close and trusted friends and professionals I had consulted so far about the two options I had originally discussed with him. I knew he initially wanted us to warn parents simply by letting the news media know what Scott had done, but wondered also if we could give the information he had provided to law enforcement agencies.

"I think the consensus is that we do not have any evidence that a crime is currently being committed, so it's hard to go to local law enforcement agencies at this point," I told him. "For the news media to have a real interest, we feel Scott's adopted son's safety is key, and we are just not sure that one can claim he is in danger simply based on the previous trial, where he was acquitted and the other charges dropped.

"We do question whether he disclosed that he had been charged with child sexual abuse when adopting a young boy here, but since adoption records are sealed, the circumstances of his adoption are private. That said, I think everyone understands that once a person abuses children, he typically does not stop and there is a great chance that sexual abuse is ongoing, which certainly concerns us greatly.

"You seem like a very likeable and credible person," I said to Ethan, "You're clearly a good communicator, polite, straightforward, and have been reliable in providing what you have said you could. The question I keep getting from the others I have asked to look at the information is: What was your motivation for pursuing this after over 20 years?"

After looking at the information Ethan had provided, everyone asked: "Was he a victim? What is his connection? What is he hoping will happen?"

Nathan felt we had to talk to Ethan to get the answers to those questions and to learn who was willing to give first-hand knowledge of what Scott had done and was possibly still doing. All we had to go on was old newspaper articles and one person telling me that the charges had been true. We would need someone willing to say that, either to the news media or to the authorities, and I wasn't sure Ethan was ready to speak publicly.

"Since you found me on a web search related to Scott, you probably know a little bit about me," I began to Ethan. "My work in public relations requires me to be careful, honest and factual, especially considering that my clients include several local elected officials. Seeing how the victim was treated in Scott's trial, I feel sure that has prevented any other survivors from speaking up, fearing that they would be similarly discredited. Without a victim speaking up...and without attributing information to you...I can share only what we can verify. Though the news articles do that well, the end result is that he was found not guilty.

"I would like to figure this out with you...if there is a probability that a child is being sexually abused, that is reason enough to care and look further," I said. "Maybe we can schedule a call sometime next week to talk. I'm interested in what you hope can come of this, and what involvement (if any) you are willing to have if someone here wants to talk to a person with first-hand knowledge of what happened there.

"I don't want to turn away from something that could be so awful going on in our city, and I'm willing to spend some personal time reading and chatting to learn as much as I can to see if we can hand it off to the appropriate people to look into it. Let me know your thoughts," I wrote.

Ethan's reply was at the same time what I anticipated he might say, but also moving closer to what I dreaded hearing.

"I think you already know what my motivation is, but if needs be, we can discuss over the phone," he said, ending the sentence with an emoticon for a wink ;). He could definitely read my thoughts.

I looked at the email for a few minutes, letting it sink in. As much as I did not want my fears to be true, I knew I was going to hear eventually that Ethan too had been a victim of Scott. Each time our conversations went beyond what Scott Rogers *was* to what he had actually *done* to someone, I realized just how dangerous he was. This was a man who had seriously hurt young boys at a most vulnerable age, leaving lasting scars. After all, here was a young man who was still pursuing him 20 years after seeing him for the last time. Of course, Scott must have abused him! Why else would he have such feelings about Scott's actions going unpunished, and more important, why would he have such concern and fear that Scott was abusing children in Baton Rouge? *He knows what Scott is capable of.*

"Feel free to call me," Ethan immediately replied. "Happy to talk with whoever you think can help. I don't yet know how far I will take this, but thank you for all your help." Ethan also had another lead. "Today I have found where Jake works. I have contacted him and left all my details. The contact is going to email him. I hope he gets in touch."

I asked Ethan if he would prefer to Skype, but because of the timing, he said a phone call would be best. So we scheduled a call for the following Monday, September 23, at 11 a.m. Central Time, 5 p.m. in the U.K., when Ethan would be finishing work.

Everyone—Nathan, Shannon, and Mary Jane—wanted to be present for the call, even though all agreed that they could simply listen without asking Ethan any questions. But that wasn't going to work for me. I had mentioned to Ethan that Nathan would probably be on the call with me, but now our group was getting a little large, and possibly intimidating. We met at my house Monday morning at 11 a.m. and took our places around my dining room table. After a few failed attempts at getting through to Ethan's mobile number, the phone rang and we waited for him to answer.

When he picked up, I asked if it was a good time to talk. "Yes, I've just gotten in the car. I'm pulling over so we can talk." Before putting him on speaker phone, I wanted to identify for him who was there. I had explained to them before I dialed his number that we would never talk to Ethan without first disclosing who was listening. "I'm going to always be honest with him," I said. "If anyone is going to listen to the conversation, I want to tell him who they are and make sure he is okay with it before we put him on speaker phone."

I felt protective of Ethan's privacy, considering what he was sharing with me. I trusted him, and I didn't want to give him any reason not to trust me. I never liked having anyone listen to a conversation without letting the person on the other end know who was in the room. The last thing I wanted to do was ambush Ethan with anything, so I first told him I had some people there who were helping me and I wanted to make sure he was okay talking with them before switching to speaker. He was, as always, very agreeable, so I switched the call to speaker phone.

"Ethan, I want to introduce you to everyone who is here with me today," I began. "Nathan Fisher is an attorney and a long-time friend of mine; Shannon is also an attorney with his firm; Mary Jane is a paralegal and investigator. I didn't want to overwhelm you with voices."

"You have quite a team," he said.

"I have quite a team, yes," I said with a slight laugh. *I have some good friends, I thought.* "I have an ongoing legal issue with 1stCo and Scott Rogers," I explained. I always liked to address that first because I didn't want anyone to hear about that and think I had discovered this information about Scott through my lawsuit.

"Okay…." Ethan said.

"Our firm worked on a project with 1stCo, and Scott stepped in at the end and billed for $15,000 of our fees and kept them," I explained. "Then he got involved with an opponent of the Mayor and went to the newspaper with a story about us that was not true. That's why I wrote the letter to the editor that you saw. Scott coughed up the funds and we are waiting to go to court for the final settlement. One of the reasons I called Nathan when I received your email is because I have an open court dispute with Scott Rogers."

"Okay, I understand," he said.

"We've had a hard time figuring out their circumstances…with them all living together," I continued. "We spent some time trying to figure out what to do with this information. We talked to John Camp and got his opinion. We all believe this abuse would still be going on here. So in full disclosure, I've seen him in action in business and know him to not be an honest person. He has adopted a child and I know the people who he said wrote letters of recommendation for him to adopt the boy. Mary Jane was asking some good questions this morning about the court case you sent records on…. Did the investigators in that case talk to you?"

"I went to Scott's school when I was 12…in the early '90s," Ethan said. "I'm 35 now. Strangely, I was never interviewed…which is very bizarre. I was never questioned by anyone. I was there at the time it was going on. I think they may have spoken to some…probably spoke to Mathew and Stuart because Mathew was living with Scott at the time. I think they interviewed those two. I've tried to get hold of Jake, but he hasn't responded. I contacted his place of work, left a message, but he hasn't gotten back to me. I just said I wanted to speak to him. He probably thinks I'm involved with Scott still, so for that reason he hasn't contacted me. Mathew joined the school a few years before me. Stuart didn't join until about a year after I joined…a bit later. But he became very involved very quickly. Mathew's family moved to France. Mathew's parents took Matt against his will to France and literally locked him in a room because he was trying to get back to Scott. Matt eventually got back to Scott and the rest is history."

We discussed the news articles for a while, dancing around the elephant in the room, which was his motive for contacting me and whether he had been a victim of Rogers. Mary Jane stepped in and asked the question that was on everyone's mind: "How is it you know this information?"

"To put it bluntly," Ethan said and his voice trailed off. "To be honest, as I told Rannah, this is the first time I've...." We all looked up quickly, our eyes darting around the table to each other in nervous anticipation of what he was about to say.

"I was 12 and I was abused by Scott for about three to four years," he said with a slight crack in his voice.

I glanced around the table and saw profound sadness on everyone's face. Nathan shook his head. There it was. No matter how much we had prepared ourselves, hearing Ethan finally say it brought about a collective feeling of sorrow. *We could never say again that we did not know....*

With this first confirmation of Ethan as a victim, we now knew why he had contacted me. We sat there with heads bowed until Mary Jane had the presence of mind to reply quickly, "I felt that may be the case...we don't need to go there. We just needed to know the information is reliable.

"Once someone does this he continues to do it," she said. "If we know how he goes about doing it, that helps to discover him, because he will follow a pattern."

I was so grateful for Mary Jane's criminal case experience that allowed her to turn the subject back to the logical reasons for needing to ask the question and away from the heartbreaking reality that this very nice young man was a victim of Scott Rogers.

"What I find interesting is that it's very similar," Ethan said, his voice steady again. "A small town, he was close with the Mayor, very close to charities in Bury. It was very similar to what he's doing there."

"That's very helpful," Mary Jane said.

"Every expert tells us they follow the same patterns," I added, glad to be back on solid ground in the conversation.

"I've obviously dealt with my demons," Ethan said, sounding stronger again. "I'm stable, I have a successful career, I'm married, I've got two kids. I'm very worried about others who aren't as strong as I am now."

Nathan spoke up, "I want to ask you...do you know any other places where he may have been in the States, like Texas?"

"I started searching for Scott about 2000," Ethan explained. "He's very hard to find. I recently found out from Rannah that he had been in Texas. He was in Bury for much of the '80s and '90s, then moved to the States around 1997."

"Let me ask you this," Nathan said. "A few years ago, he left Baton Rouge for about a year. He said he had a back problem he was trying to take care of. Do you know where he might have been during that time?"

"I'd be surprised he would come back to the U.K.," Ethan said. "I have no idea."

Mary Jane resumed asking about the court case. "Other than the boy who testified, were there others who have since come forward to law enforcement?"

"No," Ethan said. "Tim was his name. Scott was actually cleared of the abuse. Basically, there weren't loads of boys at the Academy. It's really Jake and myself who were the outsiders who weren't really locked into his manipulation. Well, we were to a certain point, but we got away. I left the Academy when I was about 16.

"He was abusing Mathew and Stuart and for whatever reason they've gone on with him," he said.

Mary Jane asked, "How many students were in this Academy?"

"He was turning over about a million pounds...there were a lot of children, but not many boys," said Ethan.

"Do you know what's happened to Tim?" I asked.

"He comes from Norwich—a county in the U.K. I haven't heard anything about him since the trial," Ethan replied. "He was the same age as me and Matt, so 35 now. I could try to find him."

"It's so unbelievable they put a victim on the stand for five days," I said. "I'm sure he has distanced himself from all of this now."

"I believe his parents lost a lot of money," Ethan said. "Tim lost the case, and they wouldn't put him through a re-trial."

"In talking to John Camp and listening to him," I offered, "he said any news value on a story like this would have to be based on concern about the child he has now...it's hard to rehash an old story. Scott could sue me for slander if I start saying he is a child molester. We all think any interest from the news media will be based on the welfare of that child," I continued. "Was Jake legally adopted?"

"I believe he was legally adopted," Ethan said. "I'm pretty sure…his name was Jake Scott-Rogers at that time. When he got away, he changed his name back to his real name. Jake probably went through the worst abuse of anyone."

"Scott's not close to our Mayor, but he has gotten close to law enforcement," I explained. "He has a concealed weapon permit. You know, we love our guns over here and he presents himself as a gun rights fan. He got certified to be a foster care parent, which is not a legal adoption, but sometimes a step toward placing an older child. He became a foster parent, then from there adopted a little boy who seems to have autism. It's disturbing to see him because Scott takes him around to functions, dresses him like a character in a play and shows him off.

"We spoke to someone in our District Attorney's office and she looked at the circumstances and came to the same conclusion we have. We talked about him starting his church and what the motives might be there. He has presented himself as an advocate of children."

"That is really terrifying," Ethan said and you could hear the emotion in his voice when the subject turned to Scott Rogers and children. "It's unbelievable that is happening."

"Do you know anyone who has contact with Scott's former wife?" I asked.

"Last I heard, she was working in a local hospital in Bury several years ago," Ethan answered.

"Is she still friendly with him?" Mary Jane asked.

"I don't know," Ethan said. "He had a strange relationship with her. He bullied her. Kim was about 3 or 4 when I met her. Scott took Kim to the States with him, and I don't know what he said to Mandie…I don't understand how she could let that happen. He's a very, very manipulative man and he obviously did something."

"I've seen this before, and sometimes it's very costly to get children back," Mary Jane said.

"I got the impression from Scott he was manipulating Kim to not like her mother," Ethan said. "Probably at some point he said to Kim, 'Where do you want to go?' and she said she wanted to live with him."

"Is she his biological child?" Nathan asked. It has long been the subject of gossip and online comments about Scott that surely she was not his biological child, but all indications were that she was.

"Yes, she is his biological child," Ethan said. "Definitely."

"He tells a story that Mandie abandoned him," I said.

"That is so untrue," said Ethan. "It couldn't be more untrue."

"We don't know where this is going," I said. "Nathan has had a sobering conversation with me about this and I have told him I am not willing to drop it. From a personal standpoint, this is someone who attempted to hurt us. It's one thing to have to take it, but it's another to have to take it from someone of his character," I said. "I think all of us look at his abuse as continuing, and I don't know how I could in good conscience not consider the safety of the child living with him."

Nathan spoke up next. "Would you come to the U.S. if necessary to talk to law enforcement officials here?"

We all looked quickly around the table at each other again, waiting for Ethan to answer, and after a pause, he finally spoke.

"Yes. I would certainly consider it," he said quietly.

Nathan hit the balls of his hands together hard in what was a strong but quiet clap that signaled his approval of Ethan's answer. For Nathan, that reply was a game changer. If Ethan would come to Baton Rouge now, as an adult, and face his abuser head-on, Nathan was fully on board. He leaned forward in his chair to speak directly into the speaker phone: "This man has to be stopped!" he said loudly.

"Absolutely," Ethan replied. "Someone said, what's my motivation. He done me wrong when I was a really young kid. The motivation is that in the first place, and protecting any children from it happening to them. I'll consider it. I'll consider anything I can do to help."

"Is there anyone else who might consider that from the U.K.?" Nathan asked.

"One is Natalie, a girl," Ethan said. "The other is Jake, if I can get him to communicate with me. Natalie…she's in Utah. She's an interesting person. I know she knows a huge amount of information. Probably more than me."

"Did she disassociate from Scott?" I asked.

"She was in the inner circle," Ethan said. She was engaged to Jake at some point. She is a friend on Facebook. I think she would probably talk."

"Would you send her a message to talk to us?" Mary Jane asked.

"I think she has about five children," Ethan said.

"She has five boys," I confirmed, quickly looking up her Facebook page on my iPad while he was talking and finding a young couple with five beautiful little boys standing around them.

"She's a good person and I think she would be happy to talk to you," Ethan said. "She's about 37 or 38…a few years older than me. I imagine she is a house mum."

Mary Jane remained focused. "Tell me what your thought is about how we should proceed in this," she said. "I take all suggestions from anyone about how to proceed."

We could hear Ethan sigh as he thought about her question. "I know it's difficult because you don't have anyone there who is ready to come forward. When I contacted Rannah, I was trying to expose him…to let people know what he's doing. Once people know, they will start asking questions. Once they start asking questions, hopefully you get answers."

I agreed with Ethan that exposing Scott should be that simple, but after talking with as many people as I had, I knew the process was in reality much harder. Still, I didn't want to give Ethan the idea that Baton Rouge would end like Bury, with Scott Rogers fooling everyone.

"We've all lived here a long time," I started explaining. "I see him working hard to make contact with elected officials. We also have those same contacts and I think even more credibility, so we just need to have something substantive. We can't go to law enforcement without some real substance. I think that's why Nathan asked if you would talk.... Even though our local authorities may not have jurisdiction over what Scott did in England, you can at least provide a firsthand knowledge of his crimes. I'm determined to not drop it...and even more so after talking to you. This guy has to be stopped. This can't continue."

I went back to his suggestion that we talk to Natalie. "You have a very good sense of who might go back to him," I said. "So I trust you on who to trust. We're trying hard not to speak with anyone who would call him. I would hate for him to pack up in the dead of night and leave here the way he left Dallas."

"We're not dropping this," Mary Jane said, "but we're going to move cautiously. Rannah's going to stay in touch with you, so if things go quiet for a day or two, don't think we're not working."

"We're making some public records requests," I said, "and that takes time. I will keep in touch with you and keep you posted. We're going to do everything we can to figure out the best way to move forward."

"That's brilliant," Ethan said.

"You're a good person for wanting to make people aware," I said. "We're going to follow up here for you...and for us." I didn't want to imply we were purely altruistic, willing to take up any cause that came our way if it appeared a noble one. I had worked in politically charged environments since I graduated from college, and I understand you occasionally have to defend yourself if someone misrepresents you. To think that someone of Scott Rogers' character had successfully convinced a major daily newspaper to go along with his made-up story about Val and me was very hard to take. At this point, listening to Ethan, I knew with certainty that Scott had done a lot of people wrong on many different levels. The time had come for Baton Rouge to face the truth about him.

"That's fantastic," Ethan said. "I appreciate everyone there."

We had talked to Ethan for about an hour when we finally ended the call, so everyone was anxious to stand up, check phones for messages, or just take a break before sitting down to rehash our conversation. Soon everyone was talking at the same time, asking questions of the group.

Mary Jane opened the discussion with a comment about the need to confirm what was driving Ethan to pursue Scott Rogers. Cautious, she had wanted to eliminate any possibility that someone with a personal grudge against Scott was using us.

Before we made the call to Ethan, she had posed the question: What if the person who had contacted me was a scorned lover? After the call, she was as convinced as I that Ethan was telling the truth.

"He has a viable motive and he has put you in the middle of his search for Scott Rogers," she said to me.

Shannon leaned back in her chair, clearly frustrated to learn that Scott had gotten away with child sex abuse in England and wondering how the courts had failed.

Nathan focused on the finances. "How much is a million pounds?" he asked. Shannon said, "Now, it's probably about $3 million…." Her estimate was high, but, clearly, a lot of money had flowed through Scott's Academy every year.

"To me, everything about him seems legitimate," I said, meaning Ethan.

Nathan commented on Ethan's saying the Academy had very few boys attending because, as he explained, boys don't typically dance at that level.

"I put Ari in ballet because I thought it would be good for him in playing basketball," Nathan said referring to his son who had been my student worker at LSU when I first met the Fisher family.

"Then you put him in karate classes, so your parenting is a little questionable here," I teased, and we laughed, knowing all too well the most famous pedophile story Baton Rouge had seen. Ari's karate instructor had been very popular until he kidnapped one of his young male students and sexually abused him. When the instructor was arrested in California and returned to Baton Rouge, the young victim's father ambushed him in the airport and shot him in the head, with television cameras capturing the death in time to report it on the ten o'clock news.

"We now have a reason, with what he told you, to follow up," Mary Jane said to me. "Because he was abused and he wants to stop his abuser. Does he have a cause of action?" she asked Nathan and Shannon. "Would he have to bring it here or in the U.K.?"

"I don't do civil work," Nathan reminded her.

Mary Jane continued, "If he has a cause of action he can pursue here...you talk about take Rogers out.... It struck me during our call to talk about a possible civil case."

"Ethan could sit right here at this table with us and have this conversation," I said. "He's credible."

"Yes," everyone said together.

"We have to talk to this girl he told us about," Mary Jane said.

"I was impressed he would consider coming here," Nathan added.

Mary Jane summed it up well: "If Scott Rogers has made a false representation at Child Services, then we go back to Immigration and he's made a false representation on his arrest, then I think we regroup at that time and decide what we do with that information."

"Yes," Nathan said, "but as I may have mentioned...if you give this material to the FBI...." He shrugged his shoulders, making a face that signaled doubt. His voice trailed off as he anticipated one of us responding.

Mary Jane finished for him, "It's going to be buried. I think if he has denied these arrests, when we get the information, we can go back to Child Services. The State will be obligated to take action. Where does that leave us? We are not in control at that time...but making Child Services aware of his arrest record would raise the stakes."

"Sue Bernie would do something," Nathan offered.

But Mary Jane was skeptical. "If we don't go with current criminal stuff, can the district attorney do anything?" she asked.

"If he has falsified documents, oh, yeah," said Nathan.

"She could go back to Child Services and tell them to cough up these records and look into it," Mary Jane ventured.

"I anticipate Child Services being another black hole," I said. "The Louisiana Department of Children and Family Services touts Scott Rogers on its website, so they're not going to be a willing participant. You hear about these kids being referred to them, then ending up dead. They have their hands full."

Nathan agreed. "It's a bitch to get those people to take action," he said.

"Right...everything goes into a black hole," Mary Jane said.

"Sue was serious about helping," Nathan said.

"She's serious and she 100 percent believes he's still abusing," I agreed. "What I didn't think was promising is she didn't offer any ideas. Her only suggestion was to get someone to go to the church because maybe he's recruiting kids there."

"She's not the investigative arm," Shannon reminded me. "Her office reinvestigates only what's brought to it. We need someone in sex crimes with the police to investigate and bring her the results."

"But I don't think I can go to someone in the police department," I said. They all knew my concerns. The Baton Rouge Police report to the Mayor, and I was afraid Scott would try to say we were using the Police to go after him after he had tried to cause problems for us. He had gotten close to the State Police and the Sheriff, but had never been able to infiltrate Baton Rouge City Police or get close to the Mayor, so I thought if they investigated our information, he would try to claim their motivation was political. Besides, Scott lived in Iberville Parish, and we had already discussed the unlikelihood of the Baton Rouge Police having jurisdiction over what we may discover regarding sexual child abuse.

"No, you can't do that," Mary Jane agreed. "First, we do the public records request. Then, once we get those documents, we'll decide where we go from there."

Shannon still had trouble accepting how Scott had managed to cover up his past. "Adoption aside," she said. "Being found not guilty aside. How in the world could he be certified as a *foster parent*?" she asked. "There has to be a question of, *Have you ever been arrested for ANYTHING.*"

"That's why I think he lied," Mary Jane replied.

"He's smart," I reminded them. "This guy said in his first email to me, 'He's a clever, evil, nasty little man.'"

"My guy told me, 'Nathan, there's something wrong over there,'" Nathan added, reminding us that when we started the lawsuit against 1stCo, he'd had his own private investigator look into Scott's background and the man had run into a dead end in Texas. At the time, Nathan was interested in only a cursory check to see if anything stood out in Scott's record, but the investigator told Nathan that Scott's time in Texas looked suspicious.

"This guy's been looking for Scott since 2000," I said. I always made a conscious effort not to say Ethan's name. I always discussed with him before sharing his identity, and he was aware that the people in the room with me knew his name. Still, I tried to get into the habit of not saying it so I wouldn't slip up at any point and, without thinking, reveal it.

"He knows how to find people online," I said. He's an amateur like me, but he's right—Scott's hard to find."

"Someone as visible as he is, you would think there's a ton of shit on him," Mary Jane added. "He's changed his date of birth. When you start changing that, it's very hard. We have a homeless lady downtown who keeps changing her birth date, so it's hard to find her benefits for her. Unless you guess the right combination of how she applied, you can't find them."

Shannon smiled, recognizing that Mary Jane was talking about the homeless lady she and Nathan dealt with near their office. "We call her Violet," she said.

Mary Jane added, "She's known as Turban Lady."

"Is that the naked lady?" I asked when I realized they made the connection. A homeless lady had attracted attention with some of her antics and was something of a legend downtown.

"Yeah...I saw her naked," Shannon laughed.

"One day, I heard Shannon saying, 'Oh, my God...'" Nathan laughed, reminding us of that day. "When she got out of jail, she asked the young guy who answers the phone for us if he would spend the night with her," Nathan said. "He was really shook up."

"She was in jail for two months for throwing bottles at cars," Mary Jane continued. "When the police arrested her, she pooped in her pants, pulled it out and smeared it all over the police car." This was the first comic relief any of us had that day, and the whole table broke out in squeamish laughter. Mary Jane and another downtown resident had started a program to help homeless people return home to family, and they now work closely with the Mayor's Office and Police Department to implement it, so we had ventured into a subject that is near and dear to her.

Shannon added, "She likes to bathe in the City Court fountain" across from their office.

"She collects a nice piece of change from lawyers," Nathan laughed, referring to her panhandling acumen.

"She's using it to buy drugs!" Mary Jane exploded. "Hear me." Because she spends her time and personal money trying to help homeless people, Mary Jane deplores those who give them a handout, which helps them remain on the streets.

"I hear you," Nathan laughed, but we could tell he was guilty of giving her money.

"What would the people at Child Services do?" I asked, moving the conversation back to the subject at hand. "Will they take the kid away from him?"

"He may still be fostering children…we don't know!" Mary Jane said.

"That's right," I replied.

"But they have an obligation to protect children," Mary Jane insisted.

"Whether they do is another story," said Shannon.

"But they will *know* that someone knows," Mary Jane shot back. "Once we gather this information and give it to someone, they have an obligation!"

"He has gotten very close to State Police and to the Sheriff," I reminded them.

"But let me tell you something…." Mary Jane said sternly.

Anticipating what she was going to say, I finished her admonition: "But nothing separates you from your friends like child abuse?" I guessed.

Shannon continued, "Yeah, it's not like having a drug problem."

"Right," said Mary Jane. "It's going to be *Oh, shit!* I also believe at some point, Kip needs to know what's going on here," she added. "And you've got to decide the right time for that," she said, turning to me.

I agreed. "I showed him the first email I received when I got it that day, and I told him I was going to pursue it and try to help the guy who emailed me and would let him know if I found out anything. He's a real stickler for pinning things down...having all the facts...so I would prefer to know the facts before I go back to him.

"I feel so bad for this guy," I said again, thinking back to our conversation with Ethan.

"I'm glad we know," Mary Jane said.

"At least we know he's legit," Nathan agreed.

"He had a supply of chosen victims," Shannon said of Scott.

"He would give kids a Russian wedding ring...crazy stuff to brainwash kids," I said. "Stuart has been living with him for 20 years. Mathew's been living with him for 20 years...I'm afraid they're not going anywhere."

"No," Mary Jane agreed.

"But after that email Ethan sent Stuart, 24 hours later, he emailed him back and wanted to contact his family," I added. "That's a good sign!" Of course, we later learned Stuart had not followed through.

"If you have a parent who has been pushed away by a child, and the child gets back in touch, the two will stay in touch at any cost," Mary Jane said. "Even if they have to accept the history."

"Sure, they will," I said.

"I would not think he is still abusing Matt and Stuart," Shannon suggested, "but the three of them might be abusing the children."

I reminded the group what local private investigator Rick Lucas—with whom I had also met and shared Ethan's information—had told me when he saw the news articles on Scott's trial. "I would stake 40 years in the business," he said of Ethan, "that he is a victim. Secondly, child sex abuse is so damaging, it's hard to get anyone to talk about it," he had said. "I know of people who suppress it for 40 years, then commit suicide. They become alcoholics, drug abusers…and even child abusers."

"There is so much focus on child molestation now," Nathan said, "I think people are more willing to believe the victims."

"A lot of kids have experienced abuse and just don't know how to stand up to it," Mary Jane said.

"I could be fooled by this guy," I added, "but to me, he seems to have a handle on what happened to him. He is managing it, but it's still there."

"The fact that he's willing to go forward…if he is willing to talk to law enforcement here, he's not snookering us," Mary Jane said, giving Ethan her vote of confidence.

"Scott Rogers will immediately cry foul if I go to the police," I said. "His attorney runs a children's foundation!"

"Well, sure," said Mary Jane. "That's why she's his attorney. But once he is outed on this, you will see a lot of people drop him."

"Shannon and I are together on this," I said. "I'm floored that anyone wants to be around him!"

"I tried to watch the show, but I had to change the channel," Mary Jane laughed.

"Ugggggggghhhhhh!" Shannon let out a long full-body shudder to punctuate her displeasure with Scott Rogers.

"He's going to be honored by Cenikor," Nathan said of the substance abuse program that had just mailed invitations to its annual luncheon.

"Isn't that amazing?" I asked.

"He has access to vulnerable children," Shannon pointed out.

Before we wrapped up, Mary Jane reminded us she had prepared a public records request for Child Services to find out if Scott had in fact lied on his application to foster children.

"You're asking for specifics?" I asked Mary Jane.

"Look at it," she said, showing me a tightly worded request to the Department. "If you leave that to a lawyer to write, it would be ten pages long."

"I'm glad we got to hear Ethan in his own voice," I said. Unlike the two lawyers and the paralegal in the room with me, I wasn't used to criminal cases, so I relied on my instincts about people and my training in journalism school. I listened carefully to the tone of a person's voice, always looking for discrepancies. I kept going back in my mind to the call we had just finished, moved by Ethan's simple honesty and logical responses.

"You couldn't have this kind of conversation with Scott Rogers," I said. "He might burst into tears in the middle of it." And yet here we sat in a city where we had all lived for many years, trying to determine how Scott had managed to get close to so many people, especially in law enforcement.

"Ethan told me, when I first asked him to explain his interest in Scott, 'It's unusual to talk about this with a stranger,'" I said, thinking back to our early emails. "He has been so brave...he doesn't know us at all."

"That's why he can be brave," said Shannon. "He's not going to see us tomorrow. He's not going to run into us at the movies."

"I feel that I know him," I said, hoping I didn't sound like the weak link in the room, the one who had let her guard down. "I've learned that you don't have to tell him to be careful...you don't have to tell him that sort of stuff. He's smart enough to know it. His instincts are good; he has the right response when you give him new information. He's been looking for Scott since 2000. That's before Scott got these children."

"He'll probably come over here, we'll meet him at the airport, and then he'll go and shoot the mother fucker," Nathan speculated, making everyone laugh. "Then get on a plane and go home."

"Well, I wouldn't tell them where he lives," said Shannon, smiling.

Clearly, I wasn't alone. Ethan had won over everyone with his honesty.

"It's a bizarre thing," I said. "Twenty years ago, Ethan couldn't have made this connection. But now, if you Google 'Scott Rogers Baton Rouge,' my letter comes up."

Actually, Ethan had been Googling Scott's name for years; finally, in 2008, when he decided to search for Mathew and Stuart instead, he found them and then Scott. Then they all disappeared from the Internet, and he searched for Scott again for another five years. He could tell from his searches that Scott was still in Baton Rouge because he would occasionally find his photo online when he attended some local function.

This time, he knew he needed to connect with someone who knew the kind of person Scott was—someone whose experiences with Scott corroborated his own. Knowing Scott as he did, Ethan knew he must have crossed someone, hurt someone. So he started expanding his searches to include phrases like "Scott Rogers lied" and "Scott Rogers deceived." He was quickly searching any words that would connect Scott with someone who knew what a nasty man he truly was.

Then a new list of Google searches popped up on his screen and he read, "Pact Story Misleading, Gray Says." Ethan clicked on my letter to the editor and began reading. When he got to the line, "That person is Scott Rogers..." he knew that whoever wrote the letter had seen the man behind the mask. That's when he made the decision to contact me.

A few hours after our call with Ethan, I got a short email. "Nice to speak with you earlier," Ethan wrote. "Thanks for the kind words. I appreciate all your help. As discussed, I will continue to search for any helpful info. Speak soon, Ethan."

I replied, "I know you don't know me, but all I can promise you is that we will pursue this information and do whatever we can to help stop the abuse from happening here. You are obviously a brave person."

I was thinking again about the warnings I'd heard that too often survivors of child sex abuse suffer a lifetime of problems as a result. Here was someone who had it all—a successful career, a loving family—and yet he had not forgotten what Scott had done to him. And, more important, he couldn't ignore what was more than a strong probability: Scott's current and continuing abuse of other children.

Was his 13-year search for justice finally about to end?

Mary Jane's notes:

After the phone call with Ethan, I sent the public records request to Child Services over my own signature. The denial response cited Louisiana Revised Statute 46:56 regarding confidentiality. I could get no information regarding Scott Rogers and his licensing as a foster and adoptive parent. The Department of Child Services took the position that because my request involved a child, the agency would not release the information. I had a discussion with the lawyers for Child Services, telling them I felt they were wrong in their denial. Their own DCFS Office of Community Services guidelines, dated July 2005, defined these confidential records as falling under this guideline: "...information concerning clients of the agency shall be confidential." The section continued: "Therefore, information regarding children in foster care and their biological families must be held in confidence by all concerned." But I was not asking about the child he adopted or the children he fostered or the biological parents. What I really wanted was to see how Rogers, who was not a client of the agency, had answered the questions about any previous arrest and trial.

In Louisiana, access to public records is considered a Constitutional right. The limited exceptions keep very few records from the public. In the Department of Health and Human Resources or Child Services, however, employees are more restrictive on what they believe they can legally give out. They can't give information on an applicant for food stamps, or medical information on children, or other information on children themselves.

What I wanted was the information from Scott Rogers' application, information that he gave to the State to foster and adopt children. Ultimately, the money the State of Louisiana paid him to take care of foster children should be public,

*because, as a foster parent, he was an employee or contractor
with the State.*

*Public record law requires that State agencies provide
personnel files and contracts to the person requesting them. Yet
this agency was refusing to give me Rogers' employment
information, the whole time praising him publically to
encourage others both to foster and to adopt. The agency itself
had made very public Rogers' participation as a foster and an
adoptive parent. That was no secret.*

*In light of Rogers' history, the agency's publicity was
completely out of line: the promotion of a pedophile to
encourage others like him to foster children. To this day, based
on Child Services' own published rules, I believe that the
information I sought is public record. And the State's hiding that
information allowed Rogers to continue acquiring children for
his sexual purposes. The same condition of secrecy had allowed
him to get away with molesting children in the U.K.*

*Unless a judge financially bites an agency for not
complying with a public record request, the agencies' initial
response always is that they "don't have it" or you "can't have
it," and then they cite, as the reason for their denial, some
bullshit rule that does not fit any defined exception. Mainly they
deny access to public records because they are lazy and don't
want to do the work to comply with the law. Normally, in an
effort to get you to back down and go away, a person with the
agency screams at you. And the only way you then get the
information is by filing a lawsuit and going before a judge,
which means that your business is now both very public and
involves a lengthy process in the courts.*

*That battle is something we did not want to engage at the
time, as it would draw attention to our investigation of Rogers.
Most important, because we feared for the kids in his care, we
didn't have the time to go through the court system.*

*But I am pissed about this denial of public information and
want to call the Child Services people out, not only for allowing
Rogers to foster and adopt, but also for proclaiming to the world
what a wonderful person he was and for using him to encourage
others to be just like him. Really! Who is Child Services*

protecting—the foster and adoptive parents or the children they are charged with protecting?

Clearly, if you are trying to protect children, Child Services is not the place to go!

CHAPTER TWENTY-ONE

THE GETAWAY

Day 29
September 25, 2013

The call with Ethan had solidified our team. Now the denial of access to Scott Rogers' application for fostering and adopting children made us even more determined to help Ethan warn the appropriate people of Scott's past sexual abuse of children.

There was no more wondering who Ethan was, no more speculation on whether he was a victim, no more doubt. Hearing his voice—reasoned, intelligent, likable—made everyone want to help him keep Scott Rogers from abusing children again. Ethan wasn't just a British accent over the phone; he was a person trying to save children from a monster.

Mary Jane went back to work on her public records search. She had found a civil suit that involved the owner of a local jewelry store, Silver Sun, suing Rogers. He had apparently placed a woman in the business to perform bookkeeping under his supervision, and the woman had stolen money from the company. Scott often portrayed himself as a business consultant, and had apparently convinced the store owner that he could provide someone to help her business succeed. Instead, the bookkeeper ended up serving jail time, and the owner sued Rogers to recover her losses.

The lawsuit files noted that Scott and Mathew had been deposed, so Mary Jane found the court reporter on the case and learned the records were still available. As she began searching them, we saw how Scott had changed his name and Mathew's, which made finding them more difficult. Scott was sometimes known as Richard Scott-Rogers, with the last named hyphenated; Kimberly Scott-Rogers used the same form of the name in official documents. Since we had searched for the surname "Rogers," we wondered if we should widen our search to include "Scott-Rogers" as the last name.

Ethan had confirmed that Mathew's name was Hodgkinson, and not Hodgkins, the name he used in Baton Rouge, and he was called by his original name in the depositions. I sent Ethan the depositions to keep him informed of everything we found, and I pressed him to remember anything he could about Scott's real name. He recalled Scott telling him he had changed his name in the late '70s or maybe the '80s, around the age of 18 to 20. Ethan said he vaguely remembered Scott's real first name as *Martin*. He also mentioned that some time ago he had contacted the archive department of the *Daily Mail* and had found additional stories on Scott and his trial.

Meanwhile, John Camp had invited Nathan and me to attend a fundraiser for O'Brien House, a local program that serves adult recovering alcoholics and drug addicts. The organization enjoys wide community support, particularly at its annual breakfast, which draws a large crowd. We were John's guests at his table, and I was seated next to Louisiana Public Broadcasting President Beth Courtney. At some point during breakfast, Beth turned to me and said, "Rannah, I have a question—who *is* Scott Rogers?" At that time, I was so jumpy over the information that had landed in my hands that I was hesitant to talk about anything to do with him, but I managed to reply, "I'm not sure, but I don't think anyone knows the answer to that yet."

Since Beth repeated the exact question asked of me by John Camp, I assumed he may have discussed it with her. Beth went on to tell me that she met Scott in the 1980s when he visited Baton Rouge with the late British actor John Inman, promoting the raunchy BBC comedy Inman starred in, *Are You Being Served?* The program enjoyed a successful run on Public Broadcasting in the U.S. after its popularity in the U.K., where it attracted audiences of up to 22 million viewers and earned Inman an award for "BBC Personality of the Year."

Inman's character on the program, the campy Mr. Humphries—along with his fame as one of Britain's most high-profile openly gay personalities—made him a gay cultural icon. While Inman was known for some of the show's funnier moments, however, gay rights advocates deplored his stereotypical portrayal of a limp-wristed gay man. Beth told me Scott Rogers came to Baton Rouge as a personal assistant traveling with Inman and later looked her up when he moved to Baton Rouge permanently and asked her if she would hire him to host a program on our local PBS station. She declined.

Ethan was surprised to learn of the Inman connection. "I would have thought he would have mentioned this," he said.

It wasn't until later that I learned many of the horrible details of Jake's attempts to flee Scott's abuse. Jake finally ran away from Scott's house on July 29, 1996. Exactly 17 years would pass before Ethan would send his email.

When he escaped to London, Jake planned carefully. He had run away twice before and had been returned to Scott. Once when Scott hit him so hard he broke his jaw, he asked his father to let him come home. But Scott had reached the father first, convincing him that Jake was having discipline problems and he should let Scott continue to work with the boy.

During one of the Academy's trips to Malaysia, Jake started to hang out with Eliza, who wasn't an Academy student but simply a girl Scott had persuaded to accompany the group to Penang for the show. Eliza and Paul, the student Scott had recruited to work in Malaysia, formed a friendship, so as she and Jake grew closer and began secretly dating, she let Paul in on their secret. Jake was unaware of the human trafficking Scott was involved with in Malaysia, but he was happy to spend time with Eliza to avoid Scott.

Paul was surprised at the budding romance, because he had believed that Jake and Natalie were the sweethearts of the

Academy. He began to realize, however, that the romance between the dance partners was just a fake fairy tale Scott made up to make the Academy sound more magical. Paul didn't know Eliza well at the time, and he always found Jake quite stoic, never tipping his hand. But Paul knew their romance wouldn't go over well with Scott.

After they all returned from Malaysia, Eliza and Paul stayed in contact, and one day she phoned him to say that Jake had turned up at her house. He had called to ask if he could see her, then told Scott he was taking the trash out, took the train to London, and appeared on her parents' doorstep.

Eliza told Paul that Jake was a mess. "Jake mustn't know that you know he's here," she explained, "because he is so scared that Scott will find him. You mustn't say anything."

Meanwhile, Scott was calling Paul in hysterics, saying, "Jake's gone missing! I don't know where he is. I'm really terrified."

"But I knew where he was, and that was a really difficult time for me," Paul told me.

Scott called Paul again, and asked him to come over to his house. When he got there, Scott was in distress. "He was again doing the whole fake crying thing," Paul said, describing it for me. "He kept saying, 'How can he do this to me?' Of course, now I realize that rather than actually caring about Jake, he was really worried that Jake would be out there exposing him for what he really was. "It was much more about protection for him than anything else.

"So I knew where Jake was, and that felt like a big secret for me to keep at the time," Paul said. "But I kept it."

Finally, after Jake had been at her house for a couple of weeks, Eliza told him she was talking to her friend Paul and had invited him to come for a visit. Paul took the train to London to see them.

"Jake was like I'd never seen him before," Paul said. "Jake was like who Jake is now. Such a different person, just a real person. And not this robotic creature that he was with Scott. So that was kind of special, to be involved in that. I felt privileged."

When Jake escaped, Scott sent the boys from the Academy to walk the streets of London looking for him. A distraught Scott, pretending to be a worried family member, went on radio and pleaded for anyone who knew where Jake was to call him. When Scott finally found that Jake was living and working in London, he would even send some of the Academy boys to threaten Jake if he didn't come back. As Jake began having some success in the West End theatre productions, Scott's minions would show up at stage doors to surprise him and let him know they could find him when they wanted. At the famous Pineapple Studios in London, dancers dropping in for classes and rehearsals would see, posted on the bulletin boards, desperate appeals for information about Jake's whereabouts. This harassment lasted for five years after Jake ran away, ending only after he hired an attorney to threaten legal action. Even then, Scott wrote long and twisted letters to Jake, insisting that he wanted only what was best for him. He even mailed him provocative photos of a teenage Kimmy wearing a swimsuit, ostensibly using her as bait to lure Jake home.

On August 28, 1996, Scott sent a handwritten letter to Jake at Eliza's home in London. It read:

> My dearest son Jake,
>
> I saw it raining today and worried about you as I knew you didn't have a coat, so I thought I'd send your Nike coat together with your faithful bum bag. I've also sent down a few little "bits"—new batteries for your shaver, some deodorant, your lucky Spiderman (hope it works) some menthols (as per our 5 things) telephone case (please use) and some change. I promise I won't call you all the time if it's on.
>
> I know things must feel very difficult at the moment for you, but don't feel sad inside. I have kept to all my promises—especially "I'll never ask of you or do anything to make you sad." I know I have to accept your

decisions—that's what we agreed. I want you to know I understand this but I also don't feel well at the moment. Please don't let "them" laugh at me anymore, don't let "them" into our world.

Would you call me to let me know you've got this—no questions asked or explanations needed anymore, just a "hello, how are you", etc. (I promise) That would mean a lot to me—I know we do miss each other.

Remember that Monday? I did exactly what I promised. I always will. Please don't forget everything—the future?

You are and will always be my 1st son and <u>best</u> friend— miss you. Speak to you soon.

Love you so much,
Dad

Scott's package was sent by registered mail to force Jake to sign for it and confirm his whereabouts. On Sunday, September 1, Scott found a package on his doorstep at 10 p.m. containing Jake's phone. He returned it to Scott because he knew it would be a way for Scott to track his movements.

This triggered Scott's anger and he sent a three-page handwritten reply to Jake on September 2 with a very different tone. The monster was awakened:

My dear son Jake,

What the hell are you doing? What are you letting them do? Last night I opened the door at 10:00 p.m. and found a NEXT bag with your phone in it together with the holder I sent on Thursday—why? I did exactly what you wanted—who did the dirty work, who convinced and planned with you, who took the great pleasure in secretly leaving it—no note, no nothing—how cruel. What have I done? I have kept to every promise. Your promises, even to Eliza are even more empty than those to me—they won't and can't last.

Why are you living off them, being controlled by them—you haven't even got the choice to call—this wasn't really your idea, they just got you to agree to it—<u>they</u> told you and convinced you. This phone (as with the CAT bag, your glasses, etc.) is <u>yours</u>!! They can't convince you otherwise—how much of a coward are you? You stay in someone else's place while they fill you full of shit against the one person who has always stood by you—me.

Up to now I have done it your way—did what you said, but now I don't care anymore or what anyone thinks. I will come down, I will go to Eliza's parents, Eliza and just tell them—I wanted to leave everything to you for you to do it your way (however long it took) but if they can control you into being so cruel and not even calling (as you promised) not even writing to each other (as promised) I've got nothing to love anymore.

You once said, "Without each other we're not complete." What's the point of me even looking to the future without a call? You could have your life there exactly as it is now with no interference—you could continue your life as it is. But whatever you <u>think</u> you've told them, however much they say they support you, if you can't give me <u>anything</u> then I have to come down to see them—I owe this to both of us.

I love you so much and I know you love me, but why allow them to shut us out—they have no right, neither do you. 12 years, Jake, 12 years. You haven't forgotten this least in your heart.

This phone is <u>yours</u>—keep your life there going, keep the things there the way they are but don't shut me out—I haven't done anything. Don't let them get you to do cruel things—fuck them—what about our love—it is still there. Please, even if it is for you—don't make me die and give everything up. You'll love Eliza, London, here, home, me. Just be kind—what's 2 minutes a day—I can't take this—in London you swore to God, to me, you'd not do this again. I'm expecting a call today—don't let me down. Don't ruin your life. I love you so much but you're killing me. I'd give everything up now.

Dx

P.S. I've included a letter I wrote last night. Please read it on your own—if you share any of this with anyone I will have to know that they have brainwashed you. Don't you remember anything.

Scott signed the letter "D" for Dad, with the "x" as a sign of affection. With the encouragement of Eliza's parents, Jake retained an attorney to write Scott and demand that the harassment stop. Scott's calls, letters and searches for Jake were incessant, filled with lies and focused solely on convincing him to return to Scott's house. But once Jake was free, he wasn't about to go back to a life of abuse.

On September 5, Scott sent a four-page single-spaced, typed letter in response to Jake's attorney that began, "We are appalled and horrified by the contents of your letter. Your comments are not only totally inaccurate and of a very slanderous nature, but lack, in the main, any foundation in the truth or in fact." In a rambling diatribe, Scott claimed the family was simply worried about Jake and believed he was being lied to by everyone except him. He used Kimmy and Natalie, referred to as Jake's "fiancée," to make tearful pleas for him to return to Scott's home. But Jake had finally escaped and he cut off all communication with anyone linked to Scott Rogers.

As Jake continued to get work in more major productions in London, two of his former Academy classmates, Gemma and another girl, went to see him in Starlight Express. The two girls, excited to see Jake in a major West End production, sent a note to him through the usher that they would like to say hello. They were disappointed not to hear back from him, not knowing what he had gone through to escape from Scott.

"We were upset, but he was obviously terrified," Gemma told me. "He couldn't risk ever talking to somebody.

"Jake was just the loveliest, most talented, and sweetest guy," she explained. "He'd already had a crappy time or he wouldn't have been fostering. He should have never ever been put into that situation."

Jake grew accustomed to former Academy students, acting on Scott's instructions, tricking him into giving information. He would bump into an old friend in London who would ask for his cell phone number to keep in touch, which Jake would gladly provide. The next day, he would receive another round of threatening calls from Scott, forcing him to change the number. Not talking to any former Academy students, regardless of how well meaning, became the safer course. Friendship just wasn't worth the risk.

In 1996 Scott placed an ad in *Stage Magazine* under the company name, "Seventh Sign Creative Arts Co.," looking for Jake. The fake ad, which claimed to have a job for Jake, was Scott's way of getting others to phone him, letting him know where Jake was. The ad read, "Seventh Sign Creative Arts Co. are urgently and still currently seeking a "Jake Scott-Rogers" for the forthcoming production and contracts. Characteristics: Excellent looks, Age 23, 5'11", Blue eyes, Short dark hair, Athletic build, Excellent dance abilities, Very talented with many previous professional engagements. Good reward if found." It included a telephone number with the word

"URGENT!" and at the bottom of the ad, a cryptic message: "We go together like carrots and peas, you can't have one without the other." *Creepy!*

The ad was placed by Diane Palladino, an American who listed her address as Scott's house on Fornham Road in Bury St. Edmunds.

By the late 1990s, Scott, Kimmy, and Mathew moved to Dallas to live with Diane. Various documents filed upon entry to the U.S. listed both Mathew and Kimmy as Scott's children. He arranged for his inner circle of Academy students, who had moved with him from Bury St. Edmunds to Gravesend in Kent, to shuttle back and forth to Dallas on 90-day visas. He had bought an old house in Gravesend and had them working to restore it so he could sell it at a profit. At any given time, some of the kids were in Dallas with Scott and some were in Gravesend working on the house.

While in Dallas, Scott was contacted again by Inman, who was enjoying a victory lap around America for his show's success. *Are You Being Served?* had ended in the U.K. over ten years earlier, but audiences of all ages were lining up to meet him in America, thanks to PBS stations still airing the program. Because only 60 episodes of the show were produced and some stations aired them five nights a week, American audiences were watching the same shows over and over.

Scott traveled to Baton Rouge to reconnect with Inman, with whom he had kept in touch. Stuart later recalled accompanying Scott to Inman's house for dinner when they were in London. While the openly gay Inman died without ever being accused of any involvement in the child sex abuse scandals that rocked the BBC, we will never know what he thought of the adult Academy principal accompanied by his young student to a social dinner. The BBC personalities who were later charged with child sex abuse were often accompanied by their young victims to elite parties and social outings, frequently mingling with England's ruling class.

Scott was finally ready to leave Dallas for a place where he could establish a home and live as a family with his inner circle, which included Kimmy, Angela, Mathew, Stuart, and a third young man. His destination wasn't the island he had dreamed of back at the Academy, but it was far enough away from any families who might interfere with him. So Scott packed up his peculiar family in a red Taurus and headed for Baton Rouge.

CHAPTER TWENTY-TWO

THE NEXT STEPS

Day 45
October 11, 2013

In my next email to Ethan, I asked whether he knew the whereabouts of Mandie, Scott's former wife, or the young boy who was the victim in the court case. Ethan remembered Mandie as a nice woman, but I told him we had trouble believing she did not know what was going on in her house. "Scott kept a lot from her, but you're right, she must have known something," Ethan conceded.

Former Academy students often described Mandie to me as "stoic."

"I don't know if she was privy to what went on back at the Academy," one student told me. "She tolerated Scott but she didn't respect him." Rumors circulated that Mandie was involved with one of the attorneys in Scott's court case, and Scott often told people that when Mandie began to openly invite men into their home, he decided to take Kimberly and build a new family for the two of them.

Mandie still teaches dance classes in Bury St. Edmunds, much to the disappointment of some of the Academy students who feel the courts should have held her, as well as Scott, responsible for the crimes children endured in her home. All of these former students agree, however, that Scott had great influence over Kimmy from the time she was born and that his treatment of Mandie resulted in Kimmy's also treating her badly. Once Scott and Kimmy moved to the United States, Scott's position to Kimmy and the others was that if Mandie loved Kimmy, she would have come with them.

Through our initial research, we found very little information on Jake, who still had not responded to Ethan's attempts at contact. Jake had gone on to success in London, but unlike most people in the performing arts, very few photos of him existed online.

By Friday, October 11, I let Ethan know that we felt ready for the next step toward informing the authorities in Louisiana of Scott Rogers' past. With Mary Jane on board, we had learned that Scott was a licensed foster parent with the State of Louisiana, which I explained to Ethan meant that he had a contract with the State to take children into his home and that the State paid him to provide temporary care.

"It appears that is how he was able to adopt the little boy," I explained to Ethan. People often keep foster children and eventually end up adopting them, should they become available. I explained that the application for a licensed foster home would ask whether the applicant had ever been arrested, charged, or convicted of any crime.

"Even an arrest without a conviction would require the applicant to provide an explanation of how the charges were resolved," I said. "We doubt that he answered that question honestly, but the State has maintained that his application is not a public record, so we have not been able to obtain a copy. If he did file a false document, that is a crime and, along with the background information you have provided us, we believe the State would have cause to open an investigation."

Mary Jane's notes:

Now I had a dilemma on my hands. I knew in my heart that Rogers would continue his conduct as a pedophile, and I knew that his son was coming of age when Rogers would probably start sexually abusing him. We suspected Rogers was already grooming him. Rannah and Nathan had asked me to help figure out what to do. Our only concern was to protect any child who was Rogers' potential victim. The State of Louisiana Child Services would offer no help.

Previously, on September 11, 2013, Baton Rouge Attorney Jim Boren and I had met in Lafayette at Assistant U.S. Attorney Luke Walker's office on another matter. Boren and I were on opposite sides of Luke Walker in Boren's case; we were adversarial. I was assisting Boren with the defense, and Walker was prosecuting.

We knew that Walker had successfully prosecuted an international child porn and sex abuse case. During our meeting with Walker, I commented how horrifying I found the facts I had just read in the newspaper and how shockingly young the victims. Those cases had resulted in sentences as high as life. That day, Walker showed Boren and me some of the pictures of the abusers. They looked to be straight from the movie **Deliverance**. The case had started in North Louisiana, where the Western District of Louisiana had jurisdiction, which is why Walker was involved.

What I learned was that for persons to join this child pornography ring, they had to commit a sexual act on a child, and that, first, the horrific nature of that sexual act and then, posting pictures of the act allowed them access to even more intensely graphic postings of criminal sexual acts on children.

Then, several weeks later, I sat in Baton Rouge Attorney Jim Boren's office, discussing the case I was working with him, the case that had brought us to Luke Walker's office that September 11. When Boren mentioned that Walker had, since our meeting, received a Department of Justice award for his outstanding work in the child porn and sex case we had discussed with him, the light went off in my brain. Bingo! Because that was an international case with ties all over the world, I knew I had found the one person who would at least listen to the Scott Rogers story, understand the situation, and offer, if nothing else, some advice and direction.

Little did I know how my meeting with Walker that September 11 would play into my first meeting with Rannah, which had taken place the evening of that same September 11. Serendipity. The moon and stars aligned. The oddity of my meeting with both Walker and Rannah on that same September day, and the later happenstance conversation with Jim Boren about Walker's award, gave me my direction. Sometimes luck is better than preparation.

While I suspected that Rogers had lied on his visa and citizenship applications, that was an immigration issue, and we were interested only in protecting any child now a victim. But for the federal government to enter any investigation, Rogers' actions must be a federal crime. At this time I believed the only federal crime was his false statement to Immigration to enter the United States. Whether that was enough for the feds was iffy. I did not know if anything else would surface. Still, I knew that even one lie could open the door for a federal investigation.

I also felt that Rogers' foster parent application to the State of Louisiana could qualify as a federal crime, especially if he had lied on the application, and used the mails to submit it. That, however, was a "could be" and not a definite, since the State of Louisiana Department of Child Services had refused to give me what I still believe is a public record.

Later on I discovered the element that absolutely made Scott's application a federal crime: To act as a foster and adoptive parent, he had lied about his past criminal arrest and prosecution. The feds therefore had jurisdiction because he was receiving federal money under false pretenses through the State because his adopted child was disabled. But we realized all of that much later.

I often come in contact with federal prosecutors in my work. Because I'm not an attorney, lawyers sometimes treat me like an outsider and a redheaded stepchild. Luke Walker is an exception. He and I met many years ago and developed a respect and liking for each other. Over the years, as Walker worked as an assistant United States attorney in Lafayette, Louisiana, he and I have had conversations about his grandfather, who came from Alexandria, Louisiana, where I grew up. Luke's grandfather and my dad were good friends, both businessmen in that small town and both about the same age. Morgan Walker, also a good friend of Camille Gravel, was one of our larger-than-life people in Alexandria, a man people admired. He owned Walker Dairies, one of Louisiana's larger dairies, as well as Continental Trailways, the bus company that moved people all over the South. The company's main terminal was two blocks from the house where I grew up.

Like me, Luke also had a very high regard for Camille Gravel, as did so many people in Louisiana.

I now felt I had someone who would give a shit. When you are looking for help in a case like this, you have to find that person who not only will listen, but who wants to do the right thing and can think outside the box.

I called him. His office is in Lafayette, where the Acadians landed and ultimately settled. Lafayette is where you find Cajun spicy food and crawfish, along with zydeco music. And you can still find French accents in many of the predominately Catholic residents. Lafayette is far enough away from the capital city of Baton Rouge, I thought, that Rogers should not have ties to law enforcement there, especially to any federal person. Besides, Walker, because of his background in child abuse cases, would have pegged Rogers immediately for what he was. I guessed that Luke Walker had never even heard of Scott Rogers, and I was right.

Luke answered my call. I told him some of the story and asked if he would meet with Rannah Gray and me about the possible sexual abuse of children. I also told him I thought the case could involve immigration fraud and possibly mail fraud in Rogers' obtaining custody of children. The question was: Where did any crime take place and was it ongoing? While the federal government would have jurisdiction over a false immigration application and mail fraud, the prosecution of any crimes would have to take place in the venue where the crimes occurred.

Rogers lived in Iberville Parish and worked in Baton Rouge—that is, in East Baton Rouge Parish. Both of those areas fell within the Middle District of Louisiana and not the Western District of Louisiana federal system where Walker lived and worked. But I knew that Rogers had lived in other places, and I knew that if Luke heard the story he would help get it to the right people if they were not in his office.

We later learned of the strong connections that Rogers had to various people in the Middle District Court system, including a federal judge and his family and at least one employee in the United States Attorney's Office. If the case had started there, we could have stepped into a big black hole.

Mary Jane had called to ask me if I would feel comfortable taking Ethan's information to an Assistant U.S. Attorney in Lafayette whom she knew, a man who specialized in prosecuting child sex offenders. I trusted Mary Jane's judgment and especially liked her suggestion of someone outside of the Baton Rouge law enforcement community, where Scott had so successfully built chummy relationships. "I like this a lot," I told her.

Then I told Ethan that Mary Jane had a preliminary conversation with an official who specializes in prosecuting sex offenders, a man we knew was receptive to helping. "The Assistant U.S. Attorney mentioned that because of the nature of 1stCo's work—web design and video production—it might also be involved in child pornography. I don't suppose you ever heard anything about videotaping children?" Ethan had not, but in the 20 years since Scott had lived in England, the Internet had changed the way video files are shared and transmitted, so we all agreed the possibility was worth considering.

To be sure we were going to the authorities with Ethan still feeling confident, I asked him, "Before I meet with the authorities, I need to ask if you are willing to speak with them by phone," I said. "I feel sure that will be the first question they ask."

We discussed how I might reach him during the interview if needed and how to confirm, on the phone, to whom they were speaking. Before we made any move, I always wanted to provide Ethan with as much information as possible so he would understand what was going on. I thought that surprising him in any way would be very unfair.

"The first place we are going will be to federal officials, so your conversation with them will be completely confidential," I assured him. "They never comment to anyone on their investigations. Since you first contacted me, a lot of work has gone into getting us to this place, and I feel we've come up with the best possible plan for moving forward. It's possible we will also give information to the news media later on, but we all feel that, because of how serious the situation appears, we must take the information first to the authorities.

"But now, I want to make sure that you and I are on the same page and that we move forward in a way you find comfortable," I told him. I reminded him that we had Nathan as a resource on legal questions, should he want to discuss anything.

Ethan's reply came immediately; he seemed assured that contacting the federal officials was the right step. "Great progress and a clear and sensible way of bringing this to people's attention," he said. "I believe we are on the same page, and I'm happy to assist with the appropriate authorities whenever you need me." Ethan again gave me his mobile phone number and the best hours U.K. time to reach him. "If possible, just give me a little time to prepare and make sure I'm not in meetings or driving," he said.

Just a few hours later, Ethan emailed again, saying he had finally reached Jake—the first time the two of them had spoken since Jake had run away from Scott's home in 1995. Ethan had been trying to get in touch with him, and Jake had not been responsive, so I think he stepped up his efforts, as we were preparing to meet with the authorities.

"He was very surprised and spooked that I had got hold of him," Ethan said. "He has had therapy, got married, and has two young children. Understandably, he does not want to go to the police, as he does not want the past brought up again, does not want it to affect his life and family. He expressed the pain, nightmares, and truly horrible ordeal he went through during his time as Scott's adopted son. He was in Scott's care for 13 years."

Thirteen years! I could not imagine the abuse Scott had inflicted that made Jake run away and work so hard to hide from him.

Ethan described Jake as still afraid of Scott and what he thought Scott could do to him. He said Jake was surprised to learn that Stuart and Mathew were still with Scott but said Scott uses them as a defense mechanism, a protection against any possible accusations. If anyone accuses Scott of doing something, he has two close eyewitnesses who can stand up and say, "No, that did not happen."

Ethan said Jake was also worried for him about his own involvement, explaining some of Scott's tactics to hurt those who can reveal the truth about him. He said Jake described the lengths Scott went when he ran away, trying repeatedly to get ahold of him, even going so far as to contact the parents of Jake's girlfriend to accuse Jake falsely of being HIV positive. In a futile attempt to get him to return, he would go to any extremes to break ties Jake developed with others. Jake worried that Rogers would even use Matt or Stuart to make up a story to get him in some sort of trouble, and warned Ethan that the same could happen to him.

Ethan said he explained to Jake about Baton Rouge, and the parallels with what Scott had done in Bury. He said Jake was interested in seeing the websites and photos of Scott that we had shared and was equally concerned that Scott had adopted a little boy.

Ethan explained how he had contacted me and where this had led us: taking the information to the authorities.

"After I put the phone down, I wrote Jake an email and explained that I was not willing to send over the articles and websites about Scott, as I think they would really affect him," Ethan went on to say. "I don't want to put him back in that place he has been fighting against all this time.

"Obviously, let's keep Jake out of this. He may have a change of heart about getting involved, depending on how this plays out. I'll wait to see how he reacts to the email I sent him. I mentioned the possibility of talking with you to strengthen the information about Scott; we will see." Ethan had a lot of compassion for Jake. Even though Jake was the older of the two, Ethan had assumed the role of protector. He believed Scott's abuse of Jake had been more violent than his abuse of the other students, and every step of the way in working to gather information, he treated Jake with kindness and respect. *As much as he wants Scott exposed, he's protecting Jake. He knows how hard this is.*

Later that day, Ethan sent me a link to information on the victim from Scott's trial. He had also heard back from Jake, indicating that should anything change and he could remain at arm's length, he might help.

"Keep this to yourself for now," Ethan said. "I have to keep Jake protected." Every time I was confronted with the reality of the damage Scott had done to innocent young boys, I was heartbroken. The death of innocence is almost as sad as the death of a friend. It's a loss that can never be recovered. After hearing how Scott's actions still affected a victim all these years later, I felt so completely helpless. Then I felt guilty for complaining about the damage Scott Rogers had done to my professional reputation, compared to the damage he had inflicted on these young men. Getting to know Ethan and Jake was a gift I never expected, a lesson in understanding how to keep life's complications in their proper perspective.

"This is so very sad," I told Ethan. "But I think it's a great breakthrough that you reconnected with Jake. I am speechless that he was in Scott's care for 13 years. I think you handled this reconnection very well and will likely be able to build some trust with Jake because of your considerate way of dealing with him. I think as long as we move forward together, respectful of the innocent, we can hopefully put information into the hands of someone we can all trust to protect children from such horrific abuse."

I told Ethan we would probably use the next week to get everything together and would try to meet with federal authorities the following week. "As you have probably heard, our federal government is shut down in some areas because of a fight over the budget between the President and the Congress, which affects whether some federal offices are open locally," I explained. "I think you did a really good thing reaching out to Jake."

I had no way of knowing how much of our government dysfunction Ethan was following in the U.K., but we were in the midst of a government shutdown from October 1 through 16, after failure by Congress to agree on a federal spending bill before the start of the government's fiscal year. Mary Jane initially had to call the Assistant U.S. Attorney on his cell phone, since his office was closed. Admitting that we couldn't really do anything because, nearly four years after signing it into law, we were still fighting passage of the Affordable Care Act— lovingly referred to by Congress as "Obamacare"—was nothing short of embarrassing.

How should I explain this to someone who has had universal healthcare coverage his entire life, coverage provided by the largest and oldest single-payer healthcare system in the world? Sometimes when you have to tell the world what our Congress is doing on any given day, the report doesn't sound so good.

Just as we had finally figured out what to do with our information on Scott, would our dysfunctional Congress keep us from getting help because the federal offices we desperately needed were closed?

CHAPTER TWENTY-THREE

THE DEPOSITIONS

Day 47
October 13, 2013

Ethan and I were sometimes in contact several times a day at this point. "Rannah, this may be worth looking into," he wrote shortly after we discussed Jake. "One thing that might be of interest is the fact that Scott has been sectioned twice for trying to take his own life and I'm pretty sure they don't let people who have attempted suicide become an American citizen." *Being sectioned* was the equivalent of confinement to a psychiatric hospital, usually against one's will.

"Also, Scott was arrested at a Texas airport around the time of the court case—the police only released him once they had confirmation from Stuart's parents that Scott had not abducted him."

Wow! This could be helpful information. I had no idea whether a person who had been involuntarily committed for mental health reasons could become a U.S. citizen, but he sure as hell had no business adopting a child without further review— or carrying a concealed weapon!

Though I also imagined that Scott must have been detained and not actually arrested at the airport, I noted that his behavior had at least made someone suspicious.

The day after Jake and Ethan first spoke, Ethan emailed me again to say, "Jake seems keen to help." I found it amazing that only 24 hours from an initial push back, Jake had found the strength to soldier on.

"He has a lot of info on gaps I couldn't fill in," Ethan said. "Scott's real name is Martin Rogers, his wife Mandie lives in Thetford near Bury. Jake also mentioned a couple of other boys I'm going to look into." Ethan knew Scott had sexually abused others, and we had urged him to contact any of them who might come forward.

After our call with Ethan, though Nathan thought he was a strong witness, two would be better. And once Ethan got a second victim of Scott's abuse to come forward, I knew Nathan would ask him to push for another one. Each victim would help make a case against Scott even stronger.

"Adrian Randall is now detective inspector for Suffolk Police," Ethan said, "He was the prosecuting officer during the court case. Shall I get his email address and phone number?"

None of us knew where this contact would go, but Ethan was always patient, addressing one lead at a time. This was another reason I think we communicated well: I like people who take calm, logical steps and don't panic.

"Randall's contact information would be very helpful," I replied. "We will follow up from here—just get what you can that will point us in the right direction without causing you a problem."

The weekend of October 12 and 13 was a busy one, with information flying between Ethan and me and my passing it along to Nathan and Mary Jane. Updating everyone was easier now that I could email Mary Jane, but I still had to call Nathan to report each development.

When Val and I were working with Stuart and Mathew on the Homeland Security project, they had put us on the list for weekly updates on *The Around Town TV Show*. I received an email announcing that the upcoming weekend's guests included Sheriff Sid Gautreaux. Even if people didn't watch the program, Scott made sure they knew which community leaders he had landed as guests. Then, Friday afternoon, Mary Jane let me know that she was getting copies of the depositions taken in the Baton Rouge civil case, The Silver Sun, L.L.C., versus Cheryl

Bryant and 1stCo, and would forward them to me as soon as they came in.

When I read Scott's and Mathew's depositions, I told Mary Jane, "Scott's deposition was similar to the one meeting I had with him—nothing makes sense." Every time the attorney asked a question, Scott stuttered and stammered his response. The case involved 1stCo's placement of Cheryl Bryant, under Scott's supervision, at The Silver Sun to handle bookkeeping for the small jewelry store. Bryant was convicted of felony theft, forgery, and unauthorized use of a credit card related to her work at the store. A judge sentenced her to serve six years in prison. Further, Mary Jane had found evidence of 13 arrest dates for her on other charges in the East Baton Rouge Clerk of Court's records.

When she read how Scott refused to answer questions about whether he had been arrested in the U.K., Mary Jane smelled a rat, confirming to her that something he didn't want to discuss had occurred there.

When attorney John London III, representing Cathy Griffin and The Silver Sun, took the deposition of Scott, both Mathew and Cheryl Bryant were present, along with Edwin Hightower, who represented 1stCo. The record showed the deposition got under way on the morning of August 11, 2005, at Hightower's office, with Scott stating his name as "Richard Scott-Rogers."

The interview soon dissolved into a puddle of contradictions, as Scott stalled and deflected questions by asking the attorney to repeat or explain further. Cathy Griffin later told me when they arrived for the depositions, Scott and Mathew greeted her cheerfully, despite the damage they had done to her business.

"What is your relation to 1stCo?" London asked.

"I work for it. I was one of the founders of it."

Next London asked, "When did you sever your relationship; you say you worked for it— you're not an owner or...."

"Well, one of the owners, yes," Scott stated.

"You consider yourself one of the owners now?" London asked.

"No," Scott replied.

And so it went. Getting a clear and concise answer from Scott was almost impossible. He stated that 1stCo had ten original founders, but when London pressed him for names, he could remember only himself, Mathew, and Stuart. Later he was able to add his daughter Kimberly as one of the founders, although she was only 14 at the time.

Just as he had in the meeting with JoAnne, he spoke of 1stCo as if he were not sure who the principals were. He acknowledged owning an early building that had served as the office for 1stCo but couldn't recall whether a written lease between him and the company existed. "I would assume it would be at 1stCo if there was a copy," he explained. When asked if he would have reflected rental income on his income tax returns, he replied, "I would assume so."

Under questioning, Scott indicated he had resigned as president of 1stCo around the time the lawsuit was filed, and Jason Sullivan and Mathew Hodgkinson had taken over the management. Scott continued the dance.

"What was your reason for resigning as an officer?" London asked.

"Because there were people better suited to take over," he replied.

"Who were those people better suited?" London asked.

"The people who took over," Scott answered.

In another convoluted ramble, though 1stCo was a Limited Liability Company and not a corporation, Scott explained that the company name was 1stCo, Inc.

"Do you know the difference between a corporation and an L.L.C.?" he was asked.

"Absolutely," Scott had responded.

"But you held yourself out as a corporation?" London asked.

Scott explained that 1stCo was a Delaware corporation and admitted he had not registered it to do business in Louisiana until after The Silver Sun had filed the lawsuit involving Cheryl Bryant. Then a similar meandering took place over who was responsible for the day-to-day decisions at 1stCo, since the lawsuit involved responsibility for Cheryl Bryant's work.

When asked about his highest level of education, Scott stated he had earned a master's degree in fine arts at The LaRache's Institute in London, although a school in England by that name does not appear to exist. When asked about undergraduate work, he also claimed the equivalent of a bachelor's degree from the British Association of Theatre Arts, which also does not seem to exist.

He claimed never to have lived anywhere in the U.S. other than Baton Rouge, failing to mention his time in Texas, where he had married and lived with Diane Palladino, the woman who went to Bury and helped him track down Jake, and then married Scott so he could bring his daughter and several young men to the U.S. And he stated that he had never had any business other than 1stCo.

London moved on, pointing out that while, during discovery, Rogers had objected to answering some questions, now, as he was a witness, London had the right to ask him those questions.

"Have you ever been convicted of any crime?" the attorney asked.

"No," Scott replied.

"Have you ever been charged with any crime?"

The record indicates that Scott didn't respond and his attorney Hightower objected. After a brief exchange about the issue of creditability, Hightower said, "If you want to limit it to the past ten years...."

But London cut him off. "No, sir. I want to ask him questions and I'll give the basis for leading to relevant evidence."

Hightower said, "I'm going to instruct my client not to answer anything beyond ten years."

London responded, "I'm attempting to resolve by this deposition the absolute non-answers of all these questions. I'm taking the position here that this is a meeting for us to determine when appropriate response to discovery will be submitted. The objections that you made in my position are groundless. I intend to file a Motion to Compel if I don't get final answers here. So, in the process, if you so instruct him, so much the better. But, again, he's a witness, his creditability is at issue. He's also said he's been the main manager of this company. The relevancy of this is that any illegal activity in the course of operating the company will be relevant in this proceeding. Secondly, any criminal activity goes to his basic creditability that—and I'm asking about *have you ever been arrested* for purposes of determining whether or not there's any convictions. I understand in court I can't talk about anything but convictions; however, this is a discovery deposition. It can reasonably lead. Evidence of criminal activity of any type can lead. That is the basis. If you're going to so instruct...."

Scott's lawyer dug in. "Not beyond 10 years; not beyond 10 years."

London insisted he would ask the questions and file the Motion to Compel and continued, "Mr. Scott-Rogers, have you ever been charged with any offenses in the last ten years?"

"No," Scott replied.

"Have you ever prior to this ten year period been charged with any offense?" London asked.

Hightower spoke up, "The same objection I raised before."

"So you're instructing him not to answer?" London asked.

"Yes," Hightower replied.

London returned to Scott. "Now, I'll ask you some specific questions. Have you ever been accused, Mr. Rogers—Scott-Rogers, excuse me, sir. Have you ever been accused of indecent behavior with juveniles?"

The record indicates Scott did not respond.

Hightower again spoke up, "Again, I don't see that this is relevant to any of these proceedings."

"I understand," London said, "but I still want to ask the questions."

Scott stated in the deposition that he and Mathew lived at the same street address, adding "Suite 1" for Mathew's address. He admitted loaning Cheryl Bryant money to pay Cathy Griffin back what she had stolen. He also acknowledged that he and Mathew had a joint checking account, then backtracked and indicated that while Mathew was a named party and a signatory, the account was Scott's personal checking account.

Scott insisted that any money he took from 1stCo was part of his salary package, which the shareholders of the company had approved. "It's that simple," he said ironically, since his answers were anything but simple.

"Do you have a written contract with 1stCo for your salary package?" London asked.

"No," Scott replied.

"Is there a resolution authorizing your salary package and defining it?" London tried.

"I don't recall," Scott answered.

After some other twists and turns, Scott said 1stCo provided a vehicle for his use, then said the vehicle was in his name. The two went round and round about 1stCo's providing Cheryl a car, even though she was a sub-consultant.

When London asked Scott whether he knew Cheryl had a criminal record, he answered *no*. "You were never aware of it?" London asked, and Scott again replied, "No."

Then London asked, "Have you ever had conversations with anyone indicating you were aware of her criminal record?"

"I'm sorry...you're—I'm getting confused," Scott stammered.

"I'm asking you, did you ever have conversations within the last four years...." London started again.

"Yes, within the last four years," Scott finally admitted.

"Did you have conversations three years ago with any individual discussing her criminal background?" London asked.

Scott: "Three years from now; so, in 2002?"

"In 2002?" London asked.

"No," Scott said.

"You never did?" London asked.

"No," Scott replied again.

"Did you ever indicate to anyone that you were aware of her criminal background and you were attempting to help her?" London asked.

"No," Scott replied again.

"You have never made that statement?" London asked.

"If we move back from three years, no," Scott said again.

"I'm saying, let's start since Cheryl became involved in the company in 2002..." London tried again.

"Right," Scott said.

"—have you ever made that statement to anyone?" London asked.

"Yes," Scott replied.

"And when did you make that statement?" London asked.

"In the last year," Scott finally answered.

This was typical of the circuitous way Scott answered questions throughout the deposition, making it difficult for the attorney to pin him down.

Scott stated that 1stCo had several divisions—1stCo Live that produced the TV show, 1stCo IT for information technology, 1stCo Web and Design, 1stCo Books, which he claimed had closed down, and 1stCo Business Development. He explained that Jason Sullivan, whose company, Guardian Networks, 1stCo had absorbed, served as president of 1stCo between 2003 and 2004 after Scott resigned that position.

After considerable wrangling, Scott admitted more about how Cheryl Bryant ended up working with Cathy Griffin at The Silver Sun. He claimed Cathy was a close friend whom he visited on a weekly basis when she confided personal information to him. He claimed to have helped her during a relationship break-up in which he felt she had sought revenge, claiming that was now the reason she was suing him.

According to Cathy Griffin, as her business grew, she sought recommendations for small business consultant services from the Baton Rouge Area Chamber, and 1stCo was recommended to her. Within six months of hiring Scott, her business was in trouble. She later returned to the Chamber and suggested that Scott Rogers should no longer be a member based on her experience with him, but her complaints fell on deaf ears.

The deposition ended two hours after it began, and the deposition of Mathew began, lasting only about fifteen minutes.

London asked Mathew how long he had known Scott, whether he had attended the Academy, and whether Scott had ever adopted him. Mathew said he was not aware of Scott's having adopted any children, having only Kimberly, his natural child. He claimed he occupied an apartment at Scott's house in St. Gabriel and paid Scott rent personally. Mathew had been in the room during Scott's deposition, so he agreed to everything Scott had explained.

John London clearly knew to question Scott about the incidents that occurred at the Academy in Bury St. Edmunds. After we received the depositions, Nathan called London to ask him about the case. London said soon after the depositions were taken, Scott settled the case with Cathy Griffin and required that the parties sign confidentiality agreements, so he wasn't able to discuss it.

Scott knew that his secrets were out in Baton Rouge and that others knew about his past.

Later, Nathan and I heard reports that Scott had sex with married men at the *Around Town Show* studio and arranged for other men to meet for sex there, too, especially those who did not want anyone to know they were gay. He was widening the circle of people who knew some of his secrets, though probably not the worst ones.

During this time, Scott trolled gay dating sites, posting under the screen name "Lestat," the blonde vampire featured prominently in Anne Rice's *Vampire Chronicles,* said to be among Scott's favorite books. Ironically, Lestat, "The Brat Prince," worked as an actor and musician, hated his father, adopted an orphan, and although he had relationships with both men and women, is best known for the obsession he felt for his male lovers. One man who met Scott Rogers on a gay dating site told me Scott never posted photos of himself online, and had agreed to meet him in person only after chatting online for several weeks. When they met at a local coffee shop, Scott described how hard it was for him to meet men for meaningful relationships and gave the man a copy of one of his books.

During this time, to arrange sexual liaisons, Scott used, online, photos of the younger men under his control. He was solely responsible for Mathew's and Stuart's H1-B non-immigrant status visas through 1stCo. His claim that they were in the U.S. because they worked in a specialty occupation put Scott Rogers in complete control of them. If they displeased him, he could easily dismiss them and send them back to England, which is exactly what happened to one former student who had accompanied the so-called family to the United States.

Upon his discovery of the young man—soon after the group's Baton Rouge arrival— having sex with a neighbor, Scott immediately shipped him back to the U.K. and banished him from their lives. In the Scott Rogers household, daughter Kimberly was the only one he allowed to date.

Scott was playing a high-stakes game and he loved to gamble, but he knew he must maintain tight control to secure the silence of those close to him. His deposition gave a glimpse behind the curtain at the mysteries Scott held close, the trust he had in Mathew, and the power he held over him. But more important, it blew open the door to reveal secrets he was desperate to keep—secrets about his indecent behavior with juveniles, his adopting children, and his relationship with Mathew. Scott moved quickly and decisively to close that door and seal away the dark secrets, but was it too late? Had someone in Baton Rouge discovered he was a child predator? How much did they know?

CHAPTER TWENTY-FOUR

THE BEGINNING

We now knew from the depositions that someone in Baton Rouge had discovered what had happened in Bury St. Edmunds, but we didn't know how that person had obtained the information or how many others knew. Meantime, Ethan had mentioned a detailed news story he had finally located after a long search through newspaper archives. It shed new light on the life of Scott Rogers.

From another piece for the *Daily Mail* by Greg Hadfield, we learned about a young woman named Lisa Barney who had attended the Academy of Dance and Performing Arts when Scott was its principal. The article compared the Academy, whose slogan was "Follow Your Dreams," to the 1980s TV show "Fame." But Hadfield reported that under the "malignant influence" of Richard Scott Rogers, "Lisa ran away from home and was on the brink of accusing her parents Roy and Kathryn of sexual abuse." I noticed in this news story, Scott's name was not hyphenated, indicating his surname was "Rogers" and not "Scott-Rogers" as he sometimes claimed.

At the time the article appeared, Lisa was back home and talking about "the effect the Academy's intensive training and the personality cult of Scott Rogers had on her." Her story and others had forced the Suffolk County Council to act, issuing its statement warning parents not to send their children to the Academy, citing its "unhealthy atmosphere" and "levels of intimacy" between an unnamed staff member and pupils.

The article stated, "The story of Richard Scott Rogers and his dance academy is an all-too-modern tale—of celebrity-obsessed teenagers who would abandon their parents for a man who seemed to promise fame; of indulgent middle-class parents who were prepared to spend large amounts of money on their children and of an evil man who exploited the children in his care to bolster his own ego, and exploited child protection laws."[25]

There was that word again—*evil*.

Hadfield did not hold back. He described the Academy as "a forbidding red brick Victorian edifice, beside a used-car yard and behind Bury St. Edmunds railway station." Hardly a glamorous description, but he noted that to the students, the place was "infused with the untouchable glamour of the stage—even though no pupil had yet gone on to stardom."

Hadfield claimed Scott Rogers persuaded students "to use the very sex abuse laws designed to protect minors—against their own parents." He described Rogers as a "petulant Peter Pan" with "more than a working knowledge of the law" and revealed how Scott had adopted or pretended to adopt his charges.

The article read, "In 1987, he won joint custody of a pupil, Jake, then 14, after relaying unproven allegations against his mother to her ex-husband. Jake changed his name by deed poll to Scott-Rogers, but his heartbroken mother has no knowledge of him being formally adopted. She only learned of the claim in a newspaper announcement of his engagement to fellow pupil Natalie," whom the article described as his dance partner.

"Such adoption claims, by falsely implying Scott Rogers had been vetted by social workers, reassured parents, who allowed their children to attend lessons at weekends and late into the evening as well as residential summer schools."[26]

The article stated that the Appeal Court had upheld Scott's request that the trial's sordid details remain secret.

---

[25] "Fame school cult warning." Greg Hadfield. Daily Mail. Associated Newspapers Limited. 11 November 1995.
[26] Ibid.

It further expressed, "Few will be surprised to learn that Richard Scott Rogers (who changed his name from Martin) did not have a stable childhood." His parents' first baby died at 12 weeks. Scott was born on February 18, 1962, to Patricia Maureen Woodward Rogers and Graham Trevor Rogers at Ronkswood Hospital in Worcester. He was named *Martin Rogers* at birth and had an older brother named Spencer. His parents split up when Scott was just 18 months, and his mother left the two boys with their father. When Scott was age nine, his father remarried; and at 15, he accused Graham Rogers, then a social worker and mental health officer, of assault, a charge his father strongly denied. Throughout his life, Scott described his childhood as very abusive, claiming that his father both physically and verbally abused him. At age 16, he left home to live with a group of American Mormons.

Scott's father described him to Hadfield as someone who "wouldn't accept responsibility for anything. His perception was that everything that was happening to him was somebody else's fault." His father did not blame the Mormons, but "pleaded in vain with his son to detach himself from the group—just as later, parents were to plead with him for their children."

Scott would tell others that he searched for his mother when he was 17; when he found her, she was living with a man and expressed no interest in reuniting with her children. It was not the first time he would accuse a mother of abandoning her child.

In November 1981, Scott married Mandie Dobson, a dance teacher, and began putting the plan for the dance and performing arts school in place.

The *Daily Mail* article reported that in 1983, "the Academy began life with half a dozen children in the Suffolk village of Hopton. Stage schools were mushrooming around the country and the Academy soon became a large-scale business with a good reputation—until now, when the claims of parents with children at the school can finally be brought to light."

Hadfield reported parents saying Scott Rogers "would regularly invite his favoured pupils to 'slumber parties' and spend the night with them, cuddling them in their sleeping bags or under the duvet. He delighted in children stroking his hair.

Sometimes they would massage his body. He required obsessive devotion from his pupils and encouraged them to tell him their secrets."

Lisa Barney told Hadfield, "Children would tell him if their parents were splitting up. I always felt obliged to have some problem for him to grasp at because then he would feel I trusted him."[27]

The article described students working hard to gain status as one of Scott's "chosen pupils"—those who received the coveted Russian wedding rings. "Only they could join his personal development classes," Hadfield wrote. He described pupils in attendance at the Academy for up to 20 hours a week, arriving at 6:30 a.m. and returning after school; further, "From 8:30 a.m. until 6 p.m., weekends were devoted to the Academy." Some reported that students in the personal development classes often left at the end of the session in tears.

Lisa described how Scott coached the students in their acting classes on how to manipulate their parents. When her father objected to the sleepover parties, Scott coached her how to respond. "We were taught in drama lessons how to cry by thinking of something sad. Scott told me to go home, sit on the settee and talk to my parents. When they said I couldn't go, I had to curl my legs up and stare blankly at the wall, rock slightly and cry," she was reported as saying.

"Unsurprisingly, the Barneys gave in and allowed Lisa to attend as many classes as she wished," Hadfield reported.

"There was always a feeling that if you didn't do these extra classes you wouldn't be one of Scott's favorites and our aim was always to be one of his favorites," Lisa said in the article.

Hadfield describes an incident when Lisa ran away from home and her worried father called Mandie Rogers, who denied that Lisa was at her house. The father asked her to call him if Lisa appeared; about an hour later he received a call from Mandie. "Later Lisa told me she had been at the house when Roy first called," Mrs. Barney reported. "She told us that Scott had said he could ring social services and say she was being abused

---

[27] Ibid.

but that she would have to stick to the story." When Lisa refused to do that, her parents received the call asking them to pick her up at the Rogers' house, the article reported. This was the first evidence I had seen that Mandie Rogers participated in Scott's criminal conduct. So far, she had been described as a poor suffering wife whose evil husband had pulled the wool over her eyes. Maybe she was that, too, but I found it hard to believe that as an adult and a mother, she had lied to Lisa's distraught parents.

The *Daily Mail* article also detailed a story about a desperate couple whose 13-year-old son was lost to the Academy, noting that for legal reasons, they could not disclose his real name. The article refers to him as "David Brown," but Ethan told me the story was Mathew Hodgkinson's. The *Daily Mail* article describes David as a "bright and personable boy" who appeared in a show at the Theatre Royal in Bury St. Edmunds where he caught Scott's eye. "Mr. Scott Rogers had told him he was 'really good' and 'had talent.' Why not come to the grandly-titled Academy of Dance and Performing Arts?" Hadfield wrote.

The Browns were described as "professional, intelligent parents" who had fostered children themselves "with the wholehearted approval of Suffolk social services and knew the damage a dysfunctional atmosphere can cause a child. But even they were taken in by the Academy's air of respectability."

Soon, the Browns' lives would change forever.

Hadfield reported, "Every time the Browns tried to have family weekends away, they would be told that David had to attend rehearsals and auditions. Slowly the family was being pushed apart.

"The turning point came when the Browns decided to move abroad," the article reported. "David, still not yet a teenager, was reluctant to go. He warned he would run away if they insisted on taking him with them. Trying to do their best for David, the Browns decided he should remain at the Academy, staying in Scott Rogers's house and attending a local secondary school.

"David joined his parents for the first fortnight abroad," Hadfield wrote. "They still hoped he would agree to stay. But Scott Rogers telephones and said he would visit on his return from America and accompany David back on the plane to London. The Browns now believe this was a ruse to ensure he did not change his mind and stay.

"During his brief visit, Scott Rogers slept in the same room as David," Hadfield continued. "During the night the door was jammed shut with a chair. Glibly, Scott Rogers explained that he was anxious about the dark, a vestige of his childhood experiences at the hands of a 'violent' father. The Browns believed him."

In April 1992, Scott was arrested for the alleged sexual offenses against a young boy. The article describes the Browns as distraught, flying back to Britain where police showed them letters their son had written to Scott addressed, "Dear Dad." Hadfield reported the letters "begged forgiveness, apparently for being jealous of the attention the teacher was paying to another teenage boy.

"The Browns decided to take David back home," the article continued. "While on bail, Scott Rogers (and his young staff, often unpaid former pupils) repeatedly telephoned the Browns, asking for David. Scott Rogers sent presents and money, ignoring requests not to pester the family. Letters to David arrived from pupils at the Academy, many identical, others written in code.

"On one occasion, 17 arrived together. They included one from a girl pupil, also a member of the Scott Rogers 'inner circle.' She talked of mass suicide, enabling all the children to go to 'the island' they had been told about at school.

"The constant harassment had its effect. David began making secret calls. His behavior worsened after each call but he continued to ring, sometimes late into the night. The stress took its toll and Mr. Brown suffered a suspected heart attack.

"But even that failed to modify David's behavior. In June 1993 the Browns were stunned to receive a phone call from David, saying he was in Britain and was staying there. He claimed to have travelled using his cousin's passport because his parents had hidden his own. To prevent them from following him, he had stolen their passports."

The *Daily Mail* reported that a witness later came forward to give evidence that Scott had engineered David's "escape" from his parents.

"The Browns did all they could to rescue their son," Hadfield continued. "They made David a ward of court, withdrew him from the Academy and took out an injunction preventing Scott Rogers from further contact. It was to no avail. When a witness claimed to have seen Scott Rogers and David together, there were plenty of people from the Academy ready to say the witness was mistaken. Meanwhile, David began a long legal battle with his parents to have the injunction lifted. He claimed, among other things, to have been assaulted by his father with a hairdryer, saying he had the facial bruises—and a doctor's report—to prove it.

"Later, the Browns were told of an Academy pupil who had heard telephone instructions given to David before the alleged assault. The instructions were about how to bruise himself— using a hairdryer."

After a three-year legal battle, David won the right to live with Scott Rogers. During that time, he had attempted suicide while living with another family. His determination to join Scott was clear to his family. Also living in the house were at least three other pupils, Mandie Rogers, who was divorced from Scott, and their 10-year-old daughter Kimberly.

The *Daily Mail* reported that a High Court judge reluctantly lifted the restraining order that prevented Scott Rogers from seeing David, and commented on the case. Scott, however, appealed and had the contents of the judge's order sealed.

"A support group of 18 families—including four who have 'lost' their children to the school—were furious that the public was still not allowed to know the full extent of the damage Scott Rogers has done," Hadfield wrote. Several schools banned the Academy from using their premises, "But it has all come too late for David Brown.

"The Browns still hope that one day David will come back," Hadfield wrote. "'We just want our son to know we still love him and will always be here for him.'

"But the omens are not good. Scott Rogers's house is cold and dark. Rumour has it that he has left for a new life in America—and that he has taken some of his 'pupils' with him."[28]

The *Daily Mail* article concluded with a helpline number for parents who feared problems at the Academy or wished to remove their children.

The article provided another piece of evidence that Scott was someone to fear. He had torn families apart in England, even his own. And if David Brown's story was Mathew Hodgkinson's, as Ethan told me, I began to understand how easily Scott could get Mathew to lie about us. He had complete control over him. The courts and his parents had been forced to let go of Mathew and allow him to live with Scott out of fear that he would kill himself. *My, God, Mathew would rather die than live without Scott! What kind of hold does he have on him?* I wondered.

If families were powerless against Scott when their own children were at stake, what hope could we have to stop him?

---

[28] Ibid.

CHAPTER TWENTY-FIVE

THE INSPECTOR

DAY 52
October 18, 2013

We heard through the grapevine that some of the information in the lawsuit involving The Silver Sun had come from a very detailed newspaper article about Scott in Texas. No one was able to produce it, however, and I asked Ethan again if he knew anything. Stuart had once joked that they had lived in Texas for only a short time and had left rather quickly. Nathan's private investigator had found "Seventh Sign" references along with Scott's name in Plano and in Irving, Texas, but they led nowhere.

I didn't know at the time that Cathy Griffin had found an article on the Internet about Scott's arrest, had printed it and taken it to her attorney. When her attorney asked her to look further, she tried to find the article again, but it never showed up again in her searches. But that one article had led Scott to settle his case with her quickly. "You could have been me," I told her later. "If news of your lawsuit had appeared in the paper, one of his victims could have contacted you."

Now that Jake was talking to Ethan, however, we had a new source for background information. We knew that anything that had happened in Texas could help our investigation here.

"It was Dallas, Texas," Ethan said. "He did a workshop at a high school there. The woman he met there over the Internet was called Diane Palladino. She worked for Microsoft in Dallas at the time, it was right in the beginning of the Internet and chat rooms. Maybe she went to the press. She came to the U.K., I remember meeting her. It was one of the last times I saw him so around '95."

Nathan always raised the question of Texas in every conversation we had, and we all agreed that something had happened there that had led Scott to move his entourage to Baton Rouge. Our learning what that was, however, seemed unlikely.

By Friday, October 18, Nathan had a phone conversation with Adrian Randall of the Suffolk Police who had been a detective on the case that led to Scott's trial. He told Nathan he remembered the case vividly, and off the top of his head, without looking at notes, guessed that it had been tried at least 18 years ago or longer. He recalled that the *Bury Press* covered the trial daily, and he remembered Mathew's mother, Mrs. Hodgkinson, recalling her name instantly. Nathan told Randall that Mathew was now living in Baton Rouge with Scott and using the name *Hodgkins*. He explained that someone in the U.K. had contacted us about Scott, but did not reveal Ethan's name.

When Nathan asked Randall if he recalled interviewing others for the trial, he answered that the police had conducted extensive interviews, but that people were hesitant to put their children through the ordeal of testifying, so at that time they had only one victim willing to come forward. Nathan told him we were in touch with a victim who had in turn identified another, but he did not know if either would talk to Randall.

As Nathan described Scott's behavior in Baton Rouge, Randall noted he was following the same path he had in Bury St. Edmunds—attaching himself to public and law enforcement officials. Randall described Scott as clever and hard to pin down.

Nathan told him about Scott's adoption of a young son here and said we were worried about the boy's safety. "Should we be concerned?" Nathan asked.

Randall replied, "Mr. Fisher, a leopard never changes its spots."

In repeating Randall's comment, Nathan always did so in his best imitation British accent, and we all imagined Adrian

Randall as a modern-day Sherlock Holmes, maybe because we wanted him to prove as brilliant.

Nathan explained that we were trying to obtain official documents we thought would show Scott had filed false statements in Baton Rouge, both to become a U.S. citizen and to adopt a young boy from the custody of the State. Randall agreed that our plan was a good one.

When Nathan asked the detective if he would speak with the U.S. officials when we brought them our information, he said he would, as long as we went through the proper channels.

I reported this conversation to Ethan, assuring him that everyone knew we were still protecting his identity. I wanted to verify that he was comfortable with our plan, and whether he would talk to Randall, should we ask. I knew that last request was getting very close to home for him.

"Thanks, Rannah, for the detail, that's great," Ethan replied. "It's also good to know I can trust you. I think Randall gave you plenty of info, which is encouraging. His response sounds good for the future. I'm taking this one day at a time. I'm happy to assist and I think when you need me to cross certain bridges just ask and I will muster up as much strength as possible to help."

Every time the investigation took another step forward, I was reminded how difficult this process was for the victims, especially Ethan. I admired his candor, and while he occasionally revealed a slight bit of uncertainty, he always promised to do whatever he could to prevent the abuse of another child. He worried about the relationships Scott had built with local law enforcement in Baton Rouge and feared an outcome similar to Bury's, should we confront him.

"Do you think the authorities will act properly once they have all the info?" he asked. "What is your view on how they will react once they see the history of what Scott is? When are you expecting to make the next step?"

The Boys of Bury

STUART *in his own words*

Bury St. Edmunds, England
2014

Scott was never able to be honest about having done what he did to me when I was 12 years old. I was able to bring it up to him maybe two or three times. He blew it off on every occasion. Until he could at least say the words, this was not done in my mind.

So that left open the possibility that he might do it again....

CHAPTER TWENTY-SIX

THE LOCAL OFFICIALS

I understood Ethan's concerns. Both he and Jake had families to protect, and he knew Jake was not ready to come forward with him.

"That's a courageous and appropriate answer, which I completely understand," I told him. I appreciated that he had said *when I needed him*, just ask. That was the key: Don't get ahead of ourselves, take one day at a time, and ask him to come forward when we needed him. That worked fine for me, because I too preferred caution. The more I learned about Scott Rogers, the more dangerous I believed him to be. We still had no idea where our concern for a child would lead.

But as it turned out, Ethan didn't have to wait long to learn our next steps.

"The next step is happening now," I told him. Nathan had decided it was time to inform Baton Rouge District Attorney Hillar Moore, as a courtesy, that we were taking information we had received on Scott Rogers to the federal authorities. We knew that D.A. Moore could prosecute a crime if we could prove that Scott had committed one within his jurisdiction; we had made the decision, however, to take Ethan's information to Luke Walker. Nathan did not feel I needed to attend this meeting with the D.A., and I was glad not to go. This case was getting very serious, and I was so appreciative that Nathan was willing to have those conversations.

And now Nathan had thoroughly briefed Mary Jane and she provided great backup for him. I smiled, thinking of Ethan's comment about our "team." We did have a team and when you stepped back and looked, it was a damn good one. To me, Nathan and Mary Jane were friends who happened to be very good in their professions. But in truth, we had a dream team.

"They will not leave any materials with the District Attorney other than possibly newspaper articles," I assured Ethan. "Federal law enforcement officials will have more resources, more international access, and any relationship Scott may have fostered with local officials will not affect them. Mary Jane has briefed the U.S. Attorney's Office on what we are coming to meet about and they are very interested in helping. I should have another report for you later this evening. I promise you, we will be with you every step of the way."

"That is great. I'm a little emotional. ;) Good luck. I look forward to the updates," Ethan replied.

There it was again. This young man was in the prime of his life, conquering professional goals without hesitation, and yet his abuser could still conjure up in him a level of anxiety that was painful to hear.

"I understand," I replied. "You're doing something really hard, but also very, very brave. Not many people could do it. I'm nervous, too, but you have our full support. I'm just trying to get the full force of the United States Government behind you, too! More later...."

Ethan replied with an email flagged for my immediate attention. "When and if the authorities ask the boy if he has been interfered with, it may be useful to know that Scott in the past used the following technique: 'It's your fault, you have made me do this to you, if you tell anyone you will go to prison.' Scott has been described as a 'super predatory pedophile' by psychiatrists of one of his victims...I know it's horrible but may be of some use," he said. *Jake must have shared this with him! What an awful memory to relive. It's true—Scott is a monster.*

Ethan's search for peace left me feeling incredibly helpless. Sexual abuse of children was not a subject I knew much about, and I didn't know what to say other than to assure him of our support. I had no idea what the authorities would say—no clue what anyone could do legally.

Nathan had confidence in Sue Bernie's opinion that Scott was a pedophile who would still be abusing children. Now it was time to inform her boss.

Mary Jane's notes:

We now had a person who was interested in the case and in a position to do something to help us. But still we had no idea if our investigation would lead anywhere. Nathan, Rannah, and I, however, decided to put the powers in Baton Rouge law enforcement on notice, as a courtesy. We did not want to blind-side anyone, should the case move forward. Nathan and I visited District Attorney Hillar Moore.

Gone was the pink carpet from 25 years ago that D.A. Ossie Brown had installed. D.A. Moore's office was now tastefully carpeted in a dark blue, and filling the walls were many sports pictures, including lots of LSU memorabilia. Moore had started as an investigator in Ossie Brown's office, before attending law school and practicing criminal defense law.

Six years earlier, he decided to go back to the prosecution side and run for District Attorney. He won easily and is now one of the most effective and respected D.A.s Baton Rouge has seen. As he is very hands-on in his job, you often see him on television at a crime scene, after hours and on the weekends and holidays.

Nathan and I explained to the D.A. that our visit was a courtesy call to let him know what was going on with Scott Rogers. Moore's concern was the embarrassment Rogers was going to create for a lot of public officials. And he was one of those public officials. D.A. Moore told us that he went to monthly meetings of the Better Business Bureau at Scott Rogers' home and wanted to warn the BBB about him. We learned from Moore for the first time that two children were living in the Rogers house. He also described the two men who lived in the house,

Mathew Hodgkinson and Stuart Poulton, as "house boys" as far as he knew, since they served meals during the BBB luncheons.

Nathan and Mary Jane called later to tell me about the meeting with District Attorney Moore, and I relayed the information to Ethan. Their most disturbing news was that not one, but two young boys, the adopted son and a toddler, were living with Rogers. The D.A. had seen them both when he attended a Better Business Bureau luncheon at Scott's home. He also worried about the business organization continuing to work so closely with Scott if the information Nathan and Mary Jane had given him was true.

I explained to Ethan that our D.A. prosecutes crimes in East Baton Rouge Parish, but that Scott lived in the neighboring parish of Iberville. Because he had secured the adoption and the foster home license through the State of Louisiana, however, and the State Capitol is located in Baton Rouge, Moore would have jurisdiction over those matters, so keeping him in the loop was important.

"We have identified the U.S. Attorney we want to give the information to and he is an expert in this type of crime," I told Ethan. "We have requested a meeting with him next week and are waiting to find out when he can see us."

Nathan had called several civil attorneys to discuss whether Ethan might have a civil claim for damages, something he and Mary Jane had kicked around after our conference call at my house. If Ethan wanted to warn the public about Scott, that was definitely one way to do it: to spell out the details of Scott's record of abuse in a civil suit. But I wasn't sure Ethan was ready for that.

"As this moves forward, you will have options to consider," I explained to him. "As I understand it, there is no statute of limitations on sex crimes in the U.K., so it is possible you and others could file criminal charges against him there. In the U.S., they will look into his filing of false documents, the welfare of the children, etc. If they find abuse of the children, those are serious crimes. In the U.S., we think you could also file a civil suit seeking monetary damages. We've spoken to one attorney who said you would have standing to file here since it is the place of domicile of the defendant (Scott). We have no idea what his finances are, and he has surely moved to put things in other people's names, but a civil suit would spell out everything he has done and would be a public document, available to the press, which would expose him and his crimes. Those are all bridges to cross down the road, but I prefer to give you time to think about the options you may face or want to explore further. For now, we are concentrating on whether he has committed any crimes in the U.S."

After I sent Ethan a lengthy report on the meeting with the D.A., he characteristically focused on the one subject that always concerned him the most. "It's horrifying that there are two children living with him," he replied. "He will have started abusing them, I have no doubt. Thanks for the update and all the effort you are putting in. I hope he is exposed sooner rather than later. This is what he does, surrounds himself with authority in case anything happens. It's so sad."

I learned over the year of communicating with Ethan that if a report mentioned the children, they were always his first concern, regardless of what else was going on in the investigation. He assured us he had dealt with the demons, but as a young father, the notion of Scott's adopting two more young boys must summon all of Ethan's fears again.

Then Ethan asked the question we were all contemplating: "Do you think he is too well connected to expose?" *God, I hope not,* I thought.

By Saturday, October 19, Ethan had briefed Jake on the meeting, and their concern for the two young children living with Scott Rogers was causing them a great deal of apprehension. I could tell my report on Nathan and Mary Jane's meeting with the District Attorney was again calling up the horrific reminders of Scott's sexual abuse. I awoke that morning to new anxiety about the children from Ethan and Jake.

"I have been speaking with Jake about the update, we are both really concerned about the two kids," Ethan wrote. "When we were being abused, he used the technique I mentioned along with trying to persuade us that we were gay and it was our fault. Those kids will be frightened, lost, alone and confused. Scott would have 'brainwashed' them." *Ethan and Jake would know!*

Ethan's words carried tremendous weight. Who better to understand the children's vulnerability than someone who had been in their shoes?

"As you know, he has set up exactly the same model in Baton Rouge, this time it's worse as he has the police coming round his house for tea and cake!"

As awful as that sounded, I couldn't help but smile because he was right. A constant parade of law enforcement officials in and out of a house, where a man whom professionals have identified as a predatory pedophile is living with two unrelated adult males and two male children—it sounds almost too absurd to be true. But that was exactly what was happening, and the man at the center was obviously and openly manipulating everyone he had worked so hard to influence and keep in his orbit.

"I only hope the authorities can see what he is and what he is doing, with the articles we have sent," Ethan wrote. "He is doing the abuse under their noses, he is trying to build an airtight defense so no one can get at him. This is what he does, he is very experienced in this, he knows exactly what he is doing. Jake has suggested that he may frame Mathew or Stuart in some way to protect himself! He is a very, very manipulative pedophile predator who will get away with this. He will stop at nothing to carry on what he is doing. Remember Jake and I were too scared, brainwashed to say anything, until years after! I know you know all this but I just want to make sure when we approach the authorities they act with extreme care and caution. He must be stopped."

All I could think of when reading Ethan's email was how traumatic for him and Jake to hear from me that two little boys were living with Scott in Baton Rouge. I was beginning to realize that the beatings and sexual abuse were much worse for Jake, lasting 13 years and involving violent and repeated rape. Now that 20 years later Ethan and Jake had an opportunity to talk, I got the feeling they were even more aware of the danger surrounding the two young boys in Scott's control.

Ethan was always very appreciative of my time and thoughtful in acknowledging Nathan's and Mary Jane's help. We had picked up his use of the word "team" and used it jokingly, as I had managed to pull in two people with much more experience in criminal matters than I had.

Nathan's primary role at this point was advising me not to mis-step and get myself into trouble. When he had first asked me to talk to Mary Jane, he suggested I hire her to pull together enough legal research to determine if he could find any charges to refer to the authorities. I had agreed because Ethan's description of Scott's abuse of the young boys in Bury was so shocking, but I hadn't really considered how far this investigation might go or how much I might have to spend.

Soon after our first meeting, I told Mary Jane I would hire her to conduct some preliminary research to see if we had something to take to the authorities. Nathan and I both seem to get ourselves involved in causes that require a lot of time, but I couldn't ask Mary Jane to work without pay on a case just because we believed in it. I would get her started and see where it led before deciding how far I would go with Ethan's allegations.

"I'm not going to charge you anything," Mary Jane had quickly replied. "You didn't go looking for this. It was dropped in your lap, and if what this guy is saying is true, we have to do something about it." *What a good person! I'm so glad Nathan suggested talking to her.*

During our first call with Ethan, our "team" of four surprised him a little. I had decided, however, that we would not treat a child in danger as something we could sit around and discuss over a glass of wine—then go about our lives because the problem wasn't ours. We were about to take a big step by going to the U.S. Attorney, and I was thinking about that step every day. I knew plenty of people thought I should drop my examination of Rogers' behavior. But that just didn't feel right to me. If I were going to a U.S. Attorney, I wanted to present Ethan's concerns with as much backup as possible.

I could not understand the depravity necessary to sexually abuse a child. The horror of the countless Catholic priest abuse scandals made me angry at the Catholic Church for its cover-ups. Raised as an Episcopalian, I didn't have my Catholic friends' fear of and blind faith in priests. I understand the subject is uncomfortable, but I've always felt those who turn a blind eye to child sex abuse are as guilty as the abusers, for they enable them to continue their crimes.

The question for me was, *What if you have an opportunity to stop the sexual abuse of a child—would you take it? Or would you be too afraid the subject matter is too ugly, too unpleasant for your association with it? Would you just leave something this horrible for someone else to face? What if everyone did that? What if no one helped them?*

I couldn't be the person who looked away, and neither could Nathan and Mary Jane.

I thought Ethan was incredibly brave, after all these years, to go on this journey to end Scott's abuse. And if at times the journey was difficult for him, as I knew it was, we would just have to stand with him and give him the strength and support he needed to go forward. *We've got your back, Ethan. Just stay strong.*

Who could blame him for his concern about our law enforcement officials? Scott had managed to build the same relationships in Baton Rouge that had helped him escape conviction in the U.K.

"I completely understand your worries," I told him. "Based on what we have learned from you, we have discussed the same concerns among ourselves. This is why we have chosen to go to a federal official who is located in another city. He's actually in Lafayette, Louisiana—but he works child abuse cases everywhere. Keep in mind that local law enforcement officials have allowed themselves to be around Scott at his urging, but when they see the articles you've sent, I don't think they will any more. None of these law enforcement officials will defend a pedophile."

I asked Ethan again about Natalie and Angela Hills. "We haven't tried to contact either and I know you had asked us not to mention your name. I'm worried about someone they don't know contacting them about Scott, especially if they might still be in touch with him and might let him know. We will probably share their names with the U.S. Attorney and let him handle it, but if you have any other thoughts on that, let me know."

We had no idea how much the women knew about the abuse or what level of contact they continued to have with Scott, Mathew, or Stuart. We had learned that some of Scott's sexual abuse of the boys was group in nature, and that he had used that experience to threaten them. For example, when one of the boys he was abusing reached 18, he would force him to participate in sexually abusing a younger boy, then threaten him with prison if he ever said anything about his own prior abuse. "Who do you think they will believe, you or me?" he taunted them. Especially after his one public accuser was unable to get him convicted, the other victims began to think no one could stop him. In addition to the scars caused by their own abuse, some of Scott's young victims also carried the guilt of having abused other boys—and the fear of being discovered.

The mind games he played to maintain a hold on the boys was sickening. He used constant threats and brainwashing to secure their silence. *What teenage boy was any match for Scott's level of depravity?*

As Ethan grew into a man and a father, however, his fear of Scott began to subside a little. He had more confidence in himself now and was able to take that first step.

"Do you feel that Jake is getting more comfortable with helping?" I asked Ethan. "I know this has to be hard for him, too, and we don't want to do anything that causes him any further harm. Please assure him we will be respectful of his feelings, too."

During almost two months of regular communication with Ethan, I had managed to restrain myself from correcting one minor fault in his emails that journalism school had trained me to fix. Ethan always wrote "Barton Rouge," and while the misspelling didn't matter at all, I somehow felt compelled to let Ethan know. After all, we had already asked him if he would fly over here if needed. We couldn't have him looking for the wrong city!

"A minor point," I began. "Our city is Baton Rouge—not Barton. (It's French for Red Stick.) I mention it only so you don't have any trouble if you are searching online." That explanation sounded weak even to me, but I didn't want to admit that I couldn't help editing his spelling. And the correct identification of Scott Rogers' whereabouts was something I thought we should get straight before going any further.

On Monday morning, Nathan and I went to see Mayor Holden as a courtesy call to let him know that I was handing over, to the federal authorities, the information I had received on Scott. I had called to ask if I could run by the Mayor's office for a minute, and Nathan went with me since the two men are attorneys and I thought the Mayor might have some questions.

Holden was his usual friendly self, welcoming me with a kiss on the cheek and Nathan with a warm hug. He invited us to take a seat on the sofa and chairs across from his desk, and he sat in the chair closest to me.

I began by reminding him of the press conference we held almost two months ago and the email I had briefly shared with him at that time. I explained that I had followed up with the sender and that Nathan had advised me to ask him for additional information. I showed the Mayor the U.K. news articles about the trial and told him that two young men who had been victims of Scott's abuse were now providing information. The Mayor sat quietly, listening intently as I showed the articles and walked him through a very brief description of what we had learned, mentioning that Scott now had two little boys living with him.

I finished by saying we felt the information was credible enough that we should turn it over to someone who was in a position to act. When he finally spoke, Mayor Holden's first words were, "Rannah, someone has to protect those children."

Oh, how I wish Ethan could have been there with us! Finally someone else whose first words were about the children! I was so glad Nathan was sitting there with me so that no one could accuse me of casting the Mayor is a light more favorable than he deserved. People who don't know the Mayor well sometimes assume I do that. But Nathan had been in more meetings on this subject than I had, and Mayor Holden was the first person whose initial concern was for the children. His only request was that, as a courtesy, I meet with the Police Chief. He wanted Chief Carl Dabadie to know we were referring the matter to the federal authorities so that he would not be caught off guard, should charges be filed in Baton Rouge by federal authorities. Mayor Holden said he trusted his Police Chief to keep the investigation confidential if federal authorities were going to handle it. We agreed and left his office to make that call.

Chief Dabadie had been chief only since July, but he had been on the force about 28 years, most recently serving as interim chief. After our brief meeting with the Mayor, I called the Chief and caught him at his office. I explained that the Mayor had asked me to meet with him briefly, and he invited us to come right over.

Nathan and I visited Chief Dabadie in the old Police Headquarters on Mayflower Street, an abandoned school that now housed the police administration. The building's condition was so poor that a previous chief had joked it was held together by termites holding hands. Mushrooms grew in a break room where department employees ate lunch.

We climbed the steps of the old school, presumably past the industrious termites and flourishing mushroom crop, to meet Chief Dabadie in his second floor office.

He listened closely with little reaction as I explained again the information we had received from Ethan. When he finally spoke, he did not comment on the materials we had shown him, but asked that we tell the federal officials to call him personally if they needed anything from the Baton Rouge Police. "I don't know if anything will be in our jurisdiction, but if needed, I can assign an officer to help them who will be very discreet," he said.

Now that the Mayor, District Attorney, and Police Chief had been notified, Mary Jane was working to get a meeting on Wednesday with Luke Walker. Nathan wanted Mary Jane and me to take Ethan's information to Walker. He felt we could best present it, and we were following Nathan's plan—respectful of the local officials but focused on putting our information in the best possible hands to help. I sent Ethan an update on our discussions with the Mayor and Police Chief, reminding him that because Scott lived in a neighboring parish, any crimes he committed there might not come under our local city police jurisdiction. "I know our Police Chief and we can trust him to do the right thing," I assured Ethan. I felt he needed to know that Scott had not manipulated the Baton Rouge Police Department, nor had Luke Walker stopped by Scott's house for "tea and cake," as Ethan had comically, but accurately, described the behavior of other law enforcement officials.

"Thanks for the update, Rannah…Chat more Wednesday. Have a good week," Ethan wrote. Then he added, "Oh…red stick noted." Communicating with him was so easy. Having spent my entire career in the communications world, I'm always reminding people of how we often perceive something nonexistent or at least unintended, especially in emails. But here was someone I didn't know, across the Atlantic Ocean, who stayed on the same page.

After that exchange, Ethan sometimes referred to Baton Rouge as *Red Stick*, teasing me a little, I thought, about my need to proofread. A time would come, when I would finally meet him, and Ethan would recall, "You scolded me about misspelling the name of your city!" joking about my love of Baton Rouge. He explained that Barton Mills was a village in Suffolk, so he often thought of it when he wrote *Baton Rouge*. The moment when he emailed, "Oh, red stick noted," though small and insignificant, was enough for me to detect a great sense of humor deep inside this young man. But the time when either of us could laugh about anything was a very long way away.

Mary Jane had successfully scheduled our meeting with Luke Walker for Wednesday, October 23, at the federal courthouse in Lafayette. Finally we would hand over everything we had discovered to the man who could help Ethan. We had no idea what action he could take, but I was at least hopeful that Luke Walker understood child sex offenders and how they operate.

We had no evidence yet that Scott Rogers was abusing the children now living with him in Baton Rouge; we could present only the evidence of his crimes in the U.K. While a powerful indictment, would that evidence mean we could hold Scott Rogers accountable now for the brutal abuse in his past?

Ethan wanted to save the children Scott had adopted in Louisiana from the same abuse he and Jake had suffered. I couldn't help wondering, *Are we too late?*

Scott Rogers would have filled out several forms for Child Services and Immigration. All include specific questions about whether applicants have been arrested, charged, or involved in any investigation involving a child.

FOSTER/ADOPTIVE PARENT APPLICATION

CRIMINAL/CHILD PROTECTION RECORD HISTORY

***Please be advised that you will be fingerprinted by DCFS staff and the prints will be forwarded to Louisiana State Police and FBI for a criminal history report. You will be asked to explain all arrest/conviction information and possibly will be asked to provide arrest reports from the authorities involved.

Please complete for **all adult** members of the household.

Name	Arrest Record		Convicted of a Crime		Sentenced to Jail/Prison	
	☐ Yes	☐ No	☐ Yes	☐ No	☐ Yes	☐ No
	☐ Yes	☐ No	☐ Yes	☐ No	☐ Yes	☐ No
	☐ Yes	☐ No	☐ Yes	☐ No	☐ Yes	☐ No
	☐ Yes	☐ No	☐ Yes	☐ No	☐ Yes	☐ No

If **YES** to any of the above, an explanation is needed regarding the report and whether it resulted in any of the following: (Charges Dropped, Conviction, Time Served, etc.). Use Separate Pages if Needed.

Have you or a family member ever been involved in a Child Protection Investigation?
☐ Yes ☐ No
If YES, when: Where:

What was the outcome of the investigation?

Have your children ever been in foster care? ☐ Yes ☐ No

If YES, when: Where:

***Please be advised that a child abuse/neglect background clearance will be conducted on all adult members of the household. Persons who have valid child abuse histories against minors may not be certified as foster/adoptive parents. This search will include all states.

Maria Edwards' computer bag was taken into evidence at the crime scene, despite her repeated requests to retrieve it before leaving.

Scott Rogers and his extended family lived in this home in St. Gabriel, Louisiana, a short drive from Baton Rouge.

Photo by Rannah Gray

Prominent criminal defense attorney Nathan S. Fisher was the first person the author turned to for advice when she received a shocking email from England.

Photo by Marie Constantin

Mary Jane Marcantel, an experienced paralegal, was asked by Fisher to work on the investigation.

Iberville Parish Sheriff's deputies responding to Maria Edwards' 911 call found Scott Rogers in his bed with Mathew Hodgkinson on the floor nearby.

A stack of notes was left by Mathew on the table by Rogers' bed.

Several handguns were recovered from Scott Rogers' home, along with $5,000 in cash Mathew's note revealed was behind an oil painting in the bar area.

Crime scene photos by Iberville Parish Sheriff's Department

Photos by Sarah Powell

Students at Scott Rogers' Academy dreamed of achieving success in nearby London, located less than a two-hour drive south of Bury.

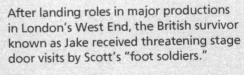

After landing roles in major productions in London's West End, the British survivor known as Jake received threatening stage door visits by Scott's "foot soldiers."

The author at The Abbey Hotel in Bury St. Edmunds in March 2015.

Abbey Gardens in Bury St. Edmunds provides a gathering place for the community.

Photos by Sarah Powell

During Rogers' early years in Louisiana, he sold himself as an international "business guru" and published motivational books and pamphlets that promoted team building.

For 10 years, Rogers hosted the *Around Town TV Show*, an early morning weekend program that aired on local cable systems.

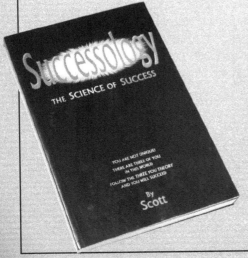

Photo by Terri Witt

Scott Rogers often volunteered to emcee events for firefighters and law enforcement.

Sex charge dance teacher 'expected arrest'

County council advises anxious parents: Keep your children away

'FAME' SCHOOL CULT WARNING

Scott Rogers' trial was covered extensively by the British press. Ethan sent the author photos of the articles he had kept in a journal.

WHERE IS SCOTT ROGERS?

By Martin Barsby and Marianne Hulland

MYSTERY surrounds the whereabouts of the former principal of a controversial dancing school in Bury St Edmunds which, it is claimed, has an atmosphere similar to a religious cult.

Richard Scott-Rogers, 33, was not at home yesterday – a week after the Bury Free Press published a five-page investigation into his influence on pupils at the Academy of Dancing and Performing Arts in Fornham Road.

Mystery of 'cult' dance academy founder

SEVENTH SIGN CREATIVE ARTS CO

are urgently and still currently seeking a

" Scott-Rogers "

for the forthcoming production and contracts

Characteristics
Excellent looks, Age 23, 5'11", Blue eyes, Short dark hair, Athletic build, Excellent dance abilities, Very talented with many previous professional engagements.

Good reward given if found.

Telephone (01284) 725527.....URGENT!!

"We go together like carrots and peas, you can't have one without the other."

WANTED

After his adopted son in Bury escaped, Rogers placed this ad as a ploy to get others to tell him where the boy was hiding.

In handwritten letters to Jake, Rogers' temper flared as he worked relentlessly to find the young man.

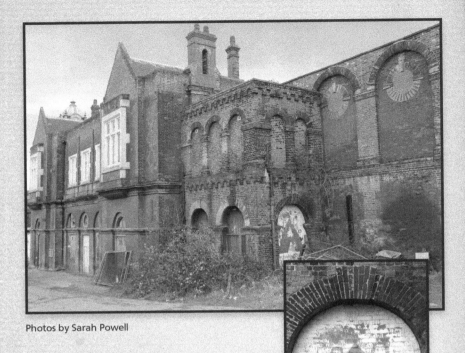

Photos by Sarah Powell

Scott Rogers' office at the Academy was to the right of the front door. The sexual abuse began in that room for some students.

The Academy was located on the back of the Bury St. Edmunds train station. Scott Rogers had the students paint the now faded mural, which featured Rogers at the center of the letter "A."

Photo by Abbott Photography

A young Scott Rogers started the Academy of Dance and Performing Arts in Bury St. Edmunds, selling dreams of fame. In 1995, the Suffolk County Council took the unusual step of warning parents about the school's cult-like atmosphere. In the U.S., Rogers insisted on keeping his real name off the Internet, and made cosmetic changes to his appearance.

Scott Rogers' home in Bury St. Edmunds, England. Living here with wife Mandie and daughter Kimberly, he often invited students to sleep over.

Photo by Sarah Powell

CHAPTER TWENTY-SEVEN

THE AUSA

Day 57
October 23, 2013

Before Mary Jane and I drove across the Atchafalaya River Basin to meet Assistant U.S. Attorney John Luke Walker in Lafayette, she sent me a news release from May 2013. The U.S. Justice Department had selected Walker for the national Child Protection Award, which he accepted in Washington at ceremonies commemorating national Missing Children's Day.

"The award recognizes the extraordinary efforts of citizens and law enforcement officers," the press release read, "who have made a significant investigative or program contribution to protect children from abuse or victimization."[29]

Walker, who serves as Project Safe Childhood Coordinator for the Western District of Louisiana, was a driving force behind Operation Delego, the largest child exploitation case ever prosecuted by the United States Justice Department. The press release noted that Walker's efforts had so far resulted in 44 convictions of Delego targets, including a teacher, a police officer, and a member of the military.

---

[29] "Western District of Louisiana Assistant U.S. Attorney Recognized at The National Missing Children's Day Commemoration In Washington, D.C." United States Department of Justice, United States Attorney's Office, Western District of Louisiana. 15 May 2013. Viewed 9 September 2015. http://www.justice.gov/usao-wdla/pr/western-district-louisiana-assistant-us-attorney-recognized-annual-national-missing

When U.S. Attorney General Eric Holder and U.S. Department of Homeland Security Secretary Janet Napolitano announced, at a press conference in 2011, the indictments of 72 individuals, they identified Walker as the lead prosecutor.

"The convictions resulted in sentences ranging from five years to life imprisonment and helped to successfully dismantle a network of individuals whose main objective was the production of hardcore child pornography involving children under the age of 12. Overseas child sex rings and commercial child pornography production rings were also dismantled," according to a statement by the Western District of Louisiana U.S. Attorney's Office.

Operation Delego centered on an invitation-only Internet site called *Dreamboard*, which Janet Napolitano described as the vehicle for distributing up to 123 terabytes of child pornography, or roughly 16,000 DVDs. Law enforcement officials in 14 countries arrested perpetrators; while investigators discovered the website's top administrators in France and Canada, they located the Dreamboard computers that stored the files in Shreveport, Louisiana.

Shreveport! A city known for its horseracing track and nearby casinos that lure deep-pocketed gamblers from Texas, just 22 miles to the west. Who could imagine Shreveport housing the computers that stored and delivered unspeakably violent child pornography images around the world?

"AUSA Walker is a committed lawyer, but it is his tireless work and dedication to the children of this community that led to his being named as a recipient of this award," said U.S. Attorney Stephanie Finley, Walker's boss.

While Operation Delego was a vast international child pornography network, at the time the convictions were going down in 2012, when Walker was nominated for the Justice Department honor, he was also working 47 active child exploitation cases. During this time, law enforcement rescued three child victims and identified an additional 24.

Walker's accolades also noted that outside the courtroom he spends time educating children and parents about the dangers of online activity, during 2012 alone making more than 25 presentations that reached approximately 3,000 children and 500 adults.

Mary Jane's notes:

On October 23, Rannah picked me up and we made that 45-minute trip to Lafayette over the Atchafalaya Basin, one of the prettiest areas of the State. The Lafayette federal building is in the downtown area, which is the old part of town that boasts many historical buildings. The new federal building is a couple of blocks off the main downtown street.

At the door of this building something very odd makes it very distinct: Large female heads called the "Urns of Justice" sit at the courthouse entrance. What's odd about them is that the tops of the heads are hollowed out and concave, as if the women have no brains. Years ago, when I first saw the new building and the heads, I commented how appropriate the busts that depicted justice. Instead of a blindfolded woman holding a scale, this courthouse had monuments to blindfolded women with no brains.

*Back then, as I walked through those same front doors, I had loudly stated how those monuments so accurately reflected how women with no brains made the federal court decisions that impact people's lives. I was quickly hushed and soon learned that a federal judge's sculptor wife had designed the statues and that the judge worked in the building. When Rannah and I, two strong, determined women **with** brains, entered the building, I told her that story.*

We walked through the glass front doors and passed through the metal detectors. The guards who work the lobby are some of the nicest you could encounter. Most of those guys are retired policemen who have been around for a long time. I had been working several cases at the Lafayette Courthouse over the past few years, so they were very familiar with me. As they called me by my first name and asked how I was doing, Rannah was a little surprised at their friendliness, so unlike what you find at many federal buildings. But that is Lafayette, Louisiana, and the friendliness of South Louisiana people.

When we reached the United States Attorney's office, we signed in and received nametags. That is the only way you get through those locked doors to every United States Attorney's office. Luke met us there and led us to his office. With me was the binder containing the 20-year-old newspaper articles and the information I had accumulated on immigration issues, as well as Rogers' deposition in the Silver Sun lawsuit, and documents from Louisiana Child Services praising him as a foster and adoptive parent.

Luke, while a very successful prosecutor, comes across as a kind, soft-spoken Southern boy. He looks like a preppie years younger than his actual age. While I have never heard Luke raise his voice, I have often heard him speak affectionately about his wife and kids. I have had conversations with him after hours while he is driving to deliver or pick up his children to or from their events. His "aw, shucks" manner makes every grandmother think of him as her grandson. But Luke Walker, with all his charm, is as lethal as a cobra when prosecuting a defendant. Do not ever underestimate Luke Walker.

I sat down in his office along with Rannah and introduced the two. We made small talk, and then I started telling him why we had come: the crimes we thought Rogers had committed when filing applications to obtain children. I told him that Rogers had been tried 20 years ago in the U.K. for sexual abuse of a child, and I told him the outcome of that trial.

That 20-year period had always been the problem in this case. That is a long time in the past, and the crime was in a different county. For the feds to have jurisdiction in the United States, Rogers must have committed a federal crime here, and the charges must be brought in a timely manner. In the United States, the statute of limitations governs prosecution. Even if a person has committed a crime, the time to prosecute him, except for murder, has expiration dates.

As I looked around Luke's office, I was familiar with what was there. Luke has a small office that contains a desk, credenza, and two chairs. A number of diplomas and awards hang on his wall.

Mary Jane had hit a home run in suggesting Luke Walker—make that a grand slam, because that's how much of a game changer he was. I found it incredible that we had someone of Walker's expertise in Louisiana and even more so that Mary Jane knew him and was able to get us a meeting so quickly. We had been like nomads wandering the desert showing knowledgeable people what Ethan had sent us, but we had not connected with anyone who could actually stop Scott's abuse. After reading about the focus of Walker's career, however, I knew he was the perfect one to trust with the safety of the children living in Scott's house.

When we reached his office, respectful of his time, Mary Jane and I quickly began walking him through the information Ethan had sent. Luke sat casually behind his desk—gray slacks, white shirt with sleeves rolled up, tie loosened around his neck—giving us his full attention.

We spent about 90 minutes going over every detail of Scott's past. We left behind only copies of the news articles, as Nathan had made sure I understood that any correspondence I shared would ultimately become the subject of discovery, should Luke file charges. I had promised Ethan I would not disclose his involvement until he was ready.

Luke explained to us the difference between *situational* child sex abusers, who when put in certain circumstances abuse children, and *predators*, who are always actively seeking control over children to abuse them. "Scott Rogers is a predator," he said, after hearing the information and reading through the articles.

Walker's vast knowledge of the behavior of child sex offenders gave us insight into the world of child sex abuse and especially its prevalence among foster children. He shared a story about a priest who was a Boy Scout troop leader in Alexandria for a group that included several boys from a nearby orphanage. Walker, who was a member of that troop growing up, said the priest had abused boys from the orphanage, children who were especially susceptible since they did not have parents paying attention. He explained to us that foster children would often accept abuse as a necessary evil to remain in a home instead of a juvenile facility, since they longed to be a part of a family. *Heartbreaking,* I thought. But I knew he was right.

Luke had spent more than 20 years investigating child sex offenders and working with adult survivors to prosecute their abusers. He was an expert on the subject. When I described my communications with Ethan, he knew exactly what to expect. "He will come to the United States if we need him to," Luke surmised. "When you give victims an opening to bring their abusers to justice, they are the most cooperative victims we work with."

I recounted my observations of Stuart and Mathew and said that I thought Stuart might come forward and tell the truth about their situation. Luke listened and made interesting observations about both young men. He thought that Stuart's personable and outgoing behavior meant he could mentally handle the abuse and that Mathew's more robotic behavior meant he needed all of his energy to hold himself together. Luke said he wouldn't be surprised if Mathew was the one who broke. Over the next year, I would have reason to think about that prediction many times. *Scott Rogers truly is a text book case on child predators!*

After listening carefully to our information, Luke laid out a plan for next steps. He explained his own workload and said he needed a couple of weeks to complete a case he was working on and gather some basic information for going forward. In about three weeks, he said, we would meet in Baton Rouge with whomever he brought in to assist him—someone from Homeland Security or the FBI, or possibly a U.S. postal inspector.

He described a female postal inspector, for example, who had worked a number of child exploitation cases with him, because child sex abuse and pornography often occur together, and because she is a skilled interviewer. He said he would make his selection based on what he could find in the records. The purpose of the meeting, he said, was the transfer to federal agents of the information we had just shared with him.

Around that time, Luke said he would like me to schedule another call with Ethan so that I could introduce him to the agents and we could together take them through the details. After that call, he explained, the federal authorities would communicate directly with Ethan, and I would have no further involvement in the investigation. *Nathan says if you can get their attention, the feds are the ones you want on a case. Luke is taking charge.* I left Lafayette feeling good about Luke Walker.

I reported to Ethan on our meeting and the direction Luke would take going forward, assuring him that he could still update me and that we would continue looking for anything that might help the investigation. "We're not going away after that meeting and will continue helping," I explained, "but obviously we will not have a role in the official investigation.

"I think we would like to talk to you before that call so we can make sure we remember everything," I said.

"Luke is personable, works extensively with children and adults who were child victims, and has great insight," I went on. "For example, from my description of Mathew as robotic and close mouthed, which he says is a defense mechanism, he believes Mathew is probably the most fragile."

When I had explained to Luke that Ethan had connected with another survivor who was not ready to come forward because Scott's mistreatment of him had included violent physical and sexual abuse, he understood. "I imagine either of these guys could kick his ass if they saw him now," Luke said. "But the fact is, if they open their door and he is standing there, they will immediately go back to the age at which he abused them and they will be afraid of him.

Mary Jane's notes:

I listened to Rannah tell Luke of her contact and three-month communication with Ethan. She gave him a synopsis of the news articles, pointing out specifics, including Rogers' crazy defense that the young boy had molested **him**. She showed him Ethan's emails and discussed our conversation with him. Luke, holding his yellow legal pad, listened and wrote his left-handed notes. I told him about finding the award from Child Services and showed him a copy. I said I thought Rogers must have lied on his immigration application to gain residency and citizenship, and those appeared to be one of the requirements for obtaining children. I told him I thought Rogers had bootstrapped the approval for residency and citizenship onto his application at Child Services, where he had personal ties through Mike Edmonson, head of the State Police.

I told Luke that if Rogers had **not** lied on his application to Child Services and had told the truth about his arrest and trial in the United Kingdom, then someone needed to investigate Child Services.

Luke mentioned a Baton Rouge postal inspector with whom he had worked in the past. He recommended putting us in touch with her. He thought that Rogers was continuing with his pedophilia.

The hook for the feds, at least as a start, was the immigration issue. During the timeframe of our investigation, immigration had grown as a big issue in the United States. Walker surmised as I did that Rogers had lied on his citizenship application. He said he would talk to the postal inspector first, and then Rannah and I would set up a meeting with her.

Luke assured me that I would like her and she would like me. He said he had worked with her on a number of cases involving children and had total faith in her. His vouching for her meant a lot to me, as well as his belief that we could get along—a very important factor for me, as I can be difficult, especially when I think others are not doing their part. The one thing I know for sure about Luke is that even if you are law enforcement, if he thinks you are lazy or incompetent, he will let you know that he does not want you around him.

I now have a pot to make the roux— now I need the ingredients.

To Ethan I reported, "I asked what you should do until we meet and he said to continue communication with Jake. Luke Walker completely understands his fear and will be respectful of that. Obviously, the investigation is going to take place here, but you two can provide helpful information.

"We do not plan to take any of this to the press at this point because that would only hurt the U.S. Attorney's ability to investigate, and I would not want him to think we did not respect his commitment. We always have that option down the road, but for now, I feel this is a good plan with the best potential outcome. After all, we don't want Scott to just disappear in the dark of night and end up somewhere else where he can abuse again.

"I hope you feel good about this," I said. "I believe this is the direction we've been looking for since you contacted me— we just needed time to find it. I left the meeting today feeling very comfortable with who will handle this investigation and the resources they have to find out the truth. Let me know your thoughts."

"Extremely positive and absolutely the right way forward," Ethan replied. "Yes, let's arrange a call, any day you think best. I'm happy to talk with the authorities moving forward, of course I will keep you in the picture with as much detail as possible. I have forwarded your message to Jake and I have asked if he will also help me speak to the authorities. Fingers crossed…I told him to think about it over a couple of days."

Ethan was anxious to hear a date for our call, even if it was just a guess on my part. I think he felt what I did—*We finally had a plan!*

When I told Nathan about the meeting, he cautioned patience. "The feds move very slowly," he said, "but they're very thorough." That was not his first reminder that federal investigations take longer than anything I had ever experienced, and he was right. But a plan to help the two boys was finally in motion.

What would Luke Walker find when he finally got a glimpse into all the legal documents Scott Rogers had filed since coming to the United States? Scott was clever, but had he lied to get custody of those two little boys?

Could Luke keep him from abusing them, too? If Scott had already begun the abuse, could Luke stop him?

CHAPTER TWENTY-EIGHT

HIDING IN PLAIN SIGHT

Leslie Todd is a licensed clinical social worker in private practice in Baton Rouge since 1991. She encountered Scott Rogers through her work with local Family Services organizations and followed the news accounts of his death, calling in to the Jim Engster Show to go on the record when one of his guests suggested that Scott had put his deviant behavior behind him. She wrote the following chapter on Scott and the behavior patterns of pedophiles without any knowledge of what others had reported about him, but with striking similarity. Her observations almost identically mirror his victims' descriptions as well as Luke Walker's.

When Ethan first contacted me, I knew very little about how child sex predators operate. Now I believe it's important for everyone to know warning signs, so they know what to do when a child needs help. Leslie provides a brief, professional introduction to the behavior of Scott Rogers, information I believe we need in order to understand fully Scott Rogers' threat to children.

Rannah Gray

HIDING IN PLAIN SIGHT
By Leslie Todd, LCSW-BACS

As Luke Walker pointed out, we may classify child molesters as either situational **molesters** or predatory **pedophiles**: that is, those who take advantage of an unusual situation (often while high or impaired), and those who are cold and calculating predators. The first category includes a spectrum that ranges from people who experience a one-time lapse of impulse control to more calculating offenders who realize that an unusual situation will allow them to intentionally (volitionally) take advantage of a vulnerable child or adult without perceived risk of getting caught.

Before I discuss Scott Rogers in particular, let me give you some general information about the two kinds of child molesters (although molestation is really a continuum), and how they operate. You can learn more at the excellent website, www.yellodyno.com, which is devoted to educating adults and children regarding missing and exploited children.

Situational child molesters are generally less intelligent than predatory pedophiles, and morally indiscriminate. They abuse people and "the system" across the board, reasoning that anything is okay if they can get away with it.

The situational molester's primary criteria for victims are vulnerability and opportunity. Children are prime targets because they are nonthreatening and easily coerced. Such a person may be a drifter, working first at a day-care where he can abuse small children, and later at a hospital, where he can abuse the mentally or physically handicapped. Because molesters of this type are generally socially awkward, they are more likely than the more polished predators to arouse suspicion and more likely to abduct victims or to murder them. The kidnapper of Elizabeth Smart is an example.

Outright predators have certain traits in common. They are generally more intelligent, and they are more socially gifted. In fact, they are often very successful and popular, making it difficult for people to believe they are guilty even when caught red-handed. Jerry Sandusky and Jimmy Saville are examples, along with Scott Rogers.

Unlike opportunistic abusers, pedophiles prefer children: they have sexual fantasies of children and are genuinely attracted to them, particularly to a certain gender and age range. However, this doesn't mean that they don't have sex with adults. They may marry as a cover (Rogers did) or even just to get close to their partner's children. They usually engage in other deviant behaviors (paraphilias), such as collecting child pornography and sado-masochism.

Scott Rogers particularly fits the profile of a "preferential sex offender":

1. Long-term and persistent pattern of behavior beginning in early adolescence; is willing to commit time, money, and energy; commits multiple offenses, makes need-driven mistakes;

2. Specific sexual interests including paraphilic preferences (sado-masochism, orgies, child pornography); focuses on defined sexual interests and victim characteristics; centers life around preferences, rationalizes sexual interests;

3. Well-developed techniques: evaluates experiences, lies and manipulates skillfully, has method of access to victims, is quick to use modern technology (e.g., computer, video) for sexual needs and purposes;

4. Fantasy-driven behaviors: records fantasies, acts to turn fantasy into reality, collects theme pornography, collects paraphernalia (videotapes, souvenirs)[30]

One reason this type of pedophile is usually more intelligent is that he is playing a "long game": He is setting up a career, not a hobby. I suspect that Rogers saw Britain's Jimmy Saville almost as a role model: a media star beloved by all, with access to the wildest of partiers—and to children. Rogers started with a dance academy in England but in America shrewdly turned to television and videotaping as his profession. What a perfect set-up for pornography and blackmail.

Pedophiles are patient because they must ingratiate themselves with the adults who are the gatekeepers to the prey: children. They might have to develop job skills that keep them in a child-rich environment. Then they must groom the children by gaining their trust, arranging for incremental touching leading to molestation. Once they actively abuse a child, they will use threats, blame, guilt, and even "love" to keep the child silent and available.

1. Pedophiles must seduce the guardians of children before they can seduce the children.

In England, Scott Rogers set up a dance academy as a front for his activities. He presented himself as a heterosexual married man devoted to mentoring youth. He created a credible reason to approach the parents of young boys: He could make their child a star. He could give the child financial and educational opportunities the parents could not provide.

---

[30] "Child Molesters: A Behavioral Analysis For Law Enforcement Officers Investigating the Sexual Exploitation of Children by Acquaintance Molesters," 4th Edition, by Kenneth V. Lanning, published by the National Center for Missing and Exploited Children, 38.

Other easy cover careers or volunteer positions for such predators include athletic coaching (Jerry Sandusky), church ministry, Scout leaders, and teachers. All of these positions put the predator in the midst of his prey, and in a position of respect, power, and influence with adults. All of these positions presuppose that the predator is spending many hours with his charges to teach, coach, or advise them—and it wouldn't seem unusual to single out a child or two for "special help" or to take on outings. Especially if this trusted person respectfully approached the child's parents first to praise the child's talents or potential and to offer unusual opportunities. What parents wouldn't want the best for their child?

Pedophiles identify so well with children that they are able to charm them. They are excellent at talking with, and listening to, children. While this charm creates a terrible trap for the lonely or abused child, all children are vulnerable to the attentions of a kind and interested adult.

"The biggest problem for this (type of) child molester is not how to obtain child victims but how to get them to leave after they are too old. This child molester is likely to use threats and physical violence only to avoid identification and disclosure or prevent a victim from leaving before he is ready to "dump" the victim. [31]

Scott Rogers' solution was to keep three of his victims close to him for decades. From the dance academy in Bury to his faux "family" in Baton Rouge, Rogers coerced Mathew, Stuart, and Jake through complex combinations of affection,

---

[31] Ibid, 27.

brutality, blackmail, financial support, and favoritism which shifted as needed.

2. <u>**Child sexual predators are patient, subtle, and cagey in approaching their targeted prey.**</u>

Once the predator has gained credibility with the gatekeeping adults (the parents, the school staff), it is natural that the children would think the predator is trustworthy. Predators use their charm and faux warmth to groom the children. These are the steps:

a. The pedophile hangs out with the parents long enough to be sure they are comfortable before offering to "help" with the child. This could be a casual offer to stay behind with the kids at the hunting camp while the other adults go hunting, or to take the child to the zoo when Mom is sick.

b. The pedophile then begins seducing the child with warmth, attention, mentoring, and gifts.

c. He may share hobbies and interests that are appealing to his target children. Young teen boys might love to visit a home full of video games and posters. **"The homes of some pedophiles have been described as shrines to children or as miniature amusement parks."**

d. He skillfully manipulates multiple victims through seduction, competition, peer pressure, guilt, threats, and blackmail (true of Scott's English victims).

e. He understands how to lower their inhibitions (talking semi-nude in the locker room; offering to rub their backs) He may introduce them to sexually explicit material (photos, Internet) as part of this grooming.

f. He will photograph children, even fully dressed. This may be for his sexual fantasies, but it is also a way to groom children for more explicit photographs later on.

Through these means, the pedophile gains his victims' cooperation and even consent.

How did Scott Rogers dupe so many people in Baton Rouge?

Curiously, in homophobic Baton Rouge, Rogers and his two male partners were able to pass themselves off in circles usually closed to gay men. Rogers had three smoke screens: his daughter Kimmy (in a sham marriage to Mathew), his videography business, 1stCo, which allowed him to introduce the men as his crew, and most importantly, his adopted handicapped son. This child was paraded around on his television show and at his public appearances so that the image of Scott-as-doting-father was foremost in his audience's minds. Stuart and Mathew were vaguely defined as the adopted son's uncles.

Local people who witnessed Rogers with the boy said the child was almost "like a puppet" for Rogers. Exactly.

Baton Rouge is a very family-oriented town, and is full of big-hearted philanthropists and volunteers devoted to helping children and their families. Its social service agencies are overwhelmed with the needs of children and the lack of resources with which to address them.

The Department of Social Services has a near impossible job. Social workers and other professionals are faced daily with huge caseloads of abused, neglected, or homeless children. The fostering and adoption of children is a great need. So when Scott Rogers arrives and announces that he is an experienced media professional who is devoted to children and willing to help child-centered agencies and volunteer groups, of course they would be grateful. Then he "walked the walk" and adopted his first son.

Of course, a handicapped child ostensibly would feel blessed to be fostered by such a kind and generous father. Add on the wow factor that Rogers was a "celebrity" who constantly promoted fostering and helped the overworked staff and volunteers of social service organizations.... How hard are these grateful people going to look at his credentials? There were no red flags in their line of vision. How easy, then, to acquire a second foster child.

<u>Seducing the Law Enforcement Community</u>

Besides the guardians of children, Rogers had another enormous audience to seduce: the law enforcement community. Parents, child welfare workers, and police hold a key trait in common: all of them are devoted to protecting the vulnerable, and all of the good ones are prone to question, "Am I doing enough?" Predators like Scott Rogers home in on that self-doubt and reassure the person, "Yes, you are doing a wonderful job. I see how hard you are trying, and I will help you."

The only time I met Scott Rogers was at an awards ceremony on October 18, 2007, when we were among several people being recognized for our community service as mediators. The mayor and many law enforcement officials were there, as well as various media staff who were covering the event. Scott Rogers struck me as phony from the minute I saw him with his entourage, and I was amazed at the very emotional hugs and greetings he exchanged with various law enforcement people.

However, I myself was star-struck at meeting our chief of police, Jeff LeDuff, who exemplifies the dedicated helper who never thinks he has done enough (clearly an image I identify with as a social worker). I tearfully thanked Chief LeDuff for his passionate devotion during the past five years. Baton Rouge had been terrorized first by two serial killers who were operating at the same time (although that wouldn't become clear until the second one was caught). Derrick Todd Lee murdered at least seven women before being caught in May 2003 and Sean Gillis had killed at least eight before he was caught in April 2004.

Then in August 2005, Hurricane Katrina devastated New Orleans and other areas, and overnight, Baton Rouge became the staging area for medical and other evacuee needs. We doubled in size overnight and for weeks, the air and roads were full of military convoys and emergency vehicles. Everyone had relatives or rescue volunteers staying in their homes. We struggled with infrastructure overload, insane traffic, and general post-traumatic stress disorder.

So by October 2007, pretty much all the community leaders and helpers were exhausted and vulnerable. The huge psychic toll had been enough to make this social worker weep at meeting the heroic police chief, and for the police chief to weep at embracing his stalwart supporter, Scott Rogers.

Who was always there to offer support and comfort to the exhausted, heroic law enforcement officers?

Scott Rogers.

He prayed with them. He praised them publicly. He appeared at their events. He supported their causes. He shared their politics and spoke their language. He was their brother. And their chaplain.

Sadly, as FBI expert Kenneth Lanning concludes in his research on child predators,

"Regardless of intelligence and education, and often despite common sense and evidence to the contrary, adults tend to believe what they want or need to believe. The greater the need, the greater the tendency."

How very clever and calculating. Scott Rogers hid in the midst of those good men and women who serve and protect. He had calculated his every move to manipulate these guardians to not "see" him. Instead, they saw the image he wished to project: a patriotic, pious community leader who offered his admiration and all his resources on their behalf—and always, for the children.

CHAPTER TWENTY-NINE

THE MOTIVATIONAL MOMENT

Day 68
November 3, 2013

I had continued watching *The Around Town TV Show* every weekend since Ethan contacted me, and the programs that aired on the 2nd and 3rd of November celebrated the show's 10th anniversary. Watching the recorded shows on Sunday night, I picked up the remote control and hit the pause button, then grabbed my camera to take a couple of screen shots. I wanted Ethan to see what Scott and Kimmy actually looked like over the 20 years since he had last seen them. Scott played a clip of his first show that aired on November 2, 2003, featuring him sitting behind an earlier version of his interview desk with a photograph oddly turned toward the camera for the audience to see. I thought the small child looked like Kimmy.

He showed segments that featured Kellee Hennessy, a former WAFB-TV reporter who had co-hosted *The Around Town TV Show* with Scott for a brief period. Kellee and her mother had been good friends with Mayor Holden, but she seemed distant since the 2012 Mayor's campaign. We assumed her friendship with Scott and his support of Mike Walker against Mayor Holden had affected her friendship with the Mayor.

Along with Scott and Kimmy, another co-host of the show was the African American chef named Celeste Gill, billed as "Chef Celeste," who made appearances at the Main Street Farmers' Market in downtown Baton Rouge on Saturday mornings to promote both her catering business and her regular cooking segment on Scott's show. Celeste worked hard to portray professionalism in the cooking segments on the show, but revealed her closeness to Scott's family with stories about holiday meals at his house or favorite dishes his children enjoyed. *What does she think about the family's strange living arrangements?* we wondered.

I noticed that in the 2003 segments Scott wore a large cross lapel pin; Kimmy still regularly wore, on the show, a cross on a chain around her neck. The anniversary programs included a commercial for the 13:34 Church where Scott served as pastor, which had been incorporated only a year earlier and now shared space with *The Around Town TV Show* studio. The program ended with Scott dramatically proclaiming, "God Bless America!" As the 2003 segments aired, Kimmy explained for the audience that only Scott, Angie, and she had taken part in the show in the early days.

Later in the 10th anniversary celebration, she played telephone recordings of people—one of whom was Angie—calling in to sing "Happy Birthday." I assumed Ethan was correct that "Angie" was actually Angela Hills, who had come to the U.S. with the group and remained very close to Scott. She had to know at least some aspect of Scott's abuse of the young boys in the U.K., so it surprised me that her relationship with him had lasted so long. By now, she was an adult. Surely she understood the horror of what he had done and the danger he posed now for the two little boys in his custody. *Wasn't she at Scott's house when he confessed to the group that he had raped Jake?*

At one point, Angela and Stuart, who were dance partners, had a more personal relationship, until Scott took her aside to convince her that Stuart was gay. The group abuse he had imposed on some of the boys gave him the opportunity to say Stuart was sexually involved with other boys at the Academy. And with the control he maintained over the boys, he could find one of them willing to confirm it if needed. Scott always had someone in the group willing to vouch for him.

The most disturbing part of that anniversary program was a public service announcement showcasing Sheriff Sid Gautreaux's cybercrime unit that tracks down child sexual predators. Here again was a peek inside the manipulative mind of a child sex predator—abusing children, then promoting the law enforcement officials who track down abusers.

"Unbelievable!" Ethan said when I told him about the commercial. "It's interesting that he uses blatant tactics to almost cover up what he is doing, like the child predator ad and inviting police around his house."

While we were always shocked to see Scott dancing so close to the flame—surrounding himself with law enforcement and social workers trained to identify abusers—the truth is that it was no coincidence. It is in the DNA of the child predator to create the image he wants people to believe. The child molester is typically a trusted adult—a family member, a neighbor, a coach, a minister— someone, who, to all appearances, is trying to meet the emotional, physical, and spiritual needs of a child. Meantime, however, he is secretly fulfilling his own sexual desires.

Scott Rogers knew exactly where he needed to place himself: in the midst of trusted adults.

On that same show, Scott interviewed Greg Dicharry, with Magellan Health Services, the company that manages the Louisiana Behavioral Health Partnership, of which the Department of Children and Family Services is a member. Dicharry was promoting a program for troubled youth, including foster kids and children with behavioral problems.

I also sent Ethan a shot of the closing credits for *The Around Town TV Show* in case he recognized any other names. I had told him that one other British guy might work on the show, but I didn't remember his name....maybe Randy? I was trying to remember everyone Scott and his staff had mentioned. The closing credits showed only David Nall, and I remembered that David sometimes operated one of the cameras on the segments JoAnne and I taped at the studio.

"I'll check out David and see if there are any U.K. connections," Ethan replied. "I didn't think Randy was a very British name. LOL...."

This exchange reminded me how comfortable Ethan had grown by this time. Of course, "randy" has a much different meaning in the U.K., referring to someone who is always looking for sex, a use popularized in the U.S. when the British tabloids dubbed Prince Andrew "Randy Andy" during his playboy days. Obviously, *Randy* would not be a common British name! But as Ethan and I communicated mostly by email, I often forgot our divide, both in miles and culture.

"I think David Nall is local," I told him. "I know of a Nall family here and I think he may be related to them. Funny about 'Randy'—I didn't think of that because it's a common name here...which I guess says a lot about the Americans. LOL...."

The more I thought about the time I spent in the 1stCo studio with JoAnne and her staff, the more I believed that Mathew, Stuart, and Kimmy were the only British people we met there.

Ethan seemed to appreciate getting the photos. I'd had second thoughts about forcing him to confront Scott again in his current appearance, but he always said that any and all information was good, which was exactly how I felt. Whatever we could learn about Scott was important.

As Nathan, Mary Jane, and I built our case, however, I sometimes felt I had taken Scott's attack on me too much in stride. I always advise clients to protect their reputations: Correct the record if anyone tries to misrepresent you, never let an untruth go unanswered. I had written my letter to the editor based on those beliefs, but challenging a front page story in the Sunday newspaper with an inside letter on the editorial page was so inadequate.

Now, as I learned how deliberately he had set out to manipulate people, I was disappointed that a man of his character had been a credible source for so many people—people I knew well. *How had they fallen for his antics? Why didn't they see through his phony pretenses?*

As the real harm he had done to others unfolded, however, I found I could more easily put aside my own problems with his behavior.

Only about ten days had passed since Mary Jane and I had met with Luke Walker, and he had said it would be two or three weeks before we met again. Ethan and I were both anxious to hear something, while Nathan and Mary Jane knew we were in for a wait. In the meantime, Ethan and I speculated about tactics. "Do you think the authorities will consider surveillance on Scott?" he asked.

"I don't know what they will do, except they did tell me they would interview anyone with information," I replied.

We had discussed how Mathew, Kimmy, Stuart, and Scott might respond if interviewed, and the consensus was that the authorities would consider Mathew and Kimmy hostile witnesses, most likely covering up for Scott. "What steps they take next will depend on the information they get from the documents he has filed—foster parent, adoption, U.S. citizenship, concealed weapon permit, and any other documents they can examine."

The Sunday program on the weekend the 10th anniversary show aired included a segment involving merchants at a local Christmas marketplace. When Scott interviewed a woman who sold baby items, he grew excited about her different colored rubber ducks for bath time and said he was going to the market because "I think my little baby would love that." Such excitement over bath toys for the little boy seemed sinister, considering what we were learning about the father. Beyond that, I didn't know if the baby Scott mentioned was the toddler the District Attorney had described or, worse, a third child in his custody.

Then Sheriff Gautreaux appeared in his Baker Police Chief uniform holding a box of Wheaties cereal with a photograph of Scott on the box in place of the usual sports personality photo, above the familiar slogan, *Breakfast of Champions.*

"This is Baker Police Chief Sid Gautreaux," the segment began. "I'd like to ask if any of you have seen this man, please contact your local Police Department immediately. This is really a dangerous individual; he's not stable. And if you see him, please contact your local authorities immediately."

You could see Gautreaux trying not to smile as he delivered his lines, but the fake TV spot foretold the truth we were all learning about the dangerous man the Sheriff was describing.

On Sunday editions of *The Around Town TV Show,* Scott ended the hour with a "Motivational Moment," which I can best describe as a segment similar to Comedian Al Franken's Saturday Night Live performance of the fictional Stuart Smalley. Franken's character, an effeminate man with perfectly coiffed platinum blonde hair, grew out of a meeting he attended for recovering alcoholics.

As Smalley, he typically wore a yellow shirt with a bulky, light blue cardigan, similar to the coordinated outfits Rogers wore for his show, often shirts with vests or coats of the same colors. Franken's character had a number of popular catchphrases rooted in the teachings for recovery from various addictions, including his most popular, "I'm good enough, I'm smart enough, and doggone it, people like me."

Just as Al Franken used the psychobabble derived from self-help teachings for humor, Scott used it in earnest to spread his own brand of false spiritualism.

The opening to Scott's "Motivational Moment" featured fall leaves cascading down the screen to the notes of a syrupy instrumental tune. This Sunday, he recited a reading about the difference between strength and courage, saying, "It takes strength to endure abuse. It takes courage to stop it."

That might be the only point we agree on, I told Ethan.

"Scary stuff," he replied. "He is a very ill man!"

Scott was always manipulating someone, even his television audience. He must have found some perverse entertainment value in teasing publicly the subject of abuse, all the while surrounded by children and law enforcement officers.

"You're only as sick as your secrets," the Stuart Smalley character often said.

CHAPTER THIRTY

THE POSTAL AGENT

Day 86
November 21, 2013

Time passed slowly for all of us, as we waited for the next meeting with Luke Walker. I was out of town November 13 through 19, first for a leadership conference that included Suzy Sonnier, the State head of Children and Family Services, and then for a trip to Disney World with my niece Melissa and her family. At least I would get a break from the waiting game. By this time, I had gotten to know Suzy well through the leadership program; if the timing had been different, I would have talked to her about Scott. But now that I had taken the information to the federal officials, I could no longer say anything to anyone about the case. Nathan had made it clear that we could not do anything that would interfere with their investigation.

What better place to clear my mind than Disney World with my niece's three-year-old twin girls? What better way to remind myself of the innocence of children than a visit to the Magic Kingdom? *Anything that keeps my mind off waiting for the next step!* Melissa's twins watching the real life Disney princesses in action only reminded me that my instincts had been right: We had to help Ethan stop Scott Rogers' abuse of more little boys.

I had let Ethan know I would be out of town, but always available by email. The day before I returned from Florida, Mary Jane got a call from D.A. Moore asking for an update on the investigation. He told Mary Jane that the community "Night Out

Against Crime" event was coming up and that Scott had been invited to serve as the emcee. The evening involved all of the various law enforcement agencies. After hearing from Nathan and Mary Jane, the D.A. was obviously uncomfortable with Scott's participation.

When Mary Jane called Luke Walker to let him know, the investigation suddenly jerked to a start like boxcars on a long freight train when the engine begins to roll. Walker arranged for Mary Jane and me to meet with a U.S. Postal Agent in Baton Rouge on Thursday, November 21, so the slow train was gathering speed again. I returned home late on the 19th and emailed Ethan.

"Walker explained to us earlier that postal inspectors have been a great help to his office on child exploitation cases since apparently abusers frequently use mail and the Internet," I told him. "I guess I will learn more when we meet. I'm going to spend some time tomorrow afternoon preparing so that everything we have discovered from sharing information is fresh on my mind. Have you learned anything new from Jake or do you have any other thoughts these last couple of weeks that I should include?

"I will let you know how the meeting goes on Thursday and may learn more about what they have found and when they might like to talk with you. We are all pleased on our end that this is starting to move again," I said. "I hope you are staying strong."

"Thanks for the update, Rannah," Ethan replied. "Sounds very positive. I last spoke with Jake about a week ago and he is keen to see this developed. I will update him today and make sure he is in the right frame of mind.... If Jake is happy to speak too, this will add real gravitas to the whole thing.... Remember he will need massive assurance of privacy should he go ahead."

Although Ethan had connected with Jake and they seemed to develop a good rapport, Jake had not yet been willing to talk to us. Scott had abused and traumatized him so severely that his first concern was the protection of his family. We would later learn that he was afraid Scott would go so far as to have someone kidnap his children from school to silence him.

When Jake was younger, Scott had used his followers to threaten him and return him when he tried to run away. When it came to the monster he had known, Jake was not willing to take any chances with his family's safety. As we all felt that encouraging Jake to come forward, too, was crucial, Nathan urged me to work for his cooperation. So far, we had to respect his wishes to remain in the background.

I met Mary Jane in a downtown parking lot, halfway between her office and mine, at 8:15 a.m. Thursday morning for our meeting with Allyson Hoffine, an inspector with the U.S. Postal Inspection Service. Her office is in the old Downtown Post Office, across the street from the federal courthouse. Mary Jane sent a text message to let her know we were there, and Allyson met us downstairs to take us up the creaky elevator to her office. Allyson is a pretty, dark-haired woman in her 30s who has the tall, lean body of a runner. Mary Jane says she looks like Jennifer Garner, and we both agree that since she was once a street cop, she is also tough. She was wearing khaki-colored slacks and a blouse with a sweater pulled around her when she met us, her attire disguising both her strength and her looks, most likely on purpose. She had the serious demeanor of a law enforcement officer, with a framed poster on her wall reminding us that hers was the oldest federal law enforcement agency in the country. That reminded me of all the TV westerns we watched as kids, and the bad guys always holding up the U.S. Mail.

Allyson is a single mother of a young son, and she has spent her entire career in law enforcement, the past seven years working primarily on child endangerment cases with Luke Walker.

Allyson's job with the U.S. Postal Inspection Service involves investigating cases of child exploitation that use the mail in some way—for example, thumb drives or gift cards mailed to kids. She works directly to protect the U.S. Mail. She works major mail fraud and mail theft cases, usually involving identity theft or embezzlement and typically associated with other crimes.

Once again, I began the story of Ethan's email, explaining how he had found me and sharing the information he had provided. Mary Jane had her binder with her, the same information she had brought to the meeting with Luke Walker, with copies of the news articles and specific items highlighted in yellow. The main story she had highlighted dealt with Scott Rogers' defense at the trial that a child had molested *him*. Mary Jane began to explain how she came to contact Luke Walker and what led to our meeting with Allyson.

As Allyson shuffled through folders containing information she had pulled together for the meeting, she held up enlarged copies of drivers' licenses and asked me to confirm the identities of Mathew Hodgkins and Stuart Poulton. Mary Jane and I spent the next two and a half hours showing her the news articles and explaining what we had learned from Ethan. Luke had filled her in, so at times we could tell she had additional information we did not have. She was serious and methodical in gathering the information she needed.

Like Luke, Allyson said that Scott's pattern was very typical. She was not at all surprised that he had worked at getting community groups to give him awards and certificates, saying that child sex offenders usually create a persona they want people to believe —to keep their true nature secret.

Allyson seemed as frustrated as we were by the news coverage of Scott's trial in the U.K., especially Scott's blaming the victim and the length of time the young victim was required to testify on the witness stand facing his abuser.

Mary Jane told her about the immigration application, noting the question where she felt he must have filed a false statement. Since he had gotten his U.S. citizenship in Baton Rouge before Judge Frank Polozola, Mary Jane thought jurisdiction could be the Middle District of Louisiana. She also told Allyson she felt his application to Child Services was falsified.

Allyson asked me where Ethan worked, and while I had not asked him directly, I told her where I believed he worked based on a simple Internet and social media search. As I explained later to Ethan, we jumped into the back and forth email exchange so quickly, I developed a trust in him before I got around to asking basic questions one would ordinarily want to know when meeting someone new. Mary Jane and I agreed that Allyson spoke in her own code, saying little aloud while she thumbed through documents, stopping short of revealing more than she wanted, leaving us to guess about details.

She was puzzled about one bit of preliminary information she was looking into, as it was incomplete. She asked if we thought it possible that Kimberly Rogers could be the person who had adopted the boy. We didn't think so, since Scott publicly claimed to be his adoptive parent, but we agreed that was a possibility. She had apparently found only one criminal background check when Scott adopted the older boy, and that was for Kimmy.

We discussed whether Scott had put 1stCo in Kimberly's name to show an income that would indicate she could support a child. Allyson let us know that, unfortunately, a special needs child such as the older boy who was autistic might be easier to adopt under unusual circumstances, such as the group's living arrangements. Another possibility was that Scott and Kimberly had not reported Mathew and Stuart living with them. These were all questions she would have to research to get more information, since Louisiana Child Services had refused to produce Rogers' application to adopt the first child.

She was interested in the information about Scott being "sectioned," as the concealed weapon permit he had obtained a few years earlier would have required that information. Allyson seemed to have looked into the unusual corporate structure of 1stCo, including the various names Scott had used—enough to understand the kind of person she faced.

She said that her initial focus would determine whether a "chargeable offense" had occurred, that is, whether Scott Rogers had committed a crime in the Middle District of Louisiana. Once she exhausted the leads we had discussed, she said she would consider interviewing some of the people around Scott. Before she did, she would rank them in priority based on what information she could gain from them versus what she could risk. She explained that the strategy works only if the victim is ready to talk.

From my description of Scott, Mathew, and Stuart, she considered Stuart a possible interview but recognized that if he were ready to talk, he could contribute a lot of information, but the risk was also very high. We agreed it was impossible to know whether she could trust Stuart to talk. If Scott had that much control over him, Stuart might report back to Scott and he could pack up the family and disappear again. Since the safety of the children was our primary concern, this possiblility was frightening.

From the background information she had gathered and the meeting we had with her, Mary Jane and I both felt Allyson was invested in the matter and not simply meeting with us to satisfy a request from a U.S. Attorney in another jurisdiction.

"I knew Luke Walker would come through, and boy did he!" Mary Jane said. "Another person who gives a shit and who works in government!"

We left the meeting with an understanding of how we would communicate going forward. Mary Jane would communicate with Allyson, I would continue talking with Ethan, and we would remain tight lipped. Though I talked to both Mary Jane and Nathan every day, usually several times, this plan kept all of us from having to repeat information too many times, at least for the two most important people now: Allyson and Ethan.

I explained to Ethan that Allyson's conversation with him was for background purposes, as her focus was the charges the federal government could bring against Scott here. I assured him I had not given her any copies of our emails, but had used them only for reference in my explanations. I told him Mary Jane and I both liked Allyson, and felt she believed the information we had shown her. I was relieved to meet another person who knew how to deal with child sex predators and who felt our own instincts were correct.

"I think you will find her easy to talk to," I told Ethan. "She would prefer the call to be via Skype so that you can see her and know exactly who she is. She wants to give you confidence that she represents U.S. law enforcement officials you can trust."

Allyson had said she could show him her badge to make him comfortable with her role. I also liked the idea of a Skype interview for the same reasons I had wanted to introduce Ethan to everyone in the room during our first telephone call. Because Scott had deceived and manipulated these young men, I was never going to be anything but open and honest. I knew that building trust with Ethan was important; for that reason, we needed always to tell the truth and avoid surprises. While I realize investigations aren't always conducted that way, I wanted to feel certain that I could trust Ethan and he could trust us. All of us.

"I do believe this is going to take time because she has to dig deep and be very specific," I told Ethan, "and Scott is every bit as clever as you have warned. But I still think we are dealing with the people who are insulated from any political persuasion."

Ethan was happy to talk to Allyson via Skype when she was ready to schedule the call and offered to provide any additional proof that he had attended the Academy if she needed to verify further his identity. He confirmed that in my search for him, I had found the company where he had worked for 14 years, but he had only a couple of weeks earlier resigned to start his own business.

Meanwhile, Ethan stayed in touch with Jake, keeping him informed. He said that at some point he thought Jake, too, would speak with Allyson. He planned to talk to Jake the following week and would look for more details on Scott's sectioning.

Then he asked if Allyson had revealed anything about what had happened in Texas.

"She did not say anything about Texas, but I did give her Diane Palladino's name and the information you gave me, and I could tell she is working on that," I told him. "I had to sit and go through the emails with her and let her take notes so that she could follow up. Her office prefers that I point out, from what you have told me, what areas to investigate. We need to let her people build their own case until they are ready to talk with you.

"The other thing to keep in mind is that they are not going to give me a lot of feedback moving forward, and once they talk with you, their communication is going to be with you and not me. The postal inspector said that one of the reasons she works so much with the U.S. Attorney on child exploitation cases is that her office is very low key. The likelihood of anyone knowing what she is working on is less than with cases that involve the FBI. That made sense to me because I wasn't aware of the postal inspectors in Baton Rouge and yet they are also federal law enforcement agents...but we know the names of the FBI agents because their cases are in the media."

I told Ethan I thought Jake's cooperation was good news. "I don't sense any doubt or skepticism at all about your truthfulness or Jake's. The federal officials look forward to talking with you and letting you know that you can trust them going forward. Both Luke and Allyson say that Scott appears to present a textbook case and that everything they see fits the pattern of a child predator. Their goal is to find a 'chargeable offense' here in Baton Rouge without a victim coming forward. But Allyson describes herself as one who will dig for the truth, and I found her very sincere and ready to work.

"Next week is Thanksgiving here, so offices are closed Thursday and Friday," I explained, again trying not to sound like someone who assumed Ethan had no knowledge of America. I felt sure he was aware of Thanksgiving, which, after all, is rooted in English tradition. "She did say she planned to go to Scott's church on Sunday, but I doubt I will hear from her again until after Thanksgiving, unless I have something to report. By then, she should have looked at additional files."

A quick note back from Ethan said, "I just wanted to thank you for not passing over the info and keeping all private...."

"You're very welcome," I said. "I know the subject matter is sensitive and could hurt if we handled it any other way. I don't want to overplay my role in this, either. I'm very lucky to have close friends I trust, an attorney and a legal researcher, who can advise me in areas where I'm not knowledgeable. And Nathan and Mary Jane helped prepare me for the meetings with the federal authorities so that I could keep information private."

Ethan's politeness always touched me, especially considering the anxiety I knew he must feel. "We don't really know each other," I said, "but it's amazing that you reached out to me, with no idea that you had stumbled upon such a stubborn woman. I had an almost instant feeling that you were honest. And everything you have done has held that to be true. I'm going to do whatever I can to protect you and try to see that goodness prevails."

"I think this whole event is a strange coincidence," he replied. "We will see. ;-) "

That night, I thought about where all this was going and realized we had just taken a very serious step.

November 21, 2013. That's the day I became a confidential informant on a case that now included two federal law enforcement agencies and would ultimately involve at least two more in the United States along with the State of Louisiana and other police agencies in the U.K.

Everyday conversations took on a new formality, an added pressure to maintain confidentiality, and a level of intensity I had never before experienced. My days were bookended by phone calls and emails about Scott Rogers, with, in between, some semblance of normalcy, as the three of us, Ethan's "dream team," went about our work as usual. I talked to Nathan and Mary Jane every day, usually several times, and we kept discussions confined to our small group of trusted people, which now included Allyson. Only occasionally did I give a very general update to family members that the investigation was "ongoing," which was my answer now to anyone with whom I had spoken about Ethan's first contact. Close friends were almost completely left out, with a few exceptions of those close enough to have gone through the initial Scott Rogers saga with me and who knew only that it wasn't over. Since Ethan's first email, we had been looking for the right person to act on his information. Now that we had entered into this more serious phase, now that the federal authorities had taken over, I had to avoid talking to almost everyone.

Before we met with Allyson, however, I decided I needed to have one more conversation. Over dinner with my mother at a restaurant in Hammond—a small college town about an hour east of Baton Rouge—I told her about the investigation that was about to begin and my involvement in it. She had decided to remodel her kitchen at Evergreen Oaks, and I knew I would be in the middle of that, since renovating a 163-year-old house is never easy. I didn't know where the case would go, I thought, so I'd better let her know I could be called away at any moment.

"I have something to tell you," I started, "but before I do, I want you to know that when I get to the end of it, you cannot say to me, *Don't get involved,* because it's too late for that." She laughed, probably because we both knew that, like me, she was not one to do what she was told. But when I finished the story, she didn't hesitate in responding.

"Scott Rogers intentionally tried to hurt you and Val by lying about you in the newspaper," she said, "and now look at what kind of person he is…abusing children! You should do everything you can to stop him," she said as she tapped her finger lightly on the table.

At 83, my mother was strong, energetic, and as brave as anyone I had ever known. She didn't respond as the lawyers had, advising Nathan against my involvement.

"A child molester!" Mom said. "Rannah, you all have to *stop* him."

Meanwhile, a federal agent was beginning to build her case for doing just that.

Where would this lead? And what would Scott Rogers do when he found out federal agents were looking into his past?

CHAPTER THIRTY-ONE

THE INTERVIEW

Day 97
December 2, 2013

On Monday morning, Allyson contacted Mary Jane to ask that I set up a call with Ethan on Thursday of that week. She asked further that I be present for the call, or at least part of it, so we could help each other fill in gaps in the timeline she wanted to create. Then I was to bow out of the conversation so that she could speak privately with Ethan.

I asked if he could be available between 3 p.m. and 5 p.m. London Time, which was between 9 a.m. and 11 a.m. Central for us. I guessed the call would last over an hour, and I told Ethan that after taking his statement, Allyson would most likely discuss with him what would come next. "I know this is a big step," I told him, "so if you have any questions, just let me know. I want you to be as comfortable as possible moving forward."

By the time I confirmed Ethan's availability with Allyson, she said something had come up and asked if we could make the call at the same time on Friday, December 6. The next day, Mary Jane heard from Luke Walker, who said that Allyson alone would conduct the interview. Because she makes the cases for him, he said, he wanted her to speak directly with Ethan. The following day, we rescheduled again and moved the call to the afternoon, or 8 p.m. for Ethan. I told him that Mary Jane and I would be present at Allyson's office, until the time for him and Allyson to speak privately.

The previous weekend, *The Around Town TV Show* guests had included a man who works with Parker House, the Volunteers of America home for abused children. Further, the show had aired an ad for the 13:34 Church that promoted a "free children's church," which I noticed because both Allyson and Sue Bernie had worried that Scott was using the Church to attract children. On that show, Scott also interviewed a woman from the Louisiana Attorney General's Office about cybercrime, immediately mentioning his close ties to Attorney General Buddy Caldwell. When interviewing another one of the guests, Scott mentioned having an 18-month-old baby in addition to his older son.

Concerned about the children, Ethan asked if I knew whether the younger boy was adopted; I told him I did not, but that Scott now referred to his two children a lot on the show. I hoped once I connected Ethan with the federal authorities, they might be able to share with him more information from the investigation.

Before leaving my office for Allyson's, I emailed Ethan one last time, just to make sure we were in synch. "We will be calling you in about 40 minutes," I wrote.

"Thanks, Rannah...speak then," he replied.

Through the magic of video chatting, we would finally meet the mysterious Ethan, who by now felt like someone I had known for a long time.

Allyson took Mary Jane and me to a room where a computer and recording devices waited on a table. In front of the monitor were the chairs where Allyson and I would sit for the first half of the interview, with a third for Mary Jane just out of camera shot. When we started the call and Ethan came onto the screen, he was waving hello to us, seated in a child's bedroom, talking to us through a pink princess telephone.

I was finally meeting the person with whom I had been communicating almost daily for the past three months. There he was—a handsome, dark-haired young man with an easy smile, who appeared genuinely glad to see us, as if he had just run into an old friend he hadn't seen in a while.

In the background, we could see a child's bed with stuffed animals, and he quickly explained that he was alone at home with his two children and had just started a movie for them, and that he would need to check in on them during the call.

In fact, the children checked in on their Dad, who excused himself a couple of times to step away from camera view, though we could still hear him patiently and lovingly answering their questions. Hearing the young father talking to his children, Allyson, Mary Jane, and I exchanged quick looks, recognizing how their presence in his life must awaken old fears of people who harm children. "That speaks volumes about who he is and how important children are to him," Mary Jane said as we watched him give his children's questions his full attention before they ran off to continue watching their movie.

After making introductions, Allyson and I settled in front of the camera as she went through the formalities of explaining the agenda for the call. She asked Ethan to retell his story for the record, and she asked me to help fill in the gaps, since the two of us had been talking for several months. For the first hour of the call, Ethan and I gave Allyson the timeline of the events the two of us knew, with Mary Jane occasionally popping into camera view to add a detail.

When we had documented all that we could, Allyson explained that from this point forward, her questions would focus more on Ethan's personal experience of the abuse. She told him that I knew what she hoped to accomplish and that she had suggested he would want me to leave at that point and that I understood. But she also added that the decision was entirely his, to which he replied, "No, I think she should stay."

After the interview, I learned that Ethan's answer was a strong signal to both Allyson and Mary Jane that I would need to stay more involved going forward than any of us had anticipated.

Ethan's trusting me to go through that very difficult portion of the interview with him made me even more committed to help him complete this journey we were now on together.

"He wanted Rannah there and her staying involved with everything," Mary Jane observed. "He had come to trust Rannah and wanted to keep her in the picture. From then on, that is how the investigation proceeded. Any time a question needed an answer, Allyson would ask me, I would pass it on to Rannah, and she would talk to Ethan, and the information would flow back. There came a time when the agent was communicating directly with Ethan, but he stayed in full contact with Rannah, keeping her apprised of everything that was going on and the conversations he was having with Allyson, and then Rannah would pass the information on to Nathan and me."

This system of communicating originated with Nathan's and Mary Jane's efforts to protect Ethan and me, since all of us assumed that the investigation could lead to charges against Scott and a legal case to follow. The process we developed worked well for all of us.

Ethan began by telling us that as a young boy, he wanted to be an actor, like the James Bond or Arnold Schwarzenegger characters he saw in action films. To the three of us listening, he certainly had the good looks to make that ambition realistic. He explained how his parents had enrolled him in The Academy of Dance and Performing Arts, run by Scott Rogers, in their town of Bury St. Edmunds.

Ethan signed up for acting classes. But soon, Scott took notice of the handsome young boy and approached him about taking a dance class. Though Ethan explained that he had no interest in dance, Scott persuaded him to reconsider, reminding him that his parents were paying a lot of money for him to attend the Academy. If Ethan would take both dance and acting classes, Scott said, he could put him on full scholarship, which would also make his parents very proud.

To a 12-year-old boy, the plan sounded like a good one, as it would save his parents money, so he began taking both dance and acting classes. The new arrangement, however, gave Scott the opportunity to come in closer contact with him through the dance class, calling him into his office for one-on-one sessions, helping him stretch, and assisting him with his dance exercises, all of which entailed putting his hands on Ethan's young body. And so began four years of sexual abuse.

For the next hour, Ethan painstakingly described the abuse that took place in Scott's office...at the Academy...in a car, a pattern of abuse that painted an even darker picture of Scott Rogers.

Though Ethan's voice was steady as he answered every question Allyson asked of him, we could hear the raw emotion as he addressed the most personal aspects.

I sat in front of the computer monitor with Allyson as she worked through her list of questions and as Ethan patiently answered each one. I knew this interview was a necessary part of Allyson's investigation, but it was difficult for everyone. Somehow Ethan found the strength to tell his story.

Pedophiles groom children for abuse, and Scott Rogers was truly a textbook case. While they differ in the children to whom they are attracted in terms of age, appearance, and gender, all pedophiles look for victims who are in some way vulnerable. We had heard of Scott's seeking out children in foster care and targeting those whose communication skills might not be strong due to autism, delayed speech, or dyslexia, any of which might make a victim hesitant or uncomfortable about speaking up.

To gain control of their victims, pedophiles collect as much information as possible. Ethan told us, for example, that Scott befriended the parents to learn all that he could about the families and to discover their weaknesses. Students at the Academy described how he almost forced them to tell intimate secrets about their parents if they wished to secure a place in his inner circle.

Next, pedophiles work to fill a need in the child's life. Scott Rogers offered full scholarships to working class families to make children feel they were helping their parents; promises of fame to fulfill their fantasies of stardom; tokens of secret affection to boost their self-esteem; and the false image of a loving family for those who were alone.

As for Ethan, he had enjoyed playing in the Abbey Gardens with his friends, pretending he was an action hero from the latest movies. Knowing that, Scott used the boy's dreams against him for the worst possible reason.

Pedophiles begin by lowering a child's inhibitions about sex, so the stretching and warm-ups needed for dance class gave Scott an excuse to put his hands on the boys' bodies and thus gradually introduce them to sexual activity.

Ethan later described sessions in his office—with Scott questioning him over and over, wearing him down mentally. "What are you thinking?" was his favorite question, and no answer was complete enough to satisfy him. Ethan described how the mental abuse lasted for hours, but he always knew how it would end—with sexual abuse. *Where had Scott learned these brainwashing techniques? He had certainly mastered them.*

He explained to us that he had not yet told his wife everything that was going on or even that he had contacted me, which made him very uncomfortable, as he didn't want to keep anything from her. He said when he emailed me, he simply thought I might get the information out to the news media, to warn parents in Louisiana who might allow their children to associate with Rogers. At that point, Ethan didn't even know that Scott had adopted a son—and had access to other children. He said he didn't know how far he was willing to go with this investigation, but he was willing to give this statement in hopes that the authorities would investigate Scott further.

Allyson was professional, but very direct. She asked all the hard questions, but in a way that made it clear she was documenting the information she needed to go further. In the second half of the interview, she asked details about the sexual abuse, and Ethan remained strong in answering. She let Ethan know she had requested Scott's immigration records and was waiting to receive them.

Allyson pressed Ethan to encourage Jake to speak with her, since Ethan had described Scott's abuse of Jake as much worse than his own. She wanted to get as much evidence as possible to proceed, and two victims would make a stronger case than one. She floated a lot of possibilities, including the victims in the U.K. pressing charges there and the U.S. deporting Scott to face them.

We all agreed that a lot had changed in the past 20 years and that the courts in the U.K. were unlikely to subject a 35-year-old man to the same treatment the young victim in Scott's trial had endured. On the other hand, we were asking young men with families, young men in the prime of their careers, to walk out into the light of day and let the world know a sexual predator had gotten away. The trial would no doubt open old wounds, but it might also heal some. It would be a stunning revelation on both sides of the Atlantic. But it would also pose a significant disruption of many lives. From what I had learned of Ethan, he would consider all options and make the best decision for himself, which would be what he deemed best for his family.

The 90-minute interview left me mentally exhausted, and I still had to review the conversation with Nathan. Mary Jane was far more accustomed to interviews in criminal cases than I was, but the reality of the horror Scott Rogers had inflicted on the lives of young boys remained in the back of my mind. Scott had committed terrible crimes and gotten away with them, leaving in his wake victims just trying their best to build successful careers, to raise families, and to live good lives, all the while enduring an unresolved secret.

Hearing Ethan's story left a quiet undercurrent of anxiety running through me. Scott's portraying himself as the exact opposite of what he was to so many reputable people gave his crimes an even more sinister air. He wasn't just hiding in plain sight, as the saying goes. He was working overtime to self-promote a false identity for himself—hosting a television show for all to see. When we were kids we had a saying, "You can fool all people some of the time, and some people all of the time, but you can't fool all people all the time." Scott was obviously unaware of that third category. *How long did he imagine his charade could go on? Did he imagine he was so clever he could fool everyone? Forever?*

Allyson had pushed Ethan to take action, while the conversations Nathan, Mary Jane, and I had pursued had involved simply receiving information and trying to figure out what to do with it. She made it clear he should pursue Scott to the fullest extent of the law in both the U.S. and England. Now he had some tough decisions to make.

Several hours after the call, when I'd had time to think about all we had heard, I met Nathan and his wife Francine for an early dinner to discuss the interview, hoping that would clear my mind of the sad details.

Then I sent Ethan an email before we each headed into our weekend: "One last thought on today," I said. "The good news is that Allyson knows what she is dealing with in Scott and wants to stop him from harming children." She made that clear to both of us.

"I know she threw out a lot of possibilities, and I don't know where this investigation will take her, but I know when the time comes, you will make the best decision for yourself and for your family and I will support whatever that is."

As angry as I was for Ethan after learning more about what Scott had done to him, I also felt that this journey was first and foremost Ethan's story, and his pursuit. I had one unpleasant encounter with Scott Rogers, a destructive act that was entirely deliberate on his part, but that had served only to put me on a path to learn the real harm he had done. Ethan's participation in the investigation and beyond wasn't my call. My responsibility was to support whatever he decided. And at that moment, depleted by the tension of the interview, I had to consider that this interview might be as far as he was willing to go. And if that were the case, I wanted to support his decision. Of course, after hearing Ethan's interview, I wanted justice for him—we all did. But at what price? *I have to support his decision—whatever it may be. He has been hurt enough and may not want to go any further.*

I told Ethan that I had spoken to Nathan about his interview, and that Nathan encouraged us to keep pushing Allyson to get the U.S. documents that would show fraud on Scott Rogers's part. "Things move slowly here, but they will move because her office commands respect," I assured him.

We knew the raw truth now. We knew how Scott manipulated young minds, how he slowly seduced them with his power at the school, and ultimately how he took advantage of them for his own perverse sexual desires.

I had believed Ethan from the beginning, but after hearing details of the abuse, no question remained: We had to stop Scott Rogers' abuse. We all agreed the most important step was to protect the children currently in his care. If Ethan couldn't go any further, we would have to find another way. But at this point, he was the key.

Talking with Allyson had made one path clearer: Ethan and the other victims could press charges in the U.K., which has no statute of limitations on child sex abuse cases, and U.S. authorities would cooperate in deporting Scott to face those charges in court. Ethan and the other boys could have another chance to convince a jury of what he had done to them, and this time, no one would stand alone.

They could press charges together, no longer vulnerable to a seasoned attorney carrying out a strenuous cross-examination against a single defenseless child. But a trial would carry with it a circus atmosphere, and so the question remained as to whether the victims would subject their families to that level of publicity. The British press had covered Scott's U.K. trial like a celebrity trial and would no doubt do so again.

A second path was to find what the federal authorities referred to as a "chargeable offense" in the United States, but that would most likely involve fraud, which might or might not result in Scott's losing custody of the children. That would be for a judge to decide.

Allyson told us we might have to accept a victory that would mean getting the children away from him and his getting away from us, disappearing before we could make a case against him. He could even leave the country.

We agreed, hoping that a paper trail on revoking his custody might prevent him from adopting any other children, at least in the U.S. But what if he ran with the children? Would the U.S. authorities follow him to protect them? *How many children fall through the cracks because predators like Scott pick up and move—and change their identities?*

And there was always the other thought we all considered, a concern we talked about often: What if he attempted suicide, or worse, a murder-suicide, to take the children with him?

Ethan had much to consider. Had this investigation gone too far for him? Was he feeling the impact of having tossed the grenade of information about Scott?

Was he ready to walk away rather than stop Scott Rogers? Rather than expose his wife and children to a trial that could hurt them? *Are you ready to do what it takes to stop him, Ethan? This is only going to get more difficult.*

CHAPTER THIRTY-TWO

THE HARDEST MONTH

December 2013

Ethan is obviously a lot stronger than I anticipated. While I was feeling concerned for him after the interview, he was taking steps to move things forward. While I went to bed early, mentally drained from what he had gone through, Ethan sat down and composed a long email to Jake explaining what he had done and asking him to come forward.

Ethan told him Allyson knew what Scott was and assured him she had a great deal of experience with this kind of case. He told him the federal authorities were taking a look at where Scott lives and with whom and his patterns of behavior. Ethan described further how Scott was running some sort of "weird church" and the authorities were attempting to learn what he was up to.

"They are aware of his friendships with local law enforcement and local politicians and how this fits with his behavior as a predatory pedophile," Ethan said. He explained that the process was in its early days and would take a long time. He told Jake he thought the federal authorities would, at some point, charge Scott with fraud and then remove the children from his home and begin investigating him more fully.

Ethan said that since he and Jake were both U.K. residents, their main role would be to provide information and that he felt the U.S. authorities would get enough on Scott to charge him. Then he asked Jake if he would agree to a Skype interview with

Allyson. "I think it will help massively for them to pull the full picture together of who they are dealing with," he told him. "Make it clear to them exactly how you want it to go, your involvement, and they will respect that," he assured him.

As it turned out, the prospect of an interview revived old fears in Jake that we could not have expected. While he considered Ethan's interview a step forward in bringing Scott to justice for his crimes, it brought to mind all the times Scott had used his young protégés to retrieve Jake when he had tried to run away and to help punish him upon his return.

"I don't think, as you said, anything from us could be used in evidence and as you know I am very paranoid about the whole situation," he emailed Ethan. "I'm not worried about people finding out what happened to me, as all of my family knows, and my friends, etc. So I'm not nervous on that score. What worries me is retribution from either Scott or his cronies that would directly affect my life and family. As you can imagine, I'm hyper-protective over my kids and as mentioned I have been threatened so much in the past. If it were only me concerned, I would say 'fuck it' and fly to the states to bloody witness! As it is, I think I would be happy to be contacted by email, then I can check credentials of anyone contacting me, then I could answer any specific questions they may have. I think you have to remember that you have built up a trust in your team and they have become friends and allies to you. I obviously don't know any of them and I've only spoken to you recently. This wasn't something I would have ever pursued myself, and as I said to you in the beginning, I tried to get as far away from The Academy as possible. I am a complete coward about speaking to someone on Skype who I don't know and have never been in contact with before, especially when conversations can be recorded. I am aware that I sound like a paranoid freak but I also find this time of year quite difficult, as this was when Scott always tried to make contact with me, leaving messages via his 'followers' at stage door or leaving Christmas messages on my phone (fuck knows how he got the number). You could call it my 'paranoia month'!

"I promise you I'm not usually a big girl's blouse about anything else in my life," Jake told Ethan. "This is just like having my worst nightmares surface and I am desperate to help bring him down but also petrified of it ruining mine and my family's life. I haven't had the buildup or communication or initiation with contacts of my own volition so this is tough for me. I hope you understand, Ethan. I'm OK with you letting the postal woman have my email (I'm sure she could get it herself if she really needed). I can't guarantee that I will respond, but think I will be a lot happier answering anything slowly.

"Cheers, mate. Have a good weekend," he signed off.

Ethan shared Jake's apprehension with me, expressing concern about Allyson emailing him, as the emails could become evidence later on. "We have to protect Jake as much as possible," Ethan said.

I found Jake's reaction entirely understandable. Everything he said made sense. I talked with Nathan and Mary Jane before responding so that Mary Jane could keep Allyson in the loop. Yes, we had to protect Jake. He knew exactly what kind of violence Scott had committed. So while Jake's speaking with Allyson would be helpful, if he were willing to communicate with her only by email, we had to discourage that, as email communications were subject to discovery if Scott went to trial. I knew neither Ethan nor I wanted to risk exposing Jake, should the authorities charge Scott with a crime. This is where Nathan was so valuable: He knew the consequences of our methods of communication and had advised me from the start to watch what I put into the hands of the federal agents. *We have to protect Jake—even if it slows down the investigation.*

Jake had run away from Scott twice before the third attempt was successful. Each time, Scott sent Stuart and other boys from the Academy to hunt for him and bring him back. Each time, Scott had convinced Child Services to return him to Scott's care, and to the brutal punishment that awaited him.

"I've been thinking about Jake this morning," I told Ethan. "It's obvious Jake needs a little more time to build trust. His feelings are very understandable and clearly he's another intelligent man and strong communicator who I feel sure would have a lot of credibility with the federal authorities here. He seems impressive in his resolve, too. You've brought him a long way, since at first he would not respond to your emails.

"What if you suggest a phone call, without Skype, with you and Allyson?" I suggested. "That way, he might not feel that his every reaction is being observed. Jake has apparently been threatened and stalked, so maybe we need to move a little slower for him to feel comfortable. I agree with him that we had the benefit of a lot of email discussion, a phone call to introduce ourselves, and finally the Skype call.

"Another thought would be for us to suggest that Allyson talk with Adrian Randall, the U.K. detective, and he could perhaps help facilitate a call between her and Jake. I don't know how Jake would feel about that, but that arrangement would at least assure him who Allyson is and confirm her credentials for him.

"Also, maybe he doesn't want to deal with this during Christmas because of the reminders," I said. "If Allyson can review the immigration and citizenship documents and find what she suspects she might, that might give Jake a greater sense of comfort, knowing that his background info is helping make a strong case. I think that would encourage all of us.

"I'm just throwing out some ideas for your feedback. I've spoken with Nathan again this morning because his advice is helpful in protecting everyone's privacy. He agrees that we don't want to ask Jake to email with Allyson...you should share that with him so he understands that we are looking out for his privacy.

"I thought we might all think about this over the weekend and I could call Allyson on Monday to discuss, so if you have any other thoughts, feel free to share. I shared this with Mary Jane because she also has a relationship with the prosecutor and I wanted her to discuss with him."

Ethan agreed to have a long think about Jake's response and get back to me on the best way forward. By Monday, he had spoken to Jake again and just didn't think he was ready. "I think at best, at some point he would be happy to communicate and give info...but that is as far as it goes.

"My initial reason for contacting you was to expose Scott and raise awareness in your community of who he is," Ethan told me. "I never expected to give evidence or take it as far as perhaps I have. As you know I have not yet told my wife I am communicating with you on this matter. Obviously, I need to talk with her and then think about the impact on my family and me. At this point, I am happy to help with info and gap filling but I don't want to waste anyone's time or hard work that will be needed here, not to mention the mental efforts needed to pursue this in the right way.

"I suggest that the next step should be to see if there is a real chance to arrest him, then review and speak with Jake. I really hope there is a way to catch Scott and save those kids...I hope this all makes sense," Ethan said.

This was not an unexpected response following Allyson's interview, which was difficult and surely revived old memories that Ethan had put behind him. Allyson asked for a lot, possibly hoping to settle for whatever Ethan and Jake were willing to share. I was not surprised that the old memories stirred by Ethan's interview made both men retreat a bit.

Meanwhile, that weekend Scott appeared on *The Around Town Show* with a woman named Mari Presedo to announce that the 13:34 Church would hold a "mass wedding" on Valentine's Day, meaning that she would be conducting weddings and same-sex "commitment ceremonies" all day long. Oddly, for this segment, Scott pretended to have nothing to do with the church and presented the wedding promotion as something Presedo and her pastor had arranged, without any hint that he was the pastor.

Scott also announced he would host the broadcast of the Baton Rouge Christmas Parade, which the Cortana Kiwanis Club put on each year, with Veronica Mosgrove as his co-host.

Mary Jane and I talked on Sunday and I asked her to relay Ethan's thoughts on going forward to Allyson.

After the long weekend of thinking about Jake's and Ethan's reaction to Allyson's requests, I sat down near midnight on Monday and responded to Ethan. "You and I are completely on the same page," I began. "Mary Jane had a long talk with Allyson and she understands as well. Although she asked a lot of questions, she does not realistically see you as a witness. Her reason for gathering as much background as possible on the U.K. situation seems to be that while she can charge Scott if she finds fraud on his immigration papers, to get the kids out of his house, she still has to find cause to suggest abuse. Because the two little boys are not able to communicate reliably or at all, I think she felt that false statements coupled with information from previous victims would help make the case for removing the kids.

"In terms of exposing him, there is always the last resort of handing the news articles over to the news media and other officials, which was what I initially thought might be the way to go. The reporters I spoke with were a little worried that an old story where he was acquitted might backfire without any new information. As you know, we've worked hard to get this information into the right hands. But if this approach fails, we have a few more options before we resort to carpet bombing news articles.

"You have done everything we asked of you and I think we need to wait to see if the postal inspector can find more information. No one wants to cause problems for you. We're trying to help, not hurt.... Allyson said she will probably email you just to let you know that she understands your position, but will also understand if you say little or nothing in reply via email.

"Let's just give her time. If she comes back with fraud on the immigration papers, that should give her reason to go to the Child Services office to look for fraud on the adoption or foster care papers. Nathan says the filing of false information on government documents is a serious crime with very serious penalties of jail time. He believes she can make progress against Scott and the others living in the house if she can bring fraud to light.

"I'm just so sorry this process isn't simpler," I said. "All I can say is that I believe it is worth the effort."

"Thanks, Rannah, sounds good," Ethan replied Tuesday morning. "Let's await the findings of the postal inspector. I know the process isn't easy and I do appreciate all your amazing efforts...speak once we know more. Let me know if you need anything in the mean time."

Perhaps December was just too difficult a month to dredge up old memories for Jake and Ethan. In the past, Scott had taken advantage of this emotional time of year, when people who are away from families and loved ones are especially vulnerable, to track down Jake and bring him back into the fold. Those close to Scott have said Christmas was a huge holiday for him. *Of course it was, since Christmas is such a magical time for children.*

We would later learn that after Jake had finally escaped from Scott, he had actually spent time living on the streets, even sleeping in a *skip*—British slang for a dumpster—for two nights in the bitter cold, wearing only a T-shirt. That was the last time he ran away; he was determined to do whatever was necessary to evade Scott. Again, on Scott's orders, the boys from the Academy formed a search party, walking the streets, looking for Jake to drag him back to Scott.

Now Ethan and Jake were young fathers, and Christmas for them was a time for creating treasured memories for their families, whom they wanted to protect at all costs...even if they had to put aside their own search for justice.

As 2013 was coming to a close, I was working every day on the production of Red Stick Revelry, the New Year's Eve celebration for Baton Rouge, glad to have a break from Scott Rogers. Still, I couldn't help wondering what the New Year would bring. Mary Jane and I knew that Allyson was doing all she could to find out whether Scott had lied on federal documents to get control of children. Waiting for her results, however, was hard.

Would she finally get justice for Ethan, Jake, and the others? Could she save the two young boys in Scott's care from suffering the same fate? Once we get past the emotions of the holiday season, will the truth begin to surface? As the countdown to a new year began, the reality of a predator's insatiable hunger for violence and manipulation was becoming clear. Ethan and Jake were real men with real lives—and a genuine fear that Scott would destroy them rather than allow the truth about himself to be revealed. Every time there was a reason to pause and reconsider, Ethan emerged stronger, ready to take the next step, just as he had promised. *Can he do it this time? Will Jake—with terrifying memories of Christmases past flooding over him—be able to do the same?* We waited to see.

The Boys of Bury

JAKE *in his own words*

England
2015

I was 11 years old when I was placed under Scott Rogers' care. I was taken away from my parents and placed under his care.

He is a master manipulator, an expert at brainwashing and a predatory pedophile.

At first he was very nice to me...but gradually things started happening...the sexual abuse. At first it was terrifying. I was beaten if I didn't comply. I was trapped under a roof with this man. I was abused...all the time. If you didn't comply, you would be held hostage...beaten with various implements. When you're a child and faced with that type of monster with that type of intelligent mind, you don't stand a chance.

CHAPTER THIRTY-THREE

THE PRIVATE INVESTIGATOR

Day 106
December 11, 2013

Just a few hours after I had promised to be patient and wait for Allyson's results, I received a strange message from a man who identified himself as Nick Graphia, a private investigator who wanted to ask me some questions about a case he was working. I returned the call, but had to leave him a message. When I phoned Nathan and Mary Jane to let them know, in case the call had anything to do with the Scott Rogers investigation, both cautioned me to be very careful. Both worried he could be working for Scott, possibly to find out why we were asking questions about him.

When we finally connected on Wednesday, December 11, Graphia told me he was working for a client who was considering a large donation to a church and had asked him to run a background check on the pastor and his daughter. In conducting his research, he came across my name in a newspaper story linked to the man and wanted to ask me if the story was true.

My letter to the editor! The gift that keeps on giving had now sent a P.I. to talk to me right in the middle of our investigation. When I asked Graphia the pastor's name, he said "Scott Rogers." He said he believed Scott also hosted a television show, had one church, and was exploring opening another one in the Highland Road area.

He said his client was considering a six-figure donation, and he had questions based on his 40 hours of research on Scott, as he had found information he thought strange. He asked me if I knew the Scott Rogers who was a pastor, and I replied that I knew *a* Scott Rogers who I understood was affiliated with some sort of church in Cortana Mall, but I was not sure if he was a pastor.

He went right to the newspaper article, asking if it were true. I told him if he was referring to my letter to the editor, which mentioned Scott, I had written it to correct inaccuracies in an earlier story, which contained numerous mistakes. I told him that because I had a lawsuit pending against 1stCo, a company with which Scott Rogers was involved, I could not comment on him.

Graphia said he had been researching Scott Rogers and had found several listings with the Secretary of State's Office that linked him to various corporations and different versions of his name. He said he had traced him to Texas, where a social security number was issued to him when he was around 38 years old, which he found strange because he could not find a domicile for Scott Rogers in Texas.

He also found it odd that the Highland Road address listed on all of his legal documents was a rented mailbox in a strip mall.

As I mentioned again that I could not talk about Scott, Graphia said he understood because he had attorneys in his family, then asked me if I could tell him if Scott came from England and whether he was black or white.

I felt comfortable answering those questions, since anyone willing to set an alarm for 5 a.m. on a weekend could easily discover the answers. You didn't have to be a private investigator to turn on your TV.

Graphia mentioned again that his client was wealthy and that Scott had been working him hard for a donation. The man was seriously considering giving him a large sum. At that point, I offered to have my attorney speak with Graphia and said that if I were he, I would pursue the questions because of the amount of money involved.

When Graphia ended by saying maybe we could help each other find out more about Scott Rogers, I told him the only way I could help further would be if he called my attorneys. I gave him phone numbers for both Nathan and Bill Lowrey, who had filed the 1stCo suit for us.

We never heard from Nick Graphia again.

By December 20, it had been over a week since I had heard from Ethan, but I didn't have anything to report and was starting to think we wouldn't hear anything from Allyson until after the New Year.

Then around mid-day, I got an email from Ethan's iPhone saying, "I hope you are well. I just wanted to wish you a Merry Christmas and a Happy New Year. I hope you and your family have a great time. Speak soon."

On Christmas Eve I replied to wish Ethan and his family a wonderful Christmas, too. "A bit of irony to share with you...the day I got your first email, I was less than an hour away from a press conference where I announced with the Mayor of Baton Rouge that we would hold our first official New Year's Eve celebration called "Red Stick Revelry" this year, so I remember the day well. Now I'm producing the event, which includes dropping a large Red Stick at midnight. "

I shared the website link so he could see the music video we produced, which included a quick shot of Mayor Holden playing Father Time. *This may explain to him why I was so vigilant about the spelling of Baton Rouge,* I thought.

"A good bit of excitement is building now, and Scott has called some of the sponsors to find out more about the celebration. He even invited one sponsor to go on his show to talk about it. When the man asked me if it was okay to appear on Scott's show, I told him sure, since I'm trying not to rock that boat just yet." Several people told me Scott was trying to get involved in the New Year's Eve event, but they had no way of knowing that he knew not to call me. Since I was the primary contact, he tried to convince others he was doing what he could to promote New Year's Eve in downtown Baton Rouge.

"Stay strong as you are…we will likely be rocking that boat in 2014," I continued, "but I believe it's going to be a good year. I hope Santa is very good to you and yours tonight!"

Ethan replied on Christmas Eve morning with the best news I had heard so far. "Thanks, Rannah. I'll check out the link. By the way, I have told my wife everything and she is behind me 100 percent. I'm more confident now with her in the picture so here's to 2014. Have a good one."

Merry Christmas, Ethan. Merry Christmas. Could it be you just got your groove back?

CHAPTER THIRTY-FOUR

THE NEW YEAR

Day 126
December 31, 2013

Baton Rouge's first New Year's Eve celebration in Town Square was more successful than anyone had imagined. We had tried to guess how many people would come out to see the 10-foot LED lighted Red Stick drop from 60 feet above the crowd at midnight. Some guessed 2,000, considering it was our first year. Others thought maybe 5,000. By 11 p.m., police estimated more than 15,000 people had crowded into Town Square, while even more packed the restaurants and bars along Third Street, as well as the local rooftop sushi restaurant that sat atop the arts center building.

It was an incredible night; looking out from the stage, I was proud of what we had accomplished. But it had been a tough year. The New Year's Eve crowd reminded me of that steamy August day when we had held the press conference to announce this event—just after I had received my first email from Ethan. I spoke with Mary Jane several times a week now, some weeks every day. Her Spanish Town neighborhood had a long-running tradition of hosting a New Year's Eve progressive party that moved to several homes before ending at the State Capitol for bell ringing and champagne. From the beginning, I wanted Spanish Town to be part of our Red Stick Revelry, and Mary Jane was one of the organizers getting everyone in Spanish

Town downtown for the first dropping of the Red Stick at midnight.

Just after the New Year, Kimmy and Scott were back on the air for the first *Around Town Show* of 2014. On the Sunday edition, Scott wished a happy birthday to Mathew Hodgkins, and I noticed in the production credits at the end of the show a listing for Ladonna Ward, a name I had not heard before at 1stCo. LaDonna's online resume described her as the Executive Director of the West Side Visitation Center in Plaquemine, which was in Iberville Parish where Scott lived. Iberville is one of the parishes divided by the river, so getting from Plaquemine to Scott's house in St. Gabriel could take an hour if the ferry wasn't running, even though the two were just across the Mississippi River from each other. The West Side Visitation Center is a non-profit organization that provides court-ordered supervised visitation and safe exchange services for families with domestic violence, child abuse, and other family conflicts. I found it odd that Scott had now managed to get someone associated with Family Services to work on the *Around Town Show,* but I had learned that with Scott Rogers, all roads lead to children.

The holidays came at a good time for Ethan to take a break from his interview, but now, with his wife's support, he seemed refreshed and ready to move forward. On Monday, January 6, he sent a short email saying, "Hello, Rannah, happy new year. I hope the Red Stick event went very well. When we spoke with Allyson on Skype, I believe the next move was to get Jake to do an interview with Allyson, is that still the case? If so, I will start to make some moves and see if I can persuade Jake to go ahead."

Wow! This was welcome news, since I felt Jake's push back was understandable. Perhaps Ethan had reason to believe he would reconsider after the initial ask.

"Happy New Year to you, too," I replied. "The Red Stick drop drew over 15,000 people and was a huge success. Our local TV station carried it live, so thousands more got to watch us ring in the New Year in Baton Rouge. Now we're just bracing for some cold weather tonight."

I called Allyson to let her know Ethan seemed willing to ask Jake again to agree to an interview. As I hadn't spoken to her since our Skype call, we talked briefly about how tough the decisions were for Ethan going forward. She wanted to wait for an interview with Jake until she'd had a chance to review the information she was gathering. I thought that was a good call. Since he was hesitant to talk, better for her to have more information in hand when they discussed his options.

While I had trouble understanding why the research was taking so long, Nathan and Mary Jane had lower expectations for how quickly anything could happen, while still maintaining optimism that Allyson would get the information she needed. From what we could tell, she had asked to look at the immigration papers on Scott and the others. Mary Jane thought that giving her until the end of the month before checking back with her was a reasonable plan, so we went into a few weeks of radio silence, patiently waiting for Allyson to let us know of any irregularities in Scott's immigration to the United States.

Weeks passed, during which most of the U.S. was experiencing a harsh winter. On January 27, Ethan checked in to see if we had heard anything. "I hope you are well and not freezing like much of the U.S.," he wrote. Apparently stories of our big chill had made the international news. "Communication going well here with Jake, have you had any feedback regarding the fraud?"

Ethan's email gave us a good reason to check in with Allyson, and as we had fallen into the routine of Mary Jane handling the communication with her, I talked with Mary Jane before replying. "As a matter of fact, the weather is causing some of the delay here," I sent back. I explained that in the South, ice storms shut down roads and government offices, and the weather had apparently delayed Allyson's access to some of the records she had requested. We had a rare occurrence of snow and ice, and many of our roads, elevated over Louisiana swamps, were closed. But I explained that we had been pushing Allyson to use the information he had provided to expand her investigation.

At the same time, I began to notice an unusual change in Scott Rogers on his *Around Town TV Show*. He was revealing more personal information than I had noticed in the previous four months of watching him.

He started off the New Year with a number of segments focused on kids: one for Volunteers in Public Schools; another on Winnie the Pooh Day, since Pooh was turning 100 years old; and segments on the East Baton Rouge Public Libraries and the YMCA, all featuring kids' activities.

Scott and Kimmy reviewed a movie showing police in a shoot-out followed by a car chase, during which Scott commented, "That's what I'm like when I'm out on the street doing my Sheriff work," reminding everyone that he was a reserve deputy for Sheriff Sid Gautreaux.

In another movie review about a woman having a baby that was somehow possessed, Scott commented to Kimmy, "When your mother was having you, all she had to do was give birth and I was terrified." He opened each program by playing a clip of a song that was number one on the charts that same week years ago. On this same program he played "Mandy" by Barry Manilow, saying, "That is also the name of my first wife." *Stop!* I hit the pause button on my DVR to rewind and play that comment again.

His first wife? What an odd choice of words, as we had never heard that he had more than one wife. But if Scott called Mandie his "first wife," he must at least have had a second wife. This comment would give Allyson something else to look for, something that would prove a very interesting piece of the Scott Rogers *coming to America* story.

On this last weekend in January, Scott also welcomed another regular guest, Ken Graham with the National Weather Service. I had met Ken when JoAnne Moreau invited him to participate in the Red Stick Ready program. Soon after, Ken began appearing on Scott's show as part of Veronica Mosgrove's segment for GOHSEP and later became a regular on *The Around Town TV Show*. Scott seemed to have grown close to Graham, asking about his children and inviting him to bring them to the show on his next visit, which he later did.

We knew from the conversation with Ken on the air that Scott had lived in Baton Rouge for 13 years, so Allyson should look for his arrival in Baton Rouge around 2000.

I shared this information with Ethan to let him know what we had gleaned from Scott's comments. Each week I watched the program and shared with Mary Jane anything I found of interest. She in turn discussed my observations with Allyson. From what I could tell, their minds operated on the same legal wave, while I tended to gauge people and events based on their level of public interest.

After Mary Jane relayed to Allyson what I had picked up from watching the shows, Mary Jane would call me with their ideas or requests from Allyson, which I would in turn share with Ethan and he would share with Jake. Somehow this back and forth flow of information worked well, allowing us to get what we learned both locally and from the U.K. to Allyson to aid her investigation.

Ethan was sympathetic about our inability to deal with cold weather in the South. "When we have snow the whole country closes down!" he said. "Then you see how Sweden deals with snow and realize just how ridiculous our reaction is."

January ended without our hearing anything from Allyson about possible fraud on Scott's immigration papers. On Friday, January 31, the highways around Baton Rouge had opened, but some government offices remained closed for several more days. By Monday, February 3, we learned that Allyson was out of the office, we hoped reviewing the documents whose contents we awaited so anxiously.

With a federal agent finally getting a look at Scott's official papers, would we at last learn whether or not he was in the United States legally? If he had lied on his immigration papers as we suspected, could he face deportation? But, most important, what would happen to the children?

Mary Jane's notes:

Louisiana weather is unique. From January 1st to the end of the month, our weather gets nasty. If you were to describe a winter in Louisiana, you would describe that month. January 2014 proved even worse than usual, with bitter cold, snow, and ice. While we all bundle up for the cold temperatures, the snow and ice shuts us down. Pipes freeze and break and roads become impassable. People from the North would laugh at us, should we describe the impact of our "winter" weather.

Allyson had been waiting to review Scott Rogers' immigration records, which were now two hours west in Lake Charles, delayed by closed roads. We were all anxious to see how Rogers had answered the question concerning prior arrests. If he had lied, the feds would have jurisdiction—and now Mother Nature had done us in!

Finally, the weather allowed for travel, and Hallelujah! The feds had jurisdiction. He had not told the truth on the immigration form; he had lied about his arrest in the U.K.

We also learned that when he arrived in Dallas, he had actually married Diane Palladino, apparently to gain entry to the States for Kimmy, Mathew, and himself. The marriage was not a traditional one, as there had never been any intimacy between the two of them.

Once Scott had U.S. residency, he and Diane went their separate ways, and she moved to Atlanta. Before she left, however, she made sure Scott and Kimmy got green cards, after which she and Scott filed for divorce.

Meanwhile, Rannah continued her communication with Ethan. Though she told him that the feds were now moving forward, she sensed his anxiety over the investigation's slow pace. He was, she told me, beginning to believe that the entire federal investigation might die. The one point that Ethan understood, however, was that the federal government was involved in the investigation; that seemed to have more significance for him than a local investigation. That one fact helped sustain his belief that we would save the children in Rogers' care.

CHAPTER THIRTY-FIVE

THE FEDERAL JUDGE

When Mary Jane finally talked to Allyson, she wasn't able to tell us anything about her investigation except that the review of the documents gave her enough information to keep moving forward. She would have to discuss her findings with Luke Walker, who had asked her to look into Scott, to determine next steps. *That's all we needed to hear!*

"As long as she doesn't tell us it's a dead end, we feel we should let the investigation continue without interference," I told Ethan. "At least the first step allows her to move to the next one, and everyone has agreed again that the goal is to save the children from harm. I'm anxious, too, so I can only imagine that you are. But even though our federal government moves very slowly, we still feel the agents are trying to help."

"Thanks, Rannah," Ethan replied. "That's good news. I understand that the wheels of law are sometimes slow but I'm feeling confident. Looking forward to whatever the next step is."

I was encouraged that Ethan was putting his confidence in our federal government, considering he had witnessed first-hand how Scott had evaded justice in the U.K. by surrounding himself with community leaders who vouched for him, even against the young boy accusing him of the most damaging and horrific crimes.

I kept assuring Ethan that I believed that the people to whom we gave his information would do the right thing. Now that federal authorities were investigating Scott, we could not jeopardize their work. If fact, interference with their investigation would be a crime, so we just had to be patient and keep quiet.

Ethan was glad to hear of progress. "It's a good sign that there's meat on the bone!" he said. Though February dragged on with little or no information on the investigation, I continued to update Ethan on anything we discovered, and Mary Jane checked in with Allyson every week to give her anything we had learned that might prove helpful. Nathan kept encouraging me to be patient, reminding me again that federal authorities would not move quickly.

Meantime, each year, Scott emceed a western-themed benefit for children sponsored by Family Services of Greater Baton Rouge, whose staff and volunteers were frequent guests on his show. He billed his adopted son as co-emcee with him, and dressed him in an almost identical outfit of matching western shirt, oversized cowboy hat, western boots, and bolo. He showed photos from the event on *Around Town*, and I took a screen capture to share with Ethan as we waited to hear from Allyson. Ethan kept in contact with Jake, informing him on our progress, or rather the lack of it.

"Creepy pics," Ethan replied, summing up my sentiments exactly. To me, Scott's young son always looked like a ventriloquist puppet, dressed for the stage with Scott's hand resting on the back of his neck as if he controlled what the boy said. When the little boy spoke, his words were well rehearsed. *So sad to watch.*

At some point in February I noticed another change on the *Around Town Show* when Kimmy disappeared both as a co-host and from the opening credits. No send-off, no mention of her departure, no explanation. She just vanished.

We weren't the only ones anxious to hear what the federal investigators might have found. In February, D.A. Moore cornered Mary Jane at a party to ask the status of the investigation. He told her he had been trying to call Luke Walker for an update but was having difficulty reaching him.

The next day Mary Jane contacted Allyson and asked her to call D.A. Moore and give him some sort of status report. Mary Jane and I were very guarded with the factual information we had about the investigation and at this point made sure we let the federal authorities provide any updates to local law enforcement.

By the first of March, Baton Rouge was starting to warm up, with only an occasional cold day when temperatures dipped near freezing. But Tuesday, March 4, was one of the coldest Mardi Gras Days on record. Again, I found myself letting Ethan know of this unusual State holiday that would no doubt also affect work progress at federal offices in Baton Rouge, so I alerted him that we would probably not hear any news during that time. His response surprised me.

"I was in New Orleans in 1996 at the time of Mardi Gras," he said, "It's such an amazing place. I had a really good time staying with a friend on Royal Street a couple of blocks from Bourbon Street. I remember having my hand stamped with red ink when I was caught drinking under age! Happy times.... Never made it up to the Red Stick though."

"Whaaaaat?" I replied. "You've been to Louisiana? For Mardi Gras?" I again found myself apologizing for having described Louisiana to him as if he were from another planet, and there was his humor sneaking back in with the reference to Red Stick. "Well, if you have been on Bourbon Street for Mardi Gras, it is indeed a small world."

By mid-March, I checked back in with Ethan, sharing photos from the Family Services fundraiser, the same photos we had provided to Allyson to help her recognize the players in Scott's family life. Scott was beginning to change his appearance, in an apparent effort to remain younger looking. The most often talked about change was his teeth, which were suddenly blinding white and larger than normal. He also seemed to have had other work done on his face. In a photo of Scott, Kimmy, and Scott's young son, the father and daughter could pass for a couple with their child. Maybe that was intentional, to distract from the oddity of Scott's adopting young boys. When Kimmy was in the picture, the impression was a more acceptable one, but now that she was gone, the family unit had a more peculiar appearance.

Ethan said he checked in with Jake every few weeks during this time and remained confident that when the time was right, he would help. "Scott was always trying to look younger than he is," Ethan commented on the photos. "Those white teeth and the whole look is creepy!"

I said again how surprised I was to hear he had visited Louisiana. "We were worried in the beginning of this journey that you might need to come here to meet with an investigator and that would be a huge request of you," I said. "Another odd coincidence…that you have been to Louisiana and this is where Scott ends up living."

I could never get over the coincidences that led to Ethan and me connecting on Scott Rogers. Albert Einstein said, "Coincidence is God's way of remaining anonymous." Whether you believe in fate, luck, or divine intervention, something beyond our control put Ethan and me in touch with each other.

"I will be happy to travel to Louisiana," Ethan said. "Such a cool place."

Throughout March, Mary Jane checked in with Allyson every couple of weeks to make sure the investigation hadn't died. In one of her calls, Allyson said she had tried to contact Adrian Randall, the U.K. police detective with whom Nathan had spoken, but he was not responding to her emails.

"How about picking up the phone and calling him?" Mary Jane asked. She told Allyson Nathan had reached him by phone and Randall had said he would gladly talk if requests went through proper channels. Then Mary Jane called me. "I think there is some problem that prevents Allyson from making international calls to Randall," she told me.

"Take her to Nathan's office," I quickly said. "He hasn't had any problem connecting with him and will gladly help her."

Mary Jane talked to Nathan and he called Randall and found out he was available. So Mary Jane told Allyson to get in the car immediately and get to Nathan's law office and he would make the call. "We literally dialed the number that he previously called, handed her the phone and walked out of the room, leaving her and her partner, Jon Helluin, to talk to Adrian Randall in Nathan's conference room," Mary Jane reported.

After they made that initial contact, Randall and Allyson started communicating by email.

Later in March, I found mention online of a series of children's books that were no longer in print or available, but had been written by Scott and published by 1stCo. They were entitled, *Once, Once More,* and *The Little Red Boat.*

Scott had apparently also published *Successology,* a book based on his motivational speaking, and another entitled *Opinionated. Successology* was edited by Mindy Brodhead Averitt, daughter of the late Bob Brodhead, a former LSU Athletic Director whom Nathan knew well. On the cover, Scott was listed as the author by his first name only, "by Scott." *Was this done to keep his full name secret?* In the acknowledgements for the book, the list of names included his victims from the Academy, with the statement, "Appreciation to the many people who have contributed to my development and success...." *How could he thank them after hurting them so deeply?*

It was no surprise that former LSU Basketball Coach Dale Brown contributed a statement endorsing Scott's book only because it was promoted as a motivational tool. Coach Brown, a nationally renowned speaker, would of course encourage the positive image Scott falsely portrayed. I worked with Coach Brown for many years at LSU and was disheartened to see that Scott had taken advantage of his good intentions.

Ethan noted that Scott had been a big fan of *Jonathan Livingston Seagull,* the 1970s book that popularized self-help and the pursuit of perfection through a story about a nonconformist seagull. In his Academy days, Scott had always mentioned that he would write books some day. Ethan too had come across the books online when he found Scott a few years back and had noticed a comment posted by one of the former Academy students who was close to Scott. "He was one of Scott's 'boys' in the '90s," Ethan warned. "He threatened Jake after he left. I noted that he made a comment as late as 2006. Jake and I were looking for possible people who could give evidence if needed, but we decided he was probably still loyal to Scott in some way."

Promotional blurbs for *Successology: The Science of Success* describe it as "the first guide of its kind to address personal and professional success and its attainment through accessible vital skills and processes using the Three You Theory." This was apparently some self-improvement jargon Scott had created.

"No other guide is easier to understand, implement or is so universally beneficial," it claims. "Place yourself into the hands of award-winning international life coach and business facilitator Scott Rogers." He loved to call everything "award-winning." The announcer who opened *The Around Town TV Show* also referred to it as "award-winning," without any explanation of what those awards might include.

"This book is your secret guide to success. It provides the processes needed for you to benefit from every other personal development book you'll ever read. Learn how to implement self-change and grow. Each purchase of *Successology* (the first book in the Xology series) also provides you access to the amazing *Successology* website for dynamic ongoing support, testing, planners, and much more to help you define your goals and achieve."

I found 18 used copies of *Successology* for sale on the Internet at 29 cents each. Apparently, *Successology* did not achieve *Jonathan Livingston Seagull* success.

Mathew Hodgkinson was listed as the book designer for *Opinionated*, using the original spelling of his name. The books were published in 2000 and 2001, so Mathew must have changed his name some time after that.

Opinionated lists Sheri Vutera as its editor. Sheri is the daughter of the late U.S. Federal Judge Frank Polozola, notorious for presiding over the criminal trials of former Governor Edwin Edwards, former Louisiana Agriculture Commissioner Gil Dozier, and LSU Heisman Trophy Winner Billy Cannon. At the time of the Edwards trial, Polozola had his own lawsuit pending as a result of an automobile accident that he claimed left him in pain, impaired, and using OxyContin, a narcotic pain medication. When Edwards' lawyers challenged whether Polozola should have been presiding over his trial in that state, citing what they called the judge's erratic behavior, Polozola blocked their access to any of his personal injury court records by sending federal marshals to seize them from the State courts and bring them to his federal court where he sealed them.

The New York Times reported on this highly unusual move, quoting former U.S. Attorney Harry Rosenberg as saying, "I have never seen that sort of situation before, but I've only been practicing for 30 years. It's beyond the cutting edge of jurisprudence and legal maneuvering."

When Scott became a United States citizen, Judge Polozola spoke at his citizenship ceremony and administered his oath; at that time Scott changed his name again, this time to Scott Tobius Rogers.

Judge Polozola's son-in-law, Dana Vutera, one of the first people Scott met when he arrived in Baton Rouge, became a regular sponsor of Scott's *Around Town TV Show* through his insurance business. With Scott Rogers, he has also been involved with the Cortana Kiwanis Club and its Downtown Christmas parades. When Scott decided to adopt a son, Dana was one of the people who provided a personal reference for him.

1stCo developed the website for Dana Vutera and Associates, and Mathew Hodgkins and Stuart Poulton wrote three of the six testimonials the website lists. "M. Hodgkins, Television Producer" wrote, "Dana has provided me with excellent, hand-selected insurance products for over 10 years, always with value and excellent service when I needed it. Thanks, Dana."

Another testimonial by "M. Hodgkins" states, "Dana is a rare true professional and a gentleman…traits that are as important as the insurance and investments that he provides to my family."

A third testimonial, this one by Stuart Poulton states, "I refer all my family and friends to Dana."

Scott remained friends with the Vuteras, and when their son married in the summer of 2014, Scott, Mathew, Stuart, and both children attended. The three men and two young boys strolling into the reception hall that evening, with Scott carrying the two year old, struck some in attendance as unusual.

Scott was drawn like a moth to the flame to those who hold power in a community. Was it possible that Judge Polozola facilitated Scott's immigration process, perhaps triggering his application for citizenship to receive less scrutiny than it would have ordinarily? *Did Scott target the Vuteras for friendship because of their relation to a powerful federal Judge?*

CHAPTER THIRTY-SIX

THE RESOLUTION

Often, when I suspected the investigation was at a complete standstill, Nathan would remind me that I had to be patient. "I've told you, Rannah, the feds are slow but they are very thorough," he reminded me. "We have to let them do their jobs." When weeks went by without our hearing anything, I would go back over the information we had compiled, looking for anything we could have missed. I was ready to shed the cloak of silence, ready to speak freely about what I did every day and with whom I spoke. I thought everyone involved must want their lives back. *I know I do!*

One night in early March, I walked into my birdcage office and sat in front of the computer for several hours, playing around with different Google searches, hoping to get lucky and find something new that might help us. Lights from surrounding houses floated among the black limbs of the oak trees like stars, with an occasional flash of red or blue from the lights of emergency vehicles streaking down nearby Government Street. I came across a mention of a Louisiana Senate Resolution by Senator Sharon Weston Broome, commending Scott for his work in the community. I had noticed a few times in online searches a resolution the Senate had passed, but I hadn't bothered to read it, assuming it was another certificate Scott had managed to get local organizations to give him, praising him in some exaggerated way.

That night, I clicked on the link and opened the following commendation, so over the top that I thought he must have drafted it himself. Later, when I met a few of his former Academy students in London, they recalled finding the Resolution online and sharing it with each other, acknowledging the same suspicion: "Scott wrote this!" they all declared with complete confidence, recognizing his effusive writing style and glorified accolades.

Among other claims, the Senate Resolution credited him with donating the proceeds from the sale of his books to Habitat for Humanity and the Earl K. Long Children's Wing, a charity hospital in Baton Rouge that closed its doors in 2013. Though the books did not appear to have sold many copies, Scott must have thought his self-promotional gesture would make him sound like a great philanthropist.

At this stage, however, the resolution provided a look behind the curtain at the organizations Scott sought to infiltrate, as well as another odd reference to his career as a "worldwide business consultant."

LOUISIANA SENATE RESOLUTION
2011 Regular Session

To commend Scott Rogers for outstanding and exemplary service to the Baton Rouge area Community.

WHEREAS, a successful career as a marketing and production consultant worldwide brought Scott Rogers to the United States throughout the 1990s and he decided to immigrate to Louisiana from England in 2000 with his daughter, Kimmy, becoming American citizens in 2009; and

WHEREAS, Scott's outstanding abilities as a motivator and bridge builder have been put to good use over the last decade through hundreds of charitable events, thousands of personal hours given, and hundreds of thousands of dollars raised due to his actions in the state; and

WHEREAS, Scott Rogers is a formidable advocate for the state and civic and charitable groups that have sought his assistance; and

WHEREAS, in 2003, he developed and financed the creation of the award-winning Around Town Show—itself a vehicle for positive news across the capital region; and

WHEREAS, Around Town has produced over 800 editions bringing free exposure to nearly five thousand different civic and charitable events, groups, and endeavors and has become known for its support of critical local volunteer groups and provides free airtime as well as coverage to promote their causes; and

WHEREAS, Scott Rogers has served as judge for Capital Area United Way Jambalaya Cookoff; Z-Fest (Zachary Idol); LSU Art Show; and Baker Buffalo Wing Competition; and

WHEREAS, he has been a member of, involved with, or assisted the Board of Directors for the Pride Fire Department; Kiwanis International (held "Regional Motivator" office for three years) and spoke to over thirty regional civic groups over three states; Circle K & Key Club (Youth Division of Kiwanis International); The Jaycees; Dreams Come True—Honorary Chairperson for two years; Arthritis Foundation; The Chamber of Commerce of Greater Baton Rouge; Governor's Abstinence Program; Baton Rouge Family Law Division; United Blood Services; Aneurysm Outreach, Inc.; Capital Area Corporate Recycling Council (CACRC); Golden Magnolia Awards; Keep Baton Rouge Beautiful; Links to Literacy; Northdale Magnet High School; Louisiana Council for Tobacco Free Living; Sweet Adelines; River Parishes College; Polaris Awards; East Baton Rouge Medical Society; Louisiana State Bar Association; Cat Haven Annual Banquet; Baker Police Department (dog runs and rest rooms and new bulletproof vests); Baton Rouge Parents Magazine; Cenikor; Friendship Force of Baton Rouge; Protect Our Dogs; McMain's Children Developmental Association;

National Black Home Educators Resource Association; Louisiana State Troopers Association; Cystic Fibrosis (Golden Rose Awards and Celebrity Waiters); Festival of Lights; and Office of Community Services (state adoption/fostering), as well as serving as guest chef at Southside Gardens; and

WHEREAS, he has emceed for Seize the Day, Epilepsy Foundation event for five years; LSU Mike the Tiger new housing fundraiser; Virginia College grand opening; Friendship Force Baton Rouge; House of Blues New Orleans; Louisiana Fallen Firefighter's Memorial event for five years; USS Kidd Memorial Day Service; Meanwhile, Back at Café Du Monde; Casas for CASA; Louisiana Tea Party Lt. Governor's Debate; Baker Buffalo Festival; Fall Couture Bridal Show; Lagniappe Women's Club; Better Business Bureau "Ethics in Business Award" Dinner for two years; ARC Luncheon and Style Show; and Epilepsy Walk; and

WHEREAS, Scott Rogers has been a speaker at CEO Women's Group; Metropolitan Community Church; Unity Church of Baton Rouge; and American Business Women's Luncheon; and

WHEREAS, he has donated the use of equipment and his time planning and implementing the 2010 Downtown Christmas Parade while co-hosting the parade with the proceeds going to the Cortana Kiwanis; and

WHEREAS, Scott Rogers donated proceeds from his Once children's books to the Cortana Kiwanis Club with the money being used to help equip the pediatric department of the Earl K. Long Hospital with some desperately needed infant-sized hardware; and

WHEREAS, he has also donated the profits from The Little Red Boat to Habitat for Humanity to help build houses for families who might otherwise never have them; and

WHEREAS, Scott Rogers spear-headed a campaign which raised $25,000 to air condition the Northdale Magnet Academy Auditorium and at the Northdale Magnet Academy, an alternative school for at-risk students, Scott also donated his own time and paid his staff's time to teach these students career and technology skills; and

WHEREAS, Scott Rogers is a truly unique individual, who through his long standing, dedicated, outstanding and exemplary service to his community, strives to improve the condition of his fellow citizens and it is of such individuals that the strength of our communities, the quality of life in the state of Louisiana, and the overall vitality of American society depend.

THEREFORE, BE IT RESOLVED that the Senate of the Legislature of Louisiana does hereby recognize and commend Scott Rogers for his outstanding and exemplary service to the Baton Rouge area community.

BE IT FURTHER RESOLVED that a copy of this Resolution be transmitted to Scott Rogers.[32]

Senator Broome is Baton Rouge's senior State Senator serving in the seat previously held by Mayor Holden. She is the first African American woman to be elected to the number two post in both the House of Representatives and State Senate, where she served as President Pro-Tempore. She is a conservative Democrat who can hold her own in a church pulpit against any preacher and was an occasional guest on Scott's *Around Town TV Show* where he flattered her and played to her strong religious convictions by emphasizing his role as pastor of his own church.

---

[32] Louisiana Senate Resolutions, 2011 Regular Session by Senator Sharon Weston Broome. Viewed 9 September 2015. https://legiscan.com/LA/text/SR31/id/293458/Louisiana-2011-SR31-Enrolled.pd

Apparently Scott had been busy in the summer of 2011. While he was orchestrating the story against our firm and Mayor Holden, he was spinning a very different tale to Senator Broome.

The Boys of Bury

JAKE *in his own words*

England
2015

It was the process of being made to feel that it was my fault that was one of the strongest influences at the time. I didn't know how it was my fault. But I totally believed that it was my fault because I'd been told by this person, "You're making me do this." And I didn't want to make him do it.

But I didn't know how to stop it from happening, and that is something that is very, very confusing as a child. Because not only do you feel shame, but you feel guilt as well, and guilt is a huge emotion that you feel. It's something that I didn't process that I was feeling until I was a little older.

And that is a really big contributing factor as to why you stay silent.

CHAPTER THIRTY-SEVEN

THE SECOND ADOPTION

Day 214
March 29, 2014

On a final *Around Town TV Show* episode in March, during an interview, Scott announced some news that would ultimately make a big difference in the investigation.

As he spoke with yet another person advocating for abused children—this time a man promoting an upcoming event at the State Capitol—he disclosed personal information about his own family.

Many abused children, the guest said, just need an adult to speak up for them. Scott kept nodding in agreement and saying, "So true...so true."

Unbelievable!

Then the guest praised Scott as a real "hero" who had fostered and adopted children. At that point, Scott opened up, explaining that he was currently in the process of adopting a little boy, though he could not yet discuss it on camera, as the child was still technically a ward of the state. He told viewers how much he loved his little boy.

Perhaps this was the younger child the District Attorney reported seeing at Scott's home, I thought.

The importance of this disclosure was that the adoption process was current, not six or seven years old and final. I relayed Scott's statement to Nathan and Mary Jane and then to

Ethan, who had continued to exhibit patience and understanding about the investigation's slow pace.

"A new adoption means new dates have started running on the statute of limitations, which opens up more doors for a federal investigation," Mary Jane said. "If Rogers filled out the old documents falsely, he would have to falsify the new ones to be consistent." Mary Jane called Allyson to discuss the possibilities of the new information and the new child.

The following week, Scott conducted another round of interviews with child advocates, starting off the Saturday show by announcing that April is Child Abuse Awareness Month. I had watched his program every weekend for seven months now, and I realized that he had increased the number of segments on children's programs. He now had a child from Dunham School, the local Christian school his oldest son attended, deliver a message at the end of the show and announced that more children would appear in the coming weeks.

We heard reports from parents at the school that Scott was cantankerous when taping the program segments, often snapping at the children. They said that his behind-the-camera demeanor was quite different from the positive image he portrayed on his TV program and that he actually had a very bad temper around the children. *The man behind the camera is not the same as the one in front!*

Scott also announced on the show that he would participate in the Crime Victims Night of Remembrance with the Sheriff's Office that week. The Sheriff's April newsletter had included a photograph of Sheriff Gautreaux with Scott Rogers and Chef Celeste on the set of *The Around Town TV Show* to promote the event and Scott's association with it.

Shannon Mathews with the Louisiana Department of Children and Family Services was the first interview of the weekend, reporting that in January 2014 the State had investigated over 2,000 reports of abuse and neglect in Louisiana.

In what seemed an obviously scripted question, Scott asked her to divulge the children's fate, when her office investigates and has to remove them from their home. "Where do they go?" he asked.

This was Ms. Mathews' cue to say that she wanted to take the opportunity to thank Scott because he is "one of our very special foster parents and we really appreciate you serving in that role."

Scott replied, "I don't normally talk about this on air, but then you came on many years ago, and I realized that even as a single parent, I could be a foster parent, so I've taken children in, temporarily, who have been abused and sometimes it just makes you want to cry when these children arrive and they're confused.... But you give them a loving place to come to.

"How could folks maybe open up their homes to maybe being temporary foster parents and take a child in for a few days or a week or longer?"

Watching Scott talk about comforting abused children, when I knew that he was himself an abuser, I could find few words strong enough to describe my feelings. He worked so hard, feigning emotion, to convince his viewers that he represented a safe harbor for abused children. Considering the young people in England who reported how he had coached them to lie to authorities and say their parents had abused them, and knowing the abuse he had inflicted on the young boys at the Academy, I could barely stand to watch.

Shannon Mathews ended her interview by giving the qualifications for foster parents and the contact information for how to become one. She mentioned that potential foster parents must agree to a background check and attend a series of courses.

Scott encouraged viewers to consider fostering children, saying, "It's really simple, folks. You don't have to be a millionaire. You don't need a mansion. You just need a loving home. Now what about folks who can do that? How can we get more information and get involved in these efforts for child abuse?"

"By listening and being attentive to children," Ms. Mathews said as Scott continued to nod sympathetically.

The second interview that weekend was with Captain Blair Nicholson of the East Baton Rouge Parish Sheriff's Office who discussed the reserve deputy program. This segment gave Scott the opportunity to boast yet again that he served as a reserve sheriff's deputy. He said he had first been a Reserve Police Officer in Baker when Sheriff Gautreaux served as Police Chief there. Scott laughed and again told the story he loved to share about making traffic stops. He told Captain Nicholson that everyone recognized him from his TV show and wanted his autograph, so Gautreaux ended up assigning him to a desk job.

Once Gautreaux was elected Sheriff, he continued, he began working with the Sheriff's Office and now served as one of its chaplains. When he told Captain Nicholson that Sheriff Gautreaux would appear on the program in the next couple of weeks, he added, "In a way, I'll be interviewing my boss." Scott Rogers was letting Captain Nicholson know he was close to the Sheriff.

"We want you to take it serious, folks, because you are serving the Sheriff's Office and that's very important for you to understand," Scott said. "So to become a reserve deputy, you have to go through all the rigorous background checks, and psychological tests to carry guns, and go through all the training…."

"But once they are cleared, and go through the Academy, where might they be assigned?" he asked Captain Nicholson.

During one show, Scott had described two programs in which he participated and claimed both require thorough background checks. Nathan, Mary Jane, and I couldn't help wondering who was responsible for the background checks and psychological tests he claimed he had undergone.

In the same program, he also interviewed Evelyn Gibson with Family Services of Greater Baton Rouge. She explained how her agency provides individual and group family counseling and child custody evaluations.

"You do all the things that people don't like to talk about, but it's crucial because it's making families healthier," Scott told Ms. Gibson, portraying his own family as a healthy one. I recalled Allyson's warning that pedophiles create for others an image that is often the exact opposite of what they truly are.

On another show, Scott interviewed two victim assistance coordinators from the District Attorney's Office, Kirsten Bowers and Kristen Raby. He talked about District Attorney Moore's creating the victims assistance unit and how we must "empower the victim." The irony of this statement was inescapable. Scott's own victims had grown into young men who were now husbands and fathers, empowered by their own desire to protect other children from the fate they had suffered at his hands. While he had the audacity to talk about empowering victims, his victims now had the courage to come forward to stop his abuse of children.

Later in that same show, Scott announced that as chaplain for the Sheriff's Office he would participate in the mid-week "Crime Victims Evening of Remembrance," an annual event hosted by the Sheriff.

"On Wednesday, there is the Night to Remember," Scott said. "I'm actually going to be acting pastor for that. I'm the Sheriff's chaplain and a pastor. I don't talk about it much on TV, but I'm so honored that they asked me of all people to be the pastor for the evening."

Yes, you of all people! Despite Scott's efforts to create a positive image for himself, if you listened very carefully, the truth was often hidden in his own words. Professionals say that because pedophiles know the truth, it is often impossible for them to lie without fail. Every time he said, "I don't talk about this much on TV," you better believe it was a message he wanted viewers to remember.

"Scary stuff," Ethan commented when I shared Scott's remarks. "It does seem as if he is covering his tracks in an unbelievable way. Very clever and soooo dark!

"If there is anything I can do to speed anything up, let me know," he said. "I could go to the police here in the U.K. and make a statement. Are they definitely investigating him and taking it seriously?"

Though I could understand his frustration, I was glad to hear he might be willing to make a statement to the U.K. police. I explained that we had other options, such as going to the State Child Services Department where Scott was adopting the children, but that once we gave our information to the feds, we had to be sure we did nothing to hinder their work.

After hearing all of Scott's recent news, I called Mary Jane to let her know he was definitely in the process of adopting the second little boy and the adoption sounded close to completion. She went to work making calls to Allyson and Luke, bringing renewed pressure for some movement in the investigation. She reminded them that a second adoption would generate a new round of applications and opportunities for Scott to file false documents with the State. She impressed upon them that we felt some urgency to not let the adoption become final before the State could investigate. And she reminded Allyson that if her office was not planning to take action, we would put the information in the hands of others, such as the press.

Everyone was frustrated. What happens if he adopts another little boy? Getting the children away from him just gets harder and harder. I could only imagine how exasperating Ethan would find this stalemate. We had to do something, and now Mary Jane had told Allyson we would go to Plan B.

On the first weekend in May, Scott opened his show by sending out birthday wishes to several people, ending with a *Happy Birthday* to Poh Rogers, whom he identified as his "newly adopted son" who had turned two that week. *Newly adopted son!* My heart sank. *He has two little boys now.*

He looked directly into the camera and said, "I love you, son," in that melodramatic voice he used when he wanted to portray his group as the typical All-American family. At the end of the show, he came back on and explained that *Poh* was not the child's real name but just a nickname and that he could not give his real name because, technically, he wasn't adopted yet. He said the adoption should be final by the end of May and he couldn't wait to show photos of his son and bring him on the show so everyone could meet him. *So it isn't final!*

Surely this new pending adoption would give the authorities some deadline for stepping up their efforts. That weekend, I also looked through the staff website of the State Department of Child Services and noticed that it listed Charlie Dirks as general counsel. I had met Dirks when he served for a number of years as legal counsel for the Baton Rouge Union of Police. During Mayor Holden's three political campaigns, I had worked with the police union board members and become friends with its president, Chris Stewart. Dirks had always seemed like a good guy, and I knew Chris had complete confidence in him.

Knowing that Dirks was general counsel to Suzy Sonnier increased my hope that the federal agents would find the State department helpful in stopping Scott's adoption of another child. Though my involvement in the case prohibited me from talking to Charlie—or anyone else—I asked Mary Jane to let Allyson know I thought she could trust Charlie Dirks. Allyson had asked that we allow her office to handle communication with the State, and Nathan always insisted that we cooperate with the federal authorities. "There is no way Charlie will allow this adoption to continue once he knows the truth," I told Mary Jane. "Please encourage Allyson to work with him before it's too late."

We knew the Louisiana Department of Children and Family Services had its plate full with internal problems. The U.S. Attorney's Office was investigating the entire department, and had accused three department auditors of embezzling money from the State, using departmental credit cards to pay for hotel rooms in New Orleans during Mardi Gras and the NBA All-Star weekend. Most important, as is too often the case, parents or friends of parents had killed children after others had filed complaints. The Department of Children and Family Services appeared to be in disorder. We had only to read the newspapers to know that a federal subpoena for information on Scott Rogers' foster parent and adoption files would grab the attention of the press. That could work to our advantage.

The suggestion that we give our information on Scott Rogers to the press continued to float through our discussions, but considering Child Services' problems, we worried that Scott's case could get lost in the chaos, or that the press might sensationalize it for the sole purpose of exposing the department's turmoil. I thought Suzy Sonnier and Charlie Dirks should have the opportunity to address, through proper legal channels, how Scott Rogers came to have custody of two young boys, and whether they were safe with him.

Mary Jane called Allyson to talk through the second adoption before it became final. She told her a door had just opened that could be helpful, but the investigation needed to start moving before Rogers adopted the second child. "Once children are adopted they become just like a biological child of that person and removing them from Roger's care becomes almost impossible, even if he has lied to Child Services. Once they approve him and the judge signs the adoption order, Poh will be his," Mary Jane explained. Then Mary Jane told her that before the second adoption took place, she, Nathan, and I were going to have to move to Plan B to stop it. She told her we needed to know if the federal government was not going forward, because if not, we were!

The frustration was beginning to wear on all of us. For Ethan, the delay in the investigation over the first two months of the year, however, was fortunate. During that time, after his interview with Allyson, the stress of confronting Scott began to build within him. As for me, I felt helpless knowing that while everyone believed Scott's 10-year-old son was already in danger of abuse, Scott was close to adopting a second little boy.

After talking to Allyson, Mary Jane called Luke Walker to tell him about the second adoption. "You need to have a conversation with these people and boot them in the ass about this investigation moving or it will become a missed opportunity," she told him.

What was Plan B? We didn't know! But Mary Jane reminded me that although the federal authorities Allyson was consulting did not know our names, they did know we had put together Plan A, which was to hand over all of the information to Luke Walker, and we were sitting on the same information they had. "Our goal is protecting those children and if Plan B is nothing but an embarrassment across the board for everyone who's not doing their job, then so be it," Mary Jane said.

In truth, while you couldn't really call our Plan B a plan, Nathan, Mary Jane, and I knew what it meant. The idea was to make sure Scott Rogers' past was exposed—either through the news media, or the State Department of Child Services, or by any other means necessary. Plan B simply meant we would move forward ourselves without waiting any longer. Plan B meant we were taking matters into our own hands! We had discussed plenty of options, and once we decided to move, we would huddle and agree on the easiest path to making Scott's past known. *How can we sit back in silence, knowing what we do, while Scott adopts another little boy?*

Allyson asked that we please do nothing until she got back to us, and we agreed. Another week passed, then Mary Jane received a call letting her know the investigation was starting to move forward. I guess all that talk about Plan B caused the feds some concern, because they were beginning to take some action. Personally, I thought Mary Jane's boot-in-ass call to Luke Walker probably hadn't hurt either.

On a warm, rainy Saturday, I relayed all this latest information to Ethan. I also told him I had learned that the attorney for the State Child Services department was someone I thought we could trust to do what was right.

"It's a rainy weekend here, but I'm feeling more optimistic than I have since we started," I said to Ethan.

"It's a rainy weekend here, too," he replied. "Thanks for the sunshine. I guess once anyone looks closer at Scott it becomes more obvious what he really is.

"There is a lot on the news here at the moment about abuse," he added, "by '70s and '80s celebrities who have now been exposed as child abusers. It's all very disturbing, sad, and shocking that these types of crimes go unreported for years, all for the same reasons, and these abusers know how the victims will react, how they won't say anything.... I think the worst thing is that children are so precious and the rest of their lives depends on those experiences in the very first few years."

In two corners of the world, both raining, we seemed like two friends having an easy Saturday chat. But once again Ethan pointed to his own children, to why stopping Scott was so important to him: "I type this as I watch cartoons with my 5 and 7 year olds," he said. "A reminder to me to know exactly what they are doing and who is looking after them all the time.

"I don't have the words to thank you enough for all your help," he said. "I guess *thank you* will have to do."

How do you accept thanks for helping someone stop a pedophile? I knew Ethan was appreciative because for all those years he had looked for Scott on his own, trying to figure out a way to stop him without even talking his own abuse through with anyone. But his thanks always made me feel uneasy. I knew he was sincere, but I didn't think we deserved gratitude. We were all doing what we had to do. Still, I could tell how much our help meant to him and I appreciated his kind words. *I just wish I could go back in time and somehow prevent this from ever happening. Then I might deserve the thanks.*

I wondered whether we could ever understand how an adult who has survived child sex abuse truly feels.

CHAPTER THIRTY-EIGHT

THE BRITISH CHILD SEX RINGS

Ethan's mention of the sex scandals involving so many British celebrities, including BBC television stars, got me to thinking. And as Louisiana's temperatures began to rise again, days and weeks dragged on without a word about the investigation. Warm summer breezes signaled we had been talking about Scott Rogers for too long. Then one day, Mary Jane sent an article about the British pedophile rings. "Have you been reading about this?" she asked.

Ethan had mentioned it, and a friend of mine, Sue Kaplan, who had worked in television news in Lafayette, Louisiana, had also brought it to my attention. Though Sue has been out of television news for a number of years, she is still the best source for current events, in part because of her nose for news and also because of her voracious desire for information that completes a story. Sue had mentioned the incredible story of Jimmy Savile, a popular British TV star who used his fame to lure underage children into sex.

"I've heard of it, but haven't read much," I told Mary Jane.

"It's amazing how similar these stories are to Scott's," she pointed out.

Scott's life and public persona followed interesting parallels with the child sex abuse scandals that had taken place in the U.K. at the same time he was running the Academy of Dance and Performing Arts. Savile—who was close to the Royal Family and to members of Parliament and had even received a Papal Knighthood from Pope John Paul—was a pedophile.

He hosted a BBC program called "Jim'll Fix It," in which he encouraged children to write him letters about their dreams; then he would choose to make some dreams come true for lucky children. Savile wore his hair bleached platinum blonde, and he dressed outlandishly. He worked very hard to make friendships with politicians, religious leaders, police officials, and anyone else in a position of influence.

In truth, Savile procured children for many of these high-ranking politicians, which no doubt helped him secure protection from prosecution. When he died in 2011 at the age of 84, more than 600 victims of child sex abuse came forward, providing details of Savile's six decades of crime. Some of his victims were foster children whom Savile convinced child service agencies to let him take from their schools for overnight stays at his home where he and his prominent associates sexually abused them.

Savile portrayed himself as a patron of children's charities, raising money for causes, serving as master of ceremonies for charitable events, relentlessly promoting himself as someone who just cared about children.

In his book "In Plain Sight—The Life and Lies of Jimmy Savile," Dan Davies wrote that Savile "seemed to enjoy keeping people guessing about his sexual orientation. The crazy attire, the dyed hair and the conspicuous lack of a regular woman in his life gave rise to gossip. In his mind, though, any publicity was a good thing. His attitude was therefore, 'If they're talking about it, let 'em think.'"[33] Somehow he rationalized that the circus atmosphere he created would detract from what he was really up to.

The book also describes how a small group of police officers visited Savile regularly in his London apartment and how Savile went "out of his way to cultivate close relationships with police officers wherever he was."

England's libel laws, among the strictest in the world, discourage both victims and the news media from making public

---

[33] Dan Davies, "In Plain Sight—The Life and Lies of Jimmy Savile," Quercus Editions Ltd., 2014.

statements about alleged pedophiles and thus played a role in keeping Savile's victims quiet for so long.

As of December 2014, Scotland Yard was investigating claims that the police were covering up the activities of at least five pedophile rings that involved members of Parliament and other high-ranking personalities. Over the last three decades, investigations have linked the names of 22 politicians—including three current members of Parliament, three members of the House of Lords, and 13 former cabinet ministers—to child sex abuse.

Incredibly, the Minister of Health had appointed Savile to head a task force in charge of a hospital that treated mental patients. The result was that Savile ended up sexually abusing patients, most of them female.

Gary Glitter, whose real name was Paul Gadd, was a rock star in the 1970s, famous for his song "Rock and Roll," the crowd-participation "Hey" song that various teams played at sporting events. Some might wonder why we no longer stand and sing "Hey" at sporting events after instrumental segments of Glitter's familiar song. After law enforcement officials charged him with possession of child pornography and child sex abuse, the NFL and other leagues called a halt to its performance. Glitter stood to make hundreds of thousands of dollars in royalties at the 2012 Super Bowl because the New England Patriots typically played the song after every touchdown, but the NFL banned it just days before the big event. Glitter had served three years in a Vietnam prison for child sex abuse before his arrest in 2012, as part of Operation Yewtree, on eight sex offenses that occurred between 1977 and 1980, including one involving a 13-year-old girl in Jimmy Savile's dressing room at the BBC studio. He was subsequently found guilty on February 5, 2015, of attempted rape, four counts of indecent assault, and one count of sex with a girl under the age of 13. At 70 years of age, Glitter was sentenced to 16 years in prison.

Most people believe celebrities like Jimmy Savile and Gary Glitter got away with decades of child sex abuse because they operated within the circles of the BBC, the British Parliament establishment, and the Royal Family, connections that afforded them the arrogance to behave in a flamboyant and bizarre manner without scrutiny.

Stuart Hall, host of the BBC television comedy game show "It's a Knockout," pleaded guilty in 2013 to having sexually assaulted 13 girls, ages 9 through 17, between 1967 and 1986. The prosecution of Jimmy Savile inspired one of Hall's victims to come forward and name him as her abuser. Despite his guilty plea, Hall denounced his accusers as gold diggers and liars, an accusation that resulted in a judge increasing his sentence.

In December 2014, Chris Denning, a former BBC radio disc jockey and record producer, received a sentence of 13 years in prison after pleading guilty to 40 sexual offenses he committed between 1967 and 1987 involving 26 male victims, the youngest only 9 years old. Denning helped develop the careers of Gary Glitter and the popular Scottish pop group, the Bay City Rollers, known for hits like "I Only Wanna Be With You."

When Jonathan King, British singer, songwriter, TV host, and one of the original producers of "The Rocky Horror Picture Show," was found guilty in 2001 of sex offenses involving five boys between the ages of 14 and 15, the judge accused him of using his fame and success to attract impressionable youngsters. Surrey Police alleged that between 1969 and 1989, King had approached 10,000 to 20,000 boys for what he described as "research," but what police believed was his technique of grooming them for sexual abuse.

Rolf Harris, singer, songwriter, comedian, actor, and TV personality known for his musical composition, "Tie Me Kangaroo Down, Sport," and popular BBC children's program "Rolf's Cartoon Time" was found guilty in June 2014 on 12 counts of indecent assault, including seven charges relating to a sexual relationship with one of his daughter's friends when she was between 13 and 15 years old. One charge involved his sexual assault of an 8-year-old girl when she asked for an autograph. Since his conviction, more victims have come forward.

Ray Teret worked for Savile as a DJ and assistant and lived with him for a period of time during which Savile referred to Teret as his son. In December 2014, the 73-year-old Teret was found guilty of seven rapes and 11 indecent assaults and sentenced to 25 years in prison. During his trial, four more victims came forward. Afterwards, Detective Chief Inspector Graham Brock said, "After decades of hiding behind the veneer of being a distinguished radio presenter, Ray Teret has finally been exposed as the manipulative and dangerous sexual predator that he is."

Max Clifford, the celebrity publicist whose clients included comedian Freddie Starr and English television talent judge Simon Cowell, was arrested four times in the wake of the sex abuse investigation surrounding Savile before officials announced they would not prosecute him. When Clifford was convicted in 2014 of eight counts of indecent assault against four victims, Cowell finally dropped him. The Director of National Services for the National Society for the Prevention of Cruelty to Children said, "Max Clifford has rightly been unmasked as a ruthless and manipulative sex offender who preyed for decades on children and young women."

In early 2015, the public learned that Cyril Smith, a Member of Parliament who died in 2010, had been arrested in the 1980s and held briefly at a police station for his participation in sex parties with young boys. His arrest followed an undercover investigation that charged Child Services facilities with providing young boys to Smith and other top British officials for sex. After Smith had spent a few hours at the police station, however, the undercover officers were ordered to hand over all evidence, including photographs and video exposing his crimes. The cover-up was allegedly ordered by a representative of the Director of Public Prosecutions, the most senior prosecutor in England and Wales. Smith was released and the police officers were threatened with losing their jobs if they spoke again of his arrest. As of September 2015, Scotland Yard was still investigating the extent of the cover-up.

David Smith, former driver for Savile and other BBC celebrities, was one of the first people police charged with child sex abuse after the revelations about Saville's history. Smith, who was a prolific sex offender with 22 previous convictions of sexual abuse against young boys, was arrested in late 2012 but committed suicide prior to his scheduled 2013 court appearance.

One of the leading attorneys representing 60 of Savile's victims said, "This was the chance for the client to be vindicated and be believed, and he will feel cheated of that. It is a major blow for the victim, he doesn't get to see justice being done." A spokesperson for a support group for victims of child sex abuse also released a statement calling Smith a coward. "It is so rare that a case actually makes it to court and therefore a feeling of injustice is a big issue for the survivors of childhood sex abuse," she said.[34]

Is that lack of a resolution where Ethan was headed? Everyone involved in the investigation recognized that Scott could pack up the family in the middle of the night, leave Baton Rouge, and show up in another town under a different name. Would the federal government follow him? We also knew he might commit suicide, since he had attempted it before, when he stood trial in England for abusing his young student.

Would he deprive his victims of seeing him punished for his crimes or, worst of all, would he commit some final act of depravity by hurting other innocent victims?

---

[34] Nazia Parveen, "Saville chauffeur suicide has cheated me of justice." Daily Mail. 29 October 2013. Viewed 9 September 2015. http://www.dailymail.co.uk/news/article-2479244/Jimmy-Savile-chauffeur-David-Smiths-suicide-cheated-justice.html

CHAPTER THIRTY-NINE

THE LAST FATHER'S DAY

Day 292
June 15, 2014

The days passed slowly in May, with little new information and a continuing focus on children in *The Around Town TV Show* lineups. More and more guests worked with children through volunteerism, law enforcement, or public office. Still, we continued to think that this shift could simply reflect Scott's desire to surround himself with public support.

At some point, however, we began to worry that he was increasing his efforts to paint an acceptable picture of his role in the community. *Had someone tipped him off?*

I kept assuring Ethan that the federal investigators had kept our names confidential. Should they begin questioning Scott, we had no reason to believe he would learn of our involvement. I knew Ethan and Jake were always fearful that he would find a way to retaliate against them, especially by hurting their families. Because I did not have their experience with him, I was never afraid of Scott. I didn't know to be afraid of him.

But as the days dragged on and we knew the investigation was building, I did consider that if I were to fear anyone, it would be Mathew. I recognized Scott's tremendous power and influence over him. After all, Scott had convinced him to run away repeatedly from his family, until the fight for Mathew broke his parents. I considered that if Scott ever learned I had anything to do with pointing the federal authorities toward him, he might make Mathew harm me in some way. I had already learned that years ago Scott had those under his control go out and hunt Jake down. So during the hot month of May, I told Ethan I was staying very quiet. I didn't want to attend any event where Scott might be the emcee, or risk running into him in public. I wanted to avoid any opportunity for him to question whether I was involved in anything that caused him a problem.

His programs that month were very mundane and of very little of interest. In a relationship that Veronica Mosgrove, press secretary for Commissioner of Agriculture Mike Strain, had helped cultivate, Strain appeared with Scott to talk about summer gardens and fresh agricultural produce. Local artists and musicians looking for any publicity they could get found a spot on *The Around Town TV Show*. I also noticed that Scott began inviting WAFB television personalities to appear on the show, perhaps in an attempt to legitimize his program and link it more closely with WAFB, which produces highly respected legitimate news programming.

Scott continued to mention his 2-year-old son, but made no comment about his pending adoption, and also talked about traveling a lot around the U.S., primarily to New York and Washington, but never disclosed the purpose of the travel. *Why does he travel around the country?*

I kept in touch with Ethan and let him know what was on the show, but mainly just checked in to provide some communication. We were again in radio silence...waiting... waiting. I reminded him that as we were going into the Memorial Day weekend with offices closed again, we would have a few days when nothing was likely to happen. I kept updating him about holidays because I imagined that he was looking for news every day.

That week I had found photos of Scott participating at events that supported STAR, the Sexual Trauma Awareness and Response organization in Baton Rouge, formerly the Rape Crisis Center, a non-profit group that raises money to help sexual assault survivors. To me, Scott was dancing dangerously close to the flame.

Photos emerged showing Scott, along with local male law enforcement officials, wearing decorative high heels for an event, billed "Walk a Mile in Her Shoes," that brought awareness to the plight of rape victims. "His audacity seems to know no end," I told Ethan, "but the experts tell me predators often try to project an image that is opposite of the truth.

"Allyson still says we should not consider acting on a Plan B at this point," I told him, "and she is continuing to gather information. We feel her searches must be getting results now because they are ongoing.

"I'm a little nervous," I admitted, "but I have a good feeling about her investigation."

Ethan said he was trying to remain patient and realistic, hoping the authorities would act before the adoption of Poh was final. "I'm still happy to go to the police here in the U.K.," he offered. "I have grown more confident about what happened and less ashamed since opening this all up." Again, in his words was the solemn reminder of how difficult this process was for him, but also the terrific news that he was feeling stronger. We had come through our coldest months, and I was especially glad to hear the shame was melting away like the winter frost as he spoke more openly about Scott's abuse. *Into the sunshine, Ethan...into the sunshine.*

If Scott were to face charges for child sex abuse in the U.K., which has no statute of limitations, that would not only help the authorities here stop the second adoption, it would also hang a perverse sword of Damocles over his head. As he pursued adoption of another little boy, he might also face new charges and even deportation. *To adopt another child, he had to be willing to tell fresh lies! Which meant commit new crimes!*

Then, on Father's Day weekend, *The Around Town TV Show* focused on fatherhood, and Scott featured his 10-year-old son, along with a counselor from the summer camp he attended. He revealed that the little boy, who had been diagnosed with Asperger's Syndrome, had attended another camp where the director had asked him to leave because of his behavior. He was, however, enjoying his new camp. As the little boy and the camp counselor demonstrated exercises they performed for his brain, Scott stood close by, always with a hand on the child's neck.

On Father's Day, Scott also included a segment on his own life, talking about what a horrible childhood he had and how many children had come in and out of his own home since he had become a licensed foster parent. He spoke of his three children—Kimberly, who he said was "off doing her own thing now," and the two boys. This was the first time he had mentioned Kimberly on the show since her departure, and he moved quickly past her to say that Poh's adoption would be legal "as soon as Child Services completes the paperwork."

Child Services must be doing something to delay the adoption, we thought. Ethan seemed relieved, but also raised a good question. "I wonder if the authorities are assessing the kids who have gone through the fostering program," he said. He worried that Scott might also have abused the foster children who had lived in his home temporarily.

We had learned that when Scott first brought his 10-year-old son into his home as a foster child, he came with a sister, whom Scott soon sent back to Child Services. *I suppose he wanted only boys.*

That Father's Day program had an especially uncomfortable feel. The segment with his son seemed rehearsed and exploitive. And we all worried that Scott Rogers was targeting children who have difficulty communicating, since he now disclosed that the 2 year old had a delayed speech problem.

Was he intentionally adopting boys who would have trouble reporting his abuse? Was that the real message we were learning from this stage-managed Father's Day tribute to Scott Rogers?

CHAPTER FORTY

CHILD SERVICES

Mary Jane's notes:

After I put Plan B on the table with Allyson, we learned that the Middle District prosecutor's office had put together a federal grand jury subpoena and served the Louisiana Department of Child and Family Services. Again because of the need to keep the details quiet, the feds had served the subpoena on Charlie Dirks, general counsel for Family Services, without an explanation. Dirks knew only that the subpoena did not involve the ongoing current investigation of the entire department. He had been working with the federal government on the investigation of several people within the department who were using State credit cards for their personal purchases and had been doing that for a while.

Then the United States Attorney's Office asked Dirks to come to a meeting. When he showed up, he found a number of people sitting around the table. Dirks was presented with binders, and as he started flipping through them, he saw the accumulated evidence on Rogers. This would be the first time that Dirks knew the background on Rogers and the investigation. He later recalled seeing the faded articles from 20 years ago on the Rogers trial. And the one detail that jumped out at him was Rogers' explanation that he had not molested the male victim but that the 12-year-old child had molested him twice. Dirks keyed in on Rogers' repulsive explanation, as I had, of why he was not guilty of a sexual abuse crime in the U.K. some 20 years earlier.

The one document I had tried to get from Child Services— unsuccessfully—was finally handed over pursuant to the federal grand jury subpoena. And what did that document show? A false statement by Rogers as to his prior arrest and trial in the United Kingdom. He had denied both on the questionnaire, as I had suspected.

The investigators were careful about involving people in the Child Services department, not knowing who was close to Rogers. Dirks included hand-picked employees within the department to work in conjunction with the federal investigators. During this active time, Dirks told the federal investigators about another program in which Rogers was taking part: As a foster and adoptive parent, he got federal money that goes to the State to help with the care of children with disabilities. So now Rogers not only chose children with disabilities, and was getting them through Child Services, he had also found a way to get money for their care. The case against Rogers—and the investigation of the second adoption involving two-year-old Poh, also disabled—now really began to start ramping up.

As Rogers went on his weekend show, telling viewers that the adoption of his second son would be final as soon as Child Services completed the paperwork, he called agency staff members and demanded that they complete the adoption.

Meantime, scripts had been written for the employees as to what to tell Rogers regarding the delay in the adoption of Poh.

The Boys of Bury

JAKE *in his own words*

England
2015

When I did manage to escape after 10 or 11 years of abuse, I was threatened into silence. Once I managed to get away, I had no one to turn to, no one to help me, I had no money. Scott controlled everything.

He would ask you what you were thinking. If you didn't have an answer, you would be put through one of his torture sessions.

Psychological torture...physical torture...you were beaten. If you refused his advances...if you refused his sexual abuse...then the sexual abuse became very violent.

It's very difficult for someone who hasn't experienced this type of abuse to understand why no one would come forward to say anything. When I escaped, I wanted to get as far away from the situation as possible. I wanted to have my freedom.

He was a monster who I felt would destroy me. I feared for my life. At one time, I was strangled into unconsciousness.

CHAPTER FORTY-ONE

THE SUICIDE ATTEMPTS

In late June, Allyson asked if we knew anything more about Scott Rogers being "sectioned." This term, which comes from England's Mental Health Act, refers to using a "section" or paragraph from the Act to detain a person in a hospital, whether or not he agrees.

Mary Jane and Nathan both explained to me that if a U.S. grand jury indicted Scott and the U.S. Attorney had evidence that he might harm himself, they would have a legal obligation to take him into custody immediately to protect him.

When Ethan told us back in October that Scott had attempted suicide twice in the U.K., we had asked U.S. authorities how many times official State or federal documents had asked Scott about his mental health history and whether he had answered truthfully. Ethan had questioned whether mental health was a factor in citizenship, and we had also urged the authorities to look at the concealed weapon permit for a disclosure of mental health issues.

We got the feeling that Allyson was finishing her report and needed as much information as possible on Scott's mental health. It was Friday afternoon, and as we understood that she would submit the report on Monday, time was of the essence. Ethan and Jake responded quickly, as always, and immediately went to work. Since Jake had been living in Scott's house at the time of the sectioning, he remembered much of what had happened.

We learned that Scott was first sectioned at the hospital in Bury St. Edmunds sometime after he had taken an overdose, which occurred after his arrest for sexual assault and indecency and after he had spent time in prison on remand. He also went in voluntarily just after the court case and again spent some time in the psychiatric ward.

Jake suspected that Scott could have contrived the sectioning to show how severely the allegations had damaged him. Scott had also told the boys at the Academy that when he was younger, he had spent time in an institution for overdosing. Ethan and Jake provided as much information as possible, because they knew it could stop Poh's adoption. By Sunday evening, the two of them were sending even more information. They provided, for Allyson's report, the contact information for Scott's doctor. If there remained any doubt about his mental stability, the authorities, we hoped, could access his U.K. records before finalizing the adoption.

Once Allyson presented the report to the U.S. Attorney in Baton Rouge, that office would have to decide whether the evidence was sufficient to proceed with a criminal investigation. This was a critical point in stopping Scott Rogers. We all felt that Allyson was working hard to compile our information, but we knew that the U.S. Attorney was the key to Scott's prosecution.

Like the action in the American television crime drama series, "Law and Order," the investigation of Scott Rogers was about to move into the next phase. Allyson and her colleagues had done their police work. Now we would wait to see if the U.S. Attorney would charge Scott and prosecute him.

To all appearances, the Middle District in Louisiana deals mainly in public corruption and drug and gun cases. We did not know if anyone in that office had Luke Walker's experience with cases of this type; we knew that few people in the U.S. could claim his expertise. But the Middle District in Baton Rouge had jurisdiction in this case, so that was where any action would take place. We took the case to Luke Walker because of his expertise and independence from local politics, but he had to hand it off to the U.S. Attorney's Office in Baton Rouge for any potential prosecution. We hoped that Luke's referral and Allyson's investigative work would assure that the case moved forward in Baton Rouge.

Allyson might need Luke's support with the U.S. Attorney, or, as the law enforcement agents say, "She might need a suit in the room." We had faith in Luke and hoped that if anyone in the Middle District hesitated, he might weigh in.

We held our breath, waiting to hear the U.S. Attorney's decision. Ethan was obviously anxious to hear any news at all, but we knew only that the investigation would begin to move more quickly now. I assured him that the safety of the children was paramount to everyone.

Allyson warned us that if Scott picked up on anything at all, he could flee with the children, making it much more difficult to keep them safe. I asked Ethan to caution Jake about talking to anyone over there, and I began talking to even fewer people outside of work, to avoid any chance of slipping up.

I didn't want to run into Scott Rogers or any of the people who circled around him like moons around Saturn, so I curtailed my activities and kept a lower profile after work hours.

Then, early one Tuesday morning, I got a text message from Mary Jane, who was at a Downtown Development District board meeting. "Sitting behind a couple wearing *Around Town TV Show* jackets," she texted. I didn't have to hear anymore. I knew it was Frances and Charles Bennett. I had seen them in the crew jackets before, but knowing what I did now, I couldn't imagine their future shock and embarrassment. *But I couldn't share any information with them. I was afraid anything I said might get back to Scott and alert him to the investigation.*

Nathan and I talked every day, trying to anticipate the next development. Mary Jane and I stayed busy with our respective work, and even though we knew either of us would call the other immediately if we heard anything, we still checked in every couple of days just to speculate on the next step. We knew the clock was ticking on Poh's adoption. *Something has to happen soon.*

Another five days passed and Allyson asked us to arrange for her to have another conversation with Ethan, this time without Mary Jane and me. She knew from her first call that he and I had developed a trust, so she asked that I encourage him to talk with her again as quickly as possible.

"We are all still here for you," I explained to him, "but speaking directly with you is important to them at this point."

"Yes, no problem," Ethan replied. "I'll mail you after the call with any info."

Allyson wanted two reports to present to the U.S. Attorney's office—one from Ethan and one from Jake. That office would then present the statements to a judge with the hope that the court could then revoke the pending adoption of Poh, take away the 10 year old, and send Scott to prison.

Ethan would talk to Jake, but he wasn't optimistic that Jake would provide a written statement. Without him, we had no assurance that Ethan's statement alone would insure the removal of the 10 year old from Scott's home. We were reminded that his adoption had been final for several years. We knew that the court would need strong evidence.

Allyson again encouraged Ethan to press charges against Scott in the U.K. She told him she had finally connected with Adrian Randall and was sharing information with him.

We had two guys sitting across the Atlantic Ocean who believed they were finally going to get justice because they had the power of the United States Government behind them. We didn't want to admit that our investigation had stalled briefly when our own law enforcement officers couldn't seem to make an international phone call.

After conferring with Randall, Allyson asked Ethan to consider speaking with him. "I truly believe it is time for Scott to face the wrongs he did to you guys as children," she explained to Ethan.

"He took something from each of you that should never have been taken. My hope is now as men, you both find the strength and courage to face the demon and make him pay for what he took from you, your innocence."

Allyson told Ethan that the legal systems both in the U.K. and in the U.S. should expose Scott. "He should have been convicted in 1993. It was wrong that he wasn't. Just trust and believe that this is a second chance."

She encouraged Ethan and Jake to lean on her for support, assuring them she had been through this prosecution with other victims, some younger and some older. "It is a tough process, but one that will leave you both stronger and finally free in the end from Scott's tangled web," she said. "You will just have to trust me on that. I've watched it too many times."

She noted that Adrian Randall's emails contained, below his signature: "Safeguarding Manager of Rowan House and Lead on West Suffolk Child Abuse and Vulnerable Adult Abuse Investigations."

Twenty years after Randall had investigated Scott Rogers for sexually abusing a young boy in Bury St. Edmunds, he had become an expert in child sex abuse cases. Could he have ever imagined he would get a second chance to see Scott prosecuted for the crimes he committed in Bury? All indications were that Randall considered Scott the one who got away.

I wasn't sure that either Ethan or Jake would be comfortable giving new statements to Randall. Ethan still hadn't sat down with his parents and brother and told them everything, and while Jake had, he was trying very hard to put his past behind him. They both felt strongly that Scott's sexual abuse of children had to end, but I wasn't sure how they felt about the prospect of his returning to the U.K.

"A lot to think about," Ethan emailed me. "I'll let you know tomorrow. I hope all is well with you."

July was coming to a close and Ethan was facing tough decisions. He always said that when we needed him, we should ask. Now Allyson was asking him to take some very difficult steps. As always, I expected he would weigh his options carefully, but I felt he would come through.

Still, I worried whether he was comfortable going as far as Allyson now asked. Was he finally willing for everything to come out? Ethan had thrown his grenade and now it was about to blow up. Was he ready for the aftermath?

CHAPTER FORTY-TWO

THE OPTIONS

After talking Allyson's request over with Jake, Ethan analyzed their options for me. Jake seemed to have little faith in the route the federal agents were pursuing. He believed that since their focus was on stopping Poh's adoption, the investigation would not impact Scott, who would simply close up when the story broke and move on to another place, where he would continue the abuse he had gotten away with for over 20 years. Jake had hoped the federal agents had enough evidence to warrant a full surveillance and catch Scott red-handed. From his experiences, he believed Scott had to be abusing someone.

As Ethan and I went back and forth on the merits of the federal agents' actions, he reminded me that until Jake was willing to help officially, theoretically he did not exist. Jake had been willing to speak only with Ethan, and Ethan was emphatic that we had to protect him. Based on his own experience, Jake always felt that Scott would retaliate against anyone who tried to expose him. Jake was understandably protective of his family, as was Ethan. Now we were asking them to face the monster. Their actions could even send Scott back to the U.K.

It was the first week in August, and, coincidentally, both men were on vacation with their families, pondering what they were willing to do. They hadn't seen each other or talked in person for 20 years, but now their peace of mind going forward would depend on the decisions they both made.

As Ethan considered his response to Allyson, he spelled out his options for me: Do nothing else and let the press expose the truth about Scott; give statements to Allyson for her report; go to the U.K. police and give a statement; if the press exposes Scott, wait to see if he worms his way out of the media fallout, then come forward with a statement in both the U.S. and the U.K.

"I'm thinking of all the options," he said, "of the best decision for me and my family and of course for those children who have been exposed to Scott. My original plan was to expose him at arm's length, but like everything in life, it's never as simple as you first thought. I'm thinking...."

As always, Ethan saw the big picture very clearly and never made rash decisions. For the next couple of days, we went back and forth as he weighed his next steps.

Mary Jane and I had heard that some action by the federal authorities should come by mid-August. Once they took official action, they said, we could involve the news media, if that was our plan. We had held off to avoid interfering with the investigation, but once the U.S. Attorney's office acted, we would be free to discuss the case.

We assumed the story would take local news media by surprise, so we would need to supply some background information to help them unravel it. Ethan had always thought the press was the way to expose the real Scott Rogers, and now, after almost a year, we thought that might finally happen. Ethan and Jake had seen the tabloid firestorm Scott's trial had created in the U.K., so they knew his story would get national attention there.

I asked Ethan if, when the news broke here, he would be willing to speak with one of our local reporters, reminding him that the press would not use his name, as he was a minor when Scott abused him. Everything we were hearing led us to believe that the next steps would come soon, and that Ethan would soon realize his hope of the public's learning the truth about Scott. He just wasn't sure he wanted to risk his own exposure. *After all these years, Scott's victims still fear him!* His punishment had always been harsh for those who displeased him, his threats swiftly made good by his enforcers or "foot soldiers," as one referred to himself.

Meantime, Scott interviewed a woman on *The Around Town Show* who had recently moved to Baton Rouge from Ohio, revealing that after his back surgery several years ago, he had bought a farm in the Marietta-Parkersburg area and intended to retire there.

I later learned that Ethan had located Stuart and Mathew in Baton Rouge five years earlier, through a video they had produced for a client who had posted it on You Tube. When he found their names, he contacted their client and asked how he could get in touch with them, knowing they would be with Scott.

Then Ethan sent a message to Scott, copying Mathew, Stuart, and Kimberly, letting Scott know he had found him and had not forgotten what Scott had done to him when he was a child. Thinking of the dreams Scott had shattered and the solace he had once found in writing poetry, Ethan decided to send an email that would make Scott think—one that would get inside his head as he had done to the boys. He scrambled the letters of his name to form an anagram for a new email address. Then he wrote his message in the form of a verse, a message that every word delivered with force.

Ethan's Email to Scott

You won't be famous if you tell.
It's only wrong in the eyes of the law.
Put on the blue coat and take off the red.
The boy becomes a man, the man becomes a boy.
What did the man do to the boy?
What will the boy do to the man?
Cometh the time, cometh the man.

As it turned out, Ethan was the only person Scott feared from his past. He knew that he had not been able to break him—that he had not been able to isolate him from his family—and he knew that Ethan would never forget what he had done to him.

When they received Ethan's email, Scott packed up the entire family and fled to Ohio, buying a house in a rural area along the Ohio River and moving everyone there, including his young adopted son. The family went into hiding, staying completely off social media and the Internet. But Scott wasn't able to find enough work there to support all of them, so gradually they came out of hiding and drifted back to Baton Rouge.

He would just have to be more careful.

CHAPTER FORTY-THREE

THE CHILDREN

Day 352
August 14, 2014

Another week passed and the discussion of the federal or State officials picking up Scott's two children intensified. Mary Jane was pushing hard on Allyson about the safety of the children, because we knew the adoption could be final soon. We got some indication that she was now working with Child Services and that someone would soon take action. We had to stand down for a little longer.

The second adoption gave Scott the opportunity to submit new false documents, so the State would not have to rely on those from the first adoption that were now eight or nine years old. Allyson had been working with Dirks at the State Department of Child Services to secure, through documents and interviews with Scott, everything that prosecutors needed to determine if a criminal case against Scott could be made. This time, no one would fast-track the process because of the people Scott knew. In fact, the Child Services people would now scrupulously review his application, because now they knew exactly who he was and what they were dealing with.

Scott kept promising on *The Around Town TV Show* that viewers would soon meet Poh, so we did not think anyone had tipped him off that anything was out of the ordinary.

Mary Jane's notes:

The plan was to call Rogers in to Child Services after he had filled out a questionnaire that contained specific questions about his past arrests and trials. Now everyone knew what Rogers' answers had to be, to be true, and they knew his answers on the questionnaire were false. They also decided to have a federal agent present along with a person from Child Services, and they keyed in on those specific questions about the past arrest and trial. Besides the false statement in a written document, a verbal denial of his past criminal arrest would constitute a false statement to a federal agent, an additional federal crime.

Then, at Child Services, when investigators asked Rogers if he had ever been the subject of any investigation regarding a child, he responded, "Well, I am glad you asked that question. In fact, I was." Everyone was stunned. They wondered if he was now going to tell the truth, and they waited for him to continue. Rogers reminded them that he had an older son, and explained that he was referring to the investigation, by Child Services, for that son's adoption. They then told him they did not mean that kind of investigation, but rather anything that would include an investigation into any type of child abuse. Rogers immediately conjured up his acting skills and feigned offense, assuring them absolutely not, going on about how horrible he considered that conduct. So when Rogers, his attorney, and Maria Edwards, the co-pastor of his church, later said that this whole investigation was about his checking boxes on immigration forms incorrectly, that was not true.

Rogers also told the people at the meeting that as soon as Poh's adoption was complete, he was going to get passports for the two children and take them to Malaysia. Previously Rogers had taken young boys from the United Kingdom to Malaysia, where, one of them said, Rogers had provided them to men for sex. In the United States, this is called human trafficking.

Prior to June 20, 2014, Thailand and Malaysia were ranked as two of "The Five Worst Countries for Human Trafficking." While these these two countries were reported downgraded to a Tier 3 by the U.S. State Department's 2014 Trafficking in Persons Report, they still did not fully comply with the minimum standards for the elimination of human trafficking, which includes children. Thailand and Malaysia promote themselves as modern, fast-developing countries, but their Tier 3 ranking puts them among the world's most lawless, oppressive, and dysfunctional countries.

In 2011, the Malaysian Statistics Department reported approximately 27.5 million people, making it the 41st most populated country in the world. Yet UNICEF Malaysia Child Protection in 2011 was aware of only 3,428 known cases of violence against children, which includes physical and mental abuse as well as injury, neglect, exploitation, and sexual abuse, with only extreme child abuse with disturbing injuries, sexual abuse, or deaths reported.

Malaysia is not a vacation spot for a child.

Several days later, Child Services called Rogers back to its offices. The investigators also decided that while he was at the meeting with Child Services, federal authorities would pick up the children and serve Mathew Hodgkinson and Stuart Poulton with federal grand jury subpoenas to appear and testify. Kimmy Rogers, the wife of Mathew Hodgkinson, and her boyfriend would also receive federal grand jury subpoenas.

On Thursday, August 14, the authorities were ready to pick up the children, and we knew this operation would have to be carefully orchestrated. Procedures under circumstances like this called for the authorities to avoid confrontations with the adoptive parents in front of the child, so we correctly assumed they would pick up the children from school when Scott was not around. Federal agents would have observed the family's daily patterns and learned that Mathew typically dropped the kids off, so we anticipated the authorities would pick them up, and we knew that could come as early as the next day.

Ethan asked Allyson if she knew whether Scott had fostered any other children over the past few years. "Yes, three or four. He also told Social Services he wants to adopt four more boys," she told him. Ethan didn't need to hear any more—he knew Scott was dangerous.

Ethan then assured her he would call Adrian Randall and asked whether she thought she could get both of the kids.

"Definitely one," she told him. "I am trying my absolute best on the other."

If we could have all held our breath until the children were safe, I think we would have done it. We had come so far. We now had the Department of Child Services knowledgeable about Scott's past and a team of federal agents working to get the children to safety. But we also had several victims who had seen Scott maneuver around the law, seemingly untouchable, and end up very vindictive.

Ethan once asked me to clarify the difference between federal agents and other law enforcement, and I explained that *federal* meant they worked for the United States Government under a U.S. Attorney who is appointed by the President. The weight of the United States Government seemed to give him some comfort. Most people expect the FBI's involvement in such cases and have no understanding why a postal inspector would head up an investigation, but Luke's decision to work with Allyson had proved correct.

Scott's plan to take the children to Malaysia raised the interviewers' anxiety regarding their safety. A more likely destination for a family trip to celebrate the addition of a new child might be Disney World. Malaysia is not exactly known as a popular vacation spot for Louisiana families.

When asked why he chose Malaysia, Scott said he had business interests there. When pressed to explain what kind of business, Scott told the group he did consulting work in the area of human resource management. He described companies paying him in excess of $20,000 to go in for a few days and work with them. A cynical person might wonder if "human resource management" was Scott's cryptic way of describing human trafficking, and, as Jake had suspected, playing a dangerous cat and mouse game with the authorities during the interview. None of us knew Scott like Jake knew him, and he felt Scott would use the interview to gain knowledge about the authorities—tricking, teasing, and deceiving them.

On Friday, August 15, Scott taped his final show with *The Around Town TV Show* crew and left shortly afterward for what he believed was a meeting with the Department of Child Services to finalize the adoption of Poh. He had no way of knowing that he would actually be met by federal authorities who would inform him that he was under investigation for mail fraud, stemming from his failure to submit truthful information on his application for U.S. citizenship, adoption papers, and other official documents.

While Rogers was being questioned at Child Services, Dirks was waiting in the wings to ask a judge in Iberville Parish for an *Ex parte* Order to pick up the children, remove them from Rogers' custody, and get them into a safe place. As soon as he learned that Rogers' interview had begun, he acted. When the judge signed the order, Dirks told the Child Services staff waiting to go get the kids.

An *Ex Parte* Order is temporary, as it is executed with only one side present, and facts are given to the judge for his consideration. On the basis of this court order, he sets a hearing at a later time, usually in just a few days in a child custody case. While Scott was learning that he was under investigation, Allyson and her partner arrived at the *Around Town Studio* and asked for Stuart Poulton and Mathew Hodgkinson. When the agents asked for a place where they could speak in private, Stuart led them into the 13:34 Church sanctuary. Although the temperature in the church was typically much colder than the studio, it was August in Louisiana and not easy to find a place where one might feel uncomfortably cold. But what took place next sent chills through Stuart.

One of Allyson's first questions was to confirm the location of the younger child, and Stuart gave her the name of the day care center. As he did, he watched her step outside to speak to someone, and he later told me he assumed the children were about to be picked up.

As the agents began explaining to Stuart the reason for their visit, as he learned that Scott's past was about to catch up with them all, he began to tremble visibly. He knew the church was cold, but he later told me what he felt that day was pure fear, and he could not stop shaking. He spoke to the agents for over an hour, and Allyson, who noticed Stuart's trembling, gave him her card when she left, encouraging him to call if he had any questions.

The interview with Mathew was much shorter. He had listened for only 15 minutes before he received a call from Scott. After that, he abruptly ended his cooperation.

In a carefully planned move, federal and State authorities executed picking up both of the children and placing them safely in the custody of the State. As the children were being secured, the federal agents were handing subpoenas to Mathew Hodgkinson and Stuart Poulton requiring their appearance before a federal grand jury on August 27, and, across town, Scott was finally learning that his past had caught up with him.

The older boy attended the Dunham School, a private school with programs for children with autism. When the Child Services officials arrived to pick him up, the headmaster, who, like Scott, was from the U.K., refused to turn him over. Dirks had to tell the man that he was sending State Police to come for the boy and that if the headmaster did not honor the court order, they would arrest him. *I knew that once Charlie knew what Scott was, he would move to protect those boys.*

The two children were now secured.

Once the boys were in the custody of the State, the process called for the 10 year old to undergo a forensic interview to obtain information for a custody hearing in Iberville Parish on Tuesday, August 19, to determine whether the children would remain in the custody of the State or return to Scott.

On his drive back to the studio, after learning that State and federal authorities had picked up the children, Scott began circling the wagons. According to those around him and records of his cell phone later obtained by the Iberville Parish Sheriff, he placed calls to State Police Colonel Mike Edmonson and other friends in law enforcement.

Colonel Edmonson is a career State Police officer, having served in the department for over 30 years. When he was selected by the Governor to lead the force, he was recognized publicly for two high-profile roles he played—chief spokesman for the State Police and security detail for LSU's head football coaches. Both of these assignments kept him in front of the cameras, where his boyish good looks and charismatic personality made him popular. To some law enforcement officers, he was an enigma—teased for his impeccable grooming, admired for his flawless people skills. As head of State Police, Colonel Edmonson would know law enforcement officials at every level, and Scott must have thought he could find out more about the State Child Services department taking the children.

When Colonel Edmonson made calls to ask what was going on, he learned that the federal government was handling the investigation.

Scott then called his daughter Kimmy. Though she had been estranged from him since moving out of his house earlier in the year, she arrived at the studio within minutes.

To plot his next move, Scott instructed everyone to assemble at the family home in St. Gabriel. He had been blindsided. He would soon learn that the Scott Rogers household would never again be the same.

As the child custody hearing the judge had ordered was fewer than four days away, neither side had much time to prepare.

Allyson moved quickly to notify Ethan that the children were safe and that she had spoken with Mathew and Stuart, who were now aware of other allegations coming forward from the U.K., although they did not know from whom. I received an email from Ethan saying, "Call me when you are free." It was getting late in the U.K., but Ethan said he would be up for at least another hour and a half, so I picked up the phone.

We were both very happy to hear that the authorities had picked up both children and not just the youngest. Ethan also told me he had spoken with Adrian Randall, and though he was moving forward on his end, he had not yet made any firm decisions.

I was surprised to hear that he had taken that step. I didn't know whether he had made the decision to press charges, but he had spoken to Randall so that Allyson could use, in the child custody hearing, information that Adrian provided.

Everything regarding the children was very confidential, so, at this point, Ethan was kept more informed on the case than I was. After talking with him, I called Nathan to update him and then went to meet Mary Jane so we could discuss the events of the day.

When Child Service officials picked up the children, federal agents were serving Mathew and Stuart with federal subpoenas, and Scott was undergoing an interview at Child Services. Because Kimmy was at work, she managed to avoid an interview on Friday, but was apparently combative with the federal agents when they tried to talk with her and expressed her support of Scott. Kimmy worked at Churchill's, a wine and cigar bar frequented by local lawyers, so some in the legal community began to hear something was up.

During this time, we learned that Mathew and Kimmy were married in January 2013 in Las Vegas. Since she had secured U.S. citizenship at the same time that Scott had, Kimmy's marriage to Mathew no doubt influenced his immigration status. But Kimmy had recently moved in with her current boyfriend— a boyfriend she had been seeing since before her marriage— leaving Scott's home and her husband behind. Her absence made the Scott Rogers family appear even more unusual, and her absence from her marriage to Mathew brought to light the likelihood that Scott Rogers wasn't the only member of his household committing fraud. No one who had been around Scott knew that Kimmy and Mathew were married. They certainly didn't present themselves as a couple. Stuart initially said he did not know they were married, but later admitted he did know that Scott had arranged the marriage to help Mathew get citizenship.

Though the State determined that it had sufficient evidence to hold the children beyond the Tuesday custody hearing, we had no way of knowing how the judge would rule.

I admitted to Ethan that Scott's craziness made me nervous but that I believed we were doing the right thing. From all appearances, the authorities' removal of the children from his home had surprised Scott and everyone around him. I imagined that he would be raging over the State's taking the children and seeing his charade undone.

"Don't worry about his craziness," Ethan said. "We have more aces than Wild Bill Hickok."

Ethan was full of surprises—he looked like a British rock star and spoke the lingo you would expect from a cool English guy in his 30s, but then he knew about the Wild Wild West in America? He also had a nice way of lightening the conversation with a little bit of humor when it turned to the dark side and what I feared most—Scott going completely crazy and going after anyone who had any part in exposing his dirty little lies. Jake's fear of him had convinced me that we all needed to take care.

Ethan felt sure Scott would now be huddling with the family, with Mathew and Stuart protecting both Scott and themselves. "They will have had a meeting by now and I'm sure Scott told them all what to say next," Ethan explained. "I hope they know what they are dealing with."

Over the weekend, Scott searched his files to show proof of his acquittal in the U.K. trial, claiming that where the Louisiana Child Service application asked if he had ever been arrested, he had simply marked the wrong box. At the same time, however, he was beginning to unravel. He took some of his so-called family members to the studio with him, and they ended up sleeping there over the weekend while Scott alternately looked for supporting documents for the custody hearing and talked about suicide, at one point tying neckties together and hinting that he would use them to hang himself in the studio.

CHAPTER FORTY-FOUR

THE LAST TV SHOW

Day 355
August 17, 2014

Over the weekend, word had spread through the tightknit 13:34 Church group that State authorities had picked up Scott Rogers' two children. One of those church members was Darla O'Connor, director of Ecumenical House, a halfway house in Baton Rouge noted as former Louisiana Governor Edwin Edwards' first stop after his release from federal prison. Ironically, Darla met Scott Rogers in August 2013, the same month Ethan first reached out to me from the U.K. She attended a 13:34 Church service and introduced herself to Scott, who was insulted that she did not know who he was. "I did not know of him, I did not know he had a TV show, and quite frankly, he was offended that I didn't," she told Iberville Parish Sheriff's deputies. But Darla began attending the church regularly, and by April 2014 she was serving on the church board.

At about 3 p.m. on Friday, Darla had received a call from another church member, Cornelia Yarbrough, to tell her she had just spoken to Scott, who told her Child Services had taken his children. Darla said she couldn't understand why, so she began trying to reach Scott. When he didn't answer, she called Mathew, who told her they needed a few days.

Over the course of the weekend, Darla kept in touch with Scott by text message, greatly concerned about him and asking, "Are you doing OK? What's going on? Do you need anything?"

Scott Rogers' last *Around Town TV Show* aired on Sunday, August 17, two days after authorities removed the two boys from his home. The program had been taped Friday morning, just before Scott was informed that he was the subject of a federal investigation. His first guest was Shelly Williamson from the Williamson Cosmetic Center, a sponsor who appeared frequently on the show. Scott had recently undergone a number of procedures with the Williamson Center, most recently to remove fat from around his waistline.

The rest of the guests almost foretold what was going on in Scott's life. The coincidences were uncanny.

He interviewed two representatives from the local chapter of the Court Appointed Special Advocates for Children, an organization that represents abused and neglected children in court. Recruitment Coordinator Jennifer Mayer and Board Chair David Faulk explained that the organization, to help raise awareness of its services, was holding a drawing for a kids' playhouse. In describing CASA, Scott credited the organization with "basically giving a child a voice in court, a very frightening place for them."

Mayer said, "Sadly, no child should have to endure any kind of abuse or neglect or abandonment of any kind," and Scott added, "And sadly, too often they do. I'm the same way—we look after our kids, and it makes it so tragic in your heart when you think there are kids out there going through this."

Scott then grew even more serious, discussing the suicide of actor Robin Williams with Dr. Ariel Lloyd, who took part in the interview on the last day she worked for Dr. Brandon Romano, another of Scott's frequent guests.

Dr. Lloyd's topic was the common triggers and treatments available for those suffering from depression. Before introducing her, Scott said, "Depression can lead to suicide. You get suicidal thoughts or you can do self-harm to yourself." After her remarks, he asked, "What should someone do?"

"Scott, I know you have some experience with this, and you know what you really wanted was support from your family, for them to show some unconditional love, make you feel like you're special, and encourage you to seek professional help."

Stop! Pause. Rewind. Play. She's talking about Scott's depression? I thought it very unusual for a psychologist to bring up someone's depression on television—unless he wanted her to.

Scott sat there nodding in agreement with a woeful look on his face.

This interview was taped the morning the authorities picked up the kids. *Had Scott known about the investigation?* There had been no indication that he had.

Dr. Lloyd later told me that just before they began taping her interview, Scott was talking with her when he suddenly asked her to acknowledge during the interview that he had suffered from severe depression. She was uncomfortable with the request, not wanting to give any impression that she had treated Scott or that she would reveal such private information about a person receiving treatment.

Though Dr. Lloyd had suspected that Scott had secrets, later she was taken aback by the layers of secrets he had kept. She had thought he was trying to hide being gay. She was not aware of the living arrangements of the three men and two little boys. Like others who had been around the show, Dr. Lloyd recalled how Rogers was charming to guests, but lost his temper quickly with the crew, especially Stuart, if anything went wrong with taping the program. She had been there when the crew had aired the wrong program introduction and had to correct the mistake. Scott fumed that the pause had interrupted the show's flow; flustered and upset, he had exploded in anger on the set.

She later explained how Scott Rogers, whom she considered a sociopath, sought out the vulnerabilities in others. She said that Scott had chosen his favorites for very specific reasons, because he saw something in them that he could exploit. "Cult leaders have a knack for doing this," she explained. "They know exactly what to do to get them on their side."

Ironically, one of Dr. Brandon Romano's specialties is the treatment of sex offenders, which leaves unanswered questions about whether Scott targeted Dr. Romano to befriend and if so, why. Did he hope to learn more about his own behavior from Dr. Romano? Or did he get some perverse pleasure in learning so much about a subject with which he was already too well acquainted? Was he playing his mind games again?

During a commercial break, another public service announcement for Sheriff Gautreaux aired—an announcement that the Sheriff's cybercrimes unit was protecting children from predators' online solicitations. "The Sheriff's cybercrimes unit works," the TV spot declared. Meanwhile, the man airing the TV spot for the Sheriff was a reserve deputy, a chaplain for the Sheriff's department, and perhaps one of the most evil child predators Baton Rouge had ever seen. *What perverse pleasure he must get from the Sheriff's announcement that the cybercrimes unit was protecting children, knowing he was fooling them all!*

The program continued with Chef Celeste poaching some pears in the kitchen and Scott sampling them and talking through a mouthful of pears to introduce his final guest, District Court Judge Trudy White, who was on the show to talk about a Re-entry Court to help rehabilitate those who get into trouble with the law.

For his Motivational Moment, Scott ended with a childish recitation of "Toddler Law," a short poem about how children are possessive of their toys. Laughing into the camera, Scott said, "I'm thinking of my baby Poh as I'm reading this."

Then Scott and Celeste signed off in their usual way, with Scott starting it off, "Until we see you again…"

"Take care of yourself," said Celeste.

"Stay safe out there," added Scott.

"God bless each of you," continued Celeste.

"And of course, God bless America…. We'll see you next weekend!"

Although he did not know it, Scott Rogers had just signed off of *The Around Town Show* for the last time.

On Monday, August 18, the day before the child custody hearing, Darla said Scott phoned her around 6 a.m. and sounded as if he had been drinking. In a rambling conversation, Scott said he had drunk a bottle of vodka, taken 40 Oxycontin pills, and was planning to kill himself. He told her he was calling to say goodbye.

Scott had always told people he had back surgery several years earlier, and while some of those close to him said he rarely complained of back pain, he had stockpiled prescription painkillers. His back surgery also enabled him to get a special license plate on his vehicle to park in spaces reserved for handicapped drivers. When 1stCo had a contract with EATEL, a telecommunications company based in Gonzales, Louisiana, company representatives questioned Scott's parking in those spaces reserved for their customers, since they saw no signs of a disability. That they would dare to question him set Scott off in one of his rages. The spoiled child in him began to deliberately engage in actions that annoyed the client, and soon, to the surprise of no one on the 1stCo crew, the EATEL contract ended.

When Scott called Darla Monday morning, she woke Tavia Crumpler, deputy director of the Ecumenical House who lives with Darla, to tell her about Scott's call. Tavia began trying to call Mathew or Stuart. When she could not reach them, she called Maria Edwards, co-pastor with Scott of the 13:34 Church. While Tavia was attempting to contact others, Darla was on the phone with Scott until his phone went dead. At that point, she called 911 and relayed the information she had. She later told authorities that about an hour after she called 911, Scott called her back and sounded perfectly fine.

"Darla, this is Scott."

"Yes?" she replied.

Scott told her he was in his room asleep when he woke to find nine people standing over him, telling him Darla thought he was going to kill himself.

"I need for you to tell them that I was only asleep or they are going to take me," Scott told Darla.

Darla spoke to a paramedic on the scene, and relayed to him what had happened. She believed Scott was suicidal and that the signs were serious enough to call 911. "I don't lightly call 911. I can only tell you what he told me. I believed he was suicidal, therefore I called you." Darla said.

But Scott told the Sheriff's deputies he was fine, and had simply taken something to help him sleep since he had been upset after his two sons were removed from his home. Before they left, the deputies noticed someone sitting alone on the patio, staring out at the nearby woods in deep thought. He never spoke to the deputies, but Stuart Poulton was beginning to have serious concerns about how Scott was falling apart, his charade unraveling. He was growing tired of all the theatrics, and did not believe Scott had the courage to kill himself, only the desire to draw everyone into his melodrama.

Did Stuart consider walking away from it all and asking the Sheriff to take him in? Ethan hadn't been able to get through to him, but with the children gone, was he ready to leave the strange life he had with Scott, Mathew, and Kimmy for the past 20 years? *Not yet.*

When, years earlier, Stuart had grown depressed about his relationship with Scott, he had wanted only an acknowledgement that the way they had started out was wrong. When Scott talked of wanting Stuart to be his partner, to marry him and share his life, Stuart wanted Scott to admit that beginning a sexual relationship with him when he was only 13 years old was wrong. But after he finally summoned the courage to bring up the subject, carefully planning what he would say, hoping for that simple admission—not even expecting an apology—Scott brushed him off and changed the subject.

So over the last few years, Stuart had shut down his emotions. He didn't have any good feelings left for Scott, and he knew if he allowed himself to love the children as if they were his own, Scott would sense his weakness and use what he cared about most when he wanted to hurt him. The reason Scott saved his harshest words for Stuart on the set of *The Around Town TV Show* was that Stuart had been challenging Scott, at times refusing his demands for sex.

Like the line from the haunting song "Waiting Game" on the charts that year, Stuart had grown distant. "What if the way we started made it something cursed from the start; what if it only gets colder?"

When Stuart couldn't get even the smallest concession from Scott, he began to imagine leaving. But he had never quite brought himself to do it.

As the Sheriff's deputies got into their units to leave, Stuart was still deep in thought, gradually withdrawing even further from the continuing drama surrounding Scott. Near the front door the deputies walked past a life-size metal knight in armor, curiously standing guard over the people Scott Rogers considered his family.

When Tavia finally reached Maria Edwards, the pastor went to Scott's house to check on him. Darla said Maria arrived before the police left, waited for them to leave, then went in to see Scott.

Later in the day, Maria called Darla and told her that Scott wanted to die. She said she needed to come by Darla's office so they could talk. When she arrived, Maria Edwards took Darla's and Tavia's cell phones and, according to Darla, told them, "You have to turn them off. You have to put them in another room, because everything we are talking about is being bugged." Even with their cell phones off and in another room, Maria had them whisper when they spoke. Maria Edwards told them Scott wanted to die, so she gave him what she called a "sacrament," which Darla assumed meant communion. She told them Scott slept for a few hours then woke up angry and made Maria leave his home. Maria asked Darla and Tavia to help her with an intervention. Darla said she and Tavia would talk with Scott, reminding her they were not members of his family and did not have any legal standing. Monday afternoon, the three women went to Scott's house and met with Mathew, Stuart, and Kimmy while Scott was upstairs taking a bath. Darla recommended they remove all alcohol from the house, but Mathew and Kimmy both thought Scott was easier to manage when he was drinking.

Darla asked Mathew, "Where is the gun? Is there more than one gun? Where is the gun?' According to Darla, Mathew replied, "I've moved the gun. It's hidden. He has not asked for it.'"

Darla asked Mathew if he was comfortable with that and Mathew replied, "For now."

Scott then came downstairs and said, "They've taken my boys. They've taken my boys. It's all lies!" He pulled out a paper from a court in England about the trial there and made his case to them: "I was acquitted! Here, look at this. You have to tell them when I'm gone that I was acquitted. I was never found guilty."

Scott continued talking about himself in the past tense, telling them he had put money up for Mathew and Stuart and was going to revise his will. Darla took Scott aside to talk to him alone and asked him if he wanted to die.

"Yes," Scott said. He told her he had been searching the Internet for information about putting a bag over his head or a belt around his neck. He said he had tried to kill himself every day since the authorities had picked up the boys.

"Scott, if you've tried four times and you haven't succeeded, what does that tell you?" Darla asked. "This either tells you this is just not gonna work, or you're just not very good at it. You don't know that you're not going to get your boys back. You've got to fight for those boys. When it comes down that you're not going to get them back, then you can revisit the suicide thing, but that day's not today. You've got a court hearing tomorrow. You've got different things going on and quite frankly, your boys deserve better than this."

Scott paced around the room until Darla called him back over and told him that if he had made up his mind to kill himself and was not willing to accept any help, this was the last time she would see him, so she wanted to pray for him. Scott sobbed and walked away.

Darla joined Tavia, who was sitting with Stuart and Mathew, and told them they had to stop letting Scott have everything he wanted. They needed to say *no* to him, Darla said, and should have put him in the car and taken him to nearby St. Elizabeth's Hospital. Darla told Mathew and Stuart that if they needed Tavia and her to help by playing the bad guys with Scott, they would do so, but she warned them that if she called EMS again, paramedics would probably take Scott to the hospital.

Mathew was his usual stoic self when talking about the court cases, but when he began talking about the boys, he started to sob, worrying about how they were being taken care of and whether they understood what was going on.

Mathew's concerns were in direct contrast to Scott's, who kept saying, "Once this hits the news, my life is over. I'm ruined!"

"But what about your boys?" Darla asked.

"That won't matter because I'm ruined," Scott told her, "and it's going to hit the news."

Scott insisted the federal government's interest in him was the result of his simply mis-checking, on an application, a box that said he had never had an alias or been arrested for a crime. As she listened to him, Darla began thinking his story simply did not add up.

When we heard the rumor on Monday that Scott had attempted suicide by overdosing on pills and that paramedics had been called to the scene, the drama was all too familiar to his victims in the U.K. "Heavy...." Ethan said. "Could be tactical. He did similar actions during the court case in '93."

If this was a strategic move, surely it would backfire, we thought. With the custody hearing just 24 hours away, no judge would allow the children to go back to Scott's house so soon after a suicide attempt. I began to think he was not planning to fight at the custody hearing—maybe he just intended to use his emotional state as an excuse to delay it.

Jake was not surprised by the suicide attempt and, like Ethan, thought it could be a delaying tactic, since it was Scott's third or fourth try. They were also curious about when the news media might get the story.

"I don't think the media can do anything as long as the court's action involves the children," I explained. "The State of Louisiana will handle the child custody issues and will seal all proceedings. The hearing is private.

"Any possible charges against Scott are federal, being handled by the U.S. Government," I explained. "We will have to wait until something occurs that can be made public. I think we are still a couple of weeks away on that.

"I agree with you that suicide threats are a pattern with him," I said, "but when he did that in the U.K., Kimmy was his only child and she had a mother at home. With the children here, a suicide attempt makes it more difficult for him to make a case to keep the children, so I think it hurts his case with the State. And I don't think the U.S. Government will delay anything because of it. The feds are just naturally slow and deliberative, but the first priority for everyone has been getting the children to a safe place."

Ethan and Jake couldn't help their skepticism about Scott's attempted suicide; they had seen that behavior before. But hearing about it sent a signal to Allyson that the federal investigation should move as quickly as possible and that if a grand jury planned to indict Scott, it should act quickly, and he should be taken into custody immediately for his own protection.

Now Nathan, Mary Jane, and I worried even more about the outcome of the custody hearing. If Scott was in fact a danger to himself, was he also a danger to the children? Everything we had heard about his cult behavior made us even more concerned that he would come up with a suicide pact and take everyone in the house with him. Scott was a narcissist, and if he ever actually acted seriously on a suicide, we were afraid he wouldn't go alone.

Ethan felt sure Scott would fight for custody of the two children, and he was anxious for someone to interview the 10 year old in depth to determine whether the abuse had begun and thus how quickly the federal authorities might bring charges against Scott. We knew a lot of time could pass before the truth came out, especially because of the 10 year old's autism, but we were hopeful that we had presented enough information to keep the two little boys safe.

CHAPTER FORTY-FIVE

THE CUSTODY HEARING

Day 357
August 19, 2014

On Tuesday morning, Scott again called Darla to say goodbye. He told her everyone was going before Judge William C. Dupont, chief judge of the 18th Judicial District Court in Iberville Parish, for the hearing on the custody of the boys. Then the phone went dead. About 20 minutes later, he called her back and said, "They're making me go to court with them. I just can't do this."

"Scott, you have to," Darla said. "It's just a day of your life. If your kids aren't worth a day of your life, come on, man!"

"I just can't do this!" Scott said, "And I don't have the courage to kill myself. Will you help me off myself?"

"Absolutely not," Darla said. "That's not a conversation for today, but absolutely not."

"I thought you were my friend," Scott told her. "I thought you loved me."

"I will support you. I will love you. And I will do what I can do, but that crosses the line," she replied. "I absolutely will not do that...and it's not right for you to even ask me to do that."

Scott continued to bemoan the loss of his kids; Darla told him to pull himself together and go to court and they would talk afterwards. The petulant child in Scott was angry that Darla would not do what he wanted, so he ignored her for a few days, sending messages to her through others.

The custody hearing on Tuesday lasted six hours. Scott arrived with Mathew, Kimmy, and Maria Edwards in tow. Stuart did not attend because in the eyes of Child Services, he was not a permanent resident of the home as the others were. At times, Scott had indicated that Mathew and Stuart lived in separate apartments on the grounds, instead of the single house. At other times, he listed only Mathew and Kimmy as living in the house with him. Bedrooms were set up to give a false impression of living arrangements— should Child Services make a surprise visit—even down to which clothes hung in which closets. On one visit by a State inspector, Scott had slipped into the kitchen where Stuart was sitting at the table talking to the children and told him to walk through and say goodbye on his way out the door. Scott told him he would tell the inspector that Stuart was a babysitter or tutor and text him after the inspector left so that he could return home.

Stuart slept on the floor in Scott's bedroom for years, and only after he had complained about his back for a long time did Scott buy him a futon. Although he spent hours taking care of both children after Kimmy moved out and Scott began to spend most evenings gambling at the casino, Stuart would serve no useful purpose at the child custody hearing and might even draw attention to the unusual living arrangements.

Based simply on his reputation with Child Services, Scott held out some expectation that the children would come back to him. But Allyson got information from her investigation into the record, and Judge Dupont ruled the evidence sufficient for the State to maintain custody of both children for the time being. Because the process allowed for appeals and rebuttals, a long-term decision would probably not come until October. By that time, the grand jury would have interviewed everyone and compiled more evidence.

Scott had a new lawyer, Seth Dornier, and the 10-year-old boy had a court appointed attorney. The hearing was closed to only a handful of people, including an observer who was beginning to question the unusual happenings on Daisy Avenue. Watching the hearing unfold, Iberville Parish Sheriff Brett Stassi knew Scott's suicide attempt was not the first time his office had been called to the house, and he was interested in the circumstances that led to State and federal agents removing two little boys from the home.

Sheriff Stassi is a lifelong resident of Iberville Parish and a graduate of Nicholls State University—"Harvard on the Bayou" they fondly call it around the south Louisiana region it serves. Stassi began his career with the Iberville Sheriff's Office after high school and then worked as an investigator for the District Attorney, bringing 30 years of law enforcement experience to the job when he was sworn in as Sheriff in 2012. Sheriffs in rural Louisiana are very powerful, and Stassi runs a tight ship. So as he listened at the custody hearing, it didn't take him long to put the pieces together.

Scott was not prepared for the information that had surfaced about his past. As the hearing unfolded, he learned that at least two of his victims in the U.K. had come forward to the authorities in the U.S. to detail the sexual and physical abuse they had suffered for years. At first, the small group of people at the hearing saw Scott roll his eyes or shake his head when agents presented information, but after realizing the volume of evidence against him, he became more teary-eyed as he listened.

If Scott was depressed after the State had picked up the children, the hearing was the clearest sign to him that someone knew exactly what he had done and what he was. But despite the evidence, the case against Scott Rogers was far from a cinch. There were issues regarding statutes of limitations, and we were constantly reminded that very possibly he would not see any jail time, even if successfully charged with fraud. The authorities would do everything they could to remove the children from his care, but they could not guarantee that the charges against him would stick.

Darla had sent a text message to Mathew at 7:16 a.m. that morning, "Praying for court this morning. Praying for each of you. I love you all so very much." Mathew didn't respond until 6:12 p.m. when they had all made it back home. "Thank you, dear. Just got back and settled. Very, very long and horrible day. Scott did great. He made it through a horrendous day. Went well. Took a small step in right direction today."

But no one knew what Scott did—that is, the truth about all the evil he had done. He was the only one who knew the full extent of what the authorities might learn about him.

Around 6:30 the morning after the hearing, I awoke to a stream of emails that had come in overnight from the U.K.

The days were long again and the morning sun was already casting soft shadows in the birdcage as light streamed through the trees. When I opened my email, six messages downloaded from Ethan, and I knew something was up. Any time the children were an issue, Ethan and Jake were most concerned. While they were pleased the children had been removed from Scott's home, they were worried to learn he would seek supervised visitation in the coming weeks.

"I think Allyson needs to know more about what Scott does in these situations," Ethan wrote. "He will be desperately trying to get in contact with the child, either through Mathew, Stuart, Kimberly, or even someone we don't know. He may even have hand signals or visual signals to the child—he's done all this before, too. He uses third parties to pass messages that even they don't know they are delivering, certain sentences that would mean nothing to anyone except the abused child!"

The next email included information he was passing along from Jake. "When Scott was arrested for sexual abuse of a minor in the U.K.," Jake wrote, "Mathew Hodgkinson was under his care. Mathew's parents lived in France, as they emigrated to open a holiday business; they immediately took their son away from Scott and brought him to France. There was a court injunction to stop Scott from contacting Mathew. Scott managed to speak to Mathew on the phone EVERY day; he convinced Mathew to say that his parents were abusing him in France. Scott sent packages to Mathew in France under the guise of "friends of Mathew" containing concealed money and false documents. This money was hidden inside CD cases and teddy bears along with messages and information. Scott managed to orchestrate Mathew running away from France back to the U.K. using a stolen passport. Once Mathew was in the U.K., Scott managed to meet him immediately and place him with a family that was "friends" of Mathew—they were really friends of Scott. With a huge court case against Scott, with an injunction in place to stop Scott from contacting Mathew…Scott managed to see him every day, hide him in a secret room in the house and unfortunately Mathew is still with Scott today."

I have never been a morning person, but I didn't need any help waking up as I read Ethan's email. What I was reading was awful, but confirmed published reports in England that came out during the trial. Scott's hold on Mathew seemed unbreakable, even destroying the bond between Mathew and his parents.

I kept reading. "Scott and anyone associated with his inner circle of friends will try to maintain contact with the child that was taken from him AT ANY COST," the email continued. "They will try messaging, phoning, leaving messages at a place only the child knows, secret phrases. He probably has the child trying to phone or contact him or one of Scott's associates—all of this to keep his control over the child, to keep him quiet and to make the child still feel that Scott is in control. Scott has so many tactics and guises to play, through third parties. He will find a way to maintain contact and abuse in my experience of him. A very evil and manipulative monster!"

I was afraid we had awakened Jake's worst fears—the little boy was temporarily safe, but he knew better than anyone that Scott would fight to get him back. And as Jake knew all too well, he just might succeed.

I moved on to the next email. "In addition to my last email, there is now also the Internet involved which is another means of contact. It's very important to state that Scott is a master at abuse and manipulation. His abuse can last a lifetime, which is evident in the case of Mathew and Stuart who are still under his control. His hands aren't tied by rules and regulations; he knows every trick in the book and uses them all to his full advantage. One more point to put across is the abused child is probably very much in the mind set of trying to get back to Scott and communicate with Scott—such is the power of his brainwashing and conditioning—the kids will do anything to try and stay with Scott! Very, very awful."

Jake's message had a raw urgency that was even more painful to process than Ethan's experiences. He was desperate to warn against the tactics Scott would employ to get the little boy back. He was speaking from the most painful experience one could imagine. He had tried to escape the abuse, only to be hunted down by Scott's disciples, beaten, and returned to Scott to be abused again.

"Sorry to overwhelm you...." Ethan said in his last email, and I had to admit I was feeling a little overwhelmed.

No one could speak from experience more powerfully than Jake. I agreed with Ethan and Jake that the authorities needed to know exactly what challenges they faced with Scott. They may deal with pedophiles every day and understand their ability to deceive, but when you combined the power of Scott's cult strategies with his success in maintaining absolute control over Mathew and Stuart for more than 20 years, I wasn't sure many local law enforcement agents had faced anyone as manipulative as Scott Rogers.

It was too early to call Nathan or Mary Jane, so I paced around the house, trying to think of how we could make sure the authorities understood Scott's depravity. Allyson would understand—at this point, she had heard most of this information and had been in touch with the detective in the U.K. who had worked on Scott's case. She knew what Scott Rogers was, and by now she had to know he should never be around children. But she wasn't in charge now. A judge would decide the custody of the children, and the U.S. Attorney's Office would prosecute Scott if the grand jury indicted him. As control of the case shifted to them, Allyson would experience an influx of other federal agencies, even though she was the one who knew the most about the case.

In my first hour of being awake on Wednesday, August 20, it became clear to me that we needed Jake to talk to the authorities, though I completely understood his hesitancy to come forward. Ethan had always said that Jake had received Scott's worst abuse. Trusting Ethan had not been easy for Jake, and he had not been willing so far to speak with the authorities in the U.S. He had seen Scott outsmart too many people, even a jury. He knew Scott was cruel and quick to retaliate. Jake had a family now, and he knew Scott would do whatever he could to get back at him, and he wasn't willing to risk harm to his wife and children.

But I knew that as a survivor of Scott's abuse, Jake had far greater standing than anyone to tell authorities in the U.S. about the real Scott Rogers. Ethan had very bravely stepped forward, but he also told us that speaking out was much harder for Jake because Scott had kept him in his house, while Ethan went home to a loving family. Even so, coming forward had been very difficult for Ethan, and took many years.

It was time to ask for Ethan's help and hope he could deliver. *He had to convince Jake to talk to the authorities.* Every step in this case was critical at this point. What Ethan and Jake had sent me overnight needed to be heard first-hand by someone who could take it directly to the judge who would decide whether two little boys continued to live with Scott. *He has to hear from Jake! The judge has to know Scott Rogers is dangerous.*

I went back to the computer and emailed Ethan, promising to make sure Allyson received all of the information that he and Jake had sent to me.

"Do you think Jake would talk to Allyson at this point?" I asked. "His name would be completely protected here, but it is very powerful for her to have a statement from a victim. Maybe he will understand how far she has come with her investigation…and help her. Because the 10 year old has been legally adopted, it's not going to be easy to take him away permanently without more proof of the harm. Yes, he has been interviewed and will continue to be interviewed, but the State appoints an attorney to represent him, and Child Services moves slowly to protect him from any further trauma."

Hoping the authorities would find evidence that would keep the children away from Scott, Ethan asked good questions about whether search warrants had been authorized on Scott's house. Nathan, Mary Jane, and I had wondered about that, too, since we had questions about a pedophile with access to the cameras and video editing equipment that a television studio provided. Our first question was whether Scott was involved in child pornography, a possible source of income for him, since no one believed the television program was a profitable venture capable of supporting the large family. In fact, Scott claimed the TV show lost money, and when he published his books, he claimed he gave away the proceeds. So we couldn't really identify his source of income other than the contracts he had been getting recently. But so far, we had not heard of the authorities executing any search warrants on the house or studio.

I pressed "send" on the email urging Ethan to get Jake to talk to Allyson directly and went to take a shower and get ready for work. When I checked emails about 15 minutes later, Ethan had replied, "Yes, I think Jake will speak with Allyson. I asked him this morning."

Again, they did everything asked of them to give the authorities the help they needed, just as Luke Walker told us they would in our first meeting.

Ethan and I spoke by phone later that day about the importance of Jake's cooperating with Allyson in the interview. I knew this was a big step for him, and I knew he would experience a lot of apprehension. Ethan provided great support for him, since we had been communicating for almost a year now and had never taken a single step that we had not first discussed, weighing options and risks before moving forward together. But Jake didn't know us and would have to trust Ethan's assurance that Allyson would protect his identity.

I felt certain the only reason he was willing to speak with her was because the issue at hand was whether a judge would allow Scott visitation with the children, especially the 10 year old. That thought had to weigh heavily on him, since he knew better than anyone exactly what could result.

On Wednesday night, the board members of Scott's 13:34 Church held an emergency meeting by conference call to discuss the situation. Scott, Mathew, Stuart, Maria, and Darla joined the rest of the board, some hearing for the first time that Child Services had taken the boys. Scott repeated his claims that the boys' removal was based on lies, and that he had simply made mistakes when filling out official paperwork. Then he mentioned that a federal grand jury would meet the next week.

Darla took immediate notice, because her experience with the federal corrections system told her that a federal grand jury was not empaneled on short notice and that when a grand jury was involved, the matter was very serious. She knew that federal grand juries took a long time to consider evidence in depth, that they met only a couple of days a month in secrecy to receive evidence on investigations, and that often people do not learn about an investigation until it is near the end.

"What is this federal grand jury about?" Darla asked.

"I don't know," Scott said. "They're just after me."

"So you don't have any idea what this is about?"

"No, I do not," Scott replied, without disclosing that he was under investigation.

"This grand jury is about the mistakes on your application?" Darla continued to probe on the call with the other board members listening.

"Yes, they are all after me," Scott snapped.

By the end of the call, the 13:34 Church board members were in lock step with Scott, telling him how sorry they were that he had to go through this anguish and assuring him they believed in his innocence. The board members decided they would tell the congregation that Pastor Scott was on vacation because he needed some time off, leaving it open ended as to when he would return to the pulpit.

Maria was sympathetic to Scott and later told authorities that his immigration attorney had informed Mathew that Scott's answers on the application constituted a lie and a major offense against the United States. Mathew said the attorney told him Scott's citizenship would be revoked, Kimmy's citizenship depended on Scott's so it would be revoked, and Mathew's depended on Kimmy's, so the chain reaction would result in loss of citizenship and deportation for all three. Maria said the family also feared that the adoption of the 10-year-old son would be invalidated because of the original paperwork.

"He was desperate, he was crying, he was not eating. He said he did not want to live without those children," Maria said. Until that time, she said, she had visited Scott's home only three or four times; now she sat with him every day.

On Thursday, August 21, Allyson and Jake finally talked for over two hours, and he opened up to her about the abuse he had suffered at the hands of Scott Rogers. His warnings about the tactics Scott would use to control the 10 year old increased her concern for the boy's safety, as did his reports of violent abuse, including broken bones. She promised to share his story with Child Services officials in hopes they could convince the judge to delay a supervised visit until the case against Scott had time to proceed.

After spending hours recalling for Allyson the horrors he had endured as a young boy under Scott's control, Jake spent the remainder of that night sick from the intense pain of a migraine headache. *After all these years, even the memories of Scott could still hurt Jake.*

The federal grand jury was scheduled to meet on Wednesday, August 27, to hear from Mathew, Stuart, and Kimmy. Diane Palladino, Scott's former wife from Texas, was scheduled to testify at a later date about the circumstances of her marriage.

"Next up will be to get a look at the weekend shows," I told Ethan. This weekend's *Around Town Show* was our first chance, after the children's removal, to see how Scott would handle hosting the show in front of the unforgiving eye of the camera. I knew it would be very hard for him to disguise his discomfort over the discovery of his past by State and federal authorities.

"We will now wait to see how things unfold before making any further moves," Ethan said.

When I spoke to Nathan, he stressed the need to provide any documentation that could help with the legal proceedings. "If Jake was treated at a hospital for any injuries he received from Scott's abuse, he could request a copy of his medical records," he suggested. "If he has copies of any correspondence from Scott, that would also be helpful." I shared this with Ethan, who would chat with Jake again over the next couple of days and encourage him to share anything that might help a court case.

How could we hope to convince Jake that this time would be any different from the years of abuse he had suffered? Why should he believe that the U.S. authorities could stop Scott when he had surrounded himself with community leaders, just as he had in Bury St. Edmunds?

The Boys of Bury

JAKE *in his own words*

England
2015

I didn't know his whereabouts...I just wanted to get away from him.

I found out he had adopted more children and I couldn't sit back and watch it happen again to innocent young children. Everybody that is close to me knows what I've been through. Now I'd spoken to a federal agent in the U.S. and I told my story because I couldn't see it happening again. I had to come forward and make a stand.

I was petrified...I thought he could somehow destroy my life again...but I had to say something.

CHAPTER FORTY-SIX

THE REALIZATION

Day 361
August 23, 2014

By the weekend, the Saturday *Around Town TV Show* opened with a greeting by Chef Celeste sitting alone at the desk, followed by Kimmy rolling into view of the camera in a chair to announce her return to the show. There she was, the dutiful daughter, back in the fold to fill in for Scott. Celeste announced that Scott was not feeling well, and Kimmy put on her best *Around Town* overly-cheerful, larger-than-life affectation more typical of Scott. At the end of the show they announced the Sunday line-up, and Kimmy said, "I hope Scott's feeling better!" I thought it unlikely he would appear on the air that weekend.

The main guest for the Saturday program was Louisiana State Police Superintendent Mike Edmonson. Clearly, Scott was doing everything he could to bolster his image by showing off his close relationships with law enforcement officials. By now, Edmonson knew the children had been removed from Scott's home and he knew a federal investigation was ongoing.

Ironically, Edmonson was at the time completing a round of media interviews touting new legislation the Governor had signed just two months earlier: a crackdown on human trafficking in Louisiana. And as he sat on the set of *The Around Town TV Show,* two victims of Scott Rogers' sexual abuse were videotaping him. These were the same two young men with whom he had interacted on numerous occasions, including at their home. Edmonson had been seen on TV sitting with the extended Rogers family at a luncheon honoring him for serving as honorary co-chair, along with Rogers' son, of the annual Active for Autism event. The little 10-year-old boy was videotaped reciting another well-rehearsed line, "When I grow up I want to be a State Trooper just like Uncle Mike."

One of the 1stCo crew members said Edmonson had an open door at *The Around Town TV Show* and could guest on the show any time he wanted. "I remember Scott telling us that once at the casino he bumped into Mike surrounded by his troopers, and Scott said how embarrassing it was that Mike would gush over him," the crew member said. "Mike had access to the show and Scott liked having access to the State Police."

As superintendent of the Louisiana State Police, Colonel Mike Edmonson could appear live on every broadcast station in Louisiana on the 6 p.m. news if he wanted or had the need. He would not need a small, independently produced TV show that airs at 5 a.m. on a weekend for publicity. But Scott, by telling those under his control that the head of the State Police was enamored with him, was able to foster the fear that he was well connected. He had always survived by developing friendships among community leaders, and law enforcement officials were his most prized catches, both in the U.K. and now in Baton Rouge. *What better way to keep your victims under control than to convince them the head of the State Police owes you some debt of gratitude?*

Baker Police Chief Mike "Snapper" Knaps followed Edmonson as a guest on the final show. Knaps had succeeded Sid Gautreaux as the Baker Police Chief, the department where Scott got his first badge—so Scott had loaded the show with law enforcement interviews.

While the final *Around Town TV Shows* were airing, Scott's paranoia grew more intense. To keep anyone from listening in on the family's conversations, he made the family members place their cell phones in an ice chest when they entered the house. He also turned the cameras in each room of the house toward the ceiling. Scott was certain that somehow federal agents might tap into his elaborate camera system to see and hear all of them.

At Sunday's 13:34 Church service, Darla conducted part of the service because a tearful Maria Edwards, after spending most of her days at Scott's house, was too emotional. Darla had been communicating with Scott by text, offering to deliver a lesson. "I know I am not ordained but I can write and deliver pretty good sermons," she had offered.

As she was getting ready to fill in for him at the Sunday morning service, she sent Scott a text saying, "Pray for me this morning. Please."

"I just did," he replied. "You are going to be amazing.... You will uplift the entire chapel. I love you. God blesses you."

When Maria arrived at Scott's house after church, he pleaded with her to stay, so she began sleeping there on a sofa and remained until Wednesday. Chef Celeste prepared a lavish meal for the family, and Scott brought them all together in a way that made Stuart ask, "What is this...the Last Supper?" Scott looked at him and dramatically nodded *yes*, but Stuart thought Scott's behavior was just another attempt to get attention and pull others into his situation.

Since the child custody hearing, realizing that the truth was coming out, Scott had continued to talk about ending his life. Stuart didn't believe he was serious until that weekend, when he asked Stuart to walk with him down the driveway to the road, far away from what he imagined were the watchful eyes of the United States Government peering into his home through his cameras and listening through the family's phones. Then Scott, who had longed for Stuart to be his partner in life, approached him about becoming his partner in death.

"You know what would really make me happy?" Scott asked Stuart. "For us to go upstairs, lie down in the bed next to each other, and shoot ourselves in the heart."

Finally, Stuart took Scott's wild threats and suicide talk seriously. He had seen Scott's violent temper. Scott had punched him in the face when he had displeased him. He had seen him smash a guitar against the wall inches from Kimmy's head just to frighten her and the others. Now Stuart looked into Scott's crazed glassy eyes and he saw a different look he was not accustomed to…a look of complete madness. He knew it was time to act. He had to get out.

CHAPTER FORTY-SEVEN

THE ALEXANDRIA CASE

Mary Jane's notes:

While we were waiting for Scott's grand jury to convene in Baton Rouge, I was distracted by a first degree murder death penalty trial scheduled for federal court in Alexandria. The defendant was charged with the murder of a 12-year-old girl in Louisiana. Prosecutors believed he had also sexually assaulted her. And he was the suspect in the murder of her mother in another state. As Alexandria is my hometown, the defendant's lawyers wanted my help in selecting a jury for the trial. They wanted someone who knew the people who lived there, who knew their families, and who knew their view on the death penalty—with the hopes of seating on the jury at least one person who would not vote for the death penalty. No other person associated with the trial was from Alexandria.

Death penalty cases are hard cases to work because of the ultimate outcome. And when they involve a child as the victim of the murder, they're even tougher. The willingness to work this kind of case involves a concern about the ultimate outcome for the defendant—the death penalty.

*Criminal defense work can cause many conflicting feelings for those who work the most heinous of crimes. And representing people who are charged with killing a child raises the emotions of the public to a fever pitch, as does representing people charged with abusing a child. That type of crime angers and repulses the public. Consequently the people even **associated*** *with such a case get attacked, slandered, spit upon, or isolated within their own community. Even lawyers who don't do criminal work find it hard to understand another lawyer's involvement with a case like that and are often critical of the involvement.*

I had, however, years ago, made the decision to do what was not popular with the public and accept the crap and criticism that goes with cases involving murder and other heinous crimes. When these cases hit the front page of the newspaper, when your neighbors read of your personal involvement, they withdraw from contact with you because they think something is wrong with you. Or they go to the extreme of literally attacking you. Again Camille sneaked into my thoughts with, "What would Camille do?" At times he had represented people in cases that made him the target of the ultimate fallout: death threats. But the threat of violence never kept him from doing what he thought was right. He opposed the death penalty. I have come around to that same position for many reasons, including this one: Innocent people wind up on death row.

After three calls from the lawyers asking that I work the Alexandria case, I struggled to make my decision. I have five granddaughters who live in Alexandria, and I knew the publicity of that high profile case would not be pretty. I told the lawyers I would talk to my kids because of the potential for fallout on them and their children, and if they were okay with it, then I would work on the jury selection. I first talked to my son, whose daughter Kristen is an adult. He said that as she does not focus on current events, she would not even realize there was a trial. My next conversation was with my daughter, who has my younger grandchildren. Her response was that, as a family, they believe that regardless of the charges, everyone needs effective representation. She told me to talk to her girls and see what they thought.

The four girls got into my car one weekend shortly thereafter to go to a family reunion. All four are vocal, and all have their strengths in different ways. Zella is the artist. Kate, who is the tall, lanky blonde, is a class officer. Violet is the spitting image of her mother and uses her own money to help homeless children she meets in school. Josie, the baby, is off-the-charts smart. Conversations with her are well above most adults' heads. At 10 years of age, she is a mini adult.

As we started toward Natchitoches, Louisiana, the oldest city in the Louisiana Purchase, the place where **Steel Magnolias** was filmed, Josie said to me, "Mom said that you wanted to talk to us." I told her I did, and started talking about the case the lawyers wanted my help with in picking a jury. I told them a man had been charged with killing a young girl. Television news would report the trial, and some of the facts were disturbing. I told them that people would say bad things about those defending this guy charged with murder, and I would be one of those people. All of them asked a few questions. I told them I wanted to know how they felt about my helping with the jury selection, explaining that I did not want them to encounter any problems or criticism due to my involvement.

A few seconds later, after I had told them what the lawyers wanted me to do, Josie started speaking in her very adult voice and very matter-of-factly said, "Well, Grandma, God teaches us that people should not be killed, so we think you should help keep them from killing him." As far as she was concerned, she was speaking collectively for all four of them. It made total sense to a 10 year old that people should not be killed and others should help to stop that. That was the end of the conversation as far as she was concerned, and it was time to move on to the next topic.

Just as Ethan was concerned about his family's reaction to Scott Rogers' sexually abusing him in the past and about that information going public—and then the fallout to his family in their community—I had worried about the fallout to my grandchildren in the town where they live, due to my involvement in this very high-profile case.

And just as Rannah experienced the critical judgment of others because she decided to step up and help a child who lived with a sexual predator, I was concerned that my grandchildren would suffer from that same critical judgment because of my work on the murder case.

Pressure from society and people in the community who sit in critical judgment sometimes makes it hard to do what is right!

CHAPTER FORTY-EIGHT

THE REQUEST FOR PROTECTION

Day 363
August 25, 2014

Allyson had been out of the office on field work and returned Monday morning for the first time in almost a week to find a phone message from Stuart Poulton asking to meet. Although six days had passed since he placed the call, Stuart had witnessed only Scott's further descent into madness. When Allyson and Jon drove to the studio at Cortana Mall to meet with Stuart, they learned that Scott had approached him the previous evening, asking that they join in a suicide pact. Scott wasn't just talking about killing himself now, but was telling Stuart that he "couldn't bear to go without him." It took the threat of death to finally break the hold Scott had over Stuart. He was terrified. His life was in danger and he wanted to leave. He was willing to walk away without anything except the clothes he was wearing.

Knowing that he had only a small window to escape before someone detected his absence, Stuart arranged to take out the trash and leave with Allyson and Jon, telling them that they had to move quickly because within 15 minutes, a 1stCo employee would miss him and notify Scott.

When Nathan, Mary Jane, and I first heard that Stuart had asked to leave with the agents, everyone's initial thought was that Scott had sent him in to scout the government's case. Ethan and Jake had warned us that if cornered, Scott would use Stuart and Mathew to defend himself, and we feared that Stuart was on an assignment. We knew from Jake that Stuart had served Scott in that role years ago, hunting down Jake to return him to the family.

"I'm not sure Allyson should trust him," Nathan cautioned.

While we were waiting to hear more, I emailed Ethan because of a vibe I got from our early conversations. I could tell he was not entirely comfortable with Stuart.

"I go back and forth on his role in the family and what we might expect of him," I explained.

"I was good friends with Stuart, we would hang out together smoking, chatting about girls, and occasionally skipping school together," Ethan recalled. "He has a nice side, but I could sense a little darkness in the way he treated his family and some of the antics he wanted to do. Stuart came out as gay when he was 15 or 16. Scott was there when he made the announcement. After that, our relationship changed, as the person I thought I knew, I didn't. Of course, I suspected Scott had got to him, abused him, and made him make the announcement, but there was also something more sinister about him. He had definitely made some kind of allegiance towards Scott in the same way Matt had. I think Scott realized that my family bond was too strong and decided to 'let me go.'

"I think the point is, Stuart has stayed with Scott for all this time, Scott has some stuff on him I'm sure, and Stuart is trapped. I would tread carefully; the years have more than likely warped him and his alliance will be firmly in place."

Stuart's cooperation could be a huge break in the case if he had come in for the reasons he said, but Nathan, Mary Jane, and I felt Allyson should proceed with caution. By now, the grand jury meetings were only 24 hours away, and we would soon know whether Mathew, Stuart, and Kimmy would speak honestly about their lives under Scott Rogers' influence, or continue to tell the stories Scott had coached them to recite.

The federal agents had arranged a hotel room for Stuart, and he had handed over his cell phone, since it had a tracking device that allowed Scott to know where he was at all times.

Soon Scott learned that Stuart was missing and began trying to call him. When he didn't answer, calls came in from the phone of a church member, and Stuart assumed Scott was trying to reach him through others, or at least through their phones.

Shortly after he realized that Stuart was gone, Scott signed over control of his personal and business affairs to Maria Edwards at 2 p.m. on Monday, August 25, in a handwritten letter witnessed by Mathew, Kimberly, and her boyfriend, Cedric Allison, and notarized by Seth Dornier.

On Tuesday, the 13:34 Church held an impromptu board meeting by phone, initiated by Maria, who wanted to bring board members up to date. Maria conducted two calls with board members by having each person connect with another by phone so she could speak to them in groups of four. She began the first call by saying, "Stuart is missing. He has been missing since Monday."

Maria then told the perplexed church members that Stuart had disappeared after taking the trash out at the studio, and when a 1stCo employee called mall security and looked at surveillance video, he saw him talking to two men around the trash receptacle before getting into a black vehicle with them and leaving. But it wasn't two men—it was Allyson and her partner, Jon, meeting him in the parking lot outside the studio. Just as Stuart had warned, he had only about 15 minutes before the others began looking for him, but Allyson and Jon had managed to get him to safety.

"Is anyone concerned about where Stuart might be?" Darla asked. "Have the police been called?"

"No...he's just missing," Maria replied. "We'll hear from him.

"We also need to let you know that Scott feels it's going to hit the papers tomorrow that he is being investigated for human trafficking and for being involved in an international pedophilia ring." *There was Scott's confession! He was the only one who knew what was out there for the federal authorities to find. The investigation involved fraud, but he knew the truth that could be uncovered.*

Everyone on the call fell into complete silence, but the pieces of the puzzle were falling into place quickly for Darla.

This is why they took his children, she thought. It was all starting to make sense.

Maria ended the call abruptly without taking any questions, telling the group of board members that was all she knew.

Darla quickly thought, *Even if this is what the grand jury is convening about, that information would be sealed until an arrest or indictment was made. This is not coming out in the papers tomorrow,* she thought. The grand jury is meeting tomorrow. She sent a text message to Mathew asking what time the grand jury would meet, but got no response.

Meanwhile, Seth Dornier notarized a document that gave Maria control over Scott and Mathew's business affairs if they were not available. *Scott was planning his exit.*

Tuesday evening, Mathew cried about the two children, wondering aloud who was taking care of the 10 year old and whether he missed his Daddy and his "Uncle Matty," or "Unkie Matty," as he called him.

According to Stuart, Scott had lost interest in Mathew sexually around 2002. As Mathew matured he had developed into a large man weighing more than 280 pounds, so perhaps his very masculine appearance was no longer attractive to Scott. But Mathew remained completely devoted to Scott, so he channeled his feelings into making himself indispensable by taking care of the business finances, the home, and the children, as he watched Scott focus his sexual interest on Stuart.

Since the children's departure, Darla had sent regular text messages to Scott, professing her unconditional love and support and assuring him she was praying for him. At the end of the day Tuesday, Scott sent her a message, "Please, I am begging you…pray for my little boys. I am so afraid they are confused and sad. This pain is unbearable at times. I feel hopeless and like I am drowning. I miss the boys terribly."

"I know you do and none of this makes any sense," Darla replied. "I am praying for all of you and I love all of you."

As the U.S. Attorney's office prepared for the grand jury, Stuart spent his second night in protective custody. The agents took precautions to keep him away from the others when he testified. We knew Allyson hoped a decision would come soon so that the federal agents could take Scott into custody immediately. We had always talked about Scott's attempting suicide, and now we too thought that if the grand jury was going to indict him, it should do so after the first day of testimony so that the agents could arrest him. Once the jury members heard from someone inside Scott's inner circle, we hoped they would move quickly to protect everyone. Allyson knew from talking to Jake and Ethan that Scott had attempted suicide in the past, and she knew we all thought that was a very real possibility now. Now Stuart could testify that Scott was talking about committing suicide every day and had asked him to die with him. *With any luck, they will see how dangerous Scott is and take quick action.*

Even with Stuart out of Scott's house, we continued to worry about Scott doing something crazy. We were assured the children were safe. And we knew his victims in the U.K. wanted him to face charges for what he had done to them. *They would finally get to face him as adults—and this time he wouldn't have the upper hand.*

But as we all stayed busy with our work, knowing we would probably not hear much from the secret grand jury, we did not believe it would deliver a decision on Wednesday. We thought more interviews would take place the next time the grand jury met, most likely in early September. Ethan and I talked about what the grand jury might hear from Mathew, Kimmy, and Stuart. We expected that Stuart would cooperate with the government, providing the investigators with their first peek behind the curtain.

Wednesday was the day Ethan had been waiting for. Twenty-four years had passed since Scott had first called him into his office, closed the door, and started a mental torture session that ended in sexual abuse. Ethan had spent 13 years looking for him, six since discovering he was in Baton Rouge, only to have him slip out of sight again. And 365 days had passed since he had sent me that first email, letting me know that Scott was a dangerous child predator who had sexually abused school boys in the U.K. before coming to America.

"Fingers crossed," Ethan said.

Would he finally get the justice that had eluded him and the others back in Bury? Would Jake and Ethan finally end Scott's abuse?

I climbed the stairs and stopped at the top to turn out the lights in the birdcage before going to bed. It would be only a few hours until I was back at the computer, its white light shining on my face, forcing me awake. I would check in with Ethan, who would be well into his day, and then we would wait. It had been an unbelievable year and the effect of the stress on all of our lives was tangible. My mind was racing with scenarios of what might happen if Scott was indicted on charges of fraud. I thought we would probably have another week to wait for a decision in his case, but I would awake early, ready for any news.

CHAPTER FORTY-NINE

THE LAST DAY

Day 365
August 27, 2014

On Wednesday, we settled in for a long day. At times we thought that if the grand jury indicted Scott, the U.S. Attorney would issue a statement. At other times we worried that the indictment could occur with no fanfare. Then we considered the real possibility of no action at all on the first day. We knew the legal case against him might prove only that he had lied to become a U.S. citizen, lied to become a foster parent, lied to adopt two little boys, and lied to obtain permits to carry concealed weapons. We hoped that would be enough to save the children, but we had no guarantee.

Ethan and Jake were anxiously waiting for the U.S. to charge Scott with fraud. Once that happened, they would file charges against him for sexually abusing them as children in Bury St. Edmunds. Facing serious charges in both countries, with a record of having attempted suicide, he would, we hoped, remain in custody until the charges made their way through the courts. What we did not know at the time was that Ethan and Jake would not be alone.

Adrian Randall had been in touch with Tim, Scott's first accuser; in the U.K., he could once again file his charges against Scott. Finally, he could get justice. He knew he could handle the court procedure this time. He was no longer a young teenage boy, standing up alone against Scott and his attorneys. He wouldn't have the pressure of his fellow students' anger for taking Scott away from them. He was a grown man, and this time he would face his abuser from a position of strength. Scott could no longer threaten him. Scott had taken something from him—his innocence. Now he wanted to take something from Scott—his freedom. He wanted Scott to stand up in court and face the tall, muscular man he now was, a man with an intellect that could easily match Scott's. He wasn't a little boy anymore. He was ready.

At Scott's house, Maria Edwards had been sleeping on the living room sofa since Sunday night. She awoke around 5:30 Wednesday morning when she heard Scott and Mathew coming in from the screen porch on the side of the house. As he had every day since Child Services had removed the children, Scott had been drinking vodka and taking pills.

Neither of the men had slept the night before; they told Maria she should go back to sleep since it was still early. She remained on the sofa until she heard Kimmy making coffee, then joined the three in the kitchen. A member of their church texted Scott that she was praying for Matt, as she had seen him in a vision, very distressed and crying.

"I got chills because that was exactly what had happened the night before," Maria said later. Scott continued texting with the church member, and Kimmy went upstairs to get ready for the grand jury hearing.

Maria felt sure the hearing would turn out fine for Scott and his family. As she'd had her own experiences with immigration laws, she did not believe that filling out the forms incorrectly would result in deportation. But she knew Scott and Mathew did not expect a happy ending. They told her they had discussed outcomes with their immigration attorney and knew what they were facing. According to Maria, they had also discussed the situation with Seth Dornier, who advised that if they were deported, they could no longer conduct business in the U.S. For that reason, Maria said, they had spent the past few days writing papers to give her authority over their financial affairs. "They were expecting, at any time, immigration was going to show up and they were going to be jailed and deported." This explanation would help her avoid admitting knowledge of what actually happened—a final act that would more plausibly warrant Scott and Mathew putting their financial interests in her name, a different ending that Maria had warned Darla and others Scott wanted.

After Maria had spent three nights with Scott and his family, she packed her things and told him she had to go home for a while. "I knew they needed me there, but I said *Let me go and I'll come back*," Maria said. But Scott pleaded, "Please stay." So Maria stayed at the house with Scott while the grand jury was meeting.

Darla sent a text message to Mathew around 8:30 a.m. asking what time the grand jury would convene, and Mathew replied, "At 9 a.m." When she texted Scott the same question, he replied that he had not been called, but needed her prayers. He told her he loved her. She then exchanged text messages with Maria Edwards, who replied that she was with Scott and assured Darla she would not leave him alone.

"I was under the distinct impression," Darla said, "that she was babysitting Scott and would not let him be home by himself."

Because Kimmy was uncertain about the time of her grand jury testimony, she got dressed and left to find out, leaving Maria alone at the house with Scott and Mathew.

"Mathew always took care of Scott, all the time," Maria said. "We were all watching Scott to make sure he would not harm himself. As long as he was with somebody, he was okay, but we could not leave him by himself, because we did not know if he would harm himself. As long as I knew them, Mathew was that person who was always protecting him, always protecting him."

Maria said that Scott grew agitated again and wanted the three of them to go to the screen porch and pray together. Then Scott and Mathew said they were so tired that they needed to go upstairs and rest. Maria stayed downstairs, and Kimmy returned, saying she did not have to testify until later in the day. Kimmy sat down next to Maria and laid her head on the older woman's lap. Maria stroked her hair and comforted her like the mother rarely present in Kimmy's life, saying, "It's going to be okay. God is in charge, God is in charge. Don't worry, calm down, calm down." Maria told Kimmy that she would come back from the grand jury, having learned nothing major, that her adopted brother would come home, and that life would return to what it had been.

When the time for her testimony grew near, Kimmy drove from St. Gabriel to the federal courthouse in downtown Baton Rouge. Maria noticed Mathew was not getting ready for the grand jury; when she asked him why, he told her that no matter what he did, they would not get the children back. Maria said she thought he was just waiting for immigration to pick him up.

After Kimmy left, Mathew and Scott went back upstairs, leaving Maria downstairs working on her laptop computer. Then Mathew came back down and said to Maria, "Scott wants you to pray with him. Scott wants to see you again."

Maria found Scott lying on his bed. He said, "Pray for me. I am exhausted. Tell me about God."

As he rested, Maria held Scott's hands and prayed with him, "It's going to be okay. God is with you." Scott soon drifted off to sleep.

Mathew told Maria he thought he would take a nap, too, and he asked her to go back downstairs and pray for Kimmy, since it was almost time for her testimony.

Maria went back downstairs to await a call from Kimmy or from Scott's attorney, Seth. She later said that every time a car or truck passed, she jumped, thinking someone from immigration had come for Mathew and Scott.

Maria sat alone downstairs praying, "Let the truth be revealed. Let the truth be revealed here, God! I believe in the system. Please show the truth!"

Five thousand miles away, across the Atlantic Ocean, young men whom Scott Rogers had abused when they were innocent little boys were ending their work day, going home to their families, hugging their children, and waiting for word on the grand jury hearing in Louisiana.

They waited patiently, putting their faith and trust in the United States Government. And they had the same simple hope that was Maria Edwards' prayer: *Let the truth be revealed.* They knew that when the United States Government uncovered the truth about Scott Rogers, surely it would not leave two little boys under his control.

All of a sudden, Maria heard a shot from upstairs. She later told authorities her first thought was, *"He did it. He got away with it."*

But what did that mean, considering what she then told the 911 operator?

Maria Edwards called 911, but because she was vague when describing what she had heard, her report appeared to involve an intruder in her home. Maria had spent the last three days in the house, listening to Scott talk continually about dying and helping both Scott and Mathew make arrangements for their deaths, and her first thought was *He finally did it.* Her own words reveal that she knows more than she is telling.

"Yes, lady, I think some people are about to do something and I just heard a noise," Maria told the 911 operator. "Please send someone to 1045 Daisy Avenue in St. Gabriel. I'm afraid they are going to do something and I just heard a noise. I just heard a noise," Maria said, her voice growing frantic. She began to cry as the 911 operator transferred her to the St. Gabriel Police Department dispatcher. As she grew more emotional, Maria's Venezuelan accent made understanding her more difficult.

When the 911 operator asked her name, Maria grew calm and replied, in a stronger voice, "Maria Edwards." Then she started to cry again and said, "I just heard another noise...oh, my God, no!" The operator completed the connection to the St. Gabriel Police Department and instructed Maria to continue. "Yes, I just heard two noises...I want somebody to come here. Can someone come here please? It's 1045 Daisy Avenue, St. Gabriel, Louisiana."

When Maria heard the second shot, she said she wondered what was going on. *"What's happening there? Are they fighting? Is one going against the other? Is this Scott killing himself? What is happening?"* Maria believed that anyone who knew Mathew would find what had happened unbelievable.

"Mathew was his protector," she said. "I was relieved when he was with Mathew, because Mathew protected him from himself."

"What's the address again?" the St. Gabriel Police dispatcher asked.

"1045 Daisy Avenue, St. Gabriel. Oh, my God...." Maria sobbed.

"1045 Daisy Avenue, and what's the matter?" the St. Gabriel Police dispatcher asked.

At this point the 911 operator interrupted, perhaps sensing the gravity of the call, and said she was transferring the call to the Iberville Parish Sheriff's Office. "I've got you, Mrs. Edwards. Don't hang up," the 911 operator instructed her.

When the Iberville Sheriff's dispatcher answered, the 911 operator said, "This is Iberville 911 with a transfer from 1045 Daisy Avenue in St. Gabriel. Mrs. Maria Edwards' residence. She heard a loud noise. Go ahead, Mrs. Maria."

Sobbing into the phone, Maria repeated, "I just heard two loud noises."

"Ma'am?" the Sheriff's dispatcher asked.

"Two guns or something. I just heard two loud noises. Can you please send somebody over here very quickly please?"

"A gun? What happened?" the dispatcher asked.

"I think, I think, I think...." Maria said. "I just heard two noises. Can you send someone over? Please send somebody over to 1045 Daisy Avenue, St. Gabriel."

"Is someone in your residence?" the Sheriff's dispatcher asked.

"Yes, Scott Rogers and Mathew Hodgkins," Maria said. "They are upstairs. I'm downstairs, but I just heard two noises. Can you please send somebody?"

"What kind of noises?" the Sheriff's dispatcher asked.

Like a *detonación* or something. Can you please send somebody, please?" and she dissolved into tears.

"I'm not understanding you," the dispatcher said.

"Like a *detonación* or something!" Maria said.

"Like a detonation? Like someone blew something up?" the dispatcher asked. "And who's upstairs that could have detonated something?"

"Mathew Hodgkins and Scott Rogers," Maria responded calmly, regaining her composure.

"Mathew Hodgkins and Scott Rogers? Can I get a call-back number?" the dispatcher asked, and Maria provided her cell phone number.

"Okay, I'll send someone out to 1045 Daisy Avenue," the Sheriff's dispatcher concluded and ended the call.

"Thank you," Maria said.

"You okay, Ms. Maria?" the 911 operator asked quickly as Maria began to cry again. "Ma'am, you want to stay on line with me until the police get there?"

"Okay," she replied.

"You want to stay on the line with me?"

"Okay, Okay, *si,* thank you," Maria said.

"Are you downstairs?"

"Yes, I'm downstairs, waiting for somebody to get here."

"You don't think they will do anything to you, huh?" the operator asked.

"No, no, no, no," Maria said. "They are going through hell right now."

"Okay. I'll stay on the line with you."

"Thank you."

"You have any children?" the operator asked, trying to calm Maria.

"No, no children at the house, no," Maria answered.

"No children…are they at school?" the operator asked.

"No, they took the children away from them," Maria replied.

"Oh, okay," the operator said, and, after a long pause, asked, "Well, how long have you been living in St. Gabriel?" clearly stalling for the law enforcement officers to arrive.

"I don't live here," Maria explained. "They live here and they're going through a very hard time so I came here just to be of support and help them…listen to them and pray with them and read the Bible with them…and uh, be of support." Maria sounded stronger now.

"Yes, I understand," the operator said. After another long pause she tried to sound positive, saying, "Well, that's a good thing, Mrs. Edwards."

"Maybe. If you were God, if you could change the world, oh, my God. Oh, my God."

"Yes," the operator said. After another long pause she added, "You know, you just keep praying."

"Yes, I'm praying right now," Maria said.

"I'm going to stay on the line with you until someone gets there."

"Okay, thank you. I'm going to pray for them right now," Maria said quietly.

C H A P T E R   F I F T Y

THE CRIME SCENE

When the Alexandria prosecutor's office completed jury selection for the murder trial there, Mary Jane returned to Baton Rouge, where she anxiously awaited news from the federal grand jury. She arrived around 11 a.m.; then, after noon, she received a call about a shooting at the Rogers house. The caller said that two people were believed dead, one of them Scott Rogers.

Mary Jane called a close friend, asking him to confirm what she had just heard and to identify the two people. Her friend called Sheriff Stassi, who confirmed Rogers' death. While they were talking, State Police Superintendent Mike Edmonson called Sheriff Stassi to inquire about the shooting.

Then Mary Jane called me. I was at my office working, and when I saw her name, I answered quickly, hoping she had some news.

"Hey, Mary Jane," I said.

"Scott's dead," she said quickly in her matter-of-fact way.

"What?" I said.

"Scott's dead," she said again, a little slower and stronger this time.

"*What?*" I said again. "I mean, I hear you...but what happened?"

Mary Jane told me that multiple agencies were responding to a shooting at Scott's home in St. Gabriel. The rumor was that two people were dead as a result of a shooting. With Stuart in protective custody, we assumed that meant Mathew was also involved.

The next reports said that two people were shot, and one was dead. *What happened?*

"Do you think it's okay to tell Ethan yet?" I asked.

"I think we should wait until something is confirmed," she said. "No one knows any details yet. I'm going to the scene—do you want me to pick you up?"

"No, no…I don't think I want to be there," I said. I had such a mix of emotions swirling in my head. I hate gun violence and it made me sick that Scott had chosen to end his life rather than face what he had done. "I'll call Nathan and let him know and call you back," I said.

As Mary Jane left for Scott's house in St. Gabriel, I dialed Nathan's number to tell him what we had heard. He had always thought Scott would commit suicide rather than face his accusers as adults. He knew that suicide was not uncommon for child sex abusers in those circumstances. They might seem brave when they are manipulating children, but when the children grow up and can fend for themselves, you see the depth of the predators' cowardice.

"Scott's dead," I told him when he answered the phone. I heard him repeat those words to his wife, Francine, in the background.

"What happened?" he asked.

"All we know is that two people were shot in his house and he is dead. We assume the other person is Mathew, but we're not sure. Mary Jane is on her way there now."

Nathan knew I didn't have the experience dealing with criminal cases that he and Mary Jane did, and he was worried that I would be upset by the turn of events, second-guessing the investigation. "You know there is nothing you could have done to prevent this, don't you?" he asked. "This is common when these people know they're caught."

"I know," I said. "But as much as we talked about this possibility, it's just hard to believe he did it." *Everyone warned that he would do this! Why am I surprised?*

"Keep me posted," Nathan said as we hung up.

I didn't know what to feel. No amount of warning and preparing ourselves for the possibility of Scott's suicide helped me deal with its reality now. As I waited for Mary Jane to get to the scene and find out more, I began checking the websites of *The Advocate* and the local TV stations to see when the news reached them.

Nathan called Mary Jane to ask if she was okay. He knew she was tough, but he also wanted to remind her that she had nothing to do with Rogers' death.

"I'm fine and you are right," she said. "I had nothing to do with his death, nor do I feel guilty about it. This is all on Scott Rogers. I'm on my way to the crime scene and will let you know more details once I get more information."

After talking to Nathan, Mary Jane called me back to get directions to Scott's house. We talked about Nathan's checking on both of us. He had always cautioned all of us that Scott would take the coward's way out rather than face what he had done. As Mary Jane drove, we recalled how many times we had speculated that he might commit suicide, since he had supposedly attempted it more than 20 years ago in the U.K. What we did not know was what had led to two deaths at his house.

As the time came for the grand jury to convene, we had assumed Mathew and Kimmy were at the courthouse, with Stuart in a separate secure location until his time to testify. In truth, Mathew had never planned to appear.

On that last day, Darla had begun to realize that the pastor she thought she had known for a year, she didn't know at all. After a lunch meeting, Darla received a call from Maria Edwards and excused herself to the parking lot to take it.

At first Maria was very calm as she spoke to Darla, then became hysterical, telling her, "There have been gunshots, there have been gunshots, and they're all dead!"

"Take a deep breath!" Darla told her. "Calm down…where are you?"

"I'm at Scott's! I'm at Scott's and they're all dead!" Maria said.

"No," Darla said. "I need you to back up a minute, take a deep breath, and tell me what happened."

Maria then told Darla she had been upstairs with Scott when he told her he wanted to take a nap. She had prayed with him until he went to sleep, standing beside him, holding his hand. Maria said Mathew came into Scott's bedroom, told her it was almost time for Kimmy to testify at the grand jury, and suggested that Maria go downstairs and pray for her. Mathew told Maria that he too needed a nap.

She went downstairs, walking across the first floor and onto the screen porch, when she heard a loud explosion upstairs. According to Darla, Maria said she immediately turned around and called 911 and, as she was talking to the operator, heard two more gunshots.

"And they're all dead! They're all dead!" Darla reported Maria saying.

"So you heard three gunshots?" Darla asked her.

"Yes," Maria replied. "I'm not supposed to go back into the house."

"Did they tell you not to go back?"

"Yes," Maria replied.

"Listen, I'm on my way down there," Darla told her, getting Tavia out of her meeting and heading to Scott's.

When Maria Edwards' call came in to the Iberville Parish 911 center at 12:52 p.m., Detective Larry Pearson and Captain James Snelson with the Iberville Parish Sheriff's Department were dispatched to Scott Rogers' house. When they arrived, Mrs. Edwards was standing outside the home at a side entrance, waiting for them. This was not the first time Pearson and Snelson had responded to the Rogers home. Both had answered a 911 call on Monday, August 18, when someone had called because she feared Scott was attempting suicide.

Upon entering the home, the Sheriff's deputies carefully climbed the stairs and entered a hallway on the second floor, where they noticed that the door to the room at the far end was closed. They cleared two other rooms as they made their way down the hall, and as they approached the last bedroom, Pearson called out, "Sheriff's Department! Sheriff's Department! Mr. Rogers, are you okay?"

According to their report, as Pearson opened the bedroom door, he saw Scott Rogers in his bed with a gunshot wound to his head and blood on both the body and the bed. Detective Snelson discovered a second man on the floor next to the bed with a gun next to his body. Snelson took a photo of the body on the floor, showing the position of the gun beside it, and then, as Snelson used his foot to move the gun from beside the body, Mathew Hodgkins stirred on the floor and sat upright.

Snelson immediately notified dispatch to call Acadian Ambulance and the coroner. The dispatcher also sent five more Iberville Parish Sheriff's units to the scene. On the floor, Mathew was moving around, and Detective Snelson recognized him from the previous week's call.

As they had entered the room, Scott was lying on the left side of the bed with his head turned to his right. Mathew had left behind, on the nightstand, blood-splattered letters along with a photograph of Scott's young son in a baseball uniform.

By 1:12 p.m., St. Gabriel Police Chief Kevin Ambeau and East Iberville Fire Department Chief John Talley, along with firemen Justin Darville and Floyd Sanchez, had arrived. Talley and Darville began administering medical aid to Mathew. Detective Aubrey St. Angelo arrived at 1:20 p.m., secured the gun, and placed it into the evidence box. At 1:23 p.m., an Acadian Ambulance unit arrived and at 1:31 p.m., the Air Med unit that would transport Mathew Hodgkinson to a trauma center in Baton Rouge touched down.

By 1:34 p.m., Major James Cox and Detective Mark Graves arrived, followed at 1:43 p.m. by Major Ronald Hebert and Detective Lori Morgan, who photographed and processed the crime scene.

At approximately 1:57 p.m. Iberville Sheriff Brett Stassi and Captain Ty Patin arrived, and by 2:06 p.m., the Acadian Ambulance helicopter lifted off with Mathew in route to Our Lady of the Lake Regional Medical Center. At 2:17 p.m., Investigator Robbie Johnson with the Iberville Parish Coroner's Office arrived.

When Detective Lori Morgan had entered the home earlier, Snelson had led her upstairs to the master bedroom and identified Scott Rogers as the dead man in the bed. Morgan had photographed Scott's body, the blood splatters on the wall and floor, the photo of Scott's young son, and the stack of handwritten notes, including a blood-spattered suicide note, presumably written by Mathew.

It read: "They broke our happy loving home. They do not get to take Scott too."

This is the only note the Sheriff would mention later at his press conference.

Mathew had also written a letter to Scott's adopted son that read:

> My dear (name redacted),
>
> I am very sorry that they took you from us. Mean people said bad things about Daddy and then they took you away. We miss you every day. It is not your fault. You did nothing wrong. We love you <u>so</u> much. We tried every day to get you back home. We love you so much that not being with you broke our hearts. We are very proud of you. You are smart, and funny and handsome. I think you're great! We have asked Maria to look after you and we have money for toys and anything you need as you grow up. Please keep reading every day, and say your prayers. Be kind and polite in all things. Please keep this letter and read it often as I will be thinking of you often.
>
> I love you, (name redacted), always,
>
> Uncle Matty
> XXX
>
> P.S. Daddy loves you too.

Mathew left a letter to Kimmy that read:

My dearest Kimmy,

I am sorry it did not work out. My greatest wish for us was to repair our problems. I knew you needed more than me. I am so sorry that you may now be in trouble just for saying "yes" to me in front of the Christmas tree. I pray for your happiness, wherever you find it. I cannot let your dad continue to suffer. I hope you can understand.

I will love you always,

Mat
X

Mathew had written a letter to Maria marked *private*:

Dear Maria,

After prayer, this is what I have decided. I realize now I will likely be separated from Kimmy and there is no chance of me being in (name redacted) life. I also cannot stand the thought of what they are doing to Scott tomorrow. How can so many loving and beautiful lives be destroyed like this? Now as executor of Scott's will (in my office on my desk I believe) I ask that you do all you can to get full custody of (name redacted). Scott is a citizen and legal parent-get Jeff to file emergency motions today, please. There is nothing left for DCFS to be concerned about. A full, loving and happy life for (name redacted) is my sole request and wish.

A few other details –
   1) I put money behind the large oil painting behind the bar-use this as needed.

2) Please cremate my remains and scatter them around the tree closest to the side porch. I don't want a service, funeral, etc. just some time with Kimmy and you as you collect and scatter my remains.

3) In light of Stuart's actions I ask that he not be allowed to see (name redacted)

4) Please call Barrett Benton and tell him we are not settling the claim with Mimi. We are closing the company.

5) Very important-1stCo owes over $200,000 in loans to Scott. Speak to Barrett and Shane Bennett about this. This should mean that any money from the liquidation of 1stCo repays Scott's loans first. This money goes to Scott for (name redacted).

Finally, Maria, please remind our church how much pain we are in for things to come to this.

Thank you for all the joy and glory you brought to our lives and family. I need you to be strong with Kimmy and David and get everything wrapped up.

Love always,
Mathew

P.S. In my office there is a pile of papers from an attorney firm in New York. Once you are (name redacted)'s guardian, please continue with this claim. It is a $200,000 claim for (name redacted) for breast growth for his taking the risperdal medication. Finish the claim for more money for (name redacted). XX

PPS-To access my gmail (redacted), password is (redacted). Please have David respond to emails.

LDAF Cooking Up Louisiana Treasures Show. Please contact Michelle Estay to cancel grant. We made 2 shows, do not bill for them.

1stCo-deposit all checks. Ask Shane Bennett to come in weekly to do Quickbooks. I use Quickbooks online.

Return all monies for September invoices.

Also, deposit church monies and write out a tithes summary and enter online.

The idea that Scott had succeeded in orchestrating a suicide pact sickened me. I knew that when the truth came out about Scott's history as a child predator, some would probably assume that Mathew had snapped after years of abuse and killed him in a rage. But that thought never crossed our minds. This was Scott's end game, his final scene. And he was the scriptwriter and director. All he had to do was get Mathew to follow his orders one last time.

Where Scott had failed to convince Stuart to die with him, he had succeeded with Mathew, who had remained loyal to Scott to the end, despite Scott's preference for Stuart as a partner.

When the police eventually read the letters from Scott and Mathew, they discovered their pact to die together and to give everything Scott had to Maria Edwards. She was now the executor of Scott's will and held power of attorney over his estate, even after his death. One of the documents Scott left behind was witnessed by his daughter Kimmy and her boyfriend Cedric and notarized by Seth Dornier.

Mary Jane commented that she had seen suicide notes in her line of work, but this was the first one she had ever encountered that was witnessed and notarized by an attorney.

Back at the crime scene, Detective Morgan moved to photograph the spent cartridges on the floor and collect evidence. One of the handwritten notes revealed that behind an oil painting in the bar area of the house was $5,000 in cash, which Morgan and Snelson located and photographed. In the downstairs bedroom, Morgan photographed another $600, two handguns, and a shotgun, before returning to the master bedroom to continue photographing Scott's body before the coroner removed it from the bed. When the crime scene investigators lifted the fitted sheet from the mattress, Morgan retrieved the spent cartridge that fell to the floor under the bed.

In the downstairs living room, Maria Edwards' laptop and shoulder bag were also collected as evidence.

When Darla and Tavia arrived at Scott's home, an ambulance was leaving. They quickly asked to speak to Maria, describing themselves as church members she had called. She walked over, and the three women huddled inside the fence under some trees, a small place of refuge in the shade, out of the way of the gathering news media.

"Who was in that ambulance?" Darla asked, and Maria told her it was Mathew, describing him as covered in blood, wearing an oxygen mask, but still alive. The ambulance drove Mathew a short distance to the helicopter waiting to transfer him to Our Lady of the Lake Regional Medical Center, the nearest level one trauma center in the area. Darla promised to stay with Maria and help her answer questions and get through the ordeal she faced.

Then Darla looked knowingly at Maria and said, "Maria, there's not another ambulance here. That tells me one of two things," Darla began to explain. "Scott is either dead or he wasn't shot. Because if he was shot and alive, there would be much more movement going on. I need you to prepare yourself for that reality."

"I can do that," Maria said.

"So what happened?" Darla asked.

Maria told Darla the same version again—that she was in the house, heard a shot, called 911, and heard two more shots.

"Okay," Darla said as she listened.

"And you know Mathew refused to go to court this morning—he refused to go," Maria told her.

"So Mathew's been here all day?" Darla asked.

"Yes, he refused to go, and that's what concerned me. Because when he didn't go, I knew he had given up," Maria said.

"So you're telling me that he was called before a grand jury and he didn't show up?" Darla asked.

"No, he never left the house today," Maria replied.

"Has anybody contacted Kimmy...do you know?" Darla asked.

"No, she's still at the courthouse," Maria said.

At that point Darla phoned a friend who works in federal probation and explained the situation. Since Kimmy would not be allowed to take her cell phone into the courthouse, they could not easily reach her. Darla asked her friend if she could contact the witness coordinator for the grand jury to make sure Kimmy did not find out about her father from the news media.

From the scene, Iberville Parish Sheriff's deputies were dispatched to the federal courthouse in Baton Rouge to notify Kimmy of the shooting.

Seth Dornier, the attorney who had represented Scott in the custody hearing, arrived at the house and began pacing up and down the street, talking on his cell phone. Iberville Sheriff's deputies told Maria, Darla, and Tavia to move outside the fenced area and across the street, since the entire area of Scott's house was a crime scene.

As Mary Jane left downtown Baton Rouge, headed south on Nicholson Drive, she drove past legendary Tiger Stadium on the campus of Louisiana State University toward St. Gabriel, Louisiana, where the crime scene was only a 20-minute drive from her home.

I was talking to Mary Jane by phone as she drove, and monitoring the news websites, when I received a breaking news alert that Scott Rogers was dead in his house and that another unidentified male had been shot. Still, we had no idea what had transpired.

My thoughts turned to Ethan. He had searched for Scott for over 13 years, and he just wanted to expose the truth so that Scott could never harm children again. But this was crazy! *What had happened?*

We did not know Scott had expected the grand jury to expose him for human trafficking and child pornography. We knew that he could have been involved in both, and that the authorities had speculated they might find evidence, but no one had mentioned it if they had. All we knew was that the grand jury would no doubt ask Mathew and Kimberly about the circumstances of their marriage, and that Stuart would have an opportunity to explain how he came to live with Scott for more than 20 years.

While Mary Jane and I were talking, the local news media were beginning to post what little information they had on their websites.

"Local TV personality shot, killed" one headline read with the dateline, "St. Gabriel."

I started reading her the breaking news and gave her some general directions to Scott's house. Nathan and I had looked up the address when filing suit against him, and the next time I was in the area with a friend, we had found the very secluded Daisy Avenue. When we passed by that day, Mathew was working on a riding lawn mower out front, and a number of trees were still down in the yard from the latest storm.

"I have to let Ethan know what happened," I said. "I'll call you back." I copied the breaking news item and pasted it into an email along with the photo of Scott that accompanied it. I typed into the subject line, "Please Read Now" and wrote a very short note above the article.

"We do not know much but you can follow the story on the websites I'm listing below the story," I said. "We can talk later." I included links to several local news outlets that I knew would cover the story for the remainder of the evening and sent the email. It was 2:40 p.m. and everything still seemed surreal. It had been only one hour and 48 minutes since Maria Edwards' call to 911 sent first responders from several departments scrambling to get to Scott's house.

"As I got closer, I could see a news truck turn off Nicholson Drive, so I knew I was in the right place," Mary Jane said later.

"I followed where the news truck turned, but when I did, I couldn't see it anymore. I had two options. The first try sent me the wrong way and I turned back, crossing a bridge over a bayou, and headed down the road, checking the streets that turn off the main road I was on."

I called Mary Jane back, trying to search online for map directions as we talked, so I could give some other street names to help her find the house. "I remember that Scott lived on a street called something like *Daisy*," and as I said those words, Mary Jane said, "I see the street sign for Daisy Avenue. I'm here." Then as she turned down the street, she saw police units, first responders, cars, and people. "I'm here," she said again. "I'll call you back once I see what's going on and have more information."

Mary Jane drove slowly down Daisy Avenue, pulling to a stop behind the last vehicle, which put her some distance from the house.

"As I got out, I looked around, not knowing where I was, or what I would find, or who would be there," she said. "I started walking. It was hot, hot, hot, since it was August 27th at the hottest time of the day. As I approached the house, I saw Allyson standing in the driveway, waiting to go inside. I texted her to tell her I was there. She texted back that she would call me later, then she disappeared into the house. Later Sheriff Stassi told me that he had to get her inside to keep the deputies' attention focused on their duties. Mathew had already been airlifted to the hospital, and the coroner's investigators had placed Scott's body in a body bag before Allyson got into the house."

At the crime scene, Scott's lawyer, Seth Dornier, walked over to Darla and said, "You need to keep the police away from Maria."

"That's not my job," Darla replied. "No. I don't know what's going on, and this is getting so crazy, I'm not sure I want to know what's going on. I'll try to keep the news media away from her, but law enforcement has to do what law enforcement has to do, and she is a person who has answers that nobody else has, because she's been here all day."

Mary Jane's notes:

As I walked closer, I saw TV reporter Kiran Chawla. She was in the news unit I had followed to the house; she saw me and recognized me. As I walked past her, she asked me if I lived in the area. I said "No" and kept walking over to where the news units were parked in a driveway across the street from the house, and where people were standing. Chawla's face showed she was puzzled as to why I was there but she did not pursue it. I was still trying to assess the situation and figure out who was there.

Yellow crime scene tape roped off the house. Two women were talking with each other, and a man was pacing and sometimes talking on his cell phone. I figured out pretty quickly that the man was Seth Dornier, Rogers' attorney who had represented him in the custody hearing three days after the kids' removal from Rogers' home. The women were walking up to him and then away. Sometimes the women were together and sometimes not.

As I stood there, I observed that one woman was highly agitated; she kept pacing back and forth. She went up to Dornier many times, telling him that he "had to get it back. The police can't have it. They can't get it. You have to get it from the house." Whatever the "it" was, she wanted it badly.

Two of my observations puzzled me. One, Dornier was the attorney for Scott Rogers, and this woman desperately wanted something that was part of the crime scene. It was as if Dornier were acting as the attorney for this woman and not for Scott. What also caught my attention was this woman's concern about whatever she had left in the house. Her agitation was all about her and this thing she desperately wanted. There was talk among the three of them about the Sheriff's moving everyone from the house side of the street to where everyone was now standing, on the opposite side, in the heat. I heard in their conversations that Sheriff's personnel had told them to go across the street and not to come back or they would be arrested. I understand crime scenes and who can be where, but this hard stance by the

Sheriff's office puzzled me. Sheriffs generally have more compassion for people affected by death cases. I figured that something had happened to cause such a tough position, but I did not know what.

*At one point, one of the unidentified ladies walked up to me as I was standing there, asking me if this was my house. I told her "No," and she walked off. I said two words while I was at the crime scene that day, both **no** and only after another person approached me. I was there to observe.*

I stood there for a while, listening and watching. Sheriff Stassi walked from the Rogers house and down the driveway, holding a piece of paper in his hand as reporters approached him. I did, too, to hear what he had to say. I was the only one in that group who did not push a microphone in his face, and Sheriff Stassi looked directly into my eyes, trying to figure out who I was. He, too, was observing, and I knew that. I was the odd man out and the new face at a crime scene, and that always piques a policeman's interest, even more so that I would be there showing such great interest. But now was not the time for me to explain who I was and why I had come.

"We received a call that shots were heard as somebody was entering the residence," Sheriff Stassi told the group of reporters. "On follow up, it was described as a murder-suicide scene and we're investigating it as a homicide until it's determined what we have here.

"It was determined that Scott Rogers was deceased and another male at the residence had received a shot to the head and was in critical condition," Stassi continued. He explained that Mathew was married to Scott's daughter, Kimmy, and said the home had been the scene of "a bunch of stress" in the past several weeks with the Sheriff's office "previously responding to calls at the home.

"It's been topsy-turvy at this residence. We responded to a couple of calls. It's been a high-stress environment for this family and looks like it culminated in this," the Sheriff said.

Mary Jane's notes:

Sheriff Stassi spoke, giving very few details of what was inside. He said that there had been a shooting in the house and that Scott Rogers was dead. He stated that another male individual in the house had been airlifted to the hospital. He was in serious condition but no name would be released until the next of kin were notified. I looked down to the piece of paper in his hand. Sheriff Stassi had written the name "Mathew Hodgkinson" and the country where Hodgkinson had originated. While Sheriff Stassi did not identify the other person, when I saw the name on the paper, I knew that Mathew was the man who was on his way to the hospital.

Seth Dornier, Rogers' lawyer, also decided he needed to talk to the press. He told the reporters that he was at his office when he got a call that he was needed immediately at the house. He stated that he certainly had not expected to find a crime scene. He said Rogers was under federal investigation over an immigration issue and not answering questions on his citizenship application properly. He told the press that certain people had been at the federal grand jury hearing at the time of the shooting. He talked about the child custody hearing about a week or so earlier and how Scott's kids had been taken away from him because of this immigration issue. He talked about what a good person Rogers was and what a loving and good father. I rolled my eyes, because I knew who Scott Rogers really was.

One of the two women I later identified as Maria, who was the co-pastor of the church with Rogers. The other was Darla O'Conner, a person with whom, over the years, I'd had a few conversations regarding people who were clients coming out of jail and into the Ecumenical House where she was director. I was always impressed with Darla and how effectively she did her job, even though I had talked to her only over the phone. She had always been very matter-of-fact but friendly and easy to talk to. Her hair was short and very wet from the heat of the day.

Knowing how crime scenes go, I knew there would be lots of activity in the house but very little outside. I stood there for a short time longer, increasingly growing hotter and hotter. The coroner had arrived and was in the driveway. Other than watching people come and go from the house, there was nothing more to see except people profusely sweating. I had heard Maria's words and continued watching her anxiety about whatever was in the house that she had to have. I texted Allyson that I was leaving but asked her to call me when she could because I had something very important to tell her. The "something" was Maria's ever-increasing anxiety over what was in the house. I wondered if the "something" had anything to do with what had just happened. I later learned that Maria's insistence on getting her purse is what got her moved across the street from Scott's house. Much later, I learned what was in that purse that had caused her anxiety.

I left, driving back to Baton Rouge. As Rannah and I talked, I told her about the crime scene and the two women and Seth Dornier's words and the Sheriff with the note in his hand. I also told her about Maria's anxiety over whatever was in the house. I asked if she had sent the news story on Rogers' death to Ethan. She told me she had but had not heard anything back yet.

We talked about how everyone knowledgeable about the investigation had discussed this possible ending, Rogers' death, and how it had come true.

When Ethan received my email and saw the subject line, "Please Read Now," his hands started shaking. He's dead, he thought. He knew it. He just had that feeling. He knew Scott had done it. Ethan clicked on the email but he began to shake so badly that his wife took his phone from his hand and read my email to him.

When Ethan replied at 2:54 p.m., he simply wrote, "Speechless. Talk later."

At the crime scene, Darla said Maria was walking around dazed when Captain Snelson approached her to come with him and give a statement. Maria immediately told him she wanted an attorney, then began complaining of feeling bad.

"All you have to do is tell them what you told me," Darla explained. "Just tell them about the 911 call and what went on here today."

"Seth says I need an attorney," Maria told Darla.

"It doesn't hurt to have an attorney," Darla said, "but I can't for the life of me figure out why you would need one. They just want to confirm what exactly happened while it's fresh on your mind. I really don't think there is anything to be concerned about. Would you like Tavia or me to go with you?"

"No, Seth says I need an attorney," Maria repeated. Paramedics on the scene began giving Maria water, oxygen, and some ice to help her cool down.

Darla had Maria's phone, which was ringing often; she was answering and screening calls, since Maria did not want to speak to anyone. Then, when Scott's attorney and friend Lexlee Overton called, Maria agreed to take the call. After speaking briefly with Lexlee, Maria handed her phone to Seth Dornier, who walked away to talk to Lexlee for what seemed to Darla about 15 minutes.

When he ended the call, Seth said to Darla, "She needs to go to Our Lady of the Lake," referring to sending Maria to the same hospital where Mathew had been taken. Soon an ambulance arrived to transport Maria, but she did not want to leave without her purse, which she said was in her car.

The detectives, however, weren't about to let anything be removed from the crime scene just yet.

"Maria, we can get all of that tomorrow," Darla explained, concerned only that she needed an ID or insurance card for the hospital. But the deputies said, "You're not going to take anything from the crime scene. It hasn't been processed."

As Maria was put into the ambulance, Darla and Tavia were getting ready to leave, when Seth Dornier again approached Darla. "You need to go to Our Lady of the Lake Hospital and make sure the police don't talk to Maria," he said.

"No, I don't have that kind of pull," Darla said. "I'm concerned about her well-being, I'm concerned about Mathew, but I don't run interference."

"Give me your phone number," Seth said, and he sent Darla a text message from his phone so she would have his number. "Someone needs to go to the hospital to check on Kimmy. She's there and she's distraught."

Darla contacted some other church members who had arrived at the hospital, where they found Kimmy and began talking with her, providing support. Then they told Darla that Lexlee Overton had arrived and made all of the church members stop speaking with Kimmy and move away from her. Then Lexlee talked to Maria and wouldn't allow any of the church members around her either.

The hospital couldn't confirm anything about Mathew's condition, and Lexlee was keeping everyone away from Maria and Kimmy, so the church members decided to leave.

Captain Snelson went to Our Lady of the Lake, where doctors told him that Mathew's injuries were life threatening. While there, he spoke with Kimmy and a man she identified as her boyfriend, Cedric Allison. Kimmy told Captain Snelson that she and Mathew had a very open relationship, and she and Cedric said they had no direct knowledge of what had happened at the house.

When the Sheriff held his impromptu press conference at Scott's house, Seth Dornier, Scott's attorney, had enjoyed his 15 minutes of fame at the crime scene. He had delivered a rambling statement to the news media about what a great father and humanitarian Scott was, but he also revealed most of the details of Scott's investigation, details that the public had never heard until then.

"It's very unfortunate," Dornier told the news media. "Scott Rogers was a great man. He was kind, honest, truthful, a great father, and a great leader. At this time, I think everybody is just shocked and deeply saddened."

From the scene, Seth did what many people do in cases involving child molestation: He victimized, all over again, the young boy who had pressed charges against Scott back in 1993.

He claimed that Scott had expelled the young victim from the Academy for using drugs and that the boy had made up the story of the molestation in retaliation for Scott's ending his career. Dornier even went so far as to claim that the young boy had confessed, during the trial, to making up the story. None of this was true, and the young boy, now a man in his mid-30s, was in England, reading news accounts of the man who had molested him as a child and terrorized him in the courtroom—the man he watched walk away from his crimes and leave for a new life in the United States, with two of his young victims in tow. Now Dornier was repeating Scott's lies about one of his victims, the one who'd had the courage to report his abuser.

Tim had been in touch with Adrian Randall as authorities in the U.K. and U.S. cooperated on the investigation of Scott Rogers. He believed he was about to get another chance at justice, since he could re-file his charges against Scott, and he planned to do just that. Today, Tim is the father of two children, a tall handsome man with the confidence he did not have as a young boy, when he stood alone in a courtroom to face his adult abuser. This time, he knew the outcome would be different, and he had looked forward to Scott's finally facing up to his crimes.

Now the justice he so badly wanted was slipping through his hands again.

Earlier, while Ethan and Jake were closely following what was playing out in the U.S., they too had agreed that once the federal authorities in Baton Rouge had charged Scott, they would press charges in the U.K., so that he would be deported to face justice there, too. Adrian Randall knew the case against Scott Rogers was coming together much stronger this time.

By around 4 p.m., however, the earliest Baton Rouge newscasts were beginning. Headlines began to tell the story of Scott Rogers that Sheriff Stassi and Seth Dornier had given at their press conference: "Murdered TV personality under federal investigation;" "Sheriff: Rogers, son-in-law were lovers."

It would be 10 p.m. in the U.K., so I updated Ethan on what we were hearing. "They just reported live from Scott's home saying that Mathew is in critical condition and that he was the aggressor—shooting Scott, then himself," I told him. "The

Sheriff's Office (not the one in Baton Rouge, but in the adjacent parish where he lived) said that deputies went to the home a week ago after receiving a call of an apparent suicide. When they got there, Scott denied that he had attempted suicide and refused treatment.

"They also reported that Mathew is Scott's son-in-law, married to his biological daughter, Kimmy. They said Scott was reportedly having custody issues over his 10-year-old son and that he may have also been facing federal charges.

"I am now hearing that WAFB-TV cancelled his TV show this week—this is from someone who was invited to appear on the show, then received a call from Scott's producer saying it would not tape due to unforeseen circumstances."

WAFB News reported that Mathew left a voicemail message on Tuesday to say that he was cancelling the show. "Scott is facing a family catastrophe," he said. "We don't know what's going on or why at this point, but I have made the decision to cancel future shows. I hope you can keep us in your prayers as we move forward."

"There will be more detailed news reports at 5 p.m., 6 p.m., and 10 p.m. our time," I told Ethan, "and they will most likely update the story. You can check those websites. I've been speechless, too. Even though we had anticipated something like this, nothing prepared me for the reality. I finally left the office and came home to watch news reports."

Before the 5 p.m. news broadcast came on, I got another email from Ethan. "He was an evil man, a coward, and what he has also done to Mathew is awful," he said. "I really hope Mat pulls through. I'm sure the truth will come out. Looks like a suicide pact or Scott got Mathew to shoot him. What's a good number to get you?"

CHAPTER FIFTY-ONE

THE RADIO HOST

On the first news reports, Scott's friends reacted to his death as if he were the person he had portrayed himself to be in public. Butch Browning, the Louisiana State Fire Marshall, went on TV, almost in tears, to describe Scott as a good friend and father. Soon after news of the shooting broke, the media interviewed Kellee Hennessy Dickerson, Rogers' former co-host, who said she had been a close friend for almost 15 years.

"He was like the little jokester that would keep people motivated and pumped up," Dickerson told *The Advocate*. "He had a big heart," she said. "He cared about people so much and he enjoyed making people laugh and he enjoyed being part of this community."

Richard Sobers, the retired Baton Rouge Police Lieutenant who had tried to involve his former department with Rogers, posted on his Facebook page a few hours after the shooting: "I am deeply saddened by the news that my friend Scott Rogers has died. I worked with the show as a volunteer and the entire staff and crew were nothing less than good people who did so many great things for the community in general."

Scott's attorney, Seth Dornier, continued to tell the news media that Scott had stood trial for molesting a young boy in his hometown in England, but had been acquitted. Maintaining that the boy had made up the story, he continued to claim that Scott had caught the 13 year old smoking marijuana and had planned to expel him from the Academy.

This was obviously the version Scott had told him and certainly not what the authorities and other victims in the U.K. had reported.

Those associated with the investigation were ready for the truth to come out. Knowing the horrific abuse his adopted son in the U.K. had suffered, we found the notion of Scott as a good father hard to stomach. Allyson couldn't say anything, and it didn't appear that the U.S. Attorney would be making any statements.

Jim Engster sent me a text message when he heard the news of the shooting, and I began to think it was time to connect him with the victims so their story could be told. Nathan agreed Ethan and Jake should be heard.

I knew that a lot of reporters in Baton Rouge listened to Jim's radio shows. He is a highly credible journalist who stays above the competition among local media for breaking news. And if ever there was a story that was perfect for radio, this was it. The young men in Bury St. Edmunds would never want to go on camera.

I suggested to Jim that they share their experience in the safe, calm environment of his radio program. I also knew Jim would conduct the interview professionally. He would ask the questions that had to be asked, but he also knew enough at this point to let the victims tell their own story. If they talked to Jim, the raw unedited truth would finally come out. He was interested in talking with any of Scott's victims who would agree to speak on his program. Now I had to see if anyone was able or willing.

I asked Jim if he could meet me Thursday evening. He had another commitment but we agreed to meet at Hotel Indigo in Downtown Baton Rouge at 10 p.m.

I emailed Ethan to discuss who would finally tell the public the truth about Scott Rogers.

"I know it's getting late there. I'm meeting a reporter friend of mine at 10 p.m. I spoke with him almost a year ago when we thought our best plan was to go to the press. He has sat on the story since then.

"He does a one-hour radio show that is highly respected. Most of the local press listens to his show because he gets such great interviews. I've been friends with him for many years.

"All of the news here is about Scott, and I want to let Jim start to get the truth out. His show airs live in the morning at 9 a.m. here, and he is going to devote a segment to the investigation in the morning. Would you consider talking to him? He would not use your name.

"Mary Jane and I are going to meet him at 10 p.m. tonight and give him whatever background we can. I agree Scott was a monster and I am so glad for you and Jake that you are free and don't have to worry about him hurting other children. You did a good thing. It must be an emotional time for you guys…it is for me. But I'm so glad it's over. One year tomorrow that we connected…."

About ten minutes later, Ethan replied. "Yes, it's been a surreal few hours. I'm going to be up for an hour or so…. I think it's too soon for me to go on radio. I'd like to see how the dust settles, what happens to Matt, Kimberly, and Stuart. What a journey…I need to let it settle in."

By that evening, WBRZ was reporting information about the trial in the U.K. The local reporters were working with ABC News and the BBC to get information for the 10 p.m. newscast. When Ethan received an email asking if he would talk, he was surprised that the local media had gotten his name. I told him that John Camp had likely tipped them off to contact him, since both Ethan and I had spoken to Camp early on, but Ethan wasn't ready to talk to anyone at this point. It was all still sinking in.

The news media reported that Mathew testified at the grand jury in the morning, then went home and the shooting occurred. In truth, Mathew had defied the federal subpoena, choosing instead to stay home with Scott that day. There was no word on his condition, but the news reports said he would be charged with murder if he survived. The Sheriff's Office reported that it was working the crime scene through the night and that an autopsy on Scott would take place the following day.

Ethan and I stayed in constant contact throughout the evening, and he was keeping Jake posted on the latest developments. If Ethan wasn't ready to talk publicly on the radio show, maybe Jake would, I suggested.

"Spoke with Jake and he is shocked. We were wondering if Matt snapped and maybe did kill him. Stuart will know everything. Be interesting to see what he says...." Within another 30 minutes, Ethan emailed that Jake had spoken with Allyson and was definitely on for the morning interview. We had also heard that Stuart would like to call in as well. They were finally ready to share their stories.

By morning, two victims of Scott Rogers, sitting on opposite sides of the Atlantic, would go on radio to tell the truth about living with him. One had escaped 20 years ago after surviving over ten years of abuse. The other had escaped only three days ago.

I was leaving to meet Nathan and Francine for dinner to talk about what had happened, when JoAnne and Don Moreau called to check on me. "There was nothing you could have done to prevent this," Don assured me. "Scott was what we call in law enforcement 'circling the drain.'" Don meant that Scott knew he was about to be exposed as a pedophile, and for the past two weeks, his life had been gradually falling apart. I agreed that only one person was responsible for Scott's death and that was Scott, but as I hung up, I appreciated Don's calling to remind me. So much tragedy surrounds Scott Rogers and the people he hurt that sorting it all out is difficult.

When I got home from dinner, I emailed Ethan, who I imagined might finally be sleeping.

"Sorry, I've been away from the computer for a while," I wrote. "I have heard unofficially that Mathew's wound is in the head and they do not expect him to survive. We have also wondered what provoked the shooting.

"I'm meeting Engster in an hour. We could have him call Jake if you want to provide a number...or if Jake is more comfortable calling him, I can provide a number...whatever he is comfortable with." At this point, we were still protecting Jake's identity, and he was still not comfortable giving his phone number.

"Jim's show airs live from 9 a.m. to 10 a.m. Central Time." I sent Ethan the link to the website for the radio station so he could listen live.

"I will wake up early to coordinate in the morning and make sure they connect," I offered.

"And I'll send an update later tonight. The television stations are running promos for the 10 p.m. news tonight, when they will air stories on Mathew and the U.K. trial. I'm recording the news shows since I will be meeting with Jim, but I'll watch and send an update afterward."

"Rannah, yes, pass me the phone details and I'll pass to Jake," Ethan replied. Apparently, he too was having trouble sleeping.

⌒⌒

Mary Jane's notes:

We didn't anticipate how the entire city would jump on the Scott Rogers bandwagon and how everyone would start talking about what a great and wonderful person he was. The press was canonizing him, when we knew all the bad things he had done in his life; we knew he was not the person the media were portraying to the world. And as the clock ticked, more and more accolades were being thrown around on the social media, and more and more people were lining up to proclaim his greatness. Now that Rogers was dead, the federal investigation would close and no one would know who he really was and what he had done to children. Rogers had duped so many people; we could not allow him to continue to dupe people even in his death. Rannah knew Mathew, and while she was not close to him, she had worked with him on the contract that started all of this. She had some emotional issues tied to this shooting regarding Mathew. I didn't know any of these people, so I had no emotional ties to who they were and was more clinical in my approach.

Rannah and I started trying to figure out how we could change the tide of all the flowery things the media and the public were saying about Rogers. Every time we heard an over the top remark, it repulsed us. All anyone knew was that Rogers was under investigation for falsifying an immigration application and his children had been taken away because of that. Totally incorrect information was being put out to the world and not a soul in any governmental agency could straighten it out. When the 6 o'clock news aired with Kiran Chawla, we heard even more about Rogers' wonderful contributions. And now they were interviewing people in the community who discussed how sad it was that such a wonderful man was dead.

Rannah and I decided that we would correct this lie so that everyone would understand why the kids were taken and who Scott Rogers really was.

One of the people Rannah had contacted before Nathan contacted me was Jim Engster. The landscape had changed now, since the criminal investigation of Rogers was over. Engster had a radio show that people listened to, including other media outlets for news. Rannah had been in touch with him and set up the meeting tonight.

Meanwhile, Allyson called me on her way back from Rogers' house. I told her about Maria's anxiety over something that was in the house and how badly she wanted it back. She said she would pass that information on to the Iberville Sheriff's office. She thought it was a computer that Maria kept trying to retrieve, to the point the investigators had put it into evidence. The police felt something was very odd with her insistence and they removed her to across the street. Allyson was going to contact the Iberville Sheriff's office and tell them what I observed.

Allyson and I discussed the media's reports on how good Rogers was and how sad his death. We knew that the federal investigation would now end because of his death, and that the public would never know the truth about Rogers and the extent of the child abuse. I told her that Rannah and I were already on that and we would be talking with Jim Engster that night. The world would know about Scott Rogers. We wanted to put some of the victims on the show and we were going to talk to Jim Engster about it that night. I told Allyson that Rannah had sent word to Ethan that we wanted him or Jake on the Engster show the next morning and the two U.K. guys were contemplating

which one would do that. As the evening went on and before 10
p.m., we had the commitment from Stuart and Jake that they
would both come on the Engster show if he wanted them. We felt
that once Jim heard their story and what we knew to be true,
they would be part of his program.

At 10 p.m. on Wednesday night, August 27, 2014, exactly
365 days after Ethan first contacted me, Mary Jane and I sat at a
sidewalk table overlooking the Mississippi River outside the
Indigo Hotel in Downtown Baton Rouge and waited for Jim
Engster. It was a warm muggy night with a breeze coming off
the river. Jim waved when he saw me and went inside to get a
soft drink before he joined us to get started.

Mary Jane was looking out at Lafayette Park and the lights
on the Mississippi River Bridge, wondering what Jim would
think of what he was about to hear.

I predictably started from the beginning in my usual "First,
the Earth cooled..." fashion and explained how, in the days after
Nathan and I had lunch with Jim the previous fall, Mary Jane
joined us to help investigate the information I had received,
which ultimately led to our turning it over to the federal
authorities.

Mary Jane jumped in and got right to the point, telling Jim
we had two victims of sexual abuse by Scott Rogers who were
willing to appear as guests on his radio show the next morning
to talk about Scott. Jim suddenly took notice of Mary Jane,
whom he was meeting for the first time. She didn't mince words
about what we knew the victims would say.

"These men are really going to tell me these things?" Jim
asked.

"Yes," Mary Jane replied.

"Jim, I'm not sure what guests you have lined up for the
morning, but...." I began.

"I'll clear the schedule for them," Jim said.

It was important that we protect Jake by not disclosing his
name and telephone number, so we arranged for Mary Jane to

connect him with Jim, since we had already arranged for Stuart to come to her house for the interview.

Mary Jane confirmed that the men's names would not be used on the show because they were sex abuse victims of Scott Rogers as minors. She explained that both of them would contact the show through her phone so that no one could get their phone numbers and call them. We confirmed that Mary Jane would call Jim at 8:30 in the morning to make sure everything was in place.

The three of us finally left around 12:30 a.m., knowing that the plan for the next morning was in place. Little did anyone know how the Jim Engster Show would change the perception of Scott Rogers around the world. I headed home to confirm everything again with Ethan.

Finally, around 2 a.m., I crawled into bed, exhausted from the day but still unable to sleep. I kept my phone close by so I could check emails and text messages. I was too wired to fall asleep when Ethan emailed to ask that I let him know when I was awake so he could call. "Call anytime...can't sleep," I replied.

Around 3 a.m. Baton Rouge time, the phone rang. After we both said we just couldn't believe Scott was dead, we agreed that everyone involved in the investigation had known for the past year that Scott might kill himself rather than face the truth about sexually abusing young boys. We knew Allyson had worried about that possibility and had been anxious to get Scott indicted and in custody to protect him from himself. If she'd had her way, he would have been in custody soon after Child Services picked up the children.

But Allyson was no longer in charge. The case was in the hands of the U.S. Attorney's Office for the Middle District in Baton Rouge, and that office would call the shots on how the investigation would proceed. And as we had learned, the wheels of justice move slowly, giving Scott time to plan his exit strategy.

"How do you feel?" Ethan asked me. "I hope you don't feel badly."

"I feel bad that two people are probably dead," I said. "And I know we have said for a year that this was a possibility, but it's still a shock when it happens. How do you feel?"

"I didn't want anyone to die," Ethan said quietly. I wanted to see him face justice, I wanted him to apologize to all the victims and face up to what he was and what he did. I guess the end justifies the means…. I do feel free, it's so surreal and so hard to describe. I feel like a new day, Rannah, and it feels good."

"I understand," I said. That was the irony. As awful as it was, for some of his victims, the day brought a feeling of freedom they had not experienced in over 20 years.

C H A P T E R   F I F T Y - T W O

THE DAY AFTER

Mary Jane's notes:

When I got up the next morning, I made a pot of coffee, not that I needed it. Jim Engster and I made phone contact.

I told him that everything was in place. The person in the United States would be the first person he had on the phone, and as I heard the interview winding down, I would get the other guy in the U.K. on the phone, and after a break he would be ready for the interview. Engster said that he was changing the format of the show and that there would be no call-in questions from the public because the story he had heard the night before needed to be told in its entirety without interruptions.

*Stuart showed up, greeted with coffee and biscuits—it's a Southern thing. We talked for a few minutes about what was going to happen, and shortly before 9 a.m. I came to my desk and made the call. I handed the phone to Stuart, who said, "Hello, Jim, this is Stuart," in his British accent. Stuart knew Jim Engster from Jim's being on the **Around Town Show**.*

The call started. Stuart took my portable phone and moved into my dining room and walked between the dining room and kitchen as he talked to Jim on the show.

Jim Engster is a Baton Rouge treasure. His radio show was the perfect place for these young men to tell their story. I knew Jim would ask the questions people wanted answered, but also have the compassion to help these two young men get through what could be one of the toughest conversations of their lives.

"This morning on the show we will discuss the life and tragedy of Scott Rogers, who came to Baton Rouge in the early part of this century and was the talk of the town," Jim began. "He was a pillar of the community, spokesperson for the Better Business Bureau, sheriff's deputy, ordained minister, and host of the popular *Around Town Television Show*." I couldn't help thinking how Scott would have enjoyed that introduction. He craved the approval of people like Jim who enjoyed such overwhelming respect.

"Yesterday, Rogers was killed in a murder-attempted suicide as a grand jury was looking into his past…that included a trial in Great Britain in 1992, in which Scott was acquitted on one count and the jury hung on five other counts," Jim continued.

"He was accused of molesting a 13-year-old boy. We will talk about this and if things go according to plan, we will hear from some people from Scott's past.

"Yesterday, at about 12:40 our time, Scott Rogers, the popular host of *The Around Town Television Show,* was killed in his home in St. Gabriel by a man he had known for more than 20 years…a man who at one point even married Scott's daughter. This man came to the United States with Scott in the early 1990s…it would have been around the mid-1990s. Scott, in Great Britain, where he was a dance instructor in a town outside of London, in Bury St. Edmunds…he was accused of molesting a 13-year-old boy and went to trial in 1992. A jury of 12 people—8 men and 4 women—after a 13-day trial, found Scott innocent or *not guilty* of the principal count of a sexual offense, but hung on the other counts involving indecency with a minor.

"Scott was a dance instructor at the Bury St. Edmunds Performing Arts Academy; he had many young men under his sway. And he, of course, now as we know, was under federal investigation. Since he became a U.S. citizen here in Baton Rouge, he had questions that were part of his process...he was asked if he had ever been arrested and allegedly, he answered *no*. Of course, the answer should have been *yes*.

"He also adopted a child...about 10 years old, and was in the process of adopting another child...who is 2 and is also a boy...reported by his attorney to be a girl, but is actually a boy. And on August 15th, these children were removed from his custody. So the last few weeks have been tumultuous for Scott Rogers and it ended yesterday with his close associate, Mathew Hodgkins, age 36, killing Scott Rogers and shooting himself. Mathew Hodgkins is in serious condition...critical condition at Our Lady of the Lake Regional Medical Center.

"In the last 12 hours or so...15 hours...we've been piecing this together with people who knew Scott and have been tied to the federal investigation," Jim continued. "The grand jury was meeting yesterday at the federal courthouse, but as the grand jury was about to convene, this terrible tragedy occurred in St. Gabriel...and with us is a man who's come forward...who knew Scott in Great Britain...has known him recently...very recently...and he is with us. Because the allegations involve minors, these people, as they come forward, and we may have more than one person today, we will not reveal their names. I know this gentleman's name, but I will not reveal it. But I think he is credible and his story warrants our attention. Good morning sir."

"Good morning, Jim," Stuart replied.

"How long have you known Scott Rogers?" Jim asked.

"I hope you can understand as I talk where I'm coming from," Stuart began very nervously. "I met Scott when I was 12 years old. I was a performer at his Performing Arts School in Bury. I grew up with Scott through the school. I attended a college that was attached to the school. From the time I was 16 to 18, I traveled around the world with him, performed in different countries...then I came to America with him in 1996–97 and have been with him in Baton Rouge ever since."

"So you've known him for 23 years," Jim said.

"Yes, the last time I saw Scott was Monday morning," Stuart said.

"How old were you when you met him?" Jim asked.

"12."

"12 years old," Jim repeated with profound sadness in his voice. "And you were a student at his dance academy."

"Yeah, he had a workshop that came to my school and my drama teacher put me in touch with him," Stuart explained. "He expressed an interest in me, saying that I had potential. He met with my parents and myself and I joined his school on full scholarship when I was 12-years-old."

"When did you become aware that Scott was under investigation?"

"Uh, I had been at the school six months...my recollection of time is a little warped, especially given recent circumstances, but it was very quick and I was aware that allegations had been made in '92, I believe it was, and that he was being investigated for allegations made by another student I did not know personally."

"Were you ever intimately involved with him?" Jim asked directly.

"With Scott?"

"Yes."

"Absolutely," Stuart said.

"And when did this begin?" Jim's voice had a gentleness not usually heard in his interviews.

"This began when I was....uh...13," Stuart said with a heavy sigh, struggling to get the words out, "and increased in frequency until I was 18...continued when I was an adult...when I was 18...through to....last week."

"Why did you follow him to the United States, follow him to Louisiana and continue to be associated with him if he did truly do what you say he did?" Jim asked, slowly moving to tougher questions.

"Uh...I've been wrestling with that myself these last few days," Stuart said. "The truth is, as I'm coming to understand it, is, um...when I met that man, Scott...I was 12 years old...and the, uh, initial relationship that I developed with him privately and not so privately was…. I was a 12-year-old kid. He informed my understanding of physical intimacy…he…he would guide me in how to speak to my parents…on what to say to people…(Sigh)…on some level, I think he raised me…from when I was 12 to 13 years old. And I think that informs your thinking when you're an adult…."

"He is…or was…an extremely charismatic individual," Jim offered.

"Yes, he was," Stuart replied.

"Through this, all these years, did you like him…as a person?" Jim asked.

"No," Stuart said firmly. "Uh…when I was about 26, I got very depressed privately and I thought about love…. I don't know that I know what love is. I know what love isn't…I had that epiphany when I was about 26ish…. From that point on, my personal relationship with Scott, although the physical side certainly deteriorated…it's still there at his request…but emotionally, I've been detached from that man since I was 26 or 27. I spent a year being incredibly depressed and not knowing who I was. And I had to think about things…."

"I understand, sir, that you have been in protective custody of some sort for a while…maybe a week. Is that accurate?" Jim asked, shifting the conversation to his current status and away from the painful past.

"A couple of days," he answered.

"A couple of days…how did that happen? What prompted you to go to authorities?

"I've been with him for 22 years," he began to explain. "I've seen him deal with pressures…I've seen him angry…I've seen him happy…I know that man better than anybody else. And starting on Saturday, he scared me. He looked desperate. I looked in his eyes and I said, *I can see right through you.* They looked glassy. He said some things to me that made me fear for my safety…and for my life. And Tuesday, a week ago, I hit a low point myself and I called a number that was provided to me by a federal agent…. That federal agent called me back Monday morning…and I pretty much broke down and asked to meet them. And they have been amazing. They've taken me out of that situation and they've been taking good care of me the last few days...but I was scared. I was scared for my safety and for my life."

"Did he threaten you?" Jim asked.

"He said that he wanted...we were walking down the driveway Saturday and he said, and he was talking about how he wants to end his life...and he looked at me and said, 'You know what I really want? You and I to go upstairs and lay next to each other...and shoot ourselves in the heart.' So if that's a threat, then yeah, I guess. So I sat with that on Saturday...on Sunday...and the agent called me when I got to the office Monday morning. And uh, I was afraid."

"When did you find out about the events of yesterday?" Jim continued.

"I was sitting, waiting to go into court to testify," Stuart explained. "I had a subpoena handed to me two weeks ago which is what started all this. And so I was sitting, waiting to go into court to tell my story and I probably found out an hour or hour and a half after it happened. The agents went out to deal with it...and they came back and put me in a room and sat me down and explained it to me."

"Well, you know better than I that Scott had become a big part of this community. He was a Sheriff's deputy...."

"Yeah, I helped make him," Stuart interrupted.

Wow. At that moment, an ocean apart, Ethan and I both thought that was a rare hint of the resentment Stuart held for Scott. The years of abuse, being scolded and humiliated in front of others for his defiance, and Stuart finally revealed that he felt he deserved some credit for Scott's success. And no doubt, he did.

"Well, how did he do it?" Jim continued with the interview.

"I don't know that I can explain the motive...I just know that Scott Rogers is a very smart man. I've always said to him, he never expresses confidence in himself. He always thinks he's worth nothing. Over the years, he can take an individual or a group of people in a room and he can make them smile...make them cry...that's his gift. I think personally, knowing him the way I do, I think he has...I don't know if emotionally he's all there. He functions like a normal person but I think there is something emotionally broken in him. I think he is wounded by demons. He knows what he did when he was 30...and he has never ever spoken about it."

"This is one of the most tragic shows we've ever done...maybe the most tragic," Jim told his audience. "I knew Scott Rogers; he was on this show March 12, 2011, and we'll hear some of that interview today." As Jim spoke, Elizabeth Dent Sumrall, who hosted a regular segment on Scott Rogers' TV show, sat near Jim in the studio with tears in her eyes as she heard the truth about her late friend. Elizabeth was a back-up guest who could speak of her relationship with Rogers if there were any problems with either guest calling in.

"Scott was on the show I previously hosted 14 times," Jim continued. "When I looked him up, he was going by the name *Scott Richards*. He was under federal investigation at the time of his death. 12:40 yesterday in St. Gabriel...Mathew Hodgkins, the man who allegedly shot Scott and then himself, is in critical condition at Our Lady of the Lake Medical Center. We're talking with a man who knew Scott 23 years and was a close associate, as you've heard, up until the last few days of Scott's life."

"Why did Scott end up in Louisiana?" Jim asked.

"Um...we initially flew into Dallas, Texas, and spent a few years living with a lady out there," Stuart explained. "I think Scott had a connection here. He knew a guy, a British comedian, who was in Baton Rouge for some reason. Then we all came by car to Baton Rouge. Why does anything happen? I don't know."

"What was the relationship between Mathew Hodgkinson and Scott?" Jim continued.

"When I was a kid, around 13 years of age, Mathew was also subjected to sexual abuse at Scott's hand," Stuart explained. "I know this for a fact because some of the abuse was group in nature. That's how I know that Mathew was subjected to the same stuff that I was. Mathew and I never talked about this stuff...no one did. But I believe Mathew's physical relationship with Scott ended sometime around 2000...2003. And I believe that Mathew has taken whatever was in his head and turned it into more of a brother relationship with Scott. That's my opinion."

"And Mathew married Scott's daughter?" Jim continued.

"Yes," Stuart said.

"Obviously this defies the imagination of some people and the host might even be included in that number," Jim said. "It's a story that if we were to make it up, people wouldn't believe it."

"I sat down last night and tried to write this down," Stuart said. "It's too much."

"Scott had a terrible childhood himself, didn't he?" Jim asked.

"I've learned not to take things at face value, but he has expressed on many occasions how he was physically abused by his father, punched in the face, beaten, put in the hospital," Stuart explained. "So yes, that's the impression I'm under."

As Stuart told what he knew about Scott's past, newspaper reports in England told a different story. Rogers's father, Graham Rogers, himself a social worker and mental health officer, had reported that Scott falsely accused him of assault. Stuart was right—it was hard to take anything at face value when it came to Scott Rogers.

"Why did he change his name?" Jim continued.

"He's told me over the years that his first name change was when he was 16," Stuart said. "He said he wanted to be a different person, which I can understand on some level. He was Richard Rogers when he came to America and in 2006; he's always gone by Scott. His full name is Richard Scott Rogers; he dropped the Richard in 2006. He did not want to be found by people back in the U.K. for obvious reasons. So that's probably some of the motivation for at least going by Scott."

"Did you live in the house with him?" Jim asked.

"Yes."

"How many people were living in that house?"

"This year... 1-2-3-4-5-6," Stuart counted.

"Six people? And was Scott intimately involved with all of them at one time? Or at some point in his life?" Jim asked incredulously.

"Would you ask the question again?"

"Was Scott intimately involved with the six people in the house at some time?" Jim repeated.

"Two of them...Mathew and myself," he clarified. "When I was 13 years of age, I was not the only person who was sexually abused by Scott. There were at least four that I know and those people were not involved in the initial allegations that Scott went to trial for in '92. The four that I'm aware of were either going on during that or came after that, and that group included Mathew and myself."

"Why would Mathew do this?" Jim asked.

"There are a couple of things I do know," Stuart explained. "The first is, that I'm just lucky that the agent called me on Monday and that went the way it did and I got out of that house because when Scott looks at me and he's distraught...as I said on Saturday, it's a madness and it's frightening. And I can only imagine Mathew...he was subjected to the same 23 years of sexual abuse...of emotional abuse...of manipulation...right down to your core...right down to your understanding of what love is...of what sex is.... So when I try to picture Mathew on Wednesday, I feel so sad for that man."

"When did Scott become a minister?" Jim asked, again, in the most difficult parts, deftly shifting the discussion.

"Um...2011, I believe?"

"His church was, I believe, called the 13:34 Church, a non-denominational church at Cortana Mall where the show was produced," Jim explained for the audience.

"Yeah, in 2011 he was involved with another church and when that ended he started up his own church. So he started it in 2012."

"He had this fabulous facility, and yet no real means of support," Jim noted. "How did he do this?"

"What do you mean?" Stuart asked.

"How did he build this mini-empire with no job of significance? I'm in this business. I know you can't build the kind of empire he did with the money that comes from hosting a one-day-a-week show that airs at five in the morning on Saturdays and Sundays."

"When I was 16, I was living with Scott Rogers and he purchased a dilapidated property just outside London, and there were probably six or seven people in our group at the time," Stuart explained. "And we pretty much rebuilt that entire house in a year with limited help from contractors."

"So he probably sold the house and made a good amount of money," Jim observed.

"Yeah, a little bit here, a little bit there. The show started in 2003 in a shed...and I think we just built it," Stuart said.

There was much speculation about how Scott financed his studio and supported his extended family. When the news of his sexual abuse of minors surfaced, authorities speculated that he was involved in child pornography, and a television studio and edit suite would have provided the perfect environment. And even though Scott told his confidantes he would be exposed for involvement in human trafficking and an international child pornography ring, his death ended the investigation, and any videos that he may or may not have made were never recovered. Of course, once the children were removed from his home, Scott had twelve days to get his affairs in order and decide what he would leave behind for others to discover.

Scott told former television journalist Leo Honeycutt, who met Scott Rogers when he first came to Louisiana, that he'd had to leave the U.K. Rogers' story to Leo was that the 1stCo company in the U.K. wanted him to leave and establish a company in the United States, almost as if a larger organization had financed his move. Leo recounted that the explanation sounded almost like a story about the Mafia and how a shadowy organization controlled his movements and funding.

"Well, he was a very talented man," Jim continued his interview. "He sold himself and his show very well. He did have many advertisers on that show, I know. But how did he go on the air—much of his show was about his faith and quoting the Bible— how did he live this double life if what you're telling us is true?" Jim asked, sounding slightly exasperated at what he and his audience were learning.

"Back at the Academy, that school was about 800 students strong, and he was very much in charge," Stuart explained. "So the structure of things made it easy for kids to be at his house, which is where a lot of the abuse took place. Over the years, to my knowledge, and I was right there next to him for all that time, the pedophilia, and that's what it is, was limited to the group at the Academy. And to my knowledge the only physical intimacy that has lasted was with me. So I think he's still the same person, but from what I've seen during this time in Baton Rouge, he has changed on whatever emotional level he functions. His relationship with me changed from one of controlling abuse when I was a child to one where on many occasions he expressed that he wants me to be his partner. I don't think a person really changes, but I think he's changed over the years. I'm having trouble getting my head around really feeling that things are real. I have messages on my phone from people expressing sorrow and general sadness, and I can't help but think it's their right to...that the Scott Rogers they knew existed...that he was real...and he did some wonderful things...but he also did some illegal things...some devastating things. All the people who knew him in Baton Rouge, all that's real, but there is a whole history that they're not privy to. It's such an unbelievable and crazy situation."

"We thank you for joining us," Jim said. "This is a terribly difficult subject."

"I have one other thing to add," Stuart started.

"Go ahead, go ahead," Jim said, making it clear that he wanted his guests to speak their minds.

"There were two adopted kids, foster and adopted kids involved in this," Stuart said. "Nothing happened to those boys. They were lovingly cared for."

"They were never abused?" Jim asked.

"No."

"That's good to know. Thank you, sir. I appreciate your time and your courage. Good luck to you."

Mary Jane's notes:

When Stuart paused and sighed, discussing his abuse by Rogers, he was standing in my dining room by the buffet. I was in another room, leaving him to as much privacy as he could have while talking on the radio to all of Baton Rouge. I saw his body language as he talked and the effect that telling his story was having on him. There was sadness, happiness, and relief. Not only was I hearing the words, I was seeing his face and body language. We later learned that people all over Baton Rouge were listening to Jim's show and to what Rogers' victims were saying. We learned that one coffee shop came to a complete silence as the one-hour show aired.

Then after a break, it was time for the other man in the United Kingdom who had been a victim of Rogers. Stuart went outside to smoke a cigarette as Jim Engster talked to the second man. As bad as Stuart's story was, the other guy's was horrific. Because I had patched the call through from the U.K. to Engster, I sat at my desk with the phone glued to my ear, listening to the horror story and hearing the other man's anger and hurt as he described what Rogers had done to him as a child—after Family Services in the U.K. had taken him from his family and placed him with Rogers. He ultimately ran away, living on the streets under a false name to escape Rogers' violence. Even then, he had to change his name to keep Rogers from finding him. The words describing the violence he suffered at the hands of Rogers as a young child made my eyes mist, and I'm not a ninny.

"Now we're joined by a man who has come forward who was also a student in that dance academy in the early 1990s, and he is joining us from across the pond," Jim continued as he introduced his second caller. From her home, Mary Jane had connected Jake, calling from the U.K., to Jim's studio.

"Good morning," Jake said, as we heard his voice for the first time.

"When did you find out about this?" Jim asked.

"You mean the current events now or about Scott Rogers?" Jake asked.

"When did you find out about his death?" Jim clarified.

"I found out about his death...I'm in the U.K., so it was yesterday evening U.K. time," Jake replied.

"And how old were you when you met Scott?" Jim asked.

"My situation is that I was 11 years old. I was placed under Scott Rogers' care by Social Services. I was taken away from my own parents for reasons that don't really need to be discussed right now...but I was placed by Social Services and the Court under the care of Scott Rogers when I was 11."

"Did he abuse you?" Jim got right to the point.

"Yes," Jake said firmly. "What I would like to be very clear about, referring to your other guest today: Scott Rogers is very, very difficult to explain, as a victim, but I've had many, many years now of speaking to psychiatrists and counselors with regard to what I went through at the hands of Scott Rogers. He is a master manipulator. He is an expert brainwasher. He is the worst predatory pedophile that you can imagine. And when you are a child and you're faced with that type of monster, that type of intelligent mind, you don't stand a chance. He's the worst kind of pedophile and the worst kind of con man. I was absolutely lost. When I was 11 years old I was taken away from a very bad situation, much like the children he has recently adopted. And at first, he was very nice to me. And he said I was going to be a very successful dancer. Then gradually...very gradually...things started happening. Sexual abuse. And at first, it was terrifying. And I didn't know how to speak up about it. You have to understand that when you're conditioned this way from the age of 11.... I was systematically beaten if I didn't comply with what was required of me. I was trapped under a roof with this man.... He was married at the time, and I was abused all the time. And if you didn't comply with him, you would be, for lack of a better word, held hostage. I was beaten with various implements if I refused." Jake was clearly ready to tell his story.

"By him?" Jim asked, seeming to take advantage of the opportunity to jump in. "You were beaten by him?"

"Yes, yes," Jake continued, his voice steady and confident. "Beaten by Scott Rogers. At the time, he was known as Richard Scott Rogers. And his biological daughter would have been three years old, I think…maybe two years old. And there was no way to get away. Once he's got you…once he's trapped you…. I had no means of escape. I had no one I could turn to. He makes you believe it is entirely your fault."

"How many were there that you know of or believe to have been abused by Scott?" Jim continued.

"That I know definitely of, I would say five," Jake replied. "That I believe there were, there could be 10 plus." *Wow.* Ethan had helped us identify six, probably seven, victims, but we knew there was a possibility of more. Since Jake had lived with Scott, he would come closest to knowing the number.

"All boys?" Jim asked.

"All boys," he replied. "Obviously the worst situation is when you are forcibly adopted by him, you are trapped, which ended up to be the case, unfortunately, with Mathew. Your previous guest was also in a similar situation. And as I mentioned to you before, you were conditioned…and brainwashed…from such an early age that it's very, very extraordinary—if not impossible—to escape from his clutches. You are made to feel extreme shame for what he did.

"When I was very, very young he made me believe that everything that was happening was my fault. I had made him do these things to me. And at first, I was threatened by Scott and by associates that were still with him. He is the only perpetrator in this crime. I don't hold anybody else accountable. But when I did finally manage to escape from him, which was after possibly 10 or 11 years of abuse…then I was threatened into silence. When I managed to get away, to escape, I had no one to turn to. I had no money…everything was controlled by Scott. Every single element of your life. One of his favorite things was asking you what you were thinking. If you didn't come up with the correct response to what you were thinking, you would be put through—I'll call it now *one of his torture sessions*. It was psychological torture...it was physical torture...you were beaten.

"There were numerous occasions where if you refused his advances, refused his sexual abuse, then the sexual abuse became very violent. This is very difficult for someone who hasn't experienced abuse under him, to explain it. You have to have a professional in this area because it's very difficult to understand why you couldn't come forward and why you couldn't say anything."

"Why didn't you come forward before today?" Jim asked.

"When I escaped, I wanted to get as far away from the situation as possible," Jake explained, continuing to gain his strength as he answered Jim's questions. "I wanted to have my freedom. I ran from him and I kept as far away as possible from him. He was a monster who I felt was going to destroy me. I often feared for my life. There were situations where I was strangled into unconsciousness."

"Hold on, hold on." Jim interrupted. "Strangled into unconsciousness...by whom?"

"By Scott," he answered. "So when I did escape, I didn't come forward because I was living in fear. As I got older, I didn't know the whereabouts of Scott, I just wanted to get away from him. And I didn't know where he was. I recently found out where he was. I found out that he had adopted more children. It got to be so much that I couldn't sit back and watch it happening again to innocent young children. I couldn't watch it happen again. I've only spoken out to people who are close to me. Everybody who's close to me knows what I went through at the hands of that monster. Now I've spoken to a federal agent in the U.S. and I've told my story because I couldn't see it happening again. When I knew it was happening again, I had to come forward and make a stand. As petrified as I was that he was going to somehow be able to destroy my life again, I had to say something."

"When did you last talk with Scott Rogers?" Jim asked.

"Probably...ah, maybe 16 years ago."

"What was the occasion?"

"I had left, and he was desperate to get me back," Jake explained. "He put advertisements in the local newspaper—a London newspaper—trying to find me. I managed to escape because I met a young lady and her parents were incredibly understanding, and they took me in. I didn't explain the full situation to them but he harassed them…and he got his associates to contact her parents and say horrible things about me. And they said to me, 'You need to find this man and speak to him.' Which I did. He still refused to leave me alone. Afterwards, I went to see a solicitor and I instructed the solicitor that if this manhunt, I'll call it, didn't desist, that an injunction would be put in place. Scott responded by saying he was very disappointed and he felt that I had been brainwashed. He made all of us call him, at some point, *Dad*, which he wasn't a father to us at all. If we were in trouble, we would have to call him *Sir*. And he would inflict some sort of punishment, whether physical violence, sexual violence, or psychological conditioning. He insisted that we address him by *Sir*."

"Was he a local celebrity in Bury St. Edmunds the way he was here?' Jim inquired.

"No, here he had a dancing school," Jake explained. "When I first met him, he worked for the local Council and his wife was a dancing teacher. He started the school and he had no dance experience at all, but he thought he was going to be a dance teacher, which is the time I was placed with him. He then grew the school. You asked your last guest how did he manage to support himself. You're talking here about a person who managed to grow a dancing school from nothing to a dancing school that was taking in on an annual basis—back in the day—well over 500,000 to a million pounds a year."

"He was a skilled man in many ways," Jim said.

"He was a master manipulator…and a monster," Jake replied. "There's no better way to describe it. And as much as I would not wish anybody any suffering, and I would not wish death on anybody…I have to say the world is a better place without that monster causing any more children any harm."

"How has your life been since you got away from Scott?" Jim asked.

"Well, my life since I've gotten away from him…. At first, it was ecstatic, because I was able to live a natural life, since I was no longer forced to do things that were absolutely horrendous," Jake said. "I could make my own decisions, I managed to make money, and I had a life. After I got from under the impact of Scott…I can't begin to describe the mental conditioning…the amount of brainwashing that you go through at such an early age. You don't know what's up, what's down. You just have no comprehension. Scott had a code that you were supposed to adhere to. You had to behave in a certain way. And finally I was able to become my own person again…to find myself through years of counseling…years of speaking to psychiatrists. I was diagnosed at one point with having Post Traumatic Stress Syndrome because of the abuse that I went through. Now I don't sleep particularly well…I have night terrors. It's still a part of me. And I was still absolutely terrified of the man. I was living in a nightmare…I was trapped there and as a child and a young adult, I had no means of escape. No way of telling anybody and nowhere to go. I finally escaped and partly due to my shame, I ran as far away as possible to get away from that monster."

"We thank you for joining us today," Jim said.

"One thing I would like to say if you have time," Jake said. "I want to make it clear that in the court case over here, Scott was not acquitted. It was a hung jury and the only reason the prosecution didn't try him again on the charges was that the victim and the prosecutor felt the victim could not go through another trial."

Jim ended the show by playing a segment from a 2011 interview with Scott, ironically on gun violence in America. It was the interview Jim had told Nathan and me about when we met for lunch almost a year before to discuss the strange email I had received. Scott had constantly asked Jim to use him as an expert opinion on his radio programs, letting him know that, to be included, he was willing to present either side of an issue. Persistence was his forte.

In the audio clip Jim played, Scott argued that if people are trying to harm others, they will use a gun, a knife, or even a hammer—they will find a way.[35]

Ethan emailed me as soon as the interview ended. "Jake found his voice," he said.

That he did. He was beyond amazing. He was honest—painfully so—confident, and very eloquent. It was as if Scott's death had finally freed him from fear, and the truth flowed out of him effortlessly. Jake was remarkable, and I knew Ethan was very happy for him, happy that he had handled the interview so well.

---

[35] The Jim Engster Show. Louisiana Radio Network. 28 August 2014. http://www.louisianaradionetwork.com/blogs/Revelations-of-scott-rogers-after-his-death#.VfEVdRFVhBc

The Boys of Bury

JAKE *in his own words*

England
2015

One of my main reasons for coming forward was that, first and foremost, I'd heard that other boys had been adopted, and I couldn't sit back and let that happen anymore, no matter how big my fear was from the past.

And secondly, to help other people realize this is the way this type of criminal operates. If I can help show people in authority that this is the type of technique they use—this is why I stayed quiet, this is how they kept me quiet, this is what happened to me—then they can recognize it more easily in other people. And maybe when other people are trying to hide certain things, they can see through that.

And also maybe my story will help them when speaking to victims, and looking out for certain signs that they are being abused, even though they aren't saying they are being abused. They don't know how to say it. How do you tell somebody when these awful things are happening to you, how can you speak to somebody and tell them that it's your fault? Even though it's not.

Even after I got away and spent so much time in fear, in a way, I still felt guilty. I still felt ashamed of what had happened.

As an adult, we beat ourselves up about the fact: Why didn't I say something? But as an adult, we forget how we feel as children. I'd forgotten how confused I felt until I'd spoken to professionals and they said, "This is why you're feeling this way and this is what was used against you to make you feel that way."

It wasn't until then that I could look at it objectively and think, Well, yeah, as a child, that's why I felt that way. And as an adult, that's why I felt guilty because I didn't know any other way to respond to it.

That's why I felt I had to speak up.

CHAPTER FIFTY-THREE

STUART

Following the radio interview, Stuart went to the Iberville Parish Sheriff's Office, where Allyson introduced him to Major Ronnie Hebert, who interviewed him about his relationship with Scott and his thoughts on what had happened at the house.

As the interview began, Hebert greeted Stuart by saying, "I'm Major Ronnie Hebert. My accent's probably going to be a little different from yours."

"As is mine," Stuart replied and the two laughed.

"It's nice to meet you, Stuart, unfortunately under these circumstances." But before he could ask the first question, Stuart interrupted and said, "If I can, in the interest of being incredibly honest, I am...I wouldn't say I'm relieved at the passing of Scott...I don't really care at this point, and you will come to understand why. I'm feeling emotionally empty, a lot's been happening.... My concern at this point is with Mathew and to a lesser degree with Kimberly, Scott's daughter. But as far as Scott Rogers, I don't consider them unfortunate events as you will come to realize."

Hebert said, "Apparently, you know what happened yesterday."

"Yes," Stuart replied. "Scott is dead and Mathew shot himself or got shot in the head...and he's in the hospital."

"Correct," Major Hebert replied. "We seem to think that he shot himself in the head, and he is in a hospital right now."

"How's he doing?" Stuart asked.

"Uh, not good," Hebert replied.

"What does that mean?" Stuart asked.

"His condition is very critical," Hebert replied. "Very critical."

"He might die," Stuart said.

"It's a possibility," Hebert said. "I'm not going to lie to you. There is that possibility that he may die. If he does not die, I don't know what quality of life he will have. I'm not a doctor…I'm just an old street cop, but his condition is very, very critical."

Then Hebert explained that he would like Stuart to give him whatever background he could that would help him understand what led to the shooting.

"I'll be frank and graphic," Stuart began. "I've done it a few times in the past two days and it's getting easier." He appeared to be running on autopilot, as he began to recite an emotionless account of his life with Scott Rogers.

Stuart began by telling Hebert he met Scott Rogers when he was 12 years old, and by the time he was 13, Rogers was sexually abusing him. He told him Rogers abused several young boys at the Academy, including Mathew and him, and because the sexual abuse was often group in nature, he knew for certain that Scott was abusing the other boys, too.

He told how Scott orchestrated Mathew's leaving his parents to live with him and how Jake had escaped to London after being abused for many years. "When Jake ran away, Scott spent a couple of weeks trying to track him down in London, literally walking the streets with about 12 students from the Academy, 16- and 17-year-old boys. Scott found him, they had a meeting, and Jake agreed to come back but never did."

Stuart told how they had moved after Scott's trial from Bury St. Edmunds to Gravesend in Kent, where Scott bought a couple of properties and lived with a handful of students from the Academy and his daughter, Kimberly.

"As for the guys in that house, we had all been abused by Scott in some shape or fashion at an early age," Stuart explained. "We never talked about it, though. But we were a tight group. I spoke to my Mom yesterday for the first time in 18 years, and I said, 'Look, Mom, don't blame yourself because the truth is, when I was 17, you could have come down with an Army and I wouldn't have left that man.'"

Stuart explained how Scott, Kimberly, and some of Scott's students came to America when Scott married Diane Palladino and how Scott's connection to John Inman had later brought him to Baton Rouge. Stuart told Hebert that getting all of the students over to America took Scott about three years, and until then they would visit him on 90-day visas.

"As for the dynamic of the family, there was myself and about three other guys that I was personally aware of who were being molested by Scott," Stuart explained. "I suspect there were at least another four or five, but I didn't see it myself. And a couple of girls were part of the group, but they weren't aware of Scott's sexual abuse of the boys. There was a girl called *Angie* who came across to America as well, and she was part of the family, but she wasn't privy to the abuse. And Kimberly has never been privy to that as well. They would sleep in a different part of the house and it wasn't discussed."

By the time they moved to Baton Rouge, he and Mathew were young men in their 20s who had been under what Stuart referred to as Scott's *guidance* since they were 12- or 13-year-old boys. "I would have said *manipulation*," Stuart told Hebert, "but right now it doesn't feel right for me to call it that."

It seemed obvious that Stuart realized exactly what it was, but he had been out of Scott's house for only a few days. Just three nights ago, he was still sleeping on a futon in Scott's bedroom and was only beginning to understand the extent of the manipulation he had endured for two decades.

"We were not living a normal life," Stuart explained. "We don't go where we want. It's never been that way where we have significant funds to pursue anything outside of the norm."

He said they worked a lot at 1stCo, and anything outside of that made Scott very upset, since he considered other activities a sign that they did not want to be part of the family.

"So a thousand little pressures like that keep us together and keep us doing what we do," he said.

"One thing worth noting is that throughout Scott's time in Baton Rouge, and in Dallas as well, he was very afraid of being found," Stuart said. "He wouldn't let us use *Richard Scott Rogers* online anywhere, since Google searches text and he could have been found in a heartbeat. So it was always 'Scott Rogers' and he dropped the 'Richard.' He made that official in 2006 with Polozola, but that was born out of fear.

"I was 25 or 26 before the whole thing stank like shit to me," Stuart said. "I couldn't ignore that whatever got me to the point I was at, I didn't want any of it. I didn't want the relationship I was in…none of it. So I've been fairly distant in my head and my heart since then, which I think actually was the difference between Mathew and me this week. There is something that I lack…or that I have…whatever, that Matt doesn't," Stuart said, as he struggled to hold back his emotions.

Stuart told Hebert he believed Scott stopped having sex with Mathew around 2002 or 2004, while his relationship with Stuart continued. "I've continued…at least once every three to six weeks there would be some form of physical intimacy between Scott and me born out of child abuse when I was 13 and my inability to break away. That's basically what it boils down to."

Stuart described how the federal authorities and State Child Services had picked up Scott's two young sons and how Scott had returned to the studio "spooked." He said Scott began drinking more than usual, although he had always abused alcohol, and spent the weekend after the children were taken drinking, throwing up, and staying in bed.

"He was a mess," Stuart said. "He was in bed, and he was moaning about it being the end for him. It was all very self-centered, and I was sitting there wondering at what point we were going to start worrying about the kids here, you know?"

Stuart described the Tuesday of the child custody hearing as a particularly emotional day for him, a day on which he had a meltdown and called Allyson, whose card he had kept from August 15, when she interviewed him at the studio.

He said that after the custody hearing, Scott's vibe changed from *"Woe is me, they've taken the kids,"* to *"This is the end for me,"* and he became gradually more suicidal.

"I've known the man for 23 years and I've seen him in all kinds of situations," Stuart said, "and I've never seen him the way I saw him on Saturday and Sunday. On Saturday, he was gradually getting more desperate. Again, we don't talk about this. We've never spoken about the abuse. But I know it happened, and he knows it happened, and it's kind of like it haunts him."

Stuart told Hebert Scott's conversations changed from talking about killing himself to a discussion of including Stuart in the process. "He said, as we were walking down the driveway and he was crying and crying, he would stop and he would look at me like a fucking madman," Stuart explained. "And he would say, 'You know what I really want? Is for you and me to go upstairs and lie down in the bed next to each other and shoot ourselves in the heart.'

"I was scared as hell," Stuart said. "We didn't leave the house on Saturday so it was pretty intense."

Stuart told Hebert that he left on Sunday to run the sound equipment for the church service and on Monday morning, he left the house at 7:30 a.m. to go to the office. Around 9 a.m., Allyson finally returned his call and he asked to meet with her. Stuart told Hebert he was genuinely concerned for his safety and went into protective custody at that time.

"The reason I feel for Mathew," Stuart explained, "is that I didn't know I would leave that house. It's just that the dynamic between Scott and me, and I assume it's the same between Scott and Mathew.... I could say this a thousand ways, but when he's desperate, he has this way of making you feel like it's your fault. It's not just a man here who is suffering, but that you can do something about this and why don't you do something about it.

"Whatever it was, I think Mathew couldn't say *no*," Stuart said.

Hebert asked Stuart if at any time while he was at the house Scott or Mathew spoke about suicide.

"Scott was very vocal about ending it for himself," Stuart replied. "He said he tried pills but it didn't work, whatever the hell that means. He carried a gun in his right pocket pretty much from the day after the children were taken." He described Scott's gun as a small one he had previously worn in an ankle holster. He said Scott and Mathew had several guns around the house— in the library, in the closet in Scott's bedroom, and in Mathew's closet.

Later, Stuart described to me an occasion when he refused Scott's sexual advances and an angry Scott got out of bed, walked to his closet, and retrieved a handgun. Sleeping on the floor, Stuart could see his movements in the dark but tried to pretend he was falling asleep. He saw Scott walking toward him with the gun and feared he might be killed that night for refusing him sex. But Scott stood over him for a moment, holding the gun, then walked out of the bedroom. *Constantly keep them on edge!*

Hebert pressed Stuart for information on Mathew's demeanor over the two weeks following Scott's discovery that he was under investigation.

"Mathew and I work together but we really don't have any meaningful relationship to speak of," Stuart explained. "Over the years, and I'm good at this, too, it has been whatever Scott's way is, everyone falls in line. And most of the time, that's negative toward me, and Mathew and Kimberly will jump on. And so their impression of me, I think they think I lie...they think I'm horrible to Scott...I'm dishonest...those kinds of things...on account of his influence over the years. So Mathew and I don't sit down and have a beer together. That's not the relationship we have. It's proximity...that's all it is.

"As Scott got worse..." Stuart continued, "Mathew loves the kids, and so do I. And I think about three or four days after the Office of Child Services hearing, Mathew made attempts to reach me emotionally; he asked how I was doing, which he never does. I did the same for him. I gave him a hug a few times. The way in our house that we check in with each other is that Scott has a concern, he then sits us all down and makes an issue out of that concern, and gets support from the peanut gallery. That's how he is. And so a typical example over the past few days...I didn't think that man trusts me. I think I told you when I was about 25 or 26, I basically hated everything in my life. I think I spent a year of just basically being depressed and lost and all that stuff. Well, I came out the other side skeptical of Scott and generally skeptical of everybody. And I think he's felt that and known that in a hundred little ways since, and so I'm not as emotionally close to Scott as I used to be. Mathew's relationship, on the other hand, developed into more of an 'I'm your brother' kind of thing, and so I think emotionally they became tighter over the past few years, and emotionally, I've become more distant to Scott and the whole situation.

"So once he got through those initial few days of being self-absorbed, and after the Office of Child Services thing…and I told him I called her on Tuesday," Stuart said as he gestured to the door where Allyson had left after making her introduction, "his hackles were up for me. *Amazing that he told Scott he had called Allyson.*

"Let's say Maria Edwards, who is a pastor at the church, would be at the house, Kimberly would be there, myself, Mathew, and Scott…. We would sit around in this circle at the end of the day at 8 o'clock and Maria, at Scott's excited direction, would go around so we could all say what we are grateful for, to each person there. And being the skeptic that I am, I would think, *He just wants to know what's in my head.*

"It's like on Saturday he would ask me, *What are you thinking?* His favorite thing to friggin' ask, for as long as I can remember, is *What are you thinking?* And I would be staring at the pampas grass blowing in the wind, and I would say, 'I'm just watching the pampas grass,' because him getting in my head bothers me. So when you talk about how you console each other…that's the typical way. The difference was that Matt asked how I was doing, he hugged me on a couple of occasions, and I did the same for him, which was new. Which tells you how crappy our relationship was."

Major Hebert asked Stuart about Maria's presence at the house on the day of the shooting and whether visiting the family was something she normally did.

"No one typically came to the house," Stuart explained. "We would have occasional functions there where people were invited, but you never just showed up to Scott's house. Now that was a unique situation. He was a mess and she obviously, through conversations with Mathew, found out that he was a mess, so it's entirely appropriate that she would have shown up there."

When Major Hebert asked about the vehicles at Scott's house on the day of the shooting, Stuart described Mathew's car, Maria's van, and Scott's leased Mercedes from L'Auberge Casino. Stuart did not have a car and typically drove with Scott. "Unless he is pissed at me, in which case he leaves me at the house and I come in with Mathew and the kids." On the day Allyson called him and he left for protective custody, Stuart said he had driven Mathew's car to the studio.

Stuart said 1stCo had provided vehicles for them, but since Scott's gambling addiction had cost him over $200,000, he had cut back on expenses and gotten rid of the leased vehicles. Mathew had recently purchased a used Chevrolet and was making his own payments for the first time, and Stuart was planning to do the same.

"I developed what I consider to be a healthy skepticism of Scott, which has become disdain over the years. I look at him sideways. I've done it for a long time. Over the past 22 years, him saying he was going to kill himself...he's done it a thousand times. If I don't do something sexually with him, it escalates to that—'*Well, I should just kill myself.*' That kind of nonsense. So when he was saying that over the past two weeks, I looked at him, then I would look at whoever was there to see *Who's the show for?* And there would be Maria and Kimberly crying. And I would think, *This is for them.* I also know that Scott at his very core is a coward. I don't think that Scott has it in him to kill himself. When push comes to shove...I don't think he...I don't know. It's just a gut thing that I have."

"You don't think he could complete the act?" Hebert asked.

"No," Stuart replied.

"You don't think he could intentionally shoot himself?"

"No."

"Do you think Mathew was capable of shooting Scott?" Hebert asked.

"Mathew hasn't got a violent bone in his body," Stuart replied. "Mathew has always been referred to as a *gentle giant.*

He is a quiet person. I've seen him lose his temper a few times, but that was few and far between. Knowing that Scott doesn't have it in him to actually do the deed, I believe that Scott, over a period of those two days, convinced Mathew that everything was going to end...that his life was over, too...that we're going to meet in the afterlife...all that kind of crap. And he got him in a place in his head where Matt saw no way out. And I believe that Matt probably did shoot Scott in whatever that moment of desperation is, and I believe then he would have shot himself."

Before ending the interview, Stuart asked Hebert if he could add something. "If the facts, which I'm not privy to, turn out that that is what happened, and Mathew recovers to the degree that he stands trial for that, I would take the stand for Mathew to attest to his mental state to whatever help I could be."

"I understand that," Hebert said. "Do you have any questions for me?"

Stuart asked Hebert if Kimberly was at the house when the shooting occurred. He told him *no*, only Maria, adding that she was not very cooperative as a witness, which he found strange.

Stuart explained that Maria had been spending a lot of time at the house over the past two weeks and he thought she was both "concerned and invested," terms that Hebert asked him to explain. Stuart said she had seen the progression, so he didn't think the deaths would have surprised her. "And I think on some level," Stuart said slowly, "Scott had maybe told her some stuff, maybe she would get in trouble or something...that kind of stuff. So maybe she was a little afraid at the time."

What was Maria afraid of? What did Scott know that could get her in trouble? Was he holding something over her head?

CHAPTER FIFTY-FOUR

THE AFTERMATH

In the days following the shooting, the Iberville Parish Sheriff's investigation concluded that Mathew Hodgkinson shot and killed Scott Rogers and then shot himself. News media reported the Sheriff as saying that Scott's body was cold when the deputies arrived. The presence of rigor indicated he had been dead for some time, which raised questions about Maria Edwards' statement that she phoned 911 after hearing gunshots. It also raises questions that can never be answered about what Mathew Hodgkinson endured between the time he shot Scott and the moment he turned the gun on himself.

Tony Clayton, lead prosecutor for the Iberville Parish District Attorney, called the evidence that Scott Rogers was a pedophile "clear and overwhelming." He said if he had not seen for himself the proof that Scott was dead, he would have questioned whether he had pulled off the ultimate trick. He described Scott's house as "Like Neverland...a haven for children...laid out perfectly for children. There were mannequins in the attic," he noted.

Bryan Cox, spokesman for ICE, the U.S. Immigration and Customs Enforcement based in New Orleans, confirmed the Homeland Security Investigations Office in Baton Rouge had assisted the Louisiana Department of Children and Family Services with removing two boys from Scott Rogers' home, pursuant to a State court order.

At 7:15 a.m. the morning following the shooting, the coroner's office performed an autopsy on Rogers; it found that the gunshot wound that killed him entered his brain in the left temple and exited the right temple. As soot was present on his skin, soft tissue, and bone, the autopsy report concluded that the shot to his head was a contact wound. It also reported he had faint bruises in his pelvis and groin area and tested positive for the presence of alcohol, Benzodiazepine, and opiates.

On the day after the shooting, Stuart Poulton sat for interviews with federal, State, and local law enforcement agencies for debriefings before boarding a plane for the U.K.

On Friday, August 29, Maria Edwards went to the Iberville Parish Sheriff's Office to get the one thing she so desperately wanted from the crime scene—her computer bag. As she was removing some personal items, Captain Snelson observed a clear Ziploc bag containing handwritten letters. They resembled the letter found at the crime scene on the day of the shooting. Captain Snelson asked her for the Ziploc bag and observed that Scott Rogers had signed one of the letters. He told Maria that the letters would be kept as evidence, so while she was able to retrieve certain items, when asked to talk to the deputies about the day of the shooting, she again refused.

Below are the letters found in Maria's computer bag:

1. A letter from Scott granting Power of Attorney to Maria Edwards:

August 25th, 2014
2:00 p.m.

To whom it may concern:

Due to current catastrophic circumstances that have recently developed in my life, I, Scott Tobius Rogers, (formerly Richard Scott-Rogers, Richard-Scott Rogers, Martin Rogers) of 1045 Daisy Avenue, St. Gabriel, LA 70776 hereby (in the absence of Mathew Allan Hodgkinson of 1045 Daisy Avenue, St. Gabriel, LA

70776 for any reason) give Power of Attorney over me to Maria Quintero Edwards (formerly Maria Elisa Quintero) of 17555 South Harrells Ferry Road, Baton Rouge, LA 70816.

Mrs. Maria Edwards may deal with all aspects of my life including (but not limited to):

- Selling my house
- Selling my chattels and personal belongings
- Close bank accounts and transfer funds into her account
- Make medical decisions over me

This document, written in my own handwriting, also extends after my death.

I understand that often "intent" is crucial in legal documents. My intent is that should I not be around, and should Mathew Hodgkinson be unavailable for any reason, Maria Edwards has full legal authority to close things down and help my son, (name redacted.)

Signed: Scott Rogers
           Mathew Hodgkinson
Witness: Cedric Allison
Witness: Kimberly Scott Rogers

2. An "Addendum to Will of Scott Rogers" which Scott wrote on Monday, August 25, and which Mathew Hodgkinson witnessed:

Due to circumstances since I signed my will on Friday, 22nd August, 2014, I write in my own hand to have Stuart Poulton deleted as my executor should Mathew Allan Hodgkinson be unavailable. I do not wish for Stuart Poulton to have anything whatsoever in my personal effects, chattels, etc. Additionally, as adoptive father to (name redacted), I do not wish Stuart Poulton having <u>ANY</u> access to my son until his 18th birthday. I respectfully sign in good faith my wishes be adhered to.

This addendum to the will was written on the day Stuart went into federal custody. As soon as Scott realized Stuart was gone, he knew he wasn't coming back.

3. A letter from Mathew authorizing Maria Edwards to act as his agent for 1stCo:

August 26, 2014

To Whom It May Concern:

This letter authorizes "Maria Edwards" to act as my agent for and on behalf of 1stCo, Inc. Should I be indisposed or unavailable Maria may act in my stead for the benefit of the company on all matters, financial, postal, contractual, property and staffing. During such time Maria may draw $2000 per month.

Yours,
Mathew Hodgkinson
1stCo, Inc.
General Manager

Witness: K. Scott Rogers
              Scott Rogers

Mathew wrote another letter to Quantum Express authorizing Maria to collect all mail for Box 7A, the mailbox used by Scott for 1stCo and *The Around Town TV Show*.

He made a handwritten list of 1stCo expenses such as leases, and left instructions for the return of laptop computers to Apple and contact information for the bank and the CPA. On a separate sheet, he wrote the names of individuals to contact about the bank accounts and automobile leases, as well as a list of expenses for the house, including gas, cable, electricity, water, and security. Mathew drew a small sketch of his office showing where Maria would find files for both 1stCo and personal business.

On another sheet of paper, he made a list of passwords for bank accounts, his iPad, and church membership files, along with instructions on how to send mass emails to the church members. Security questions for his passwords included "music group," "first car," and "mother's name," a sad reminder of the broken-hearted woman who fought so hard to save her son from Scott.

For the first time, the reason for Maria's anxiety seemed clear: She did not want the police to find the murder-suicide note that documented everyone's knowledge of the events before they occurred. She had in her possession a notarized and witnessed note giving her control of everything once Scott and Mathew were dead!

Also on Friday, Mathew underwent minor surgery to remove some blood and relieve pressure on his brain. The Iberville Parish Sheriff's Office obtained search warrants for Maria Edwards' computer and the cell phones it had removed from Scott's house as evidence.

Because she'd had surgery the day after the shooting, Darla had kept in touch with Maria through text messages. She inquired about Scott's dog and cat, and Maria said she believed Kimmy had taken them. She asked about a funeral for Scott and was told he had never wanted a funeral and would be cremated.

On Thursday, September 4, Darla visited the Iberville Parish Sheriff's Office again. She had heard on the news that Scott's body was in rigor when the emergency responders arrived at the scene, indicating that time had passed between his being shot and Mathew's being shot.

Darla couldn't sleep, so she had gone to the authorities to review the day of the shooting again. Iberville deputies agreed with her it was hard to understand why Maria needed an attorney simply to tell the detectives what she heard when she was in the house.

Rumors were flying among Scott's friends, she told them, that on Monday and Tuesday before the shooting he had shifted a lot of money around and changed the locks on the church. Mathew was in charge of Scott's business accounts, and she heard he had given that authority to Maria on Tuesday. She worried that the men had planned the shootings, and she worried about Maria's role in their deaths.

Darla told the Iberville detectives that Scott had offered to serve as a volunteer pastor at the halfway house she ran and had filled out the same application a prospective employee would complete. She found it odd that Scott claimed on the application that he had lived in all but three of the fifty states—Hawaii, and North and South Dakota. He also said he had lived in Malaysia and other countries, and she wondered how that was possible, when he had lived in Louisiana the past 10 years. The information he had provided her was not consistent with other statements he had made.

She discovered further that he had listed himself on her application as Scott Tobius Rogers, and she was not aware that his name had been Richard Scott Rogers. "It strikes me as so odd that I had known this man for almost a solid year, and had no idea...no idea," Darla told the detectives. "The thing that is the most heartbreaking to me is Stuart and Mathew are good people. For me to have no clue whatsoever.... Yeah, I thought their living arrangements were a little weird.... I thought, yeah, that's a little bit off the edge. But he had these two boys that basically he wasn't raising. Mathew and Stuart did everything for them...took them to school and did things with them. But I had absolutely no idea and I feel incredibly stupid. I'm really sorry I didn't notice anything. Eccentric? Narcissistic? High maintenance? Yeah. But some of the stuff that has come out.... I'm really sorry I didn't notice anything."

When detectives asked Darla if she knew that Mathew and Kimmy were married, she said that she had not been aware of it, but that when it came out in the news, Maria Edwards confirmed it for her.

Darla said that although Scott told her L'Auberge Casino gave him a black Mercedes to drive because he was a television personality, she suspected the loan had more to do with his heavy gambling habits. His Player's Card revealed he spent many hours playing his two favorite slot machines, hoping to win a jackpot.

"I think in his mind he was a bigger celebrity than he actually was," Darla said.

She described Scott's behavior toward Stuart as condescending. When she asked him how, as a pastor, he could treat Stuart so badly, he brushed her off, saying, "That's just the way we communicate."

"With Mathew, he would say *please* and *thank you,*" Darla said. "Mathew was a very gracious person. At Scott's last birthday party, at the Casino, Mathew kept giving Scott presents to the point that other guests were embarrassed. Scott opened six or more gifts from Mathew, all of them Waterford crystal." Darla had watched Mathew's face show visible relief when Scott was pleased. "There was definitely an adoration on Mathew's part for Scott," Darla said.

She described both Mathew and Stuart as very protective of and attentive to the two boys. "While Scott was the figurehead father, he certainly was not the Daddy," Darla said. Stuart was in charge of the children's church activities at the 13:34 Church, and at the end of the services, when he brought them in to join the congregation, he would take the youngest child down front and hand him off to Scott. But little Poh always wanted to go back immediately to Stuart. He didn't want to be up front with Scott. According to Darla, "Poh was not happy with Scott. He wanted Mathew or Stuart."

On the day Darla sat down with the Iberville Parish Sheriff's detectives, the news media reported Mathew had shown some movement indicating signs of brain activity.

On the morning of Friday, September 5, Kimberly Rogers went to the hospital with her boyfriend, presented what she claimed was a valid marriage license from Las Vegas showing that she and Mathew Hodgkinson were married, and signed an order to have him removed from life support.

He was taken off at 10:35 a.m.

Across the Mississippi River from Baton Rouge, Maria Edwards arrived at the Iberville Parish Sheriff's Office accompanied by her attorney, Chris Alexander. Finally, at 11:18 a.m., nine days after the shooting, Iberville Sheriff's deputies began their interview with Maria as Mathew lay dying.

Maria's attorney, Chris Alexander, had also figured in the Mike Walker campaign against Mayor Holden. Alexander had represented a sheriff's deputy in Oklahoma who had lived in Baton Rouge at one time and who returned to make scurrilous statements against the Mayor in the middle of the campaign. The man claimed he had received two Purple Hearts, a claim he could never prove before returning to Oklahoma, seemingly discredited. *Geeze...another coincidence that someone involved in Walker's campaign was also involved in the Scott Rogers case?*

Mathew Hodgkinson died at 12:55 p.m. on Friday, September 5. He was never reunited with his loving family, who had grieved so deeply over losing him to Scott more than 20 years earlier.

Kimberly Rogers' move apparently caught by surprise the Iberville Parish officials who were still investigating the case. There was no word from hospital officials on the steps they took, if any, to confirm the validity of the marriage license, which gave Kimberly control of Mathew's medical treatment.

"For all practical purposes, this shuts down my investigation," said Iberville Parish Prosecutor Clayton, upon the announcement of Mathew's death.

Ethan helped us get contact information for Mathew's family so that Allyson could call them. I wondered if they would hear the news since the U.K. media were following the story so closely. Allyson wanted to call them and we thought she was the best choice to deliver such heartbreaking news with compassion for the son they had lost again. Their only request was that Mathew not be buried with Scott. Kimberly reportedly had both Scott and Mathew cremated.

In the days following the shooting, Scott Rogers' former wife Mandie, described by those who know her as stoic and unemotional, visited her daughter Kimberly in Baton Rouge.

Victims wondered how she could have lived with Scott Rogers in the house where the abuse took place without knowing of his crimes. They wondered how she could let him take her daughter to another country so far away from her. But the Academy students had watched Scott poison Kimberly against her mother. Scott's victims generally described Kimberly as a brat in those days, often threatening to report them to Scott if they didn't do what she wanted. To humiliate the boys, Scott would walk past them in dancing class and pull down their pants to make the other students laugh, or walk up to them and pinch their nipples so they cried out in pain. As a little girl, Kimberly felt she could get away with the same antics her father did and joined in the ridicule of her father's students. They had no doubt that when Scott left the U.K., Kimberly would go with him. She was in every way her father's daughter.

DNA tests on the rough surfaces of the gun used to shoot Scott and Mathew revealed a mixture of DNA from at least two individuals, one major contributor and one minor contributor. As expected, Scott Rogers and Mathew Hodgkinson could not be excluded as contributors.

But there was also DNA from a third individual, inconsistent with the DNA profiles of Scott and Mathew.

The DNA profile obtained from a swab of the gun magazine revealed a mixture of three individuals, one major contributor and two minor contributors. The Louisiana State Police Crime Lab report provided no conclusions about the identity of the third individual. *Who else had handled the gun used to kill Scott and Mathew?*

Fingerprint tests indicated that Mathew had been the only person to handle the letters on the nightstand beside Scott's bed.

After Mathew's death, federal authorities announced they were closing their investigation, while the Iberville Parish Sheriff said his investigation would remain open pending autopsy results and a crime lab analysis of the computers and cell phones from Rogers' home. In January 2015, the Iberville Parish Sheriff's Office responded to the BBC that it had closed the investigation after the searches revealed no other victims.

The Suffolk Police in the U.K. also closed its investigation without any further comment.

Jake and Ethan both theorized that the suicide notes were Scott's thoughts, but that Mathew had written and signed them. It seemed odd that Scott left no note to Kimberly or his 10-year-old son, while Mathew had written to both. But Jake and Ethan thought the notes were more than likely Scott's words and that Kimberly would know that. They believed the note from Mathew to Kimberly describing the marriage proposal sounded like Scott, always concocting a dramatic scene, like the marriage proposal in front of the Christmas tree. Perhaps he was painting a scenario that would keep Kimberly from getting into trouble with immigration. They kept reminding me that Scott would have orchestrated everything about his own death, just as he had orchestrated Kimmy's sham marriage to Mathew.

Psychologists and social workers familiar with the case have called the murder-suicide pact one of the cruelest exploits Scott Rogers ever imposed on Mathew. Since he was 12 years old, Mathew had lived under Scott's control, even turning against his parents to remain with him. When the time came for Scott's final curtain call, he chose to make Mathew shoot him in the head. This meant first killing the man to whom Mathew was completely devoted—the man he had known as a father figure, a lover, and even a father-in-law—the most influential person in his life. Then once that act was complete, Mathew had to turn the gun on himself, without the support of the person he loved most to help him get through it.

When confronted by Scott with a similar request to die together, Stuart knew it was time to leave. He not only had no feelings of love or devotion left for Scott, but he had increasingly come to dislike him. Faced with Scott's death wish, Stuart chose life.

"Scott was never able to be honest about what he had done," Stuart explained. "It took me six months of building up my courage to have that conversation with him, and he ended it in just a heartbeat. Over the years, when I would try to bring it up, it wasn't humorous to him, but there was a lightness. I was aware that he never appreciated what he had done for what it was. Until he could at least say the words, 'I'm sorry for how we started,' this was not over. That's what I wanted from him—an acknowledgement for how we started. At a minimum, that's what I wanted."

But Stuart would not get that concession.

Ten years after coming to Baton Rouge, Scott Rogers' past finally caught up with him. And instead of facing his accusers— or apologizing for his crimes as Stuart had hoped he would—he chose a coward's death, an end he preferred over the loss of control he would have experienced had he gone to prison. Rather than relinquish the power he so desperately craved, Scott chose a manipulative, narcissistic death that also claimed the life of one of his victims.

Following the shooting, Maria Edwards resigned as a pastor of the 13:34 Church and as a board member, telling the board she was doing so on the advice of her attorney. She also relinquished her role as executor of Scott Rogers' estate to Kimmy.

Scott's death freed his victims in the U.K. from the fear they had lived with for over 20 years—the fear that Scott would retaliate against them for leaving him by hurting those they loved most, their own families. His death also freed them from the horror of knowing he was repeating the steps he had taken in the U.K.—bringing little boys into his home and under his control through adoption and fostering. It freed them from the nightmare that other children could have their innocence stolen, their very souls crushed, and in some cases their bodies as well.

The Boys of Bury

JAKE *in his own words*

England
2015

Scott was a master manipulator and a monster...there is no better way to describe it. The world is a better place without that monster hurting any more children.

Scott had a code which you were supposed to adhere to... it took me some time to become my own self again...to find myself again. I was treated for Post-Traumatic Stress Disorder because of the abuse I went through. I don't sleep... I wake up with night terrors.

I was trapped in a nightmare as a child and young adult. I had no means of escape and nowhere to go.

I finally escaped.

CHAPTER FIFTY-FIVE

THE MEN FROM BURY

In March 2015, I sat down, individually, with three of Scott Rogers' child sex abuse victims in Bury St. Edmunds in the U.K. to discuss their life under his control. Tim regrets he will never have the opportunity to face Scott in court again, this time as an adult. Clearly frustrated, he knows that Scott Rogers escaped justice. A second prosecution of Rogers would have been his only satisfaction. As soon as the grand jury in Baton Rouge indicted Scott—presumably on charges related to fraud for falsifying immigration and other legal documents—Tim planned to file his own charges in the U.K. for sexual abuse of a child. And although he did not know it at the time, he would have been joined by Jake and Ethan, who had also committed to pressing charges. Tim's case against Scott would have been even stronger.

Ironically, Tim lived in Baton Rouge for a short time before Scott's arrival and is familiar with Cortana Mall, where Scott's TV studio was located.

He is honest about the difficulties he has experienced as a result of the abuse. He has divorced twice, without sharing what happened to him with either wife. He recognizes that he has problems when he feels anyone is exercising any control over him. To make his current relationship work, he is determined to be honest and open about the abuse and its impact on his life, and in fact, his girlfriend accompanied him to meet me. Her support is clearly helpful to him. I watched her begin to relax as he became more comfortable talking with me. Tim believes Scott hid money away, either in the U.S. or back in the U.K. He wanted to make a claim against it, but navigating the legal system between two countries is not easy. "I don't care how much it is, I want to take something from that man because of what he took from me," he told me. When I returned from the U.K., Mary Jane and I connected him with an attorney who concluded that U.S. statutes of limitation would make it difficult for him to succeed.

While most of the students, including Jake and Ethan, believe that Scott bullied Mandie into turning a blind eye to his evil behavior, Tim feels she bears some responsibility for the horrors that took place in her house. He feels she should have questioned Scott's cuddling and sleeping with the boys while she and Kimberly were banished to the upstairs of the house. Since Mandie still teaches dance classes around Bury, Tim believes she deserves scrutiny, so that other children do not suffer, in her presence, a fate similar to his.

In Bury, Ethan took me to see where the Academy had been located in the back of the town's train station. The space the Academy occupied has been closed for over 20 years, and most people have forgotten about Scott and his trial. As Ethan and I stood shoulder to shoulder, looking in through a window now covered with wire, he spoke quietly, "This was Scott's office. This was the first place I was abused." *It's just a small dirty room now.* I turned quickly and walked away from the window, hoping Ethan would, too. *Don't look back, Ethan.*

It had been 20 years since he had seen that room, although he had driven by the Academy in the years before, at times parking his car nearby to sit and stare at the building. *We are here…at the place where it began. If we don't respond to it…if we treat it like the rundown place it is now, we can somehow take away its power to bring Ethan back to that day.* At least, that's what I thought.

My trip in March 2015 was the first time I had spoken to Jake, whom Ethan had protected from exposure, and it was the first time he and Ethan had seen each other in 20 years. We were invited to Jake's home, where we met his beautiful wife and children, clearly the reason he has recovered so well and was able, finally, to come forward to protect other children.

In his own children's playroom, Jake has a lighted cabinet full of Marvel comic superhero figures—Iron Man, Spider Man, The Incredible Hulk, Wolverine, Captain America, The Avengers. These are the comic book characters whose stories helped Jake survive while living with Scott. As a little boy, enduring the horrible physical, sexual, and psychological abuse Scott inflicted on him every day, Jake imagined he would need super powers to escape the torture. He often thought about killing Scott, but realized that would only get him into trouble. So as he read his comic books, he drew inspiration from the superheroes, who helped keep him strong. His favorites were the superheroes who conquered through adversity, against all odds. He knew their powers were his path to freedom.

As an adult, he has quite a collection, now providing a cool backdrop for his own children's playroom, while at the same time reminding him that sometimes we get inspiration from unusual places. And they give us the strength to endure.

Jake showed Ethan and me a box of random objects he had kept from his time at the Academy—some letters from Scott he had turned over to his attorney in the U.K. to help stop Scott's stalking him, old photos, newspaper clippings about the Academy. Neatly folded on top of the letters was a faded blue Houston Astros t-shirt. "This was the shirt I was wearing when I finally escaped for good," he said picking it up. "I just felt like keeping it."

Jake told a story that explains how Scott gained control over the boys. Looking at me, he said, "I hope you never experience this, but if you're ever hit in the face very hard, everything goes white and you can't see anything."

He told us about riding in the car with Scott when he was a young boy when, out of the blue, Scott hit him as hard as he could. Jake saw stars and kept trying to regain his focus. When he could see again, his lap was soaked with bright red blood as it poured out of his mouth and nose. Scott was screaming at him, "You made me do this! This is all your fault!"

As a young boy, 10 or 11 years old, Jake believed him. All he wanted was for Scott to tell him what he had done to upset him so that he would never do it again. He couldn't understand why Scott didn't just tell him. He would promise anything to avoid displeasing him again....

As an adult, Jake knows that Scott never told him because it wasn't Jake's fault. He never did anything to deserve Scott's abuse. The only person to blame...the only one at fault, was Scott.

In addition to spending time talking and sharing his experience with us, Jake had also written about finally finding Scott. Helped by years of speaking with professionals, he eloquently told of the horrors and abuse he faced while living with Scott Rogers, just as he had in the radio interview only 21 hours after the shooting. I have met six former Academy students, and it is always Jake they ask about first, remembering him as a kind young boy with amazing talent. In hindsight, they realize he was always very quiet. They all believe his abuse was the most severe, and admire his resilience. *But Jake has found his voice....*

Ethan can write about his youth with the humor and mischief he had shown as a little boy growing up in Bury, the same personality that made him popular with his classmates. But when it came to writing anything related to Scott, he filled several lines of the page with X's before recounting another childhood adventure. After a social worker's advice that talking to me would be easier for Ethan than writing, Ethan and I spent three days walking the streets of Bury St. Edmunds, talking about that time in his life, the Academy and the other students, before sitting down to talk about his personal experiences. Finally, Ethan spoke at length to me about what his 20-year journey to find Scott Rogers meant to him. It was painful to see the anguish and the impact his search has had on his life, his tears spilling from his watery blue eyes down his cheeks. But to remember that conversation for its agony does not do his journey justice. It was a moment of amazing triumph...a time to celebrate one man's remarkable quest to right a wrong. Ethan had completed his journey and was no longer a victim of one evil man's crimes against him as a young boy. He was no longer broken. I believe he was healed, his tears washing away the last remaining remnants of his fury.

Five months after that incredible visit, Ethan took the transcript of his interview and finally wrote about his journey. Those years of writing poetry and song lyrics, as an escape from the abuse, now gave him the ability to paint a beautiful picture with words.

Only Jake and Ethan can complete their own stories.

C H A P T E R   F I F T Y - S I X

JAKE

In his own words

I would like to begin by sharing my deepest thanks and appreciation for everyone involved in revealing the truth about Scott Rogers. Thank you, especially the agent I spoke to in the U.S., for believing in the few of us who were speaking up. You were so supportive and understanding of my situation that it made me feel empowered and safer in speaking about my abuse. You helped to break the cage of fear, shame, and terror that I had always been living under. Most of all, I would like to thank the one man who was brave enough to step forward, speak up, and start the investigation into Scott Rogers. He was a victim and survivor of Scott's abuse, too, but also the catalyst in his ultimate demise. I am proud to call him a friend.

To write a description of Scott Rogers as a person is very difficult; I will attempt this by using the analogy of a mask. Scott Rogers wore a mask and disguise; he created a beautiful façade for himself, his mask was shown to everyone, it conveyed a charitable man, a spiritual religious leader, a kind and caring television host who helped the community, a man who was selfless and fostered children. Under the mask he was hiding as a vile pedophile who entrapped, sexually abused, physically abused, and tortured boys. The only people to see under the mask were the boys he abused. He even tried to fool himself into believing he was a good person, but deep down he knew what he was doing was criminal and morally abhorrent.

My experience of Scott Rogers was in the U.K., where he wore the mask of a well-respected Elder from a local church, a dance teacher, and someone who taught and nurtured young people. What he was actually doing was preying on young boys who were in disadvantaged situations.

I was placed with Scott Rogers and his wife by the courts and social services in the U.K. when I was around 11 or 12 years old. Initially he always seemed very caring and kind. Gradually over the first few months of being fostered by Scott Rogers, the sexual and physical abuse began and I was helplessly trapped with my abuser. It is almost impossible to rationally explain why I was unable to speak out about my abuse when I was a boy because the manipulation, threats, physical violence, and conditioning used on me were so constant and in depth. Everyone believed in the mask Scott was wearing, and I was only a child. I was abused in every way possible by Scott over around 10 years. I tried to escape three times and was always returned to him by the authorities. I feel most of the reason I was unable to speak out was because he always made me believe that the abuse I was suffering was *my* fault! He truly conditioned me as a young boy to believe that somehow *I* had *made* him do these things to me. I felt such shame, terror, and confusion at my situation, and Scott used every manipulative tool at his disposal. I was beaten, brainwashed, conditioned, shamed, tortured, and raped over the years to maintain my silence.

I was also conditioned and taught by Scott how I was to behave in front of other people. I had to try to maintain a happy disposition and act as if everything was "normal." Everything I did was watched and monitored by him and scrutinized. The punishment, should I not adhere to how Scott expected me to behave, was brutally severe, both physically and sexually. As mentioned before, I was beaten often—he had a special stick and belt to use. I was strangled into unconsciousness, injured many, many times, and if his sexual advances were refused, this would lead to violent rape as a form of "teaching" me how I should behave. I realize now that the mental abuse I suffered was almost as equally damaging and long lasting. I would be subjected to days at a time locked in a room with Scott while I endured a barrage of his talking at me, questioning me, confusing me, and brainwashing me into submission if he was unhappy with my behavior. Even if he seemed happy with me, the mental abuse was constant.

As an adult I realize that Scott had to force his victims to behave in this way so that he could carry on with his abuse without suspicion or discovery. When I was a child he made himself omnipotent to me; his hold over me, and I'm sure his other victims, was absolute. Scott behaved as if he was a God; he always said what he did was right and everyone else was wrong. This is how he justified his crimes to himself, in my opinion. As a child I could never have a chance against such a complicated, structured, and evil abuser. Everyone fell for his disguise, manipulation, and devious subterfuge.

It wasn't until I was a bit older that I realized Scott was abusing other boys. In my naivety as a child, I hadn't thought that they were in the same situation. We never spoke to each other about the abuse we suffered at the time, and Scott made sure we never spoke of it and never developed friendships.

When I finally managed to escape from Scott, I ran as far and as fast as I could with no money and started a life for myself. It was very difficult, because he hunted and blackmailed and threatened me, obviously to try to get me back under his control. I managed to keep safe from him this time and gradually got on with my life, completely cutting all ties with Scott or anyone who knew him. I always lived with the fear that if I ever spoke about what happened to me, my life would be destroyed. This was still the fear that Scott had instilled in me over many years.

I managed to have a successful career; I got married and had a family. It was a wonderful time, having my freedom and a life of my own. I was living an incredibly happy and full life, but there was always a nagging fear in the back of my mind that Scott was still at large and was either going to try and destroy my life or was destroying and abusing others as he had me.

I spoke to no one I knew from my time fostered by Scott until last year, when I was contacted by one of the other boys Scott abused. He told me he had found that Scott was living in Baton Rouge and that he had adopted two young boys. When I heard what was happening in Baton Rouge, how Scott had again adopted a boy and was attempting to adopt more, how he had become a local television presenter and was well respected and in a position of influence within his own church, it was like a nightmare resurfacing.

I could not sit back and do nothing when I knew Scott was continuing his abuse and manipulation. When I became a parent many years ago, the full horror of what I went through as a child seemed to hit me with a new force, but it also gave me huge strength and amplified my protective nature. Scott had travelled to the United States and continued his abuse, and I would not run away from my past fear anymore. I decided it was time to stand up and be counted and tell my story to my friend here in the U.K., and he sent this to the relevant parties in the United States. When the time was right I spoke to the authorities first in the United States and then here in the U.K.

It was my fervent wish that Scott should answer in a court of law for the crimes he committed and for everyone to see him for what he was—a child molester, a tyrant to those he controlled, and a manipulator of many innocent people. As it was, Scott Rogers never faced up to his crimes. He died as he had lived, an evil coward.

CHAPTER FIFTY-SEVEN

ETHAN

In his own words

I'd always thought about it from the very first time it happened to me…the abuse. I'd always thought, I have to put it right. I have to put what's happened right. It was something I thought about every single day, from the start. It was something I lived with all my life. Until now.

I'm not going to describe some gruesome scenes of abuse. I won't talk about it. I will tell you that I was abused for four years, between the ages of 12 and 16. There was mental abuse in the form of manipulation and sexual abuse on a very regular basis. Before the abuse there was a talking session…if you didn't say *yes* to hours of questioning he would get very angry. I was brainwashed. There were times when I thought I would never get away from it. I was afraid. I was lonely. I was confused. It was fucking scary.

I was 16 when I finally managed to leave the Academy. I left just after the court case. I wanted to be an actor and study at a local college. Scott wanted me to join the Academy College, a school Scott had set up with high fees. It was more of a hoax, no real qualifications at the end. He was angry. He asked me if I wanted to wear a blue coat or a red coat. The blue coat was the Academy and my future life and the red coat was a normal life. At least that's what I got from it. I endured a few hours answering questions and Scott trying to convince me that I should stay. I had a letter my mum had written, about me leaving, and that was what I hung onto. I said that my parents wouldn't let me stay, that they didn't have the money for the Academy College. He was somehow weaker from the court case, he was losing the Academy. I felt stronger. I saw it as my only opportunity to get away from him. I don't know if it was the possibility of speaking with my parents or all the other pressures that were going on, but in the end, he agreed. I felt like someone who had crawled out of an exploding building.

About 18 months later, Jake had escaped and Scott called me in. He sent someone out to collect me. When I visited him he was delirious, confessing to abuse that he had done to Jake. It was like he was on drugs. Like he was a cartoon. Mathew told him to be quiet as Mandie was in the other room, he then started asking me to stay, to go with them, and he was talking about leaving. Selling the house and getting away from everything. When I refused Scott turned, got angry, started verbally attacking me. I darted for the door. That was the last time I saw him.

I didn't tell anyone about what had happened until I was in my early 20s. I spent a few years processing everything that had happened. Understanding why it had happened. I had separated it from my reality—that was the way I dealt with it. When I did finally tell someone it was a massive relief. It's always been a very personal experience that I have had to live with, just like everyone else in the world that has traumas, good and bad experiences. That's life, and this is mine. But I couldn't just forget about it. It was wrong. It was dark. I started thinking— *How do I deal with this? And how do I put this right?* Because I knew that I was broken in some way, and I *had* to fix it. It was more of a spiritual thing than anything else. And it wasn't really just for me. The concern was that I was letting him abuse other children.

It has always troubled me that he would be abusing other children. I think that's a natural thought for most abused children that suddenly find themselves as adults. I wanted to change that. I wanted to stop it. I couldn't just sit back and let that happen. It always intrigued me during my abuse and after, why he thought he could get away with it. Did he not know I would grow up? I never understood that.

The Search

When I reached 23, I had settled into my life. I had a good job, good potential. The Internet was in its infancy when I started searching; it wasn't a constant search, sometimes months would pass, on occasions I would get a tip from someone who would say, Scott was here, or Scott was there, but the leads always went dry. I don't think I would have had a very good strategy back then to deal with it, even if I had found him.

When I turned 30, the search intensified. I didn't want to wait until he was too old to face trial or had abused and terrorised more and more children. The Internet was more advanced, more spiders searching, searching for Scott Rogers. On the day I found him I had changed my search, I knew that Mathew and Stuart were with him, so I searched for them instead. I stumbled across an article online about a hotel they were doing a story on. They were all there, in photos. Wearing bad trousers. They were in Louisiana. I contacted the hotelier, he passed me all the details of where they were, cell phone numbers and emails. I created an email using an anagram of my name, I wrote a poem, on the spot. I don't know why but it felt like the best way to get a message through. A message I knew that he would understand, one that he would have to dig deep to figure out. I wanted him to know that I had found him. I wanted him to know that he had failed.

The next day I arrived at their website, it was under construction. Completely closed down. It stayed like this for days, then months. I figured he got my message. But what could I do? I didn't have the money, the contacts to pursue a legal case—all I had was information about what he had done to me. How do you stop a paedophile who lives 5000 miles away? I contacted the office number, but always answerphone. I knew where he was. Baton Rouge.

The reality was, I couldn't stop him. All I had was my experience of what he did to me. I didn't have the means, the power, and the contacts. I did nothing. I did nothing for five years. It took that long for me to turn up. I had advanced as a person. I was ready to face all the fears. I was sick of the secrets. I wasn't prepared to live my life and do nothing about it. These feelings that I felt, these thoughts that went through my mind didn't belong to me. They belonged to Scott and he can have them back. He can have them all back.

I knew there were other victims. Tim, Jake, Stuart, Mathew, Andy. I knew he would have access to children. The one thing Scott always had on me was a secret. A secret he was terrified of. That's what they do. Trap you and keep you quiet. All I needed to do was to expose him, contact the police in his community, warn people of the dangers. That would be enough for people to ask the question. That was all I needed to do. That's all any victim really needs to do. But it's the hardest thing in the world. I was ready and I could do something about it. All I needed was a contact. Someone I could alert of the dangers. I was searching again, Scott's website was live again, I made a list of all the people Scott had built relationships with, whether on the show or in other articles his company featured in. I was considering sending a mail shot to all of them with the stories of the court case. It just didn't seem like the best idea. I had to be cautious, anything could happen. I didn't know how Scott would retaliate against me. It was so unpredictable. It felt like a massive risk. I couldn't resist it. I knew this was the right time, everything was in place. I decided not to send to the multiple people I had found.

Instead on August 28, 2013, I stumbled upon an article by a Rannah Gray. Rannah's company had been slandered by none other than Scott Rogers. It was late in the afternoon; it just turned 5 p.m. Here I was. Standing at the cliff, nothing but darkness. As I drafted my email, I knew. This was the beginning. As I pressed *send* I felt like I leapt off the edge of a cliff into the darkness alone. As I fell, a hand caught me. A hand caught me and pulled me into the light.

Rannah

I don't know if I found Rannah, or Rannah found me. That was how it was. Rannah responded after two days. It was a relief when she did, she was very concerned, worried about the children, concerned about the community. Communicating with Rannah was very easy, we had an immediate trust and information started moving very quickly. At first, I felt like I was throwing in a grenade, exposing the truth and walking away. At first I thought I would just need to alert Rannah, allow her to pass on the information to the police and that was that. That would have been all I needed to do to alert people of the dangers. But it didn't happen like that, Rannah had taken the information and started exploring every possible angle. I soon discovered that Scott had adopted a son, now 10 years old, and was finalising on another adoption of a boy, 2, in just a few months. Then there was the church, and the fact that Matt and Stuart were still with him. As it turned out Rannah was a much respected member of the community, with powerful friends, right in the town where Scott was. She was my eyes and ears. Rannah was like my grips. I could start to climb the mountain. I wasn't alone anymore. Rannah knew more about me than anyone else in just a few weeks. My secrets exposed. I could tell her anything, I completely trusted her.

Rannah was coming up with ideas and routes to get to court that I would never have thought of. Within a few weeks Rannah had put a team together, not just any team, Rannah had some incredible contacts, all willing to help a stranger they barely knew. I don't have the words for the kindness and bravery of the whole team. We had a top lawyer, his associate, a paralegal and pretty soon the U.S. federal government investigating my information, my story. Not once did they question my truth, at least not to me. We started to build a case. My role was to supply information.

Rannah and her team worked tirelessly over the coming months. I conducted Skype interviews with the federal government, gave my statement, painted the picture of what Scott was, what he had done. What he was capable of. As the case continued and you started to see the picture of what Scott was doing, it was scary. Baton Rouge was like his business model of Bury St. Edmunds—he had befriended local judges, law enforcement, governors; he had started a church, started adopting children. He had requested more boys from the fostering agency. He was gearing up to something dark, something big.

Everything I wanted, all those boxes I wanted to check in terms of freeing myself, saving children, and giving my family answers at the end of the journey was starting to happen. It was going to be hard, last a long time, but I would have the chance to stop him and get justice for me and other victims.

I started feeling really empowered from the time I contacted Rannah. Rannah wasn't selected from a long list of possible applicants. I just stumbled across her. Everything just felt natural. There were no barriers. It just felt strangely familiar. From when Rannah came back to me a day or two after I sent the email, it was a feeling that it was supposed to happen.

At last, going through this journey, I just felt like I was starting to heal. It was like I was going back and I was putting it right. I felt that within myself, and I could feel myself growing from just going through this process of talking. Because I had never spoken to anyone so much about it.

Going through that with Rannah in which she was asking, *OK, what's your part in this? What's your motivation in this? Give us some information about this court case you're telling us about.* So now I was going through and talking about it in great detail with somebody who understood the man, who understood the abuse and understood what we needed to do.

I couldn't ever thank Rannah and her team enough for the bravery they showed. For standing with me. They risked everything. For a stranger with a story. Who does that? I have never met anyone with that kind of integrity, with that kind of kindness, with that courage. I am forever in her debt.

Jake

I needed more information. The investigators needed more. I had always thought about Jake. I knew that I couldn't take this team forward just by myself. I knew I needed more information and that was the next stage, I had to bring another victim in to share this experience with me, for them to find some answers to what had happened. I'd often thought about Jake, even though we were not great friends at the Academy. We were both in our bubbles. Looking back on how Jake was then, we were just trapped in bubbles and we were just trying to survive it. You could tell that Jake was alone. Mathew was alone. I was alone. Stuart was alone. Looking back on it now, you can see these children dealing with it, and we probably all dealt with it in very similar ways in terms of just blocking things out, separating from reality.

One of the reasons I thought about Jake was because during my abuse, Jake was brought into the scenario, which says a lot about Scott's primary abuse of his victims. While he was abusing me, Scott told me that he had done things with Jake. But also during my abuse, he would try to get me to fantasize about Jake in the abuse. So Jake was the only one I could be sure of, apart from Stuart, who I just knew was being abused because of this interaction with Scott and him telling me about it. The reason I knew Stuart was abused, was the way he came out as gay was a big clue. I thought, Scott's convinced him that he was gay like he had tried to convince me that I was gay.

So I wanted to bring Jake in, and I knew the amount of information he had was tenfold what I had, and I knew he had gone through a lot more abuse because of his situation compared to mine. I had a family, I went home at night. I had a support network. Even though my family didn't know it at the time, I drew from that strength of having a family. Because I separated my life into two—and I was able to draw strength from that and I was able to get away when I did, where Jake was in a completely different situation. So to bring Jake in, which wasn't obviously easy, I wanted to bring him into my experience and just take him with me, I wanted him to feel liberated from the abuse.

At first he didn't trust me. He was still scared of what Scott could do with him. I explained what I had done, what Scott was doing. Jake was happy to pass me information but he didn't want to talk or be involved other than that. I wanted to protect Jake. I didn't want him to be dragged in if he didn't need to be. So I kept his identity a secret, passed all his information on.

He was a huge part of the investigation, and we wouldn't have done as much if it wasn't for Jake's input. We worked together gathering information, tracking other possible victims.

It was really positive for Jake and me, because he was a victim and I was a victim and we were communicating again, and that was part of our recovery. Because not only could I talk to someone who had been through the same thing, I could talk to someone who *had been through the same thing*—with the same person, in the same place, at the same time.

Over the coming months Jake grew more and more confident. Like me. He was going through the healing process. We became good friends, had a similar sense of humor. He was a great wingman to bounce ideas off. I always had a lot of respect for Jake. He was someone that had endured years of abuse, got out. Started a new life and didn't let Scott destroy him. That takes a lot of strength. That was the kind of friend I needed.

The End.

I was preparing for everything that was coming. Having to go to the police in the U.K., going to court, telling my family. I knew that it was going to be a long process, but I had to do it. This was what the whole journey was about.

Then March, April, May got exciting because we knew that things were going to happen—that the children were going to be saved. I guess all the way through, really, if we could get those children out, that would have been enough, because he would have been exposed. These children wouldn't have been abused. And I would have felt at least I did something to help some children. At least I didn't do nothing, it was really important to me that those children did not go through what we went through, and that we stopped that.

Then it all started kicking off in August. *It's going to happen, it's going to happen.* We were starting to make good progress. Then the authorities went in on the 15th of August and took the children away and that day was incredible. We'd done that step. And if that's the only thing that happens, we've done that. The next step was making sure the kids didn't go back into his custody, which meant me putting a statement through. That was difficult because Jake was sort of whispering in my ear that we're messing with the hornet's nest. *This is going to happen if you do this and if you do that.* I was trying to persuade Jake to do a statement, too, but he didn't want to because of the risk to him and his family, and Scott finding out that Jake was involved. These worries were coming back to me as well, and it was like, *Just do the statement.* Because if you don't do the statement, those kids were going to be back in his care very quickly. At some point, I just drew the line and I just did whatever I had to do. Then Jake had a change of heart and made the statement too.

Then I thought, *How is Scott going to react now? How is he going to fight back?* And between the 15th and the 27th, we didn't really know. We knew that this process was working, and we were getting somewhere, and then it was "Let's see what happens with the court case." I was thinking, *When he is charged with the fraud and he is maybe spending a year in prison in the States, then we move on to the next stage, Scott facing his victims in the U.K.* This was scary for me because now, it was bringing it home. I was facing up and confronting all the fears I had when I was younger. I contacted the detective at Bury Police, the original officer on the case. I spoke off the record, told the officer what had happened. Asked questions, got all the options together, ready to press charges. And then, on the actual day of the shooting, it was like a white flash had gone off. At first, I couldn't register what had happened. It was like being in a daze... I couldn't fully comprehend what had occurred, as I read the article which came through on my phone, at first it was confusing, two shot. *Who's dead?* I thought. *Who's been shot?* Mathew, Scott, what's happened!? And it sunk in—Mathew had shot Scott and then shot himself. Of course, that's what it read. But I knew. Scott had Mathew shoot him and in doing so, Scott murdered Mathew, that's the truth.

That was a massive regret. I'm really sad about what happened. I hoped that he would pull through. I wanted him to escape, like Stuart. I wanted him to be free. He was a victim. Mathew endured a lifetime of mental and physical abuse. I remember first meeting Mathew at school, before I was a dancer. He was completely alone. I remember picking up on those vibes when I was younger. He was bullied at school for being a dancer. When I joined the Academy he was one of the top dancers. Scott had completely got inside his head. Smothered his mind. Mathew was lost to the world. To himself. He completely relied on Scott throughout his life. He didn't have two realities like I did. He only had one; that had become normal for him. In the end Scott had such a control over him, he could persuade him to do anything.

It was a hot day in August, everything was so surreal. In the heat of the moment I needed to get away, so I went for a run. It was always a good way to think to clear my head. As I jogged along country roads, a thousand thoughts running through my mind…I realized. These weren't the actions of a 36-year-old man. These were the actions of a 12-year-old boy. He wasn't weak, he understood the philosophy of what had happened. He knew what he needed to do. I slowed up and found a spot by a tree, and I remembered—I remembered a long walk home, after I was first abused as a 12-year-old child—lost, scared, confused, and looking for answers. I took an hour to complete a 10-minute walk home that night. I was in shock. I had to act quickly before getting home. I needed a plan. I made choices that night which I never faulted. The first was not to tell a soul. The second was to survive it, and the third was to make it right. And in that flash, I felt complete. I felt like I re-visited that kid…I went back for him…walked him home, and I made it right. Just like I promised him I would.

Who gets to do that? Who gets to live that journey? Who gets to fight that? And who gets to fucking win it?

CHAPTER FIFTY-EIGHT

THE HOTWASH

Since Hurricane Katrina exposed America's vulnerability to major natural disasters, members of the national emergency preparedness community have implemented what they refer to as "hotwash," or after-action discussions following major events, to evaluate their performance. These forums identify lessons learned, so that corrective actions can be made before the next event occurs. Any hotwash discussion on the death of Scott Rogers would reveal many unanswered questions and much room for improvement.

The shooting at Scott's house came as a shock—both to those who had observed him only from a distance, and to those in his orbit, those he deceived up close. I recall Jake's description of Scott's mask, and how only the boys he abused knew what was behind it.

But the people inside his house during those final two weeks had listened to his incessant suicide planning and endured his attempts to involve them in his death. They knew what was coming; they could not have been surprised. From our standpoint, we had worried for a year that he might take his life, and we feared he would take others with him. But the finality of it still left everyone reeling.

As is typical of those who plan suicides, Scott and Mathew put their affairs in order, signing over control of Scott's business, updating his will, providing a list of tasks for their survivors.

Mathew's notes included a drawing of his 1stCo office and the location there of documents and files, a list of passwords, and instructions for church and business matters. The personal notes Mathew left for Scott's daughter and son clearly indicated he expected to die.

On October 27, 2014, Kimberly-Anne Mary Scott-Rogers petitioned the 18th Judicial District Court for appointment as independent administrator for the estate of Scott Rogers. She filed a "Detailed Descriptive List" that claimed Scott Rogers' house was valued at $500,000 and he had $15,000 in a checking account. She listed a mortgage in the amount of $346,000 and attorney fees and court costs in the amount of $3,500 as debts. She listed the total value of Scott Rogers' estate at $165,500. [36]

Kimberly, who moved back into her father's house after his death, claimed in her petition that Scott died "intestate," or without a will. *But what about all the references to Scott's will in the notes left behind? Mathew even told Maria where to find it in his office.*

She also provided an affidavit signed by Lexlee Overton and Mandie Elizabeth Rogers swearing that Scott was married only once, to Mandie. It's almost inconceivable that none of the three knows he was married to Diana Palladino, who lived in the house with Mandie and Scott after they divorced and whose home Kimberly shared when Scott and his students relocated to Dallas.

Since Kimberly had moved back into Scott's house during the last two weeks of his life, when he was finalizing his will with great fanfare, it's hard to believe she was not aware of it. She would have been present when he talked about leaving something for Mathew and Stuart in his will before he cut Stuart out. And at the very least, she and her attorneys would have had access to Scott's addendum to his will and Mathew's directions on where to find a copy of the will at the 1stCo studio, since the

---

[36] Succession of Scott Tobius Rogers, 18th Judicial District Court, Parish of Iberville. 6 November 2014.

Iberville Sheriff's office had taken both documents into evidence.

Kimberly swore that Scott died without a will despite the addendum to his will, which states that he had signed his will on Friday, August 22, 2014. The addendum, removing Stuart as his executor, was found with the other notes at the house on the day of the shooting.

It was also rumored that Kimberly was taking steps to gain permanent custody of her adopted brother, who is possibly Scott's only legal heir, regardless of what his will says, since the child's disability would not allow Scott to leave him out of any inheritance.

One year after Mathew's death, an obituary appeared in *The Advocate* which read, "On Friday, September 5, 2014, 'Unkie Mattie' went to his final resting place, with God. Born on January 6, 1978 in the town of Bury St. Edmunds, Mathew was with us for a very short 36 years. In that time he mastered network and server security, Photoshop, videography, and carpentry. He was a self-taught carpenter who did not believe in shying away from a challenge. Never was there such a compassionate and loyal friend, as was found in this man. For 11 years, he served as Manager of 1stCo and Executive Producer of The Around Town TV Show. He is survived by his wife, Kimberly and his best friend Stuart. Among his closest friends were Celeste, Charles & Frances, David and Ladonna. Memorial donations may be made to www.brstar.org."

STAR is the Sexual Trauma Awareness and Response organization in Baton Rouge, originally founded as the Rape Crisis Center.

The following questions and more go unanswered with the deaths of Scott Rogers and Mathew Hodgkinson.

What happened to Scott's will?

It was a tool he used to control those around him—*Who's in my will and who's out?* He said in the notes he left behind that he had updated his will as recently as Friday, August 22, 2014, and he wrote an addendum on Monday, August 25, when he realized that Stuart had left the family. According to those who called on Kimmy in the days and weeks after her father's death, Scott's attorney Lexlee Overton and friend Dana Vutera were helping Kimmy sort through financial matters. In fact, Overton witnessed the document Kimberly presented when asking the court to appoint her administrator for Scott's estate.

Why did Kimberly claim her father had died without a will?
If Scott Rogers left behind any assets, his adopted son is a forced heir, since he has a disability and cannot be excluded from any inheritance, even if Scott had wished to do so. It is the responsibility of the State Department of Child Services to make sure that legal counsel represents the child to protect his rights.

How many shots were fired?
After Maria called 911 and reported hearing "detonations" at the house, she called Darla and reported "They're all dead." She told Darla on the phone and later at the crime scene that she heard a shot, called 911, and heard two more shots while she was still on the phone. Speaking with the 911 operator, she appeared to report that she heard a shot, called 911, then heard another noise.

Why did Scott's lawyer keep police from talking to Maria Edwards at the scene?
After the shooting, Seth Dornier arrived at Scott's house. He had served as Scott Rogers' attorney for the child custody hearing and had notarized the power of attorney that gave Maria control of Scott's estate. He directed Darla O'Connor to keep Maria from speaking with the police at the scene where his client, Scott, had been killed and Maria was potentially a witness. Darla refused. Then, after Maria handed him her phone and Seth spoke with Lexlee Overton, Maria was transported by ambulance to Our Lady of the Lake Regional Medical Center. There, Overton prevented church members from speaking with her. Neither of these attorneys represented Maria when she finally spoke to Iberville Parish Sheriff's deputies, and it is

unclear why they were intent on preventing law enforcement from speaking with her at the crime scene.

Why did Maria Edwards have the power of attorney documents in her possession and why was she anxious that the police not find them?

Maria's behavior at the scene of the crime casts her in a suspicious light. She was eager to retrieve her bag containing the letters, without any explanation to law enforcement, despite their repeated requests to talk to her for over a week. Since she had stated that the documents' purpose was to allow her to conduct business for Scott in the event that he and Mathew were deported, what was the urgency in keeping them away from the police in light of their deaths? Why would a witness to a terrible crime not want to cooperate with the police in their investigation? What was Maria Edwards afraid of?

Who is the third individual whose DNA was on the gun that killed Scott Rogers and Mathew Hodgkinson?

The Louisiana State Police Crime Lab report indicates that the magazine on the gun used to kill Scott and Mathew contained a DNA mixture of three individuals. No conclusion could be made about the identity of the third person.

How long had Scott been dead when Mathew was shot?

Early news reports indicated that Scott's body was stiff when police arrived at the scene, which would mean that he had been dead for some time when Mathew was shot and found alive by emergency medical technicians who arrived at the scene.

Was it a coincidence that Maria finally gave her interview with the Iberville Parish Sheriff's Office at the exact time that Kimberly removed Mathew from life support?

On Friday, September 5, Kimmy had Mathew removed from life support at 10:35 a.m. Maria's interview at the Iberville Parish Sheriff's Office got underway at 11:18 a.m., and Mathew died at 12:55 p.m. Considering that friends of Scott said Maria had been comforting Kimmy in the days following the shooting, and that Maria had refused to talk to the Sheriff's Office for 10 days, the timing is very curious.

What business dealings did Scott have in Malaysia?
    His trips to Malaysia when he ran the Academy included selling young boys for sex. Why was Scott Rogers anxious to finalize the adoption of his second son so he could take both boys to Malaysia? Was the adoption of the two boys, with a request to Child Services for four more boys, a continuation of Scott's trafficking boys in Malaysia?

Where are Scott's assets?
    Just weeks before his death, Scott took out a second mortgage on his house to repay the money 1stCo owed Mimi Fowler, whom Scott befriended when he arrived in Baton Rouge. Mathew left written instructions, however, not to pay her. Yet when Kimmy filed a list of Scott's assets with the court, she listed only the house and $15,000 in cash. Where is the money from the loan? Where is the $20,000 Rolex watch Scott had 1stCo buy him as a 50th birthday present? Where are the guns that were taken into evidence and have value? Where is his jewelry?
    Mathew said in his note to Scott's son that they left money for him. Was it secured? Scott said his will included money for Mathew and Stuart, before he removed Stuart from the will. What happened to those funds?
    Before shutting down the *Around Town Studio* at the Cortana Mall, Kimmy organized a sale and sold everything there, from TV show props to personal items including several baby strollers. One person who stopped by the sale said studio equipment such as lights and cameras sold quickly at drastically reduced prices, while curious buyers picked over memorabilia from the now macabre *Around Town TV Show* set. *What happened to the funds from that sale?*

Did Scott have assets in the U.K.?
    Because some believe he transferred money to and from the U.K., questions remain about whether he had other assets not

listed in Kimmy's petition to serve as administrator of his estate. Is the State of Louisiana protecting any assets that should go to his adopted minor son? Is the son's legal counsel moving to assure Scott's estate is not depleted and that the child's inheritance is protected for his future needs?

The Iberville Sheriff's office left the case open to allow other victims of Rogers' abuse to come forward. After six months, it closed the investigation.

Stuart went home to his family, unsure of how Scott Rogers' past was exposed. His mother called Mary Jane shortly after his return, thanking her profusely for giving her son back to her. A son she had not seen in over 16 years. A son she thought she would never see again.

When Mary Jane let Stuart know that I had been the person one of Scott's victims in the U.K. had contacted, Stuart called immediately to thank me for what I had done.

This is the first time in his life he has been truly on his own and he admits the adjustment is not easy. But Stuart, who has now moved back to Baton Rouge, is taking one day at a time talking to his family every day and trying to build a new life for himself.

In Baton Rouge, attitudes about Scott Rogers have overwhelmingly changed. A few try to ignore his abuse of children on the basis of the good he did, failing to recognize that the purpose of his good acts was to seduce the community into trusting him with its children. But that is the way it is with pedophiles. The favorable image they create for themselves often blinds their followers to the horrible crimes they commit. And Scott Rogers' treatment of his victims fits almost every professional description of a predatory pedophile.

Dr. Ariel Lloyd, who appeared on Scott's final *Around Town TV Show*, describes how sociopaths like Scott gain power over their victims. The children ask themselves, *What can I do to make him happy with me...so maybe he won't hurt me so badly?*

"Sociopaths seek out their vulnerability," she explained, "and it leads to dependency. Scott's favorites were chosen for a specific reason: There was something he could exploit. Maybe he felt they were unloved and he could exploit that and fill in that role. Cult leaders have a knack for doing this. The rituals, the gifts, they know exactly what they can do to get the children on their side."

Dr. Lloyd hopes the Scott Rogers story, by removing the stigma from an open discussion of child sex abuse, makes it easier for victims, especially men, to speak up.

We know from psychologists who work with sex offenders that basic human interaction is a game to child predators. They lack compassion; they feel no guilt. They calculate which families to target and what child to choose. They are experts in creating double lives so that no one suspects them as child predators.

"Why, after all these years, at the age of 36 or 37 years old...why couldn't they leave?" I asked Dr. Lloyd about Mathew and Stuart.

"The familiar evil..." she replied, her voice trailing off. "They were less afraid of the evil they had come to know than they were of the unknown out there in the world."

The Louisiana Department of Children and Family Services still maintains that its records are not subject to public records laws, citing the confidentiality of those who want to foster children. Even though the department recognized a monstrous predator, Scott Rogers, as a hero for fostering and adopting children, it still claims confidentiality—despite the subsequent proof of pedophilia—for all records of his application to foster children.

If we had obtained a copy of that application, we would have instantly known that Rogers lied to get custody of children. Those records do not contain any information about the children, only about the person who seeks to enter into a contract with the State to take care of children for payment. If Scott Rogers' victims—including Ethan, who was looking for him—had access to his application, they could have gone to the State with their information and asked that someone take a closer look before putting children under his control.

The people responsible for protecting children must put into place rules that actually *protect* the children. And we must hold those bureaucrats accountable for their failures to do so.

There will be people in law enforcement and Child Services who realize now that Scott Rogers duped them. There will be those who recognize their failure to protect children. We, the public, however, will never know if those failures were unintentional or a result of willful blindness. We must learn from cases like this so that the next pedophile who courts the bureaucrats, playing to their egos with offers of free publicity, fails in his efforts to seduce them.

The ongoing criminal investigation of child sex abuse in the U.K. has shocked the world. Over the past 20 years, law enforcement covered up horrific abuse and even child murders. Those guilty of this reprehensible crime include people in high-ranking positions in the courts, Parliament, and law enforcement, as well as television and radio personalities. We wonder if Scott was ever involved with any of the BBC personalities who have been charged.

Along with those who fail to protect children, you also find special people—Luke Walker, Allyson Hoffine—willing to step up. They deal with the sordid conduct of sick, depraved people daily and yet continue to function in the world while raising their own families away from the horrors they see daily. They should be proud.

And yet, people will ask them why they take on such terrible work. The answer is simple: to protect children. Instead of feeling squeamish, we should not miss an opportunity to thank them and others who perform similar work. A job protecting children from sexual abuse may be a stressful one, but it's one we must appreciate. We must hold up those who save children as heroes in our communities. As long as we cannot talk about pedophiles who sexually abuse children, our reluctance perpetuates the feelings of guilt and shame that victims feel, making it even harder for them to speak up.

The U.K. has no statute of limitations on child abuse cases. Tim could have pressed charges against Scott a second time without concern of a statute of limitations or an issue of double jeopardy. Scott Rogers knew that if he was arrested in the United States and extradited to the United Kingdom to face his victims, who were talking to law enforcement about his crimes, their testimony would put him in jail for a long time, if not for the rest of his life. He also knew that life in prison is not easy for pedophiles.

I learned that before Ethan contacted me, he had collected a list of 19 email addresses for people he found linked online to Scott Rogers in Baton Rouge. He had at one time considered emailing all of them copies of the news stories about Scott's trial to see what reaction he might get but had never acted on that idea. Included on that list were several WAFB-TV contacts: News Anchor Donna Britt, General Manager Sandy Breland, General Sales Manager Vicki Kellum, Research and Programming Manager Kathy Kedroske (also listed as a station contact for Children's Programming), Director of Digital Media Brent Ledet, Chief Engineer Dale Russell, Art Director Cheryl Craig, and the general station address for press releases.

WAFB is the Baton Rouge television station that carried *The Around Town TV Show.*

The email list also included Mayor Kip Holden's general office account; Jamie Karam, with the Louisiana Assistive Technology Access Network; Julie Preau, with Guaranty Broadcasting; Karen Kennedy with the Arthritis Association of Louisiana; Hollywood Casino; Davis Rhorer, Executive Director of Baton Rouge's Downtown Development District; the President of the Baton Rouge Tea Party; Folk Alliance International, a non-profit organization promoting folk music; Peggy Sweeney-McDonald, producer of the *Meanwhile Back at Café Du Monde* live food monologue show for which Scott served as emcee; KALB-TV in Alexandria, Louisiana; and the Louisiana Department of Children and Family Services.

When *The Advocate* newspaper named the top ten news stories of 2014 in Baton Rouge, the shooting of Scott Rogers was listed as the #3 story of the year. His death was parodied in the Spanish Town Mardi Gras parade, one of Baton Rouge's biggest celebrations, when his photo adorned two floats that mocked his offenses. When the parade rolled on February 14 in 2015, its theme was "St. Valentine's Day Masquerade;" floats featured the parade's signature pink flamingos and irreverent depictions of local celebrities. "The Masquerade is Over" was the title of one float that displayed Scott's photo and the words "#Son-in-lover." Another featured Scott as "St. Pedophilia" wrapped in crime scene tape with the caption, "Ran but couldn't hide...."

Scott Rogers had become a pathetic joke. Perhaps the mockery helped people face the truth: He had fooled Baton Rouge. He had kept his dark past secret.

Though he had once rubbed shoulders with politicians and community leaders on two continents, Scott Rogers' legacy as a child predator was now secure.

CHAPTER FIFTY-NINE

FREE

The hero in this story is Ethan, who sent one email to one person in another part of the world and a surprising friendship began. And because that one person believed him, others came to believe him, too. Ethan made it clear from the first time we talked that we shouldn't worry about him. He just wanted to make sure that Scott Rogers was exposed for what he was—a child predator—so he couldn't hurt more children.

"It takes strength to endure abuse. It takes courage to stop it."

When Scott Rogers quoted this line from a clichéd poem on his weekend TV show, he had no way of knowing the one person he feared most—Ethan—would have the courage to stop him from abusing children. The conclusion of that anonymous poem:

May the wind carry a voice that tells you,
There is a friend sitting in another corner of the world.

After meeting Ethan and Jake, I believe they will finally put the pain of their ordeal behind them without the fear that Scott will hurt them, or worse, their children. They will never forget, but they are finally free of their emotional prison, of what Jake called the "cage of fear."

Tim, on the other hand, has not found closure with Scott's death. He feels cheated of the opportunity to set the record straight about the terrible lies Scott's U.K. and U.S. attorneys told about him.

When I met Jake, he said something to me before we even sat down to talk, something I will remember for the rest of my life. "You were the only person who stood up for us, and you didn't even know us," he said. I don't write this to pat myself on the back, but to let people know that anyone can do what I did. If adult survivors of child sex abuse have the courage to come forward, we must stand with them. That's the only way to stop those who commit such terrible crimes. The next child a pedophile targets could be anyone's child.

Ethan has exciting ideas for business ventures and it's clear he will be successful in life. He also has that someone *sitting in another corner of the world* who is proud to call him friend.

"You have everything it takes to accomplish whatever you want in life," I texted him after our meeting in the U.K., on my way to Heathrow Airport for the long flight back to Baton Rouge. "With this behind you, the sky's the limit. And I know you will do great things because you lead with your heart…and it's a good heart."

"Thanks, Rannah," he texted back. "I won't let you down."

You never have, I thought.

About four months after the shooting, Nathan passed away. I know he felt tremendous pride in making sure everything we did was in accordance with the law. And although at times I complained to him that the federal investigation seemed to move too slowly, he never lost confidence in the ability of the United States Government to find the truth. Standing at his funeral services, I spotted Lance Madison, the New Orleans man wrongfully charged in the Danziger Bridge shootings, the man Nathan had represented until the eight police officers responsible for the murder of his brother and for the cover-up that followed were brought to justice. So many of us turned to him when we were looking for someone to make things right.

For 25 years, Nathan was the daily phone call I counted on to brighten the day with a few minutes of the most entertaining and insightful conversation you could ever hope to have with a friend. When I landed back in the U.S. from London, I thought how my phone would have rung the minute the pilot announced we could turn our cell phones on, and it would have been Nathan, with his perfect timing, anxious to hear all about my visit with Ethan and Jake. Like his wonderful family, I miss him.

Back on August 27, 2014, when I let Ethan know that Scott was dead, he sent me a short email before we talked later that night. It had been an emotionally draining day for all of us and we were all exhausted but couldn't sleep. His words reminded me of the enduring terror Scott had forced on some little boys who'd been having the time of their lives, enjoying being kids until he stole their innocence. Sometimes Ethan could say just a few words and their raw honesty would make me catch my breath.

The familiar evil is a powerful demon to conquer, but by finding their voices, the men Scott Rogers abused when they were children were finally released from the terror of his crimes against them. They could finally let go of the daily fear that he was abusing other children.

For Nathan, Mary Jane, and me, Ethan's words that night, exactly one year after his first email to me, made everything we had done worth it.

"I am. Jake is. Free."

EPILOGUE

DETECTIVE INSPECTOR ADRIAN RANDALL

The author received the following email from Detective Inspector Adrian Randall on October 27, 2015, after he retired from the Suffolk Constabulary in England.

Yesterday was my last day in the Suffolk Constabulary after 30 years, and I retired as a detective inspector. I can now comment upon that time when I investigated the Scott Rogers case as a detective constable based at Bury St. Edmunds criminal investigation department.

I was the officer in the case and was supported by Detective Sergeant Steve Gooda. We were both of the same mind that once we heard of the complaint from this young boy, others would speak out. In our minds there was never doubt in what he reported. You could see how troubled the boy was on what had happened, and the account he provided was never exaggerated, always matter of fact, shrouded in embarrassment and fear. He had nothing to gain from the allegations but had the courage to speak out, supported by his parents.

As investigating officers we were initially confident that others would have been abused and would disclose to strengthen the case. It has taken nearly 25 years for that prediction to come about, and then only with the death of the perpetrator.

While I have dealt with and managed many cases of child abuse over the years, this case has stayed with me for various reasons. As I was a young detective at the time, the Rogers case may have influenced the rest of my career: Ultimately I spent over 10 years working in child safeguarding specialist units and public protection roles.

Alas, such bespoke units weren't about when I investigated this case.

That's not to say the outcome would have been different, as I know I worked tirelessly on the case and was well supported in trying to get justice for a brave lad who stepped from the shadows to speak out. We left no stone unturned, but it soon became clear following Scott-Rogers' arrest that the hold he had on everyone surrounding him prevented many from speaking with the police and that the other victims feared such terrible perceived consequences.

I sampled an insight of his temper myself when I had to return some property to him at the dance academy, following his arrest whilst he was on bail. Many were around and he made the most of the opportunity to demonstrate his control and contempt for authority.

Of course, I had to remain professional and couldn't raise to the bait as he vilified me, accusing me of all sorts of impropriety. He declared—and I remember his words as clear as yesterday—"You are an evil man, Detective Randall, an evil man."

As I left, I thought two things. Firstly, I made a mistake seeing him on his territory, as that gave him an opportunity to demonstrate to others he still had power and control and could show it by speaking out at the police. My other thought was, *One day the truth will come out.*

After the investigation, the trial for justice was taken out of local Suffolk courts and held at the Inner London Crown Court. I stayed in London for the duration of the trial, ensuring all witnesses got whatever support they needed.

Our victim was supported by his family and delivered his evidence in the same way he had relayed his account to us. Because he was one victim, the jury were not certain beyond reasonable doubt and they were split. The victim, whom I have recently met again, should always remember that he was right to speak out. Following the hung jury, of course his family felt it was too much for him to go through another trial. The police and prosecuting lawyers completely respected that decision.

In some ways, however, the power and control that Scott-Rogers once exhibited over children was now under the microscope, as the Local Authority were rightly strong and publicly gave messages of concern about the way he operated. This ultimately, in my view, helped to get Scott-Rogers to move on and out of Bury St. Edmunds.

Of course, I feared this only shifted the risk, but dispersal sometimes affords evidential opportunities.

I didn't think it would be as long as it was before I heard his name again—over 20 years later, when I received a call from the Baton Rouge authorities.

I helped them as much as I could from the U.K. and had recovered all the archived case material to provide them the evidence that they needed concerning his antecedents.

In conclusion, I would describe Richard Scott-Rogers as a pied piper of children. All looked innocent from a distance. Despite no criminal allegations having ever been proven in a criminal court beyond doubt, now other allegations have surfaced. I will leave others to reflect on those past events that surrounded his behaviors at the Academy of Dance.

I hope in some way I have professionally helped some of those involved in the events that surrounded Richard Scott-Rogers and his dance academy in Bury St. Edmunds.

ABOUT MARY JANE MARCANTEL

When she went to work for Camille Gravel, Jr., almost 40 years ago, Mary Jane Marcantel was not only the first paralegal in Louisiana, but the first paralegal to do criminal work as well. Mr. Gravel, who was very well known throughout Louisiana as Executive Counsel to three of Louisiana's governors, had political ties throughout the United States. Even during her high school years, she dreamed of working for him, and that dream came true in 1977. She learned from Mr. Gravel that those who have a special ability to help others must do so without fanfare and credit. She has followed that guide both in her professional career and in her private life.

Well known among judges, prosecutors, and criminal defense lawyers in Louisiana, she has also worked with many of Louisiana's well-known defense lawyers to defend high profile white collar federal cases involving governors, senators, congressmen, sheriffs, police chiefs, and other political cases. In addition, she has helped defend people charged with murder, sexual crimes, drug offenses, and other street crimes. As a paralegal, she works alongside the lawyers in every aspect of the case, from a client's initial contact through the investigation, research, witness interviews, discovery, control of documents, trial preparation, jury selection, and sitting at counsel table and actively participating during trial as part of the defense team.

She has worked with law enforcement agencies to assist them in various matters involving issues for their agencies.

When she was asked to help a mother find out what had happened to her missing daughter, she got involved. The husband was the suspect in the disappearance. While she was working with law enforcement in this missing person's case, the husband then became a suspect in an international drug operation coming out of Columbia. And while he had been a suspect in the ten-year-old cold case of his previous wife's murder, five years after Mary Jane became involved in the investigation of the missing third wife, law enforcement credited her with "unearthing crucial evidence" that resulted in his plea to the international drug operation into Louisiana and the successful first degree murder prosecution of both him and the trigger man in a murder for hire plot to kill this second wife for life insurance proceeds.

Because of her success in the murder for hire case and her ability to think outside the box in problem solving, Nathan Fisher contacted her for help in the case involving Scott Rogers. When Fisher described Rogers' past life and a previous trial for sexually abusing a little boy, she became involved, just as she had in the murder for hire case, because someone needed help.

The information developed from Scott Rogers' prior victims in the United Kingdom was gut wrenching. With her experience in child sex abuse cases, she believed Rogers was a pedophile. She knew that any child in his care was at risk of sexual abuse. When she learned that Louisiana Child Services had placed children in his care and that those children had communication disabilities, she knew they were even more at risk. She knew she had to figure out a way to protect the children from Rogers.

Mary Jane lives in Spanish Town, the oldest neighborhood in Baton Rouge. Spanish Town sits at the base of the State Capitol and is the most unique of all the neighborhoods in Baton Rouge. It is the most diverse in economics, education, race, sexual orientation, and social culture. She is an officer for and is active in its civic association.

She is also actively involved in downtown Baton Rouge activities. With another resident, she started "The Way Home," a program that helps homeless people get back to family or friends and to jobs and a place to live. Many of these people have mental issues and criminal issues that are part of the problems for the homeless. Mary Jane is very much hands on with this program. It was so successful that the City of Baton Rouge and the Baton Rouge Police Department joined in the effort. All work together with the Capital Area Alliance for the Homeless to help people living on the streets, including children, return to a self-sustaining life.

Mary Jane is a mother of two children and grandmother to five granddaughters. She loves to spend time with both her real family and her chosen family, her friends, who are also very special to her. She loves to cook and many times gathers a number of people around her table for Louisiana foods and lively conversation. As she enjoys salt water fishing, often those fish are on her table.

My Thanks

I also extend my thanks to those Rannah has thanked.

A thank you to Nathan Fisher who called me early that morning. So much more was learned after his death. I wish he were here to know the full picture of the aftermath of that "ping" to Rannah on August 28, 2013.

And Rannah, the very gracious lady and the exact opposite of me in so many ways, who has become a close friend through this investigation.

And to the most important person, Camille Gravel. If I had not walked into his office 38 years ago and then gone to work for him, this story would not have occurred.

For Ethan and then Jake to step up as they did took a lot of courage. I thank them for putting their trust in us. I also thank those who helped them and the two children who were living with Scott Rogers. Without all of them, there would have been neither a solution nor this story. That is what it takes to stop a sexual predator: the work of lots of caring people.

*And then there is Luke Skywalker—the mythical hero we call in real life **Luke Walker**. Even in real life he is a hero to many.*

And Allyson Hoffine. Young enough to be my daughter. She is smart and tenacious in what she does. She has a big heart coupled with that tenacity.

To my family—large and small—those by birth and those I consider my chosen family. My two children, Sean and Michelle, who put up with a lot along the way of my work life. Thank you.

My grandchildren—Kristen, Zella, Kate, Violet, and Josie—who sometimes call me **Mary Jane.** *They like to play with me and me them. They tell me I'm not like a real grandmother. They tell me I'm silly, interesting, and fun.*

My brothers, Mike and John, whom I helped raise, and their wives and children and their children's children. Over the years my brothers and sisters-in-law stood in for me with my children when I was working.

And to my chosen family that I care a lot about.

Darryl, my best friend for the last 25 years. He looks after me and I look after him.

Mary Olive, my fishing buddy, who loves to introduce me as "knowing where all the dead bodies are buried in Louisiana." We have some interesting conversations.

Anna who knows my secrets and I know hers.

And to the guys along the way I like to play with—Alan, Brad, Brian, Bud, David, Donnie, Ed, Jeff, Jerry, and Pat. Some call me **Mom***. Y'all have all had an impact on my life.*

Mary Jane Marcantel

ABOUT THE AUTHOR

Rannah Gray is a public relations consultant whose career highlights include Louisiana's two favorite pastimes—politics and sports. Her work as a political media producer has been honored with numerous national awards, including three Pollie Awards from the American Association of Political Consultants and eight Telly Awards, including two Classic Tellys for outstanding television produced over the past 20 years. *Politics Magazine* named her one of the *Top 100 Influencers* in Louisiana. In Baton Rouge, *Sales and Marketing Executives International* named her *Marketer of the Year, and Business Report Magazine* listed her as one of the city's *Influential Women in Business.*

For 13 years, she served as Associate Athletic Director at Louisiana State University, where she led one of the country's most successful collegiate sports marketing programs, managing advertising, corporate partnerships, event promotions, radio and television programming, and ticket operations for 20 teams.

She previously served as Undersecretary to the Louisiana Secretary of State.

She is a graduate of LSU with both a Bachelor of Arts and a Master of Arts in Journalism. While she is a prolific writer, having served as a speechwriter, spokesperson, and image maker for clients throughout the country, this is her first book.

Rannah is a native of Chatawa, Mississippi, and resides in Baton Rouge where she provides expertise in advertising and public relations, media production, and community engagement to a broad base of clients.

PUBLISHER'S NOTE

To help safeguard children, Rannah Gray, author of *Familiar Evil*, hopes to share the experiences gained from learning how easily child predators are able to operate without detection in society. Having seen firsthand how the systems responsible for protecting vulnerable children too often fail, she plans to present the facts of this case throughout the United States and in the United Kingdom, where this story began. A portion of the proceeds from the sale of *Familiar Evil* is donated to programs that support survivors of child sex abuse.

For bulk sales of *Familiar Evil* or to contact Rannah Gray about speaking to your group, email The Lisburn Press at info@thelisburnpress.com.

James H. "Jim" Brown, Publisher
The Lisburn Press

Lightning Source UK Ltd.
Milton Keynes UK
UKHW03f1015160318
319518UK00004B/3/P

9 780578 1707